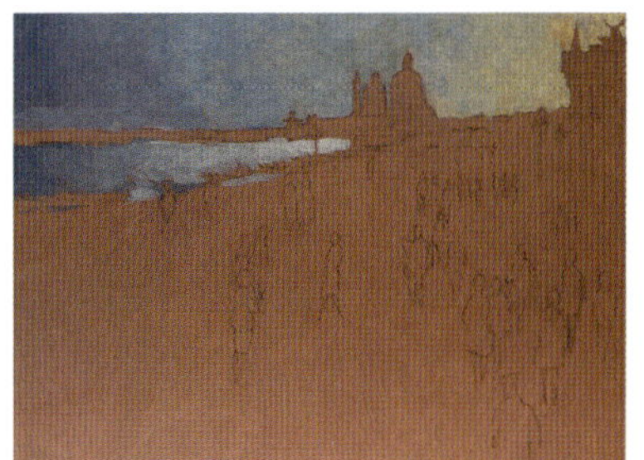

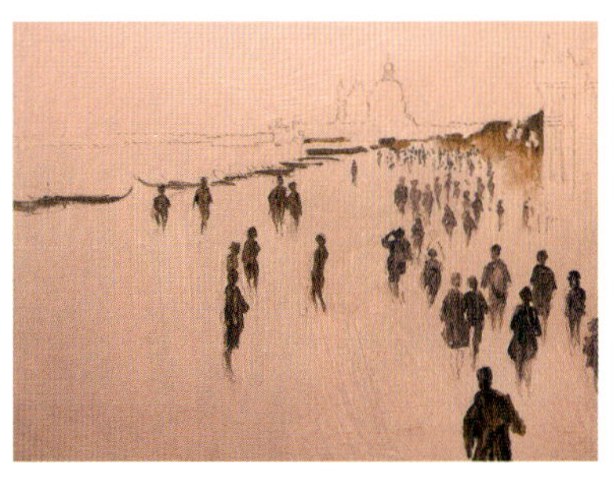

ACRYLIC PAINTING LAYER BY LAYER™

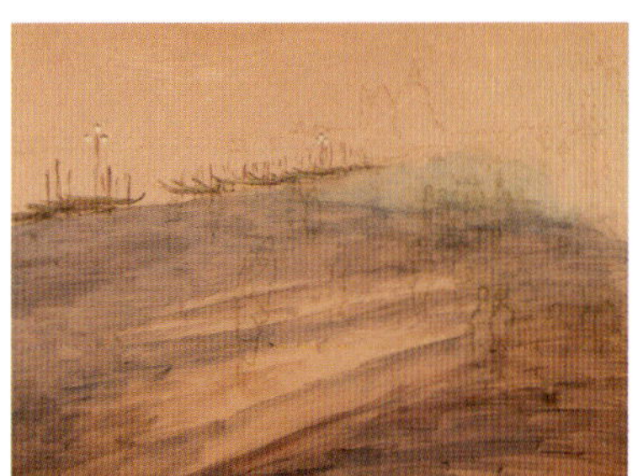

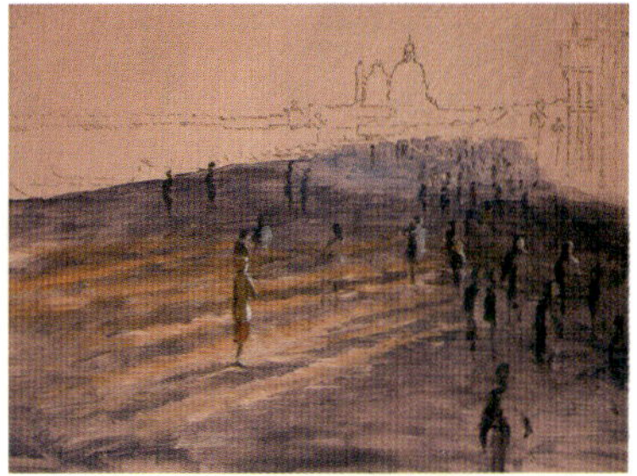

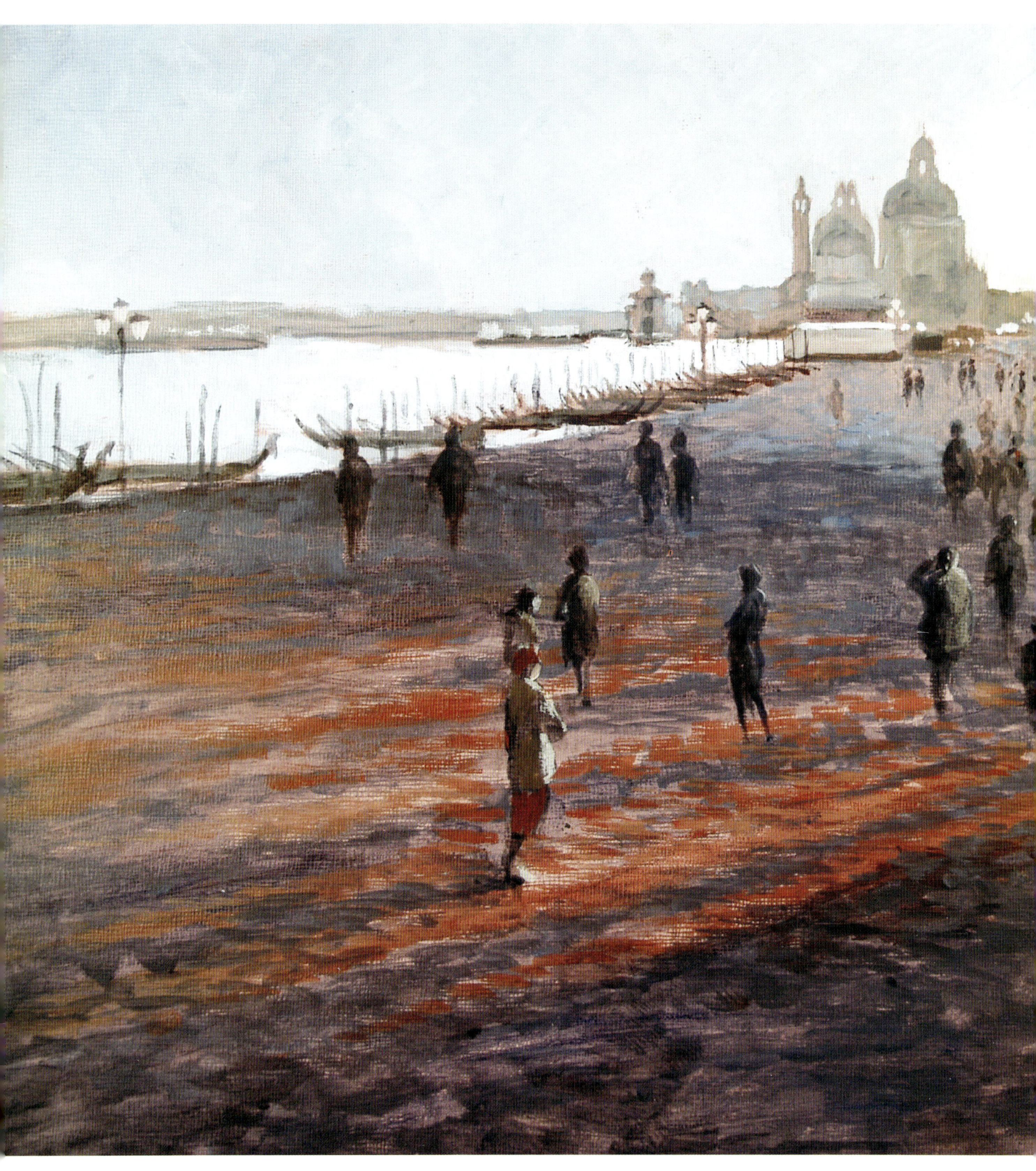

ACRYLIC PAINTING LAYER BY LAYER™

WITH THIS UNIQUE METHOD, EACH STEP OF EVERY LESSON IS SHOWN AS A SEPARATE LAYER, MAKING IT AMAZINGLY EASY TO CREATE BEAUTIFUL ACRYLIC PAINTINGS!

IAN SIDAWAY

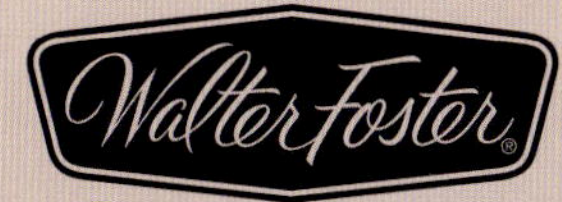

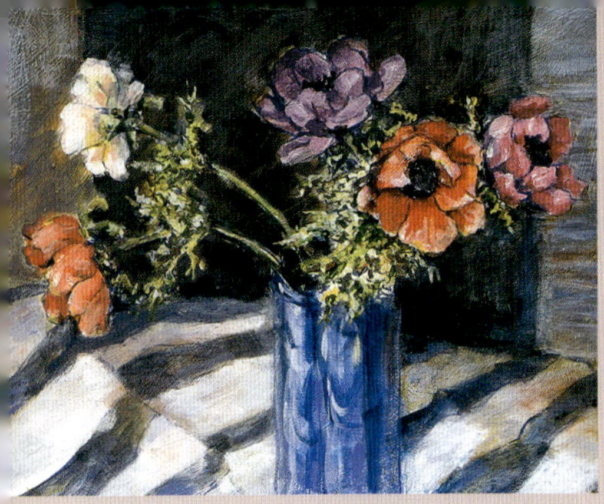
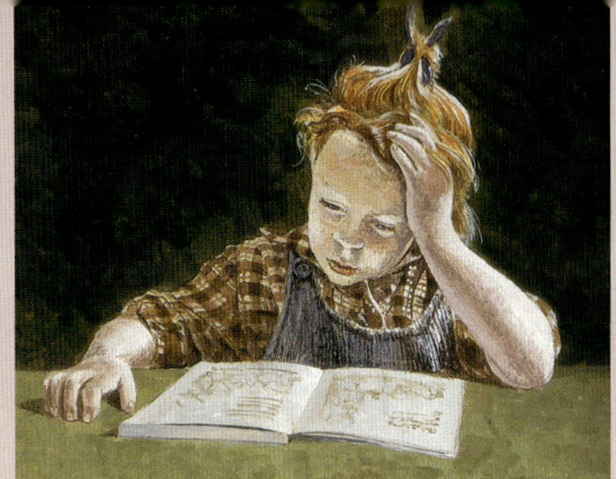
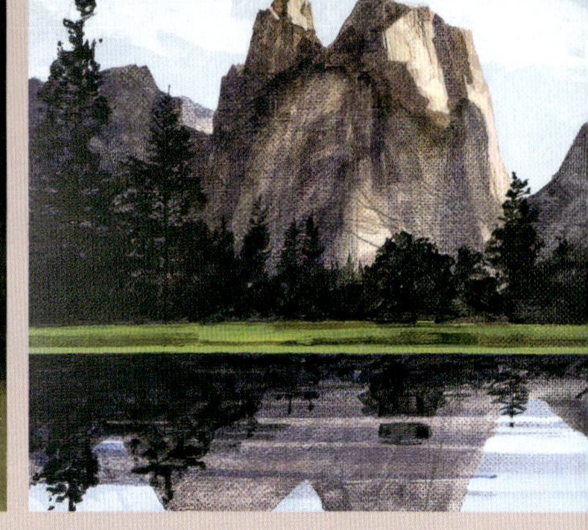
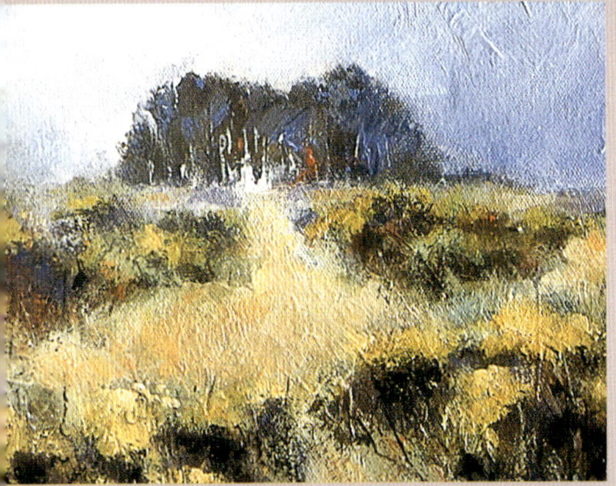
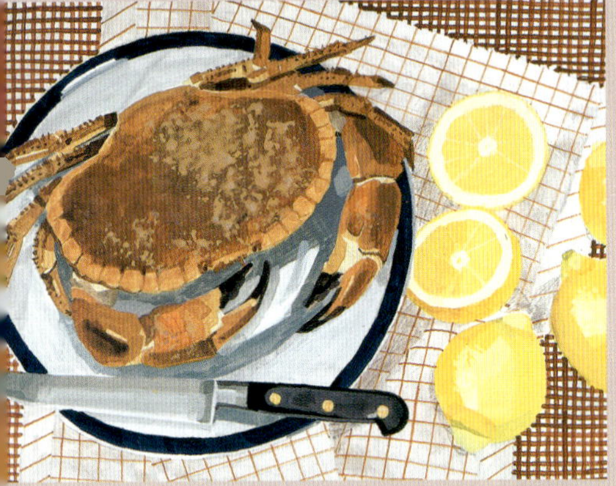
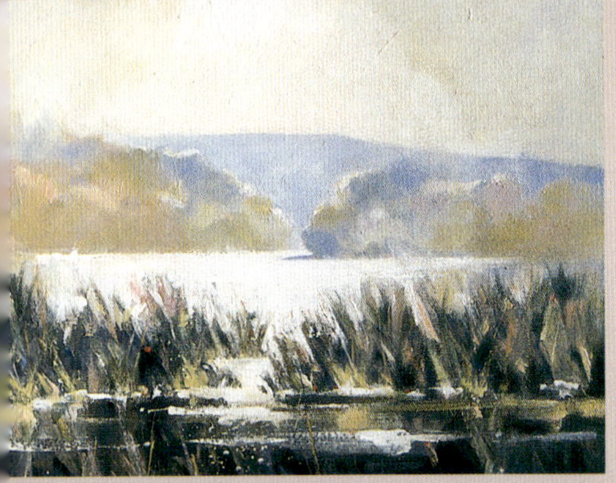
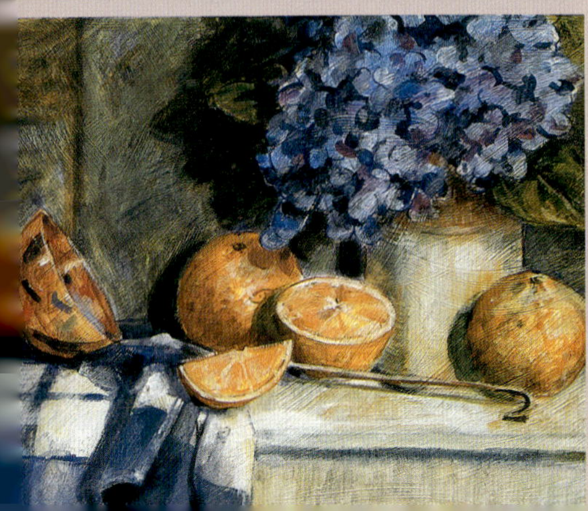

A QUARTO BOOK

First edition for North America published in 2005 by
Walter Foster Publishing, Inc.
23062 La Cadena Drive
Laguna Hills, CA 92653
www.walterfoster.com
Walter Foster is a registered trademark.

ISBN: 1-56010-905-X

Conceived, designed, and produced by
Quarto Publishing plc
The Old Brewery
6 Blundell Street
London
N7 9BH

QUAR.ALL

PROJECT EDITOR: Paula McMahon
ART EDITOR: Anna Knight
ASSISTANT ART DIRECTOR: Penny Cobb
COPY EDITOR: Carol Baker
DESIGNER: Joelle Wheelwright
PHOTOGRAPHERS: Paul Forrester, Ian Sidaway
PICTURE RESEARCH: Claudia Tate
PROOF-READER: Mary Groom
INDEXER: Geraldine Beare

ART DIRECTOR: Moira Clinch
PUBLISHER: Paul Carslake

Manufactured by Modern Age Repro House Ltd, Hong Kong
Printed by SNP Leefung Printers Ltd, China

9 8 7 6 5 4 3 2 1

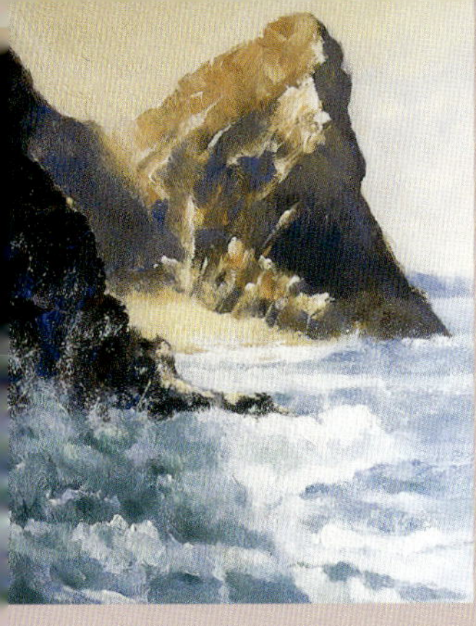

CONTENTS

INTRODUCTION

Although still relatively new as a painting material when compared with oil, watercolor, gouache, or tempera, acrylic paint has come a long way in 60 years.

An accidental by-product of industrial chemists, acrylic paint has attracted artists worldwide because of its vividness and durability. Acrylic combines the qualities of watercolor and oil painting and allows the amateur to experience the various techniques associated with each medium. Diluted with water, acrylic becomes transparent and subtle. Straight from the tube, it takes on the rich textures of oil, but without the messy cleanup.

This versatility, coupled with a fast drying time, has boosted the popularity of acrylic paint. With acrylic, the painter may combine both watercolor and oil techniques into a unified whole. And manufacturers now provide a variety of acrylic paints, including those with longer drying times, thicker or thinner consistencies, and even paints designed to adhere to hard-to-stick surfaces. Acrylic paints adapt well to working on location, making it possible not only to produce rapid sketches and color notes, but also finished works. The medium has distinct advantages for studio work, because—unlike oil paintings—acrylic needs no protection from exposure or handling. Acrylic paint's ease of use and versatility has had a somewhat liberating effect on the creative process. The sequence of building up and application is not as critical as when using other painting materials, and alterations and corrections are easily facilitated.

This book represents the combined efforts of several artists, each of whom used acrylic to create uniquely personal paintings. Each work presents its own set of challenges and rewards, and you may gravitate to one style over another. Take from the book what you can, and add your own visions. Experiment boldly and learn with confidence. Above all, enjoy everything that this exciting medium has to offer.

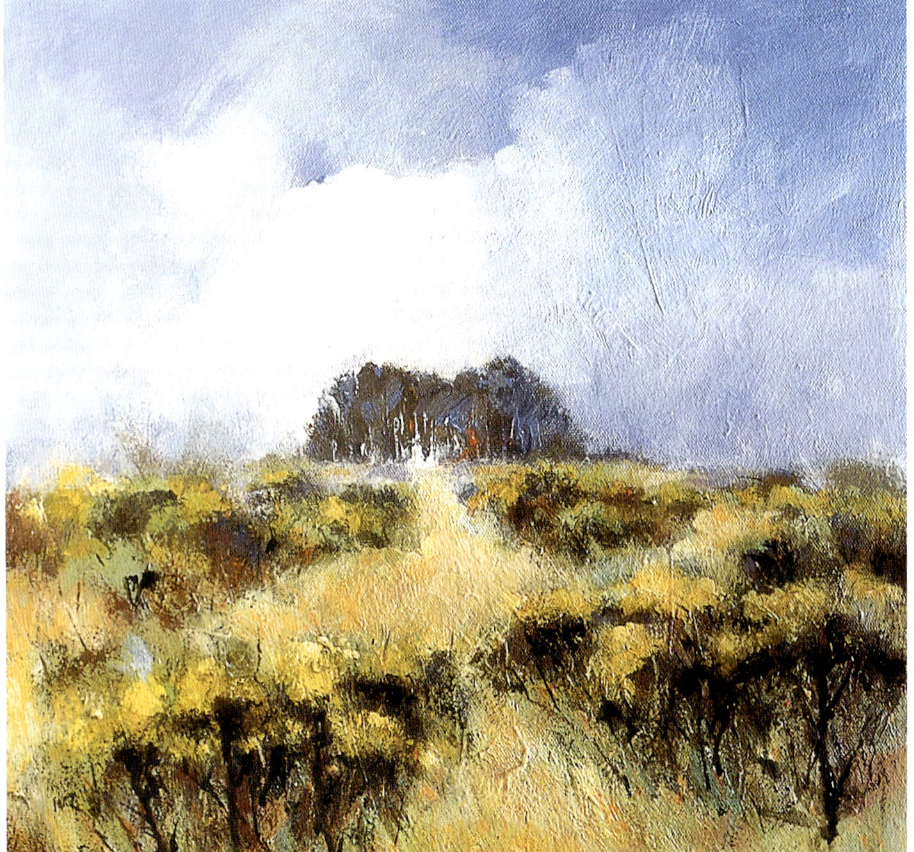

HILLSIDE IN SPRING

Textural effects and color combine to create this atmospheric image of a distant hill.

HOW TO USE THIS BOOK

Part One, Getting Started, details the paints, mediums, and other tools that you will need, as well as offering useful tips on planning your picture's color and tone. Part Two, Techniques, illustrates the painting techniques that will help you create beautiful pictures. If you study Part One and Part Two carefully, you will be able to enjoy getting inside the artists' minds as they create paintings in Part Three.

In Part Three, Exploring Themes, you will see how different artists exploit the medium to meet different moods and requirements. Each painting has been broken down into six or eight stages, or layers. This layer-by-layer technique is a way of showing each artist's thought processes and will help you understand the components of a painting.

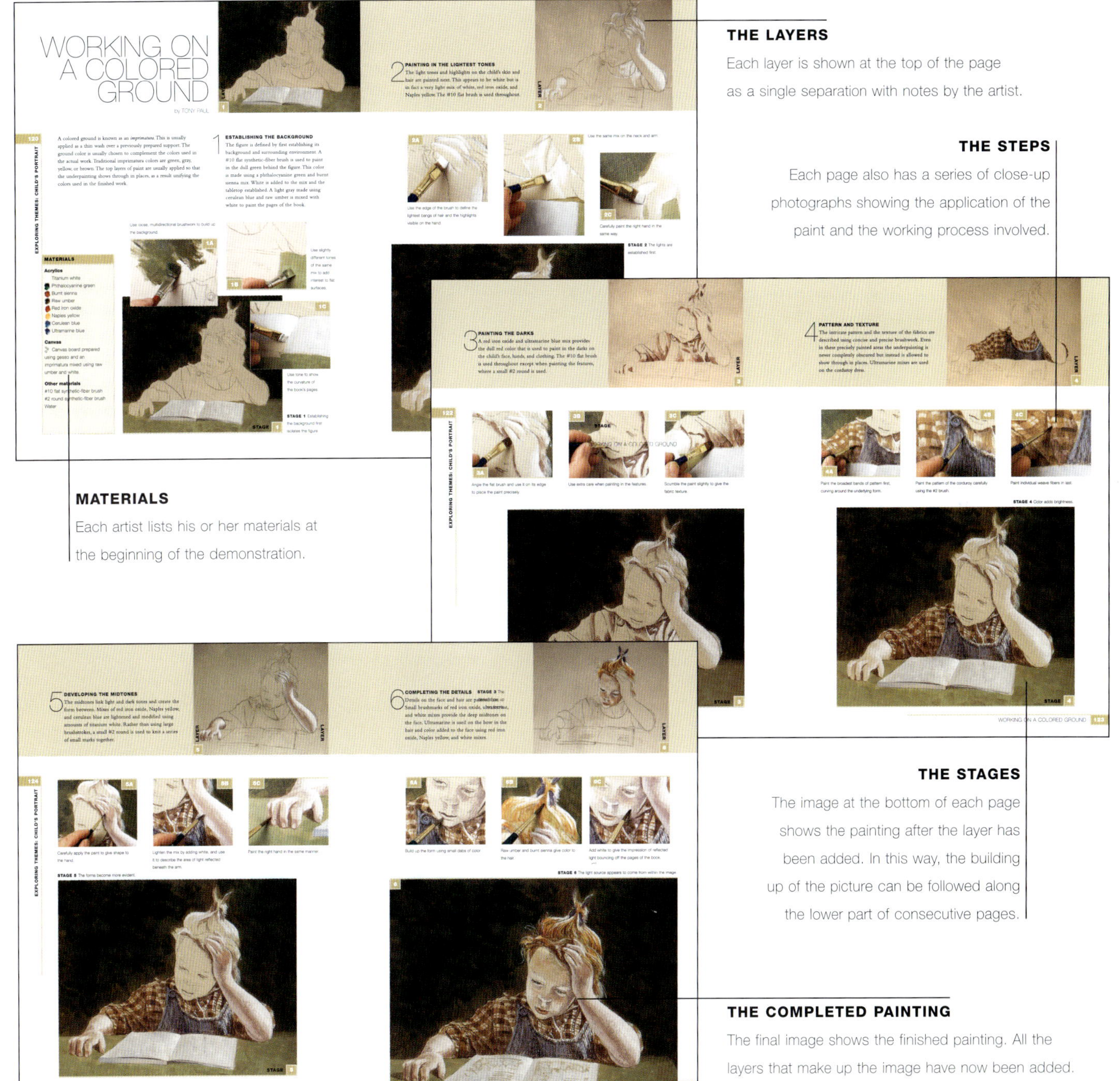

THE LAYERS

Each layer is shown at the top of the page as a single separation with notes by the artist.

THE STEPS

Each page also has a series of close-up photographs showing the application of the paint and the working process involved.

MATERIALS

Each artist lists his or her materials at the beginning of the demonstration.

THE STAGES

The image at the bottom of each page shows the painting after the layer has been added. In this way, the building up of the picture can be followed along the lower part of consecutive pages.

THE COMPLETED PAINTING

The final image shows the finished painting. All the layers that make up the image have now been added.

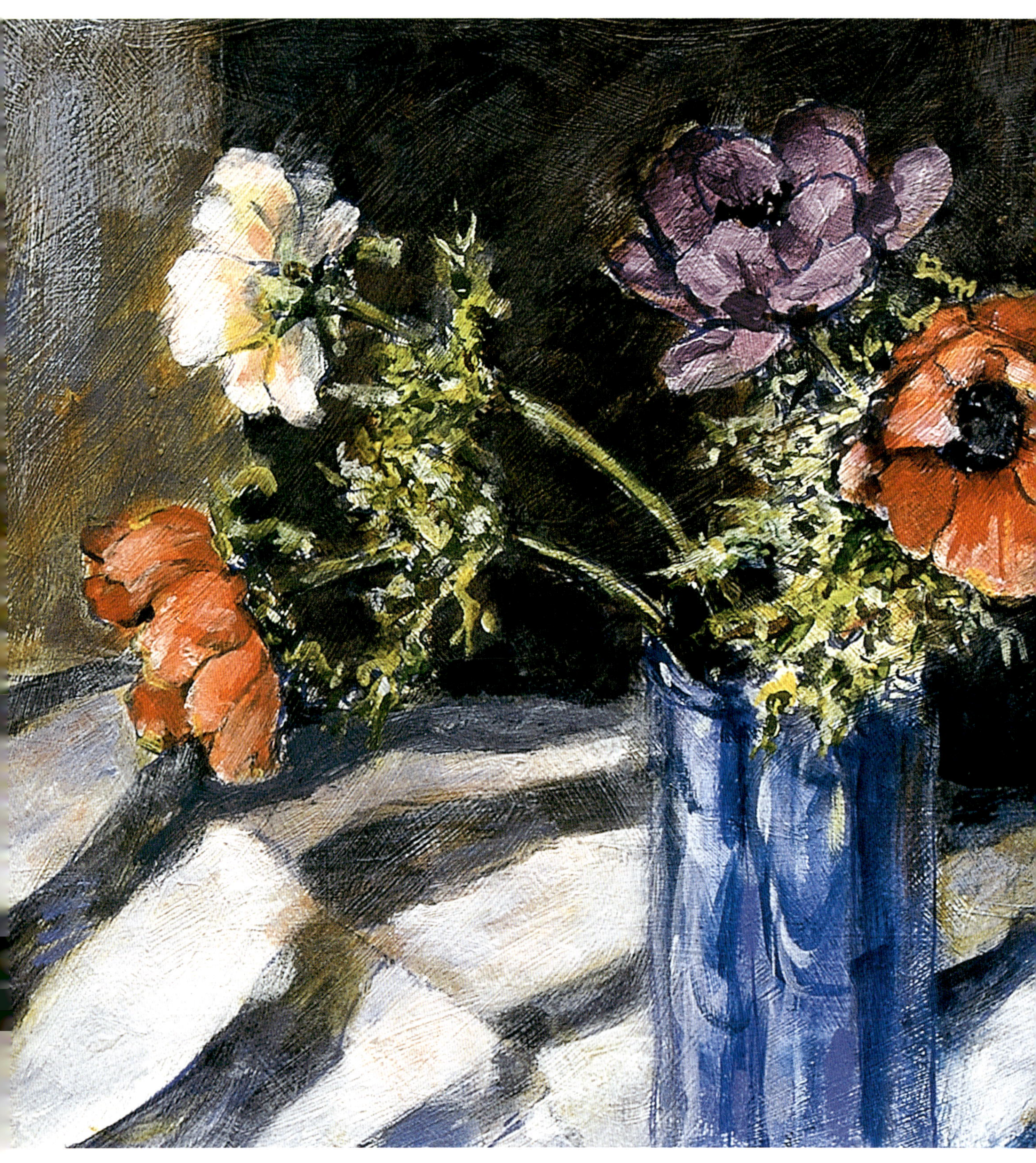

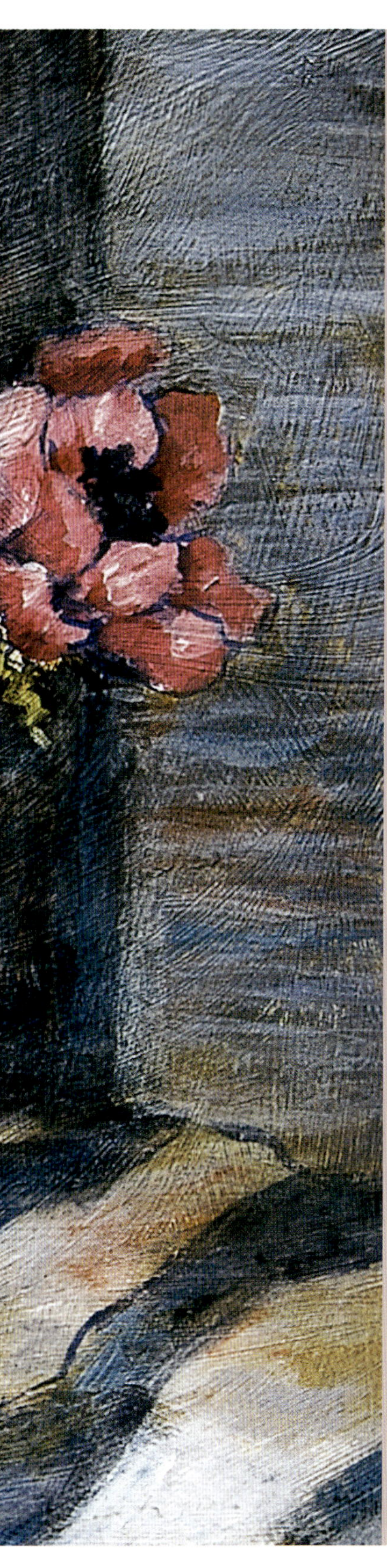

PART ONE

GETTING STARTED

A few carefully chosen colors, a brush, a surface to paint on, and a subject are all you need to get started. Simple support preparations and clean water are all that is required to thin paint or clean brushes.

ACRYLIC PAINT

Acrylic paint is made like any other paint—by mixing pigment with a binder that serves to secure and hold the pigment to the surface of the support.

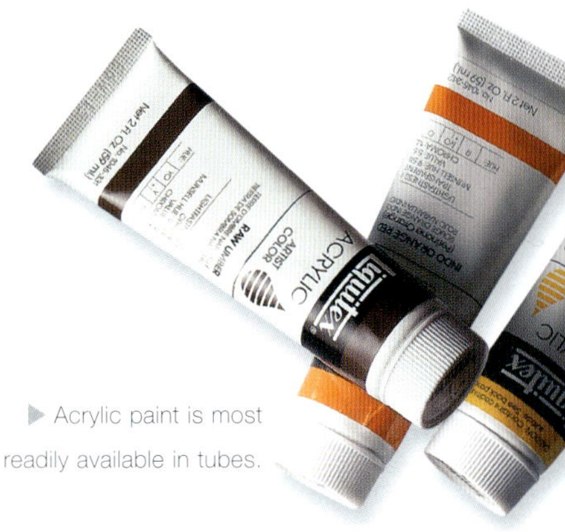

▶ Acrylic paint is most readily available in tubes.

In acrylic paint, the binder is an acrylic resin made from a solution of polymers. The resin is emulsified in water, and the paints are thinned with water. Acrylics dry as the water content evaporates; but unlike other water-based paints they form a permanent, tough, but flexible film that cannot be made soluble again by rewetting. The acrylic emulsion is "milky" in color when wet but dries clear. It is for this reason that colors look slightly lighter when wet than they do when dry. All manufacturers of acrylic paint have their own formulae and modify their paints with various dryers, matting agents, and stabilizers. However, all brands of acrylic paint are similar, and like all brands of watercolor and oil paint, they can be mixed with no adverse effects.

Paint is available in tubes and bottles. The paint dries quickly and cures to create a very hard film. To avoid having unused paint harden, always replace the cap or lid after each application of paint.

As with other types of paint, both student-quality and artist-quality paints are available. The difference is in cost, quality of the pigments, and the variety of colors.

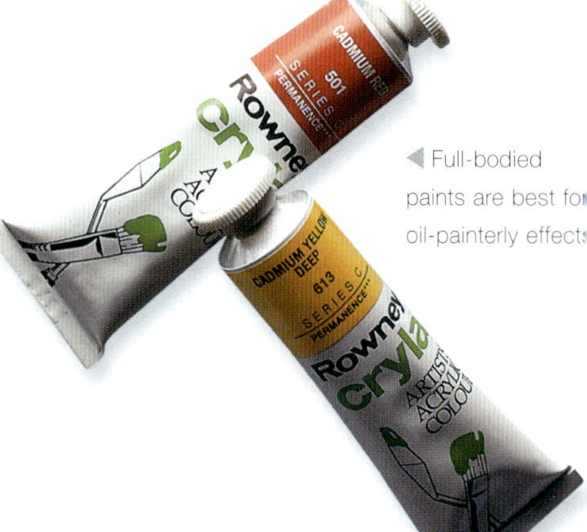

◀ Full-bodied paints are best fo
oil-painterly effect

◀ Several manufacturers offer introductory sets tha include a range of colors

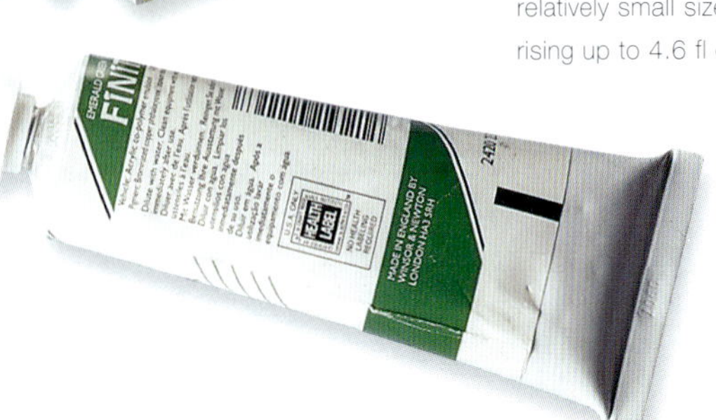

◀ Tubes of acrylic paint start at the relatively small size of 0.4 fl oz (12ml), rising up to 4.6 fl oz (138ml).

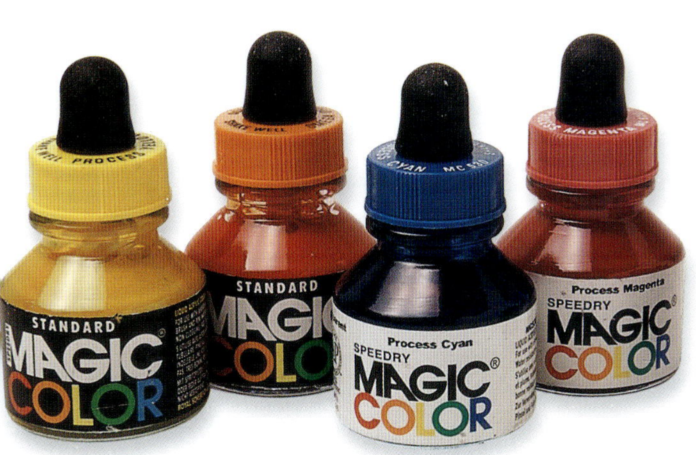

▲ Liquid acrylic paints often contain a dropper that is used for transferring the paint onto the palette.

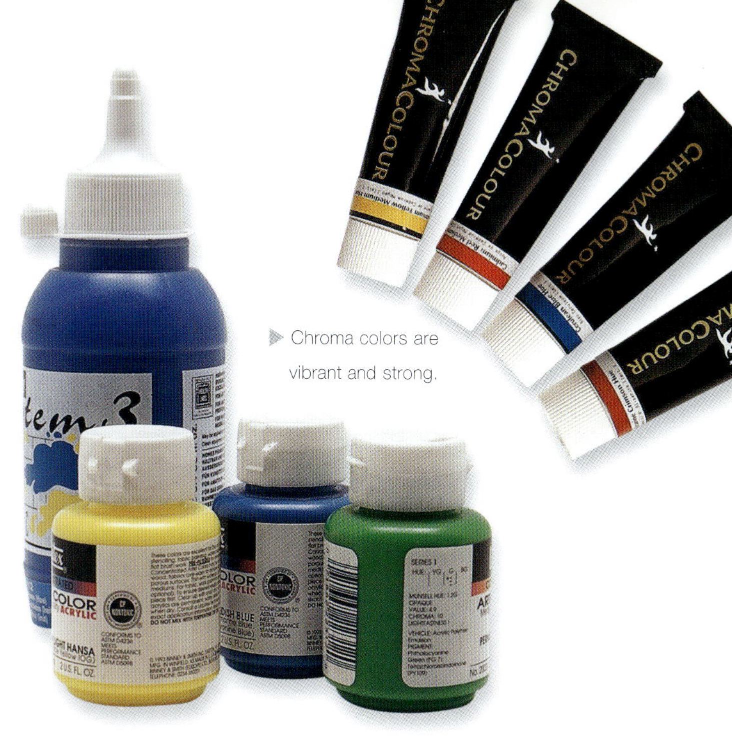

▶ Chroma colors are vibrant and strong.

▲ Squeeze bottles and cap bottles hold anything from 1 fl oz (30ml) up to 10.5 pints (5l), depending on the manufacturer.

PAINT CONSISTENCY

The viscosity of acrylic paint can vary from brand to brand. As a general rule, paint from the tube is stiffer than paint from bottles. However, it is easy for manufacturers to alter the consistency of the paint, and many offer both high- and medium-viscosity varieties. A recent innovation by one manufacturer is a super-heavy body paint, available in squeeze bottles. When used without the addition of water or mediums, the paint retains every brushstroke. You may also come across liquid acrylic inks, which are permanent when dry and can be used in thin semitransparent washes. These can also be used in pens and airbrushes without fear of clogging.

As acrylic paint dries quickly, the paint can be manipulated only for a relatively short period of time, which can make slow blending techniques difficult. But, if you work by glazing one color over another, the process is sped up because you no longer have to wait for each glaze to dry before you apply the next. Fast drying time requires the artist to clean up spilled paint immediately, place soiled brushes into water, and then clean them thoroughly once the painting session has finished. However, one manufacturer has recently introduced a paint that remains usable for many hours and stays thick for many days. Needless to say, this makes blending an easier process.

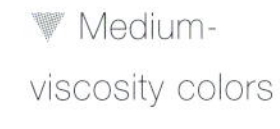

▼ Medium-viscosity colors

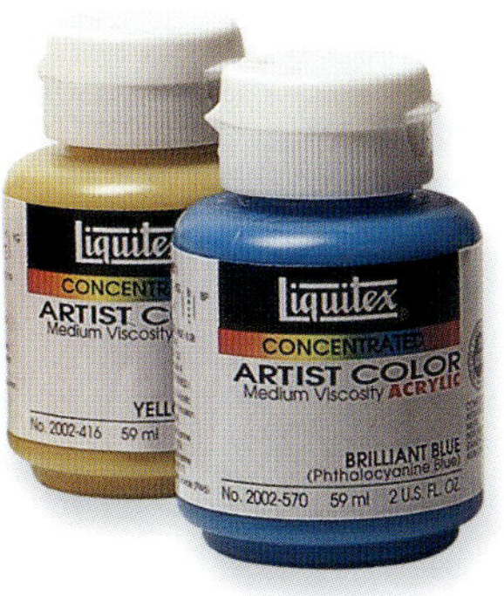

▼ Acrylic inks can be used in combination with acrylic paints. The pearlescent inks shown here produce an attractive shimmering effect.

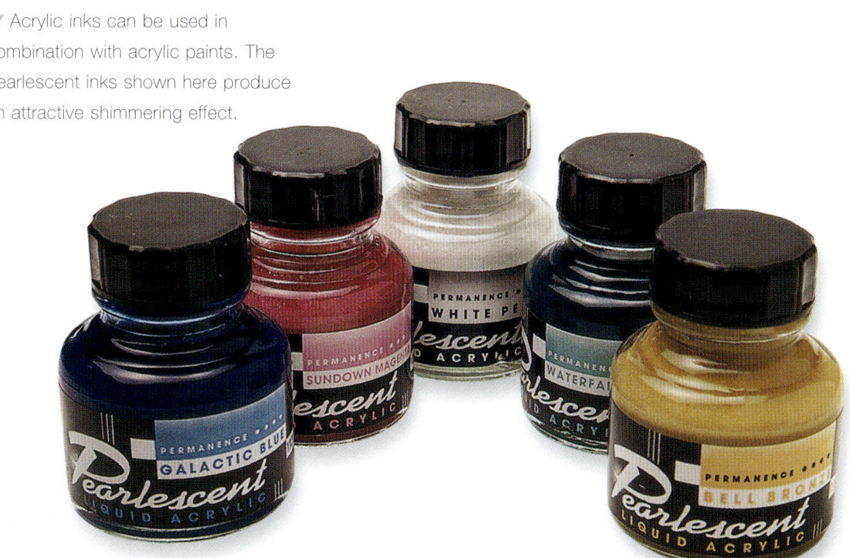

COLOR RANGE

Acrylic paints come in a full spectrum of colors. All manufacturers carry the standard color range, which includes the commonly used primary reds, yellows, and blues, along with a variety of greens and a range of earth colors. White and black are also standard.

If you look at any manufacturer's color chart, you will see that the range of different hues far exceeds the short list mentioned above. For the beginner, choosing the first selection of colors can prove somewhat confusing. However, as colors can be mixed, it is not necessary to buy one of every color but only those that suit the subject matter of the painting. Many artists work with fewer than 10 colors, and very few will be found working with more than 16.

▶ The pigments used to make acrylic paints are the same as those used to make oil and watercolor paints.

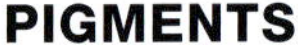

PIGMENTS

All paint colors are made using standard pigments. This makes choosing and using colors very easy. Many colors are made using a single pigment; however, some are made using a combination of pigments. Colors made from a single pigment will be pretty much the same regardless of the brand chosen, but colors made by combining several different pigments may be slightly different, depending on the brand. Examples of mixed colors are Payne's gray and sap green—attractive colors found in most manufacturers' ranges but often made using different combinations of pigments.

To ensure bright, clean color mixing, limit your mixes to just two or three colors. Whenever possible, make sure that those colors are made using a single pigment. Although inconvenient, this practice will help you mix pure colors instead of colors that are dull and subdued—a common occurrence for those new to color mixing. Note that the artists who have produced many of the examples in this book have worked with their own palette of colors, and some of these colors were made with more than one pigment.

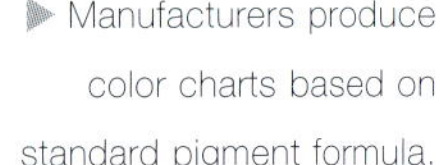

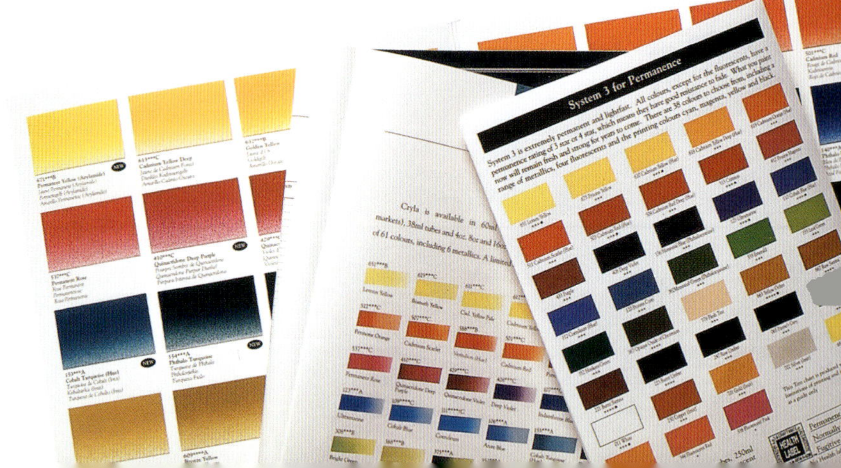

▶ Manufacturers produce color charts based on standard pigment formula.

CHOOSING A BASIC PALETTE

The twelve colors listed should meet all your needs, but feel free to add or substitute colors if you wish.

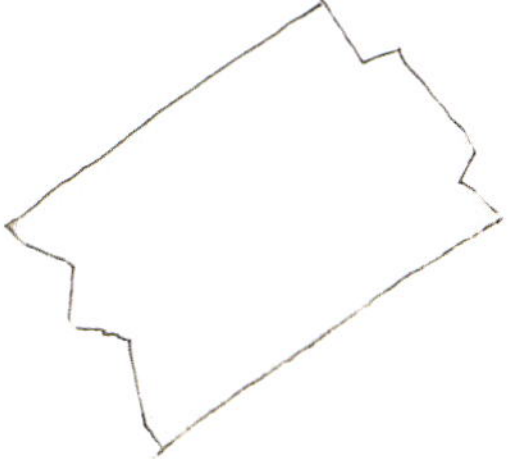

TITANIUM WHITE: PW6
Titanium dioxide. Good tinting strength. Opaque.

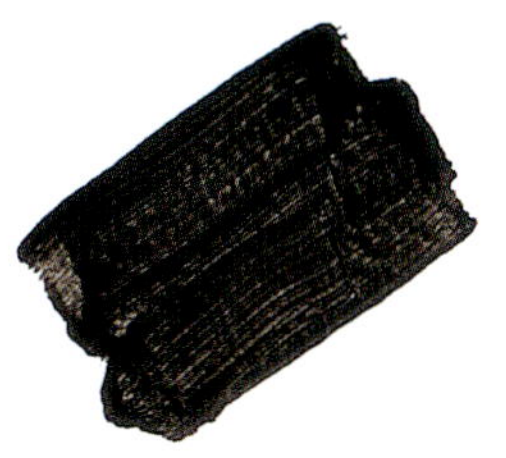

IVORY BLACK: PBk9
Amorphous carbon from charred animal bones. Good tinting strength with a slight brown tinge. Opaque.

CADMIUM RED LIGHT: PR108 **Cadmium selenosulfide.** Good tinting strength with reasonable opacity. Warm.

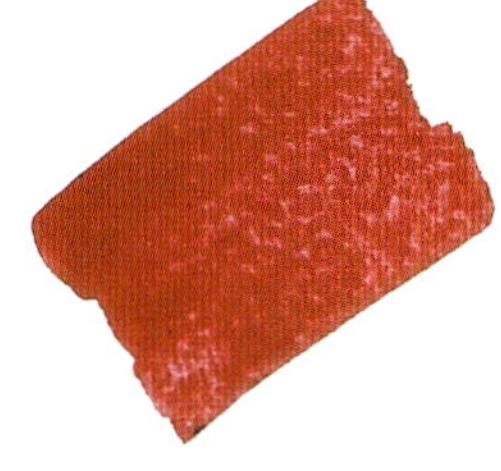

QUINACRIDONE RED: PR207 **Quinacridone.** Very high tinting strength. Transparent and cool.

CADMIUM YELLOW LIGHT: PY35 **Cadmium zinc sulfide.** Relatively opaque with good tinting strength. Cool.

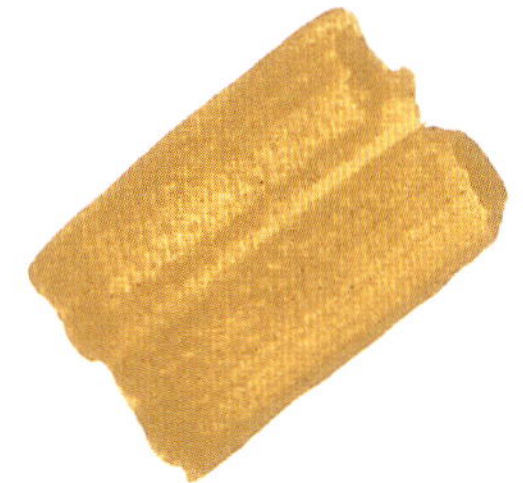

YELLOW OCHRE: PY43
Iron oxide. Relatively opaque with low tinting strength. Warm.

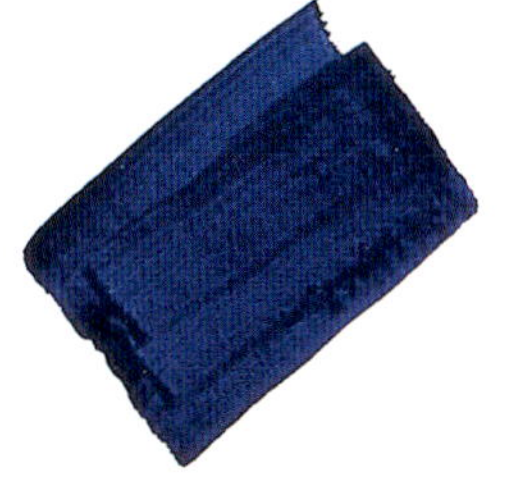

PHTHALOCYANINE (PHTHALO) BLUE: PB15 **Copper phthalocyanine.** Exceptionally high tinting strength. Transparent and cool.

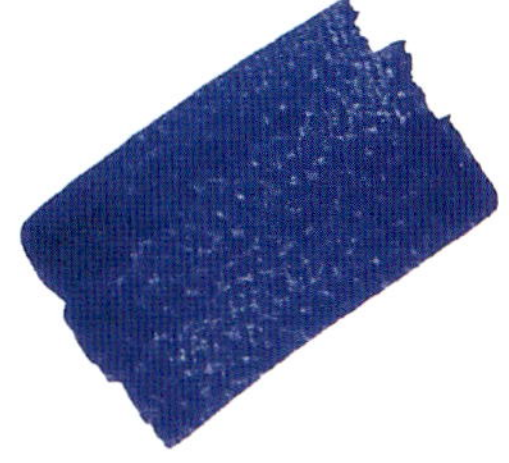

ULTRAMARINE BLUE: PB29 **Sodium aluminum sulfosilicate.** Reasonably high tinting strength. Transparent and warm.

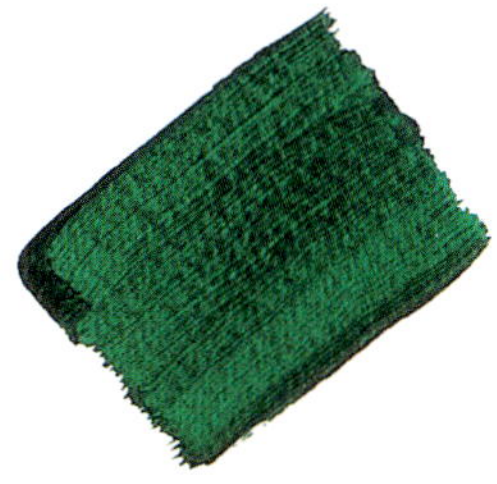

PHTHALO GREEN: PG7
Chlorinated copper phthalocyanine. Very high tinting strength. Transparent and cool.

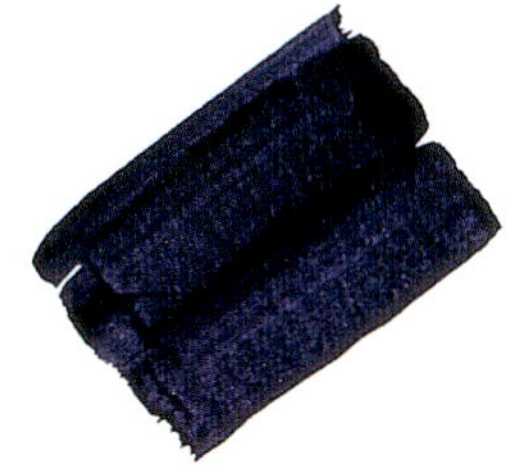

DIOXAZINE PURPLE: PV23 **Dioxazine violet.** Good tinting strength. Transparent and cool.

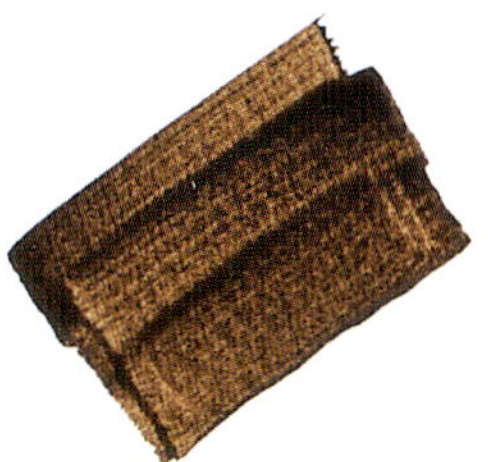

BURNT UMBER: PBr7
Natural iron oxide. Fairly transparent with a good tinting strength. Warm.

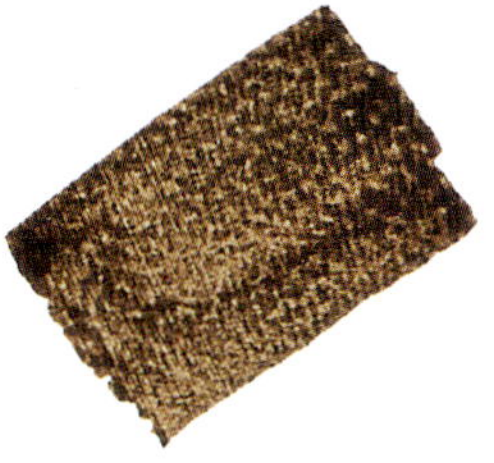

RAW UMBER: PBr7
Natural iron oxide. Cooler than burnt umber with reasonable tinting strength. Transparent.

MEDIUMS AND ADDITIVES

The versatility and potential of acrylic paint is complemented with a wide range of mediums and additives. To use the paint, just add water!

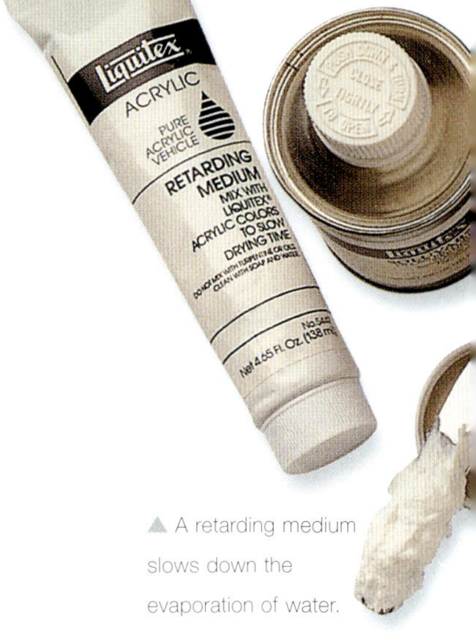

▲ A retarding medium slows down the evaporation of water.

Water is used to thin acrylic paint and spread it across the support surface. As the water evaporates, the paint will become less workable because the acrylic resin, when dry, locks the pigment particles in place. You will quickly learn how much water to use in order to mix the paint to the consistency you want, and you will also learn to judge how long the paint will remain "open" or workable. Always use clean water when mixing paint, and wash out your brushes in a container separate from that used to hold the water for mixing.

MEDIUMS

There are two main acrylic mediums available: *gloss medium* and *matte medium*. These are essentially the same acrylic resin as that used in the manufacture of acrylic paints. The mediums are milky in color but dry clear; and when they are wet, there is no way of telling them apart. The mediums are available as fluids which pour easily from the container, or in a gel form, which is stiffer and retains brush or knife marks. Heavy gel variations are also available to create very thick paintwork and are ideal for creating a range of textural marks. All gel mediums have high adhesive qualities and can be used for collage work on any type of support. All mediums when added to paint will marginally extend the drying time.

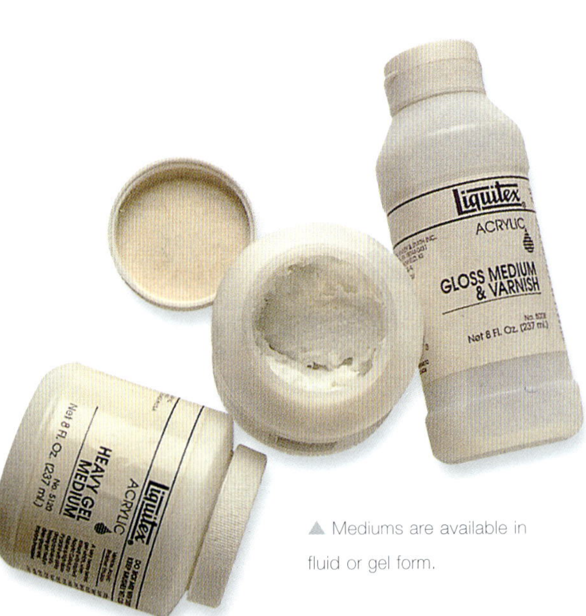

▲ Mediums are available in fluid or gel form.

ADDITIVES

The relatively fast drying time of acrylic paint can be countered by adding a retarding medium. This medium works by slowing down the evaporation of water and increasing the time the paint can be manipulated. This is useful if you are blending large areas of color or applying large washes to be worked wet into wet. As with all mediums and additives, read the instructions included with the products, as adding too much can result in poor adhesion and problems with shrinkage. Some retarding mediums are added to the paint, while others can be applied to the support surface prior to applying the paint.

The flow or the ability of the paint to spread over an area easily can be altered by adding a flow improver. Flow improvers work by reducing the surface tension of the water vehicle—in essence making the water "wetter" so that it spreads more easily. This wetting agent prevents thin washes from forming puddles or being repelled on smooth paper or unprimed canvas, a process known as cissing, and it helps thicker, creamy applications of paint to brush out smoothly.

Texture pastes add texture to the paint. These pastes are made by adding various aggregates to a heavy gel. The materials used include flint, natural pumice, sand, glass beads, flakes, and fiber. Texture pastes can be added to the paint or applied directly to the support and painted over, once dry. Very thick applications can be applied (although this is best done

MEDIUM EFFECTS

Adding gloss medium to paint results in the paint drying to a gloss finish, while adding matte medium results in the paint drying to leave a matt finish. These two mediums can be mixed to create a medium that will create a finish of various degrees of sheen, according to how much of each is used.

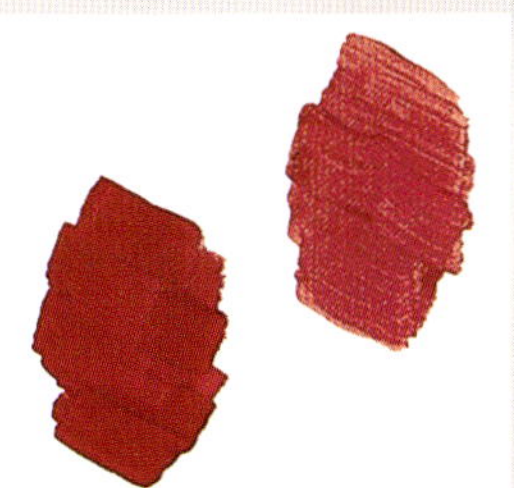

Paint straight from the tube (left). Overlaid with iridescent medium (right).

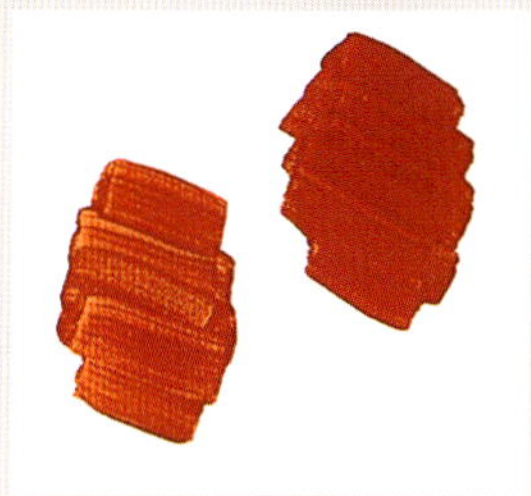

Paint straight from the tube (left). Overlaid with matt medium (right).

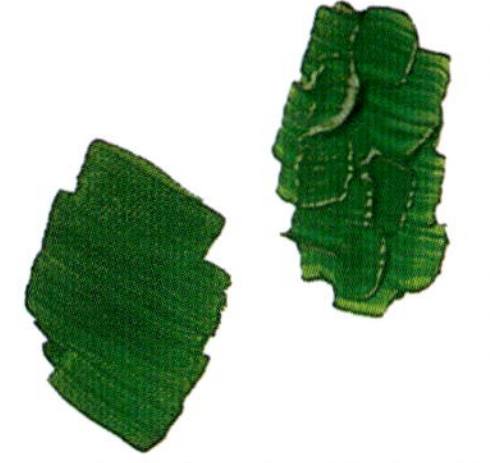

Paint straight from the tube (left). Mixed with heavy gel medium (right).

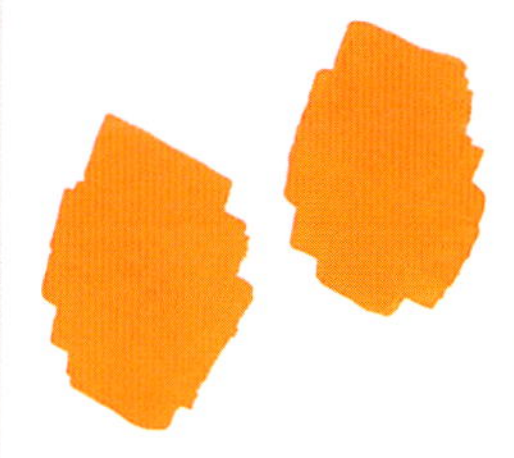

Paint mixed with ceramic stucco, a texture paste.

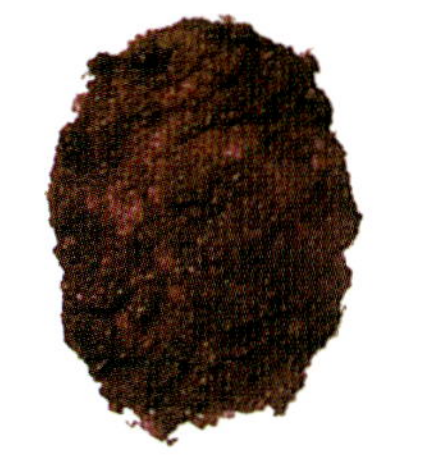

Paint mixed with resin sand, a texturing medium.

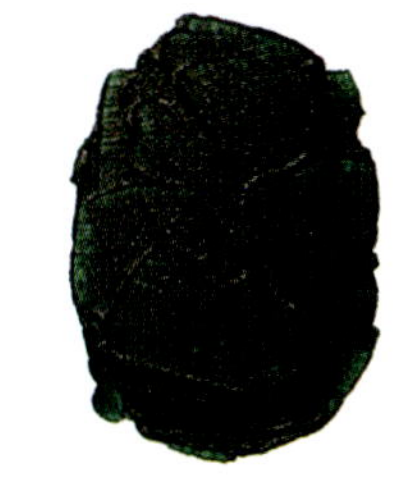

Paint mixed with natural sand, a texturing medium.

Paint mixed with blended fibers, a texturing medium.

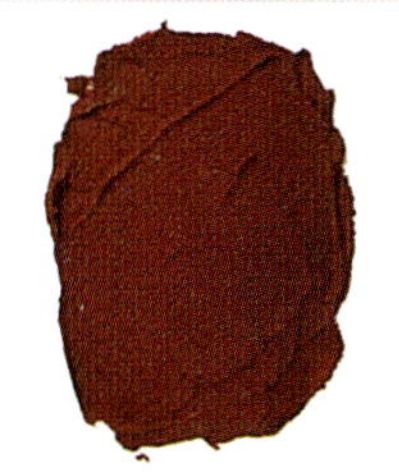

Paint mixed with ceramic stucco, a texturing medium.

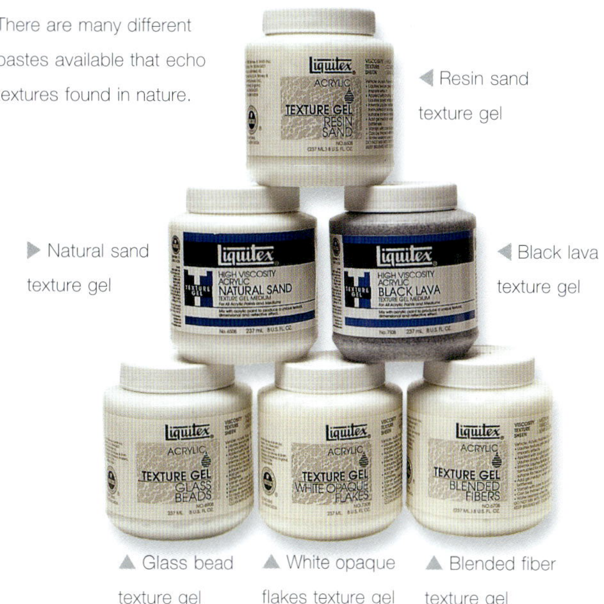

There are many different pastes available that echo textures found in nature.

◀ Resin sand texture gel

▶ Natural sand texture gel

◀ Black lava texture gel

▲ Glass bead texture gel

▲ White opaque flakes texture gel

▲ Blended fiber texture gel

by applying several thin layers), building up to the desired thickness gradually by allowing each layer to dry before applying the next. It is an easy task to make your own texture pastes by adding clean materials to heavy gel mediums. These might include pumice, which can be found in some art stores, or clean play sand available from toy stores. Modeling pastes, although similar to texture pastes, are made from marble dust and set to create a hard surface that can be sanded and carved using various tools. The material can be colored using acrylic paint or used "raw" and painted, once dry. Objects can be pressed into the layer of texture paste to leave an impression or left in place, where they will stick firm once the paste has dried. The material is best applied to a rigid support.

VARNISHES

Once the painting is dry, it can be given a coat of varnish to protect it from atmospheric pollutants and the effects of ultraviolet light. Both matte and gloss varnishes are available, which can be mixed to create a finish with a slight sheen. These are water-based varnishes and are permanent once dry.

SUPPORTS

Acrylic paint can be applied to any surface that is permeable, but it will not adhere to glass, plastic, or glazed ceramic. The surface that carries the painted image is known as the support. *Remember that acrylic paint is water-based and will not sit happily on a support surface that has been prepared using an oil- or spirit-based primer.*

CANVAS: LINEN AND COTTON DUCK

Canvas is the most widely used surface for painting. Its surface is very receptive to brushwork, and very large canvas supports can be prepared that are comparatively light and easy to handle. The two main types of fabric used for painting supports are linen and cotton duck.

Linen is made from the woven fibers of the flax plant. A dull ocher-brown in color, it has a slightly irregular weave that can be relatively pronounced in heavier weights. Linen canvas is woven in a range of weights and textures from fine and light to heavy and coarse. As a general rule, the larger the support, the heavier the grade of canvas used. Fine-weave, heavy linen can be very expensive, but linen is a pleasure to work on as the surface is springy and receptive.

Cotton duck is a popular alternative to linen. It is made from cotton fiber and is a light cream in color. As with linen, it is available in a range of weights, with the weave texture becoming more pronounced as the weight gets heavier. The weave of cotton duck is regular and mechanical. Cotton duck is considered to be an inexpensive alternative to linen, but in reality, it is used by many artists and should serve most needs. Other suitable materials include *hessian,* which is inexpensive and of a very coarse weave; and synthetic fiber fabrics such as polyester, which can be found ready stretched and prepared.

Linen

Cotton duck

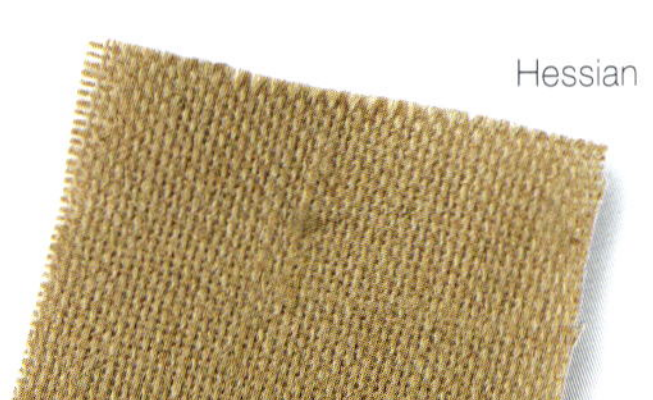

Hessian

STRETCHING AND PREPARING CANVAS

Before being worked on, canvas needs to be stretched taut over a wooden frame known as a "stretcher." Prepared canvas that is stretched, primed, and ready to work on can be found in all art stores, but preparing your own is both easy, satisfying, and economical. You will need canvas, stretcher bars, a staple gun, acrylic gesso primer, and a brush.

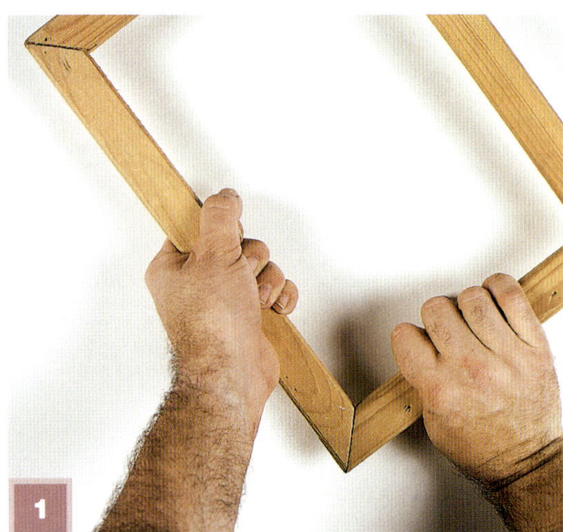

STEP 1 Assemble the stretcher bars by slotting the corners together. Make sure that the bars are the correct way up. On one side, the edges will be beveled; on the other side, they will be square. On some makes of stretcher, there is a lip on the side that goes next to the canvas. Larger stretchers have crosspieces to prevent the assembled stretcher from twisting.

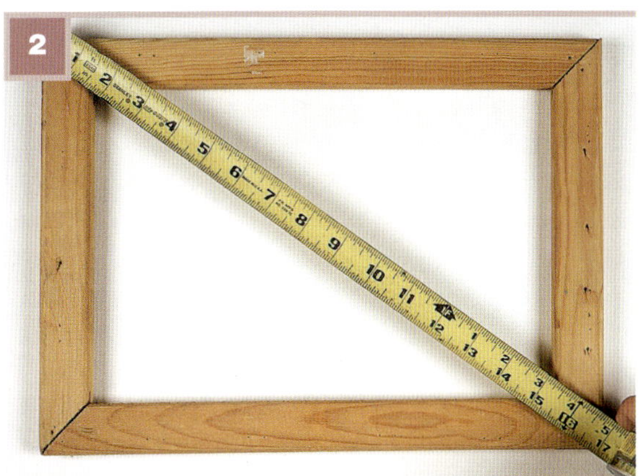

STEP 2 Make sure that the stretcher frame is square. You can do this by measuring diagonally across the stretcher frame from corner to corner. If you do not have a tape measure use a piece of string. If the measurements are the same, then the frame is square.

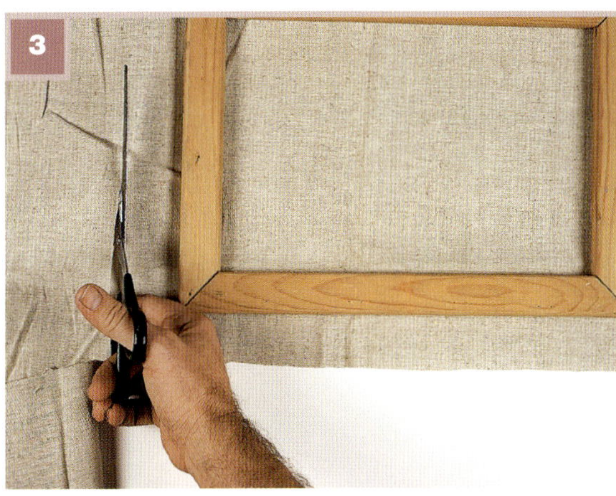

STEP 3 Place the canvas on a flat surface, and place the frame onto it with the beveled or rounded edges next to the fabric. Cut the canvas so that it is approximately 1" or 2" (2.5 or 5 cm) wider all around. This is to make sure that the canvas can be folded up the side of the stretcher bars and onto the back. Make sure that the weave of the canvas—the warp and the weft—run parallel to the stretcher bars.

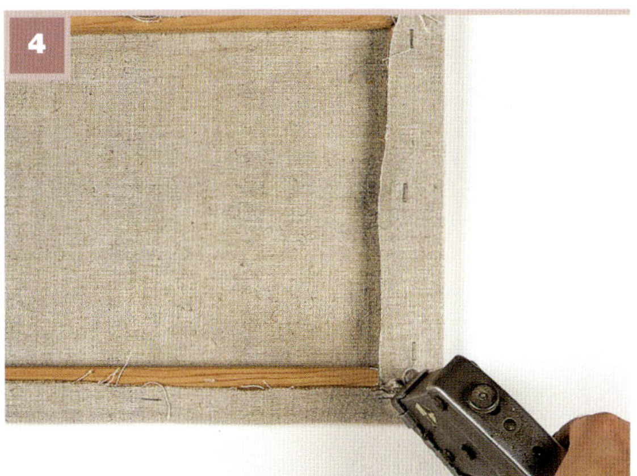

STEP 4 Secure the canvas to the back of the stretcher bars using the staple gun. Staple the canvas at the center of one edge, then pull the canvas taut with your finger and staple the center of the opposite edge. Place staples every 4" or 5" (10 or 12.5 cm) along each of the stretcher bars until you reach the corners. Do the same along the other two edges. At the corner, fold the canvas into a pleat and secure it with a staple.

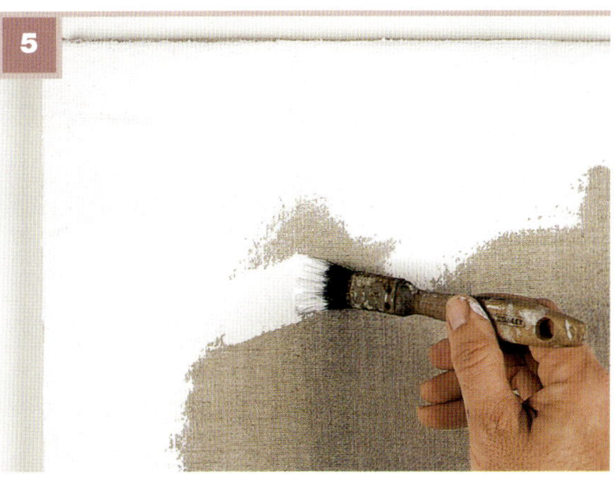

STEP 5 Prime the canvas using two or three coats of flexible acrylic gesso primer, allowing it to dry thoroughly between each coat.

Plywood

Hardboard

MDF

BOARDS AND PANELS

Both wood and cardboard panels make excellent supports for acrylic work. Prepared boards can be found at all art stores. The main wooden boards used are made from plywood, hardboard, and medium-density fiberboard. *Plywood* comes in a range of thicknesses, has a smooth surface, and is not prone to warping. *Hardboard* is available with both tempered and untempered surfaces. Tempered board has a slightly greasy surface, so use untempered boards where possible. One side of the hardboard is smooth, and the other side is roughly textured; either side can be used. Hardboard is prone to warping, so it is best used only when cut into small boards. By far the best board to use is medium-density fiberboard known as *MDF*, which is available in a wide range of thickness and does not warp. Thin sheets are ideal for making small panels, while the thicker sheets—although heavy—make excellent large panels. The surface is smooth and takes acrylic gesso beautifully. You may also apply canvas or some other fabric to the surface—a technique known as marouflaging.

MAROUFLAGING

Linen, canvas, cotton duck, hessian, or even old cotton sheets can be marouflaged onto boards. This is an ideal way to use up those cut-offs of canvas that are too small to stretch. Any board can be used, but MDF is stable and will not warp. You will need fabric, board, acrylic medium, acrylic gesso, and a brush.

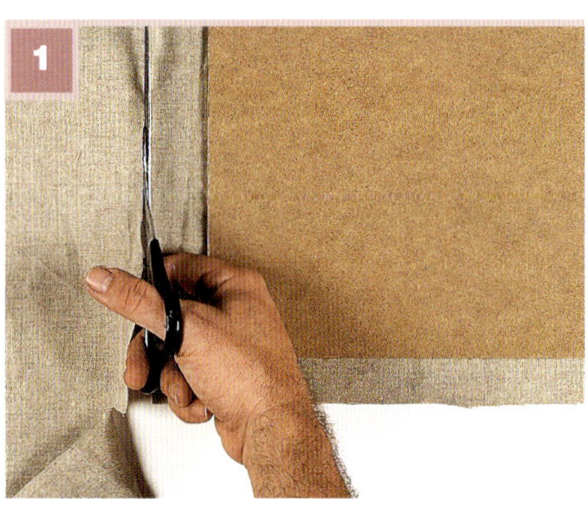

STEP 1 Cut the fabric to be used so that it is about 1" (2.5 cm) larger than the board all around.

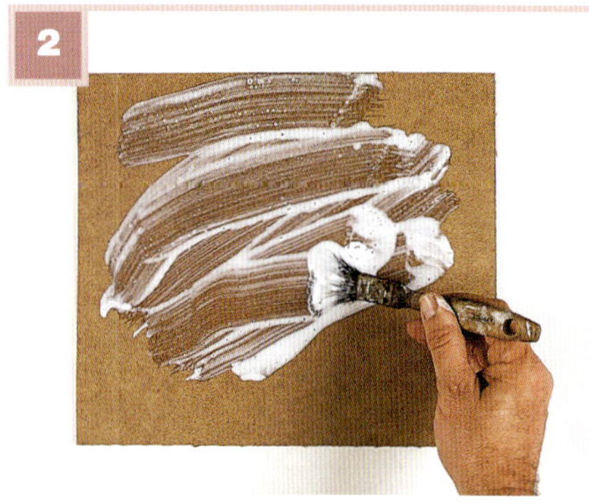

STEP 2 Apply a liberal coat of acrylic medium onto the surface of the board.

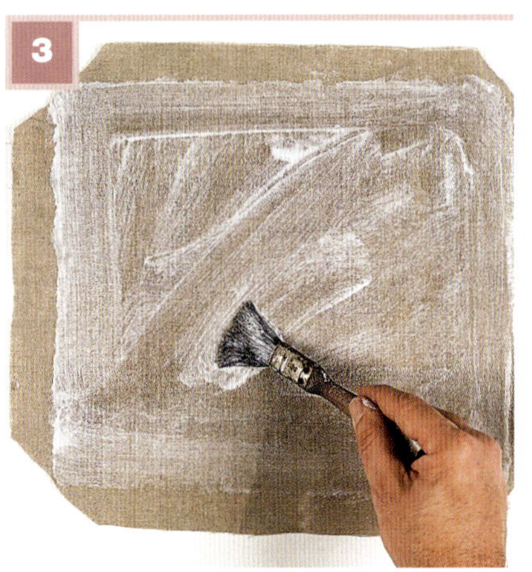

STEP 3 Apply the fabric onto the surface, and press down firmly, ensuring that there are no air bubbles trapped between the fabric and the board. Note: The acrylic medium may push through the weave of the fabric. More acrylic medium can be brushed over the canvas surface to smooth it out.

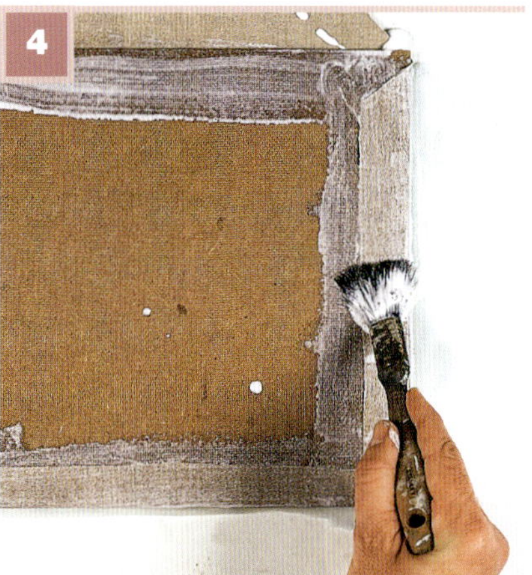

STEP 4 Turn the board over, and place it on a surface such as glass or a laminate so that it will not stick. Cut across the corners of the fabric, and apply acrylic medium round the edge of the board. Fold the canvas onto the back of the board, and press it into the medium, making sure that it is stuck firmly. More medium can be brushed on if you wish.

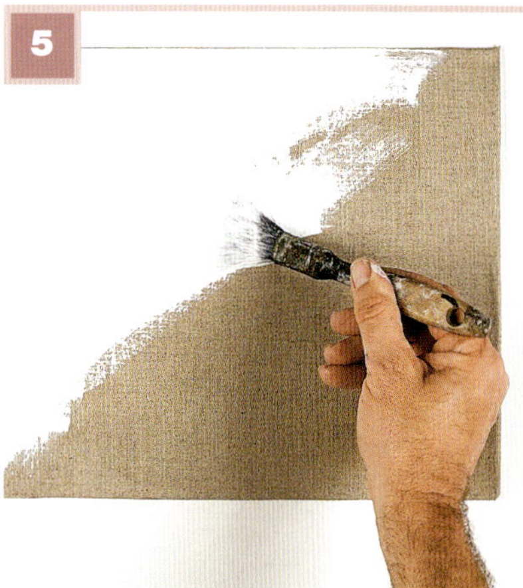

STEP 5 Turn the board on its edge, and stand it to dry against a jar so that the glued surface is not touching anything. Once dry, the board can be primed.

PAPER

Acrylic paint can be used on most papers without any need for a primer, although decorative papers with shiny laminated surfaces are perhaps best avoided. The amount of different papers available to the artist runs into the thousands, and their individual qualities of surface texture, weight, absorbency, and color will have a direct and often very apparent effect on the way the image looks. Despite the various different papers available, all can be divided into a few main types. The thickness of the paper is described in pounds (lbs) and grams (g), and the higher the number, the thicker the paper. Lighter papers should be stretched before using them, or they will buckle when you apply the wet paint. Stretching your paper before painting will give you a smooth flat surface to work on. This surface will stay flat as you work, and the finished painting will dry flat.

Hot-pressed paper has a smooth surface made by passing the freshly formed sheet through hot rollers. The surface produced is hard, smooth, and featureless. It is good for fine detail work and for drawing.

Cold-pressed paper has a slightly textured surface formed by passing the sheet through cold rollers. This type of paper is sometimes described as NOT (not hot pressed). Cold-pressed paper is a good all-around paper.

Rough paper is not passed through rollers but allowed to dry naturally between drying felts, which often impart their own texture to the paper's surface. Rough paper can be very rough, and it offers interesting dramatic surfaces full of character.

Thick or heavyweight paper can be used as is but thin paper tends to buckle when wet paint is applied. In order to prevent this from happening you will need to stretch the paper onto a wooden board.

rough

cold press or NOT

Hot press or HP

STRETCHING PAPER

To stretch paper, you will need a sheet of paper, a wooden board that is larger than the sheet of paper, brown paper tape, scissors, water, and a clean natural sponge.

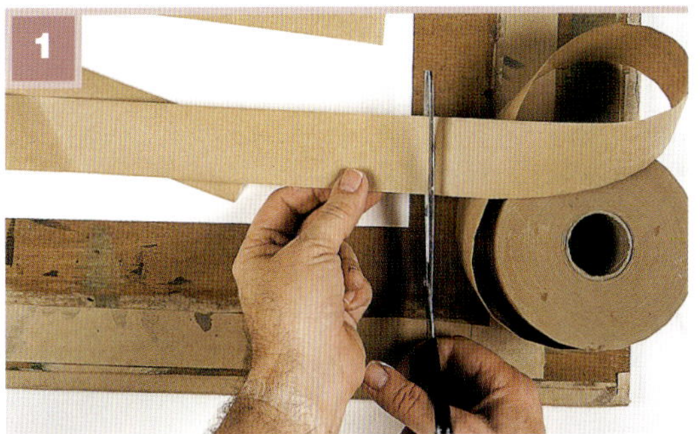

STEP 1 Lay the sheet of paper onto the wooden board, making sure that the paper is at least 1" smaller than the board on all four sides. Cut four strips of the paper tape, one for each edge of the paper.

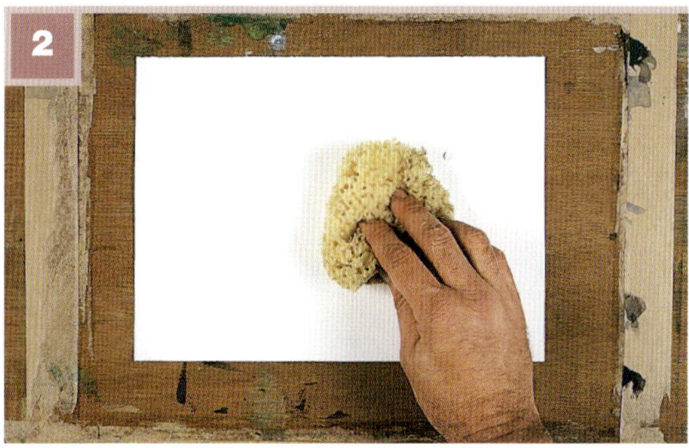

STEP 2 Wet the surface of the paper using clean water and the sponge. (Very heavy sheets of paper can be soaked in the bath then laid on the board.) Use the sponge to remove all the excess water.

STEP 3 Use the sponge to wet a strip of tape, and lay it along one edge of the paper so it half covers the paper and half covers the board. Smooth the tape down firmly.

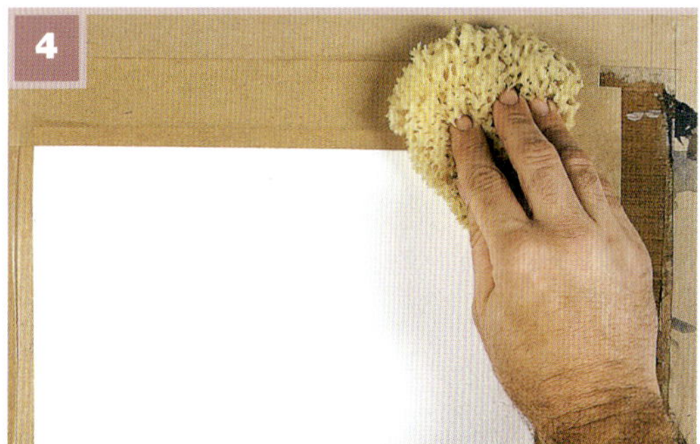

STEP 4 Do the same to the other three sides. Place the board in a warm place, and allow the paper to dry thoroughly before working on it.

BRUSHES AND OTHER TOOLS

Brushes come in a wide range of shapes and sizes and use a variety of different materials. To realize the full potential of acrylic paint, you will need several brushes. The basic brushes, tools, and materials used for acrylics are no different than those used for oils and watercolors.

BRISTLE BRUSHES

The majority of bristle brushes are made from the stiff hair of hogs, with the finest bristle coming from the Chungking area of China. Bristle is hardwearing and can withstand the abrasive action of the bristle being rubbed repeatedly against the canvas. Good quality hog bristles also hold and deliver a reasonable quantity of paint. Good bristles are split slightly at the tip; this is known as "flagging" and helps the brush deliver paint smoothly onto the support. There are five main brush shapes available: round, flat, short flat (brights), filbert, and fan.

Round brushes are useful for sketching in an image using fluid paint and for loosely blocking in large areas. They are also used for adding small areas of colored line work and highlights.

Flat brushes make precise marks that can be made to vary in width, either by turning the brush onto its side or by applying pressure to splay the bristles as the stroke is made. The corner of the tip can be used to add small dabs of color, and the end or edge used to create linear marks.

Short flat brushes are also known as "brights" and can be used in exactly the same way as long flats, although they hold and deliver less paint. They are suited to using thick heavy impasto paint in short precise strokes.

The filbert is a flat brush with a rounded tip. By turning the brush and altering the pressure of the stroke it can be made to create linear marks as well as to apply thick paint over a wide area.

Fan brushes were invented specifically for blending colors and tones together. They are extremely useful for dry brushwork and for use in landscape work, such as painting trees and clouds.

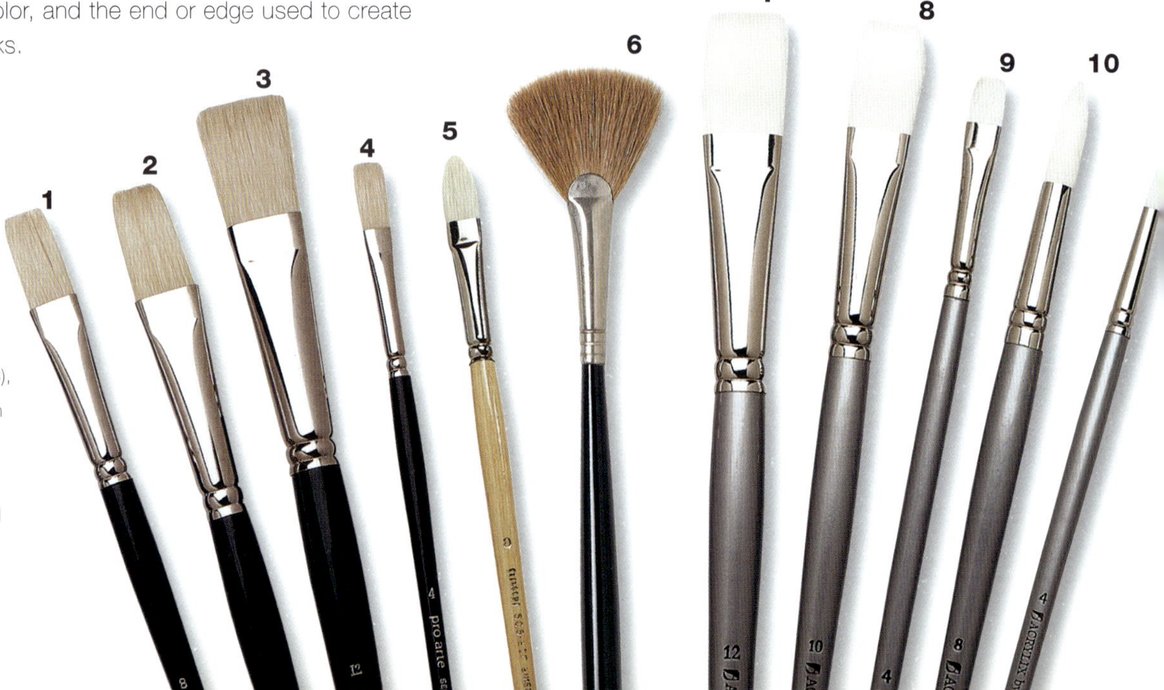

DIFFERENT BRUSHES

Medium bristle (1), Medium-large bristle (2), Large bristle (3), Small bristle (4), Filbert (5), Fan (6), Large flat nylon (7), Medium flat nylon (8), Small flat nylon (9), Medium round nylon (10), and Small round nylon (11).

NATURAL HAIR

Several different types of natural hair are used in the manufacture of brushes. Soft brushes keep their shape well and hold large quantities of paint. Soft-hair brushes are best used for acrylic techniques that require the material to be applied in thin washes, as one would when using watercolor. The same shapes that are available in bristle brushes are available in soft hair; however, you may come across a few different-shaped brushes that have specific uses.

SYNTHETIC FIBER

Synthetic fiber brushes are made using nylon filament. Today's synthetic brushes offer exceptionally good value for the money and perform almost as well as brushes made from bristle and natural hair. All the brush shapes available in bristle and natural hair are available in synthetic fiber.

BRUSH CARE

Acrylic paint dries quickly and, once dry, is very difficult to remove without using specialist solvents; so pay particular attention to looking after your brushes, or they will quickly be ruined. As you work, keep your brushes wet; this is best done using a tray and laying the brushes down so that the hair or bristles rest in water with the handles resting on the side clear of the water. After work, clean all remnants of paint from the bristles paying particular attention to the area where the bristle or hair enters the ferrule. Wash the brushes using soap or a mild detergent and rinse well in clean water.

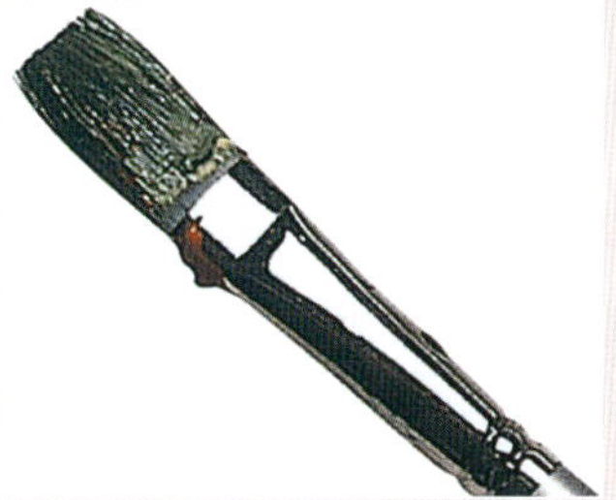

From the tip to the ferrule, brushes can become clogged with paint.

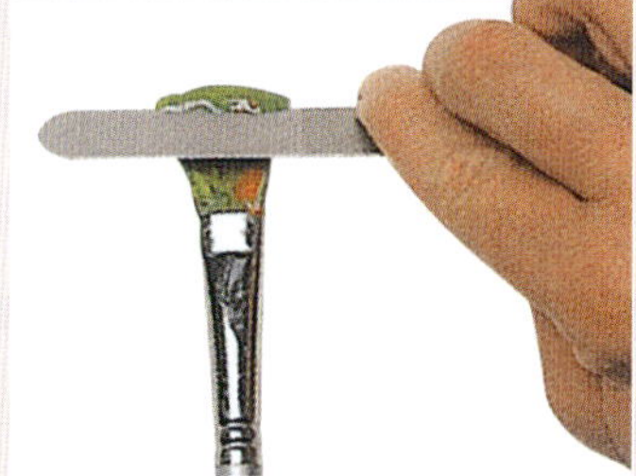

Before placing in water, remove excess paint with a palette knife.

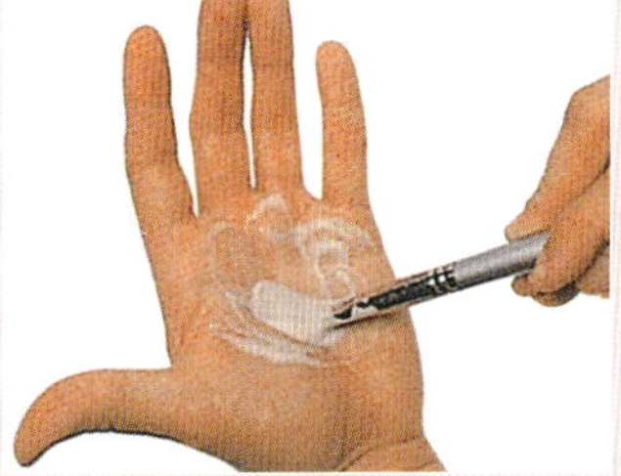

Rinse the brush in warm water and rub it into the plam of a soapy hand.

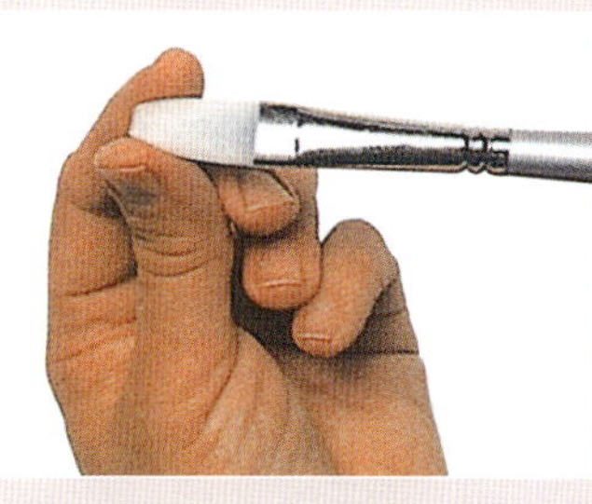

To reshape, dampen the brush and stroke it between finger and thumb.

OTHER TOOLS

Painting knives have long been used with oil paint and can be used in exactly the same way with acrylic paint. Such knives are available in plastic or stainless steel with a bent blade set into a wooden handle. The bend or crank helps keep the hand and fingers clear of the wet paint as you work. Knives come in a range of shapes and sizes, and (as with brushes) it will be necessary for you to obtain a variety of them.

Paint shapers look like conventional brushes but are made to hold a flexible rubber tip that is used to move the paint around the support surface. Shapers are available in a range of shapes and sizes in both soft and firm rubber. They are durable and easy to keep clean.

Sponges, both natural and manufactured, are excellent for applying paint and creating texture. They are available in a variety of shapes. An alternative to natural sponges is synthetic nylon sponges, available as sponge "brushes" and rollers. As with conventional brushes, these painting tools all need to be kept wet and cleaned thoroughly after use.

▼ Painting knives

▼ Palette knife

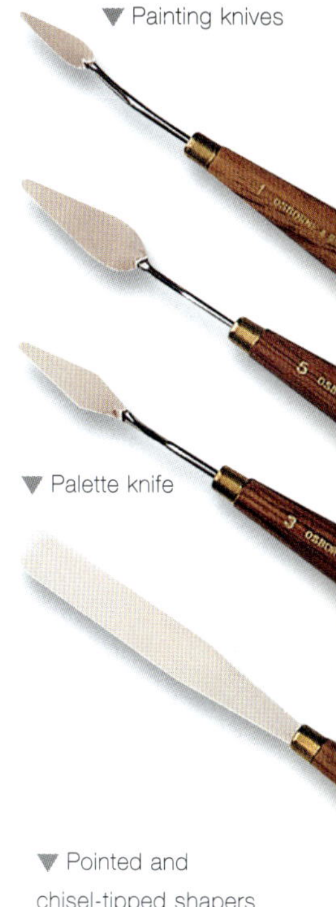

▼ Pointed and chisel-tipped shapers

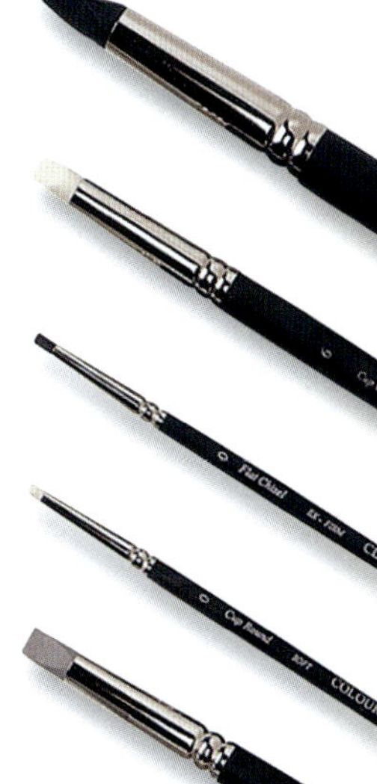

▼ Flat shapers

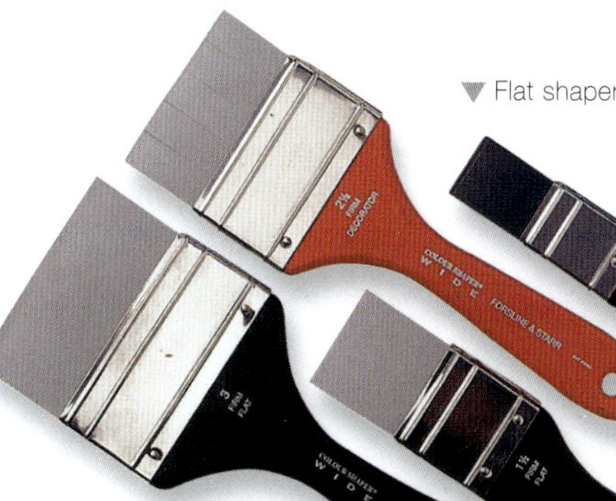

ADDITIONAL EQUIPMENT

For an artist, a palette is an essential piece of equipment. It is possible to work without a drawing board or an easel, but it is much easier if you have one or both.

PALETTES

The surface on which artists lay out and mix their paint is known as a "palette." Palettes suitable for use with acrylic paint need to be made from of a nonporous material. Glass, plastic, and ceramic surfaces are ideal. Traditional wooden palettes—unless covered in a laminate finish—are best avoided because the paint will stick permanently to their surface. Plastic palettes are intended for use with acrylic paint, but many of these tend to stain relatively quickly. Ceramic palettes intended for watercolors can be used when mixing washes but they are invariably small. Perhaps one of the best types of palette intended for use with oil or acrylic paint is the tear-off disposable palette. Another useful palette is the stay-wet palette.

The very nature of acrylic paint makes the use of improvised palettes almost obligatory. Perhaps the very best surface to choose is glass. Glass palettes are also incredibly easy to clean. Dry paint that is covered in water simply peels away. For more fluid mixes, collect and use paper, plastic, or polystyrene cups, yogurt and butter containers, or take-home food cartons.

For mixing paints on your palette, you will need to buy a palette knife or mixing knife. These are much more useful for mixing together large quantities of paint than a brush is. Knives can also be used for scraping off unused paint from the palette surface.

▼ **DISPOSABLE PALETTES**

Tear-off disposable palettes are made of sheets of impermeable paper in rectangular pads or pads that resemble an oblong palette. As each sheet is used, it is torn from the pad and disposed of.

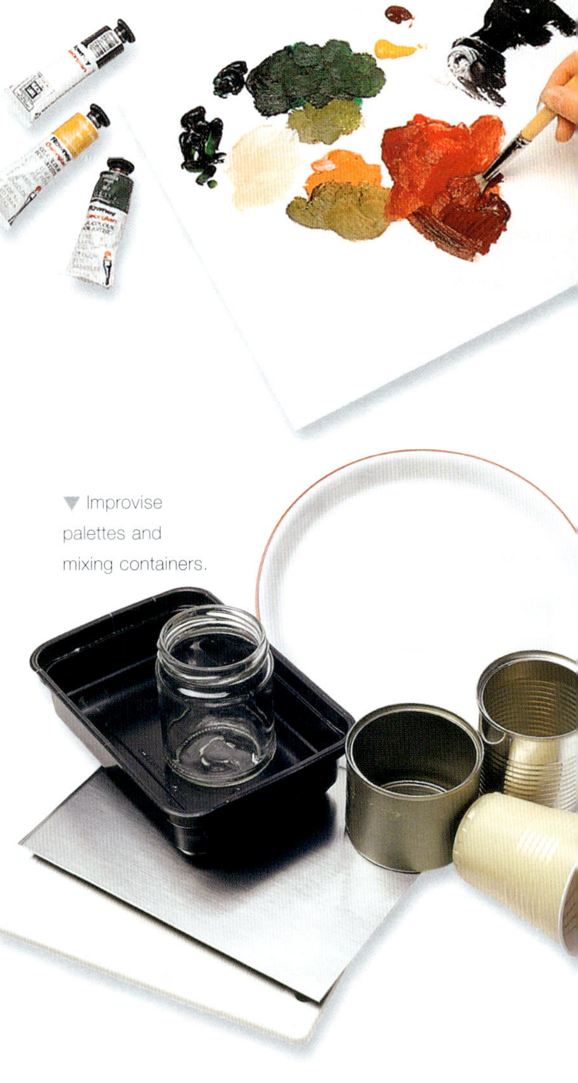

▼ Improvise palettes and mixing containers.

▼ **PERMANENT PALETTES**

You can use a purpose-made plastic or ceramic palette for acrylic paint, but many artists improvise. An old plate or a plain sheet of glass, with the edges covered with insulating tape, is fine. A sheet of thick glass can be easily purchased from a local glass supplier. This type of mixing area will be large enough to accommodate all your mixes, unlike palettes that fill with mixes very quickly.

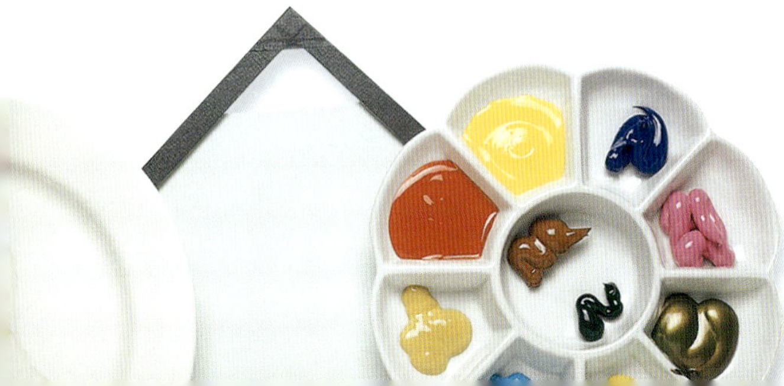

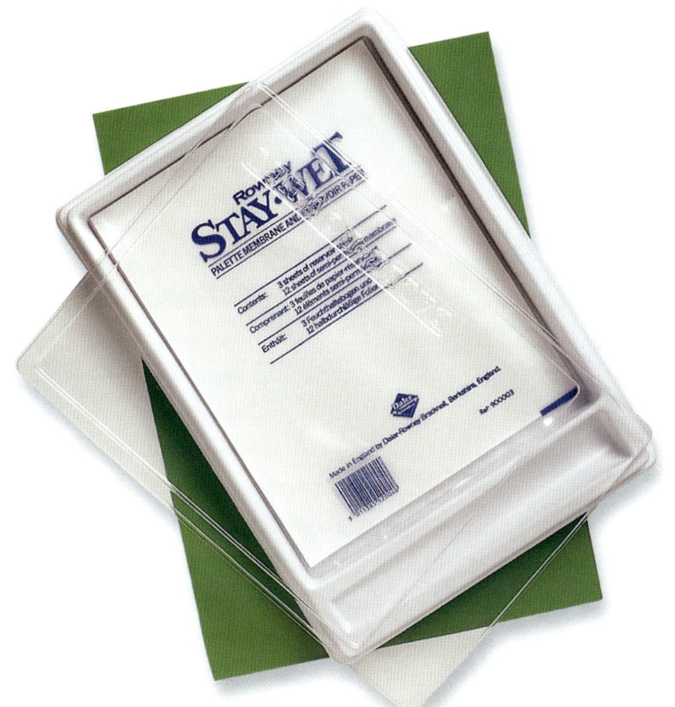

▲ **STAY-WET PALETTES**

A stay-wet palette consists of a shallow tray in the base of which is an absorbent spongelike material made damp by soaking in water. Over this is laid an impermeable, disposable paper onto which the paint is arranged and mixed. Once work is finished, a cover keeps the paint moist for days, if not weeks. As soon as the top palette paper is full, it is replaced with a clean one.

MAKING A STAY-WET PALETTE

A stay-wet palette is easily made using two or three sheets of blotting paper or a piece of capillary matting, a piece of absorbent paper, and a piece of greaseproof paper or thin tracing paper.

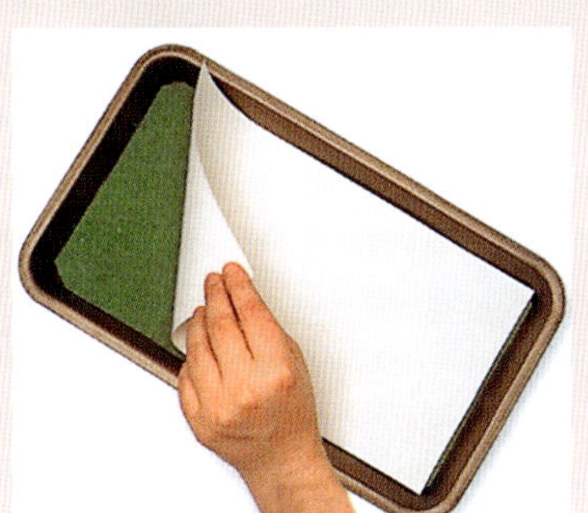

1 Soak the capillary matting for 15 minutes then squeeze it out so that it is moist. Place it in the tray base, then add the absorbent paper and greaseproof paper on top.

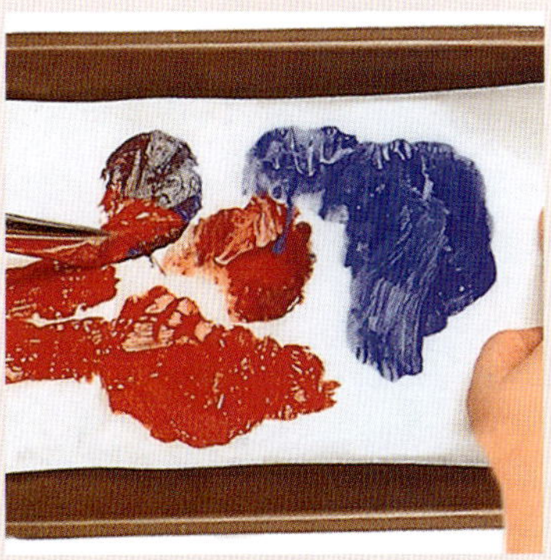

2 Place the greaseproof or tracing paper on top. To keep moist between working sessions, cover the whole tray with plastic wrap.

BOARDS AND EASELS

Boards are available in various sizes and are used to provide a solid work base for stretching paper. An easel provides a stable and adjustable support for both canvas and boards. The type you choose will depend on whether you intend to work on location and the size of paintings you intend to make. There are three main types of easel: table easels, portable easels, and studio easels.

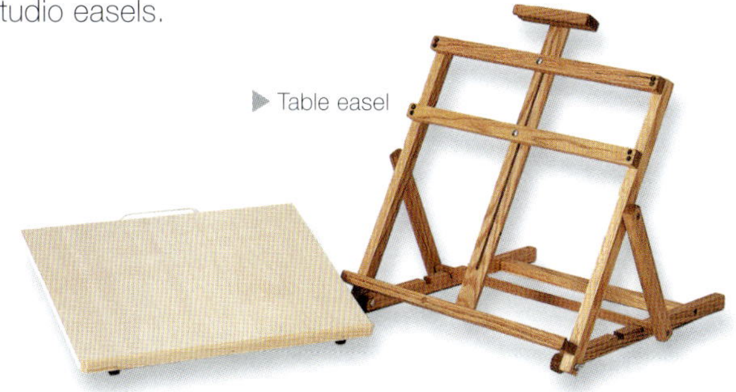

▶ Table easel

Table easels, as the name suggests, rest or stand on a table. The angle is adjustable, but they can hold only relatively small-sized supports.

Portable easels fold down to a size that can easily be carried or transported from place to place and would be the choice if you are producing work on location. They can be adjusted to hold board or canvas either horizontally or vertically, and some can accommodate supports that are of a reasonable size. They can, of course, also be used at home or in the studio.

If, however, you plan to do a lot of studio work of a certain size, then you will need a studio easel. Although expensive, it will last a lifetime. Studio easels are made in two distinct shapes based on an A frame and an H frame. A-frame easels are the smaller of the two and fold flat to rest against the wall. H-frame easels are larger and able to accommodate very large canvasses or boards. They have wheels to facilitate moving them around and either a ratchet or winch device for raising or lowering work.

FREESTANDING EASELS

The type of easel you buy must be suited to the type of work you intend to do.

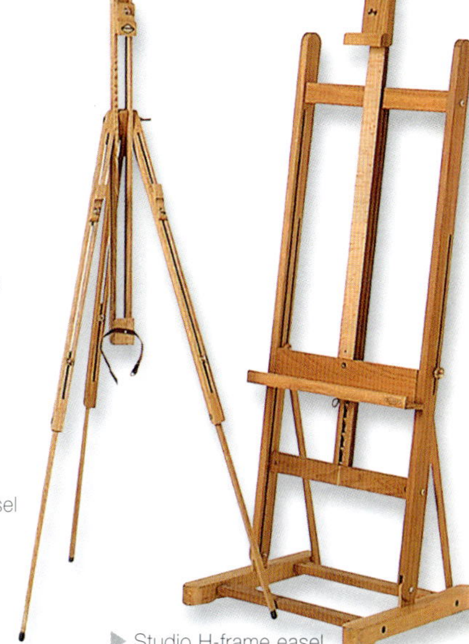

▶ Portable easel

▶ Studio H-frame easel

PLANNING THE PICTURE

Planning the picture before you begin work can save time and effort later.

FORMAT

The first consideration when planning your picture is its shape or format, and your choice will have an effect on all of your subsequent compositional decisions. There are three main formats in regular use. These are the horizontal rectangle, also known as "landscape" format; the vertical rectangle, also known as "portrait"; and the square format.

▼ PANORAMIC

Both horizontal and vertical rectangular formats can be altered proportionally to be very wide or very deep. Possible formats can be checked by making a frame through which you look by using the thumb and first finger of each hand. Alternatively, make a viewfinder (a set of cropping Ls) that can be looked through in the same way.

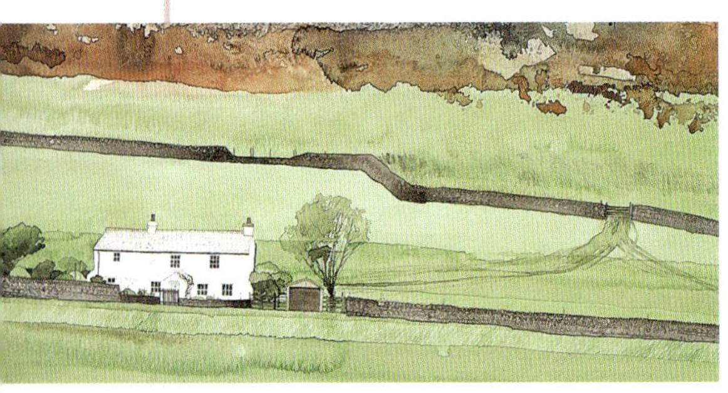

▲ An exaggerated rectangle creates a panoramic view that pulls the eye across the fields, away from the cottage.

▶ LANDSCAPE

The horizontal format is referred to as landscape format because that is the most frequently used format for painting landscapes. The horizontal format is very stable, and its shape tends to lead the eye to move across the image laterally from side to side, giving a feeling of space.

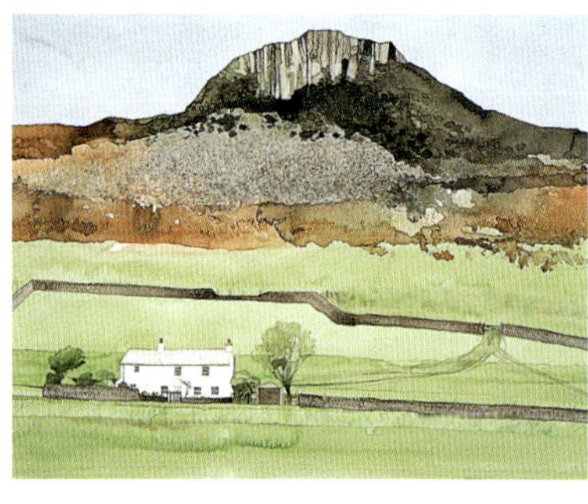

▲ A large rectangular format enables this expansive view to be accommodated.

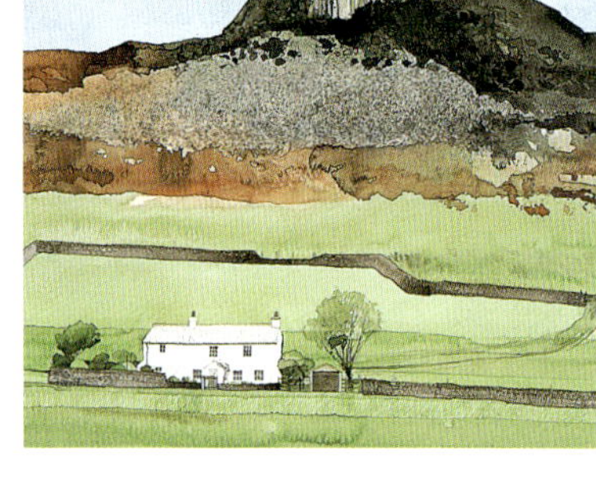

▶ Making the rectangular format smaller tightens the composition and places more emphasis on the cottage.

▶ PORTRAIT

The vertical format is the format often chosen for portrait and figure work, as it suits the upright proportions of the standing or sitting figure and gives a feeling of intimacy.

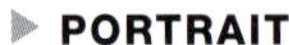

◀ An upright rectangular format of the same size adds emphasis to the height of the rocky outcrop towering above the cottage.

▶ SQUARE

The square format is perhaps the most difficult to use successfully, as the eye tends to travel both horizontally and vertically. This creates a spiraling effect, which automatically pulls the attention deep into the image.

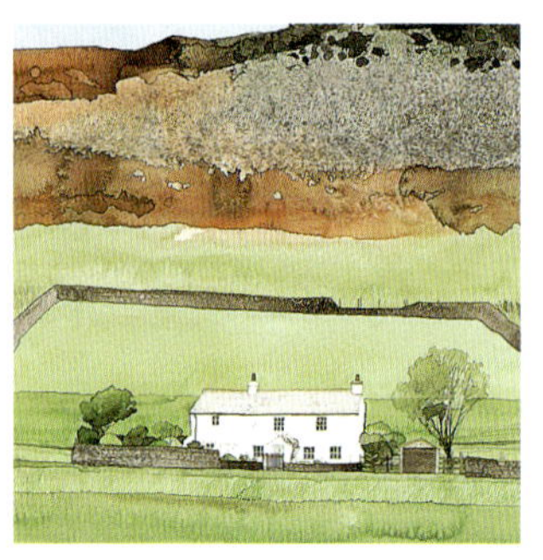

◀ An almost square format is more intimate an again draws focu to the cottage sheltered beneat the hillside.

COMPOSITION

Composition is the art of arranging all the elements to be included in the work so that a balanced design is created. Shape, scale, color, tone, and texture all play a part and need to be given equal consideration. An effective composition will not make a bad painting great, but it can make a good painting much better and so deserves careful consideration. However, it should be remembered that every rule of good composition might be and often is broken, sometimes to good effect.

FOCAL POINT

Every picture should have at least one focal point to provide a center of interest. To this end, you should always ask yourself and decide on what the main focus or point of the painting should be or what you want to emphasize or draw attention to. The focal point can be positioned anywhere within the picture area, but in a painting that is well composed, the eye—though encouraged to travel toward that focal point—will not become trapped there but will also travel round and explore the rest of the image.

THE RULE OF THIRDS

Artists have adopted or devised various formulas that divide the picture area up in an invisible grid; positioning the main elements of the image on this grid will result in a pleasing image. A similar but far easier formula is the rule of thirds, which divides the horizontal and vertical dimensions of the chosen format into thirds. By placing important elements on or about the lines and intersections, a composition can be devised that is easy on the eye, stimulating, and well balanced.

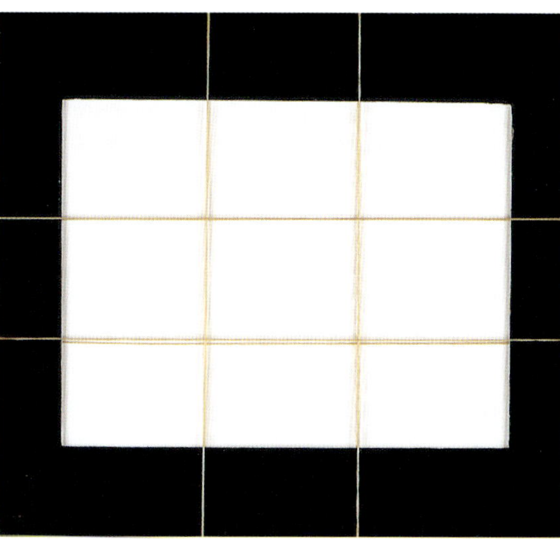

◀ A frame divided into thirds can easily be made by stretching rubber bands across the aperture cut in a sheet of cardboard. This is then held between you and the subject and will help you assess the viability and potential of the composition.

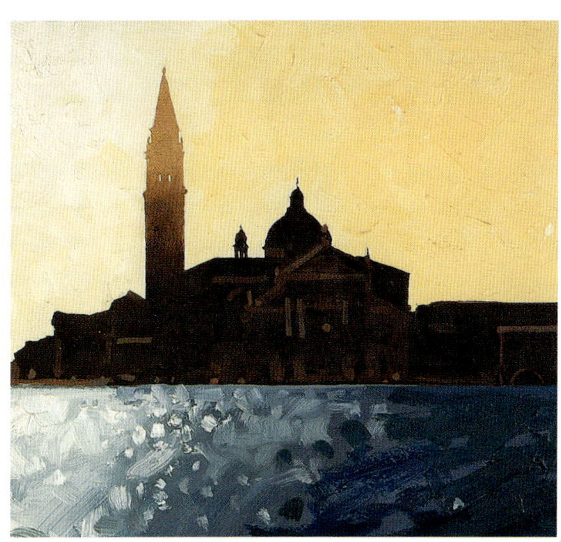

▲ In this sketch of Venice, the sky, buildings, and sea all occupy approximately one-third of the picture area, with the *Campanile* situated about one-third of the way in from the left-hand side.

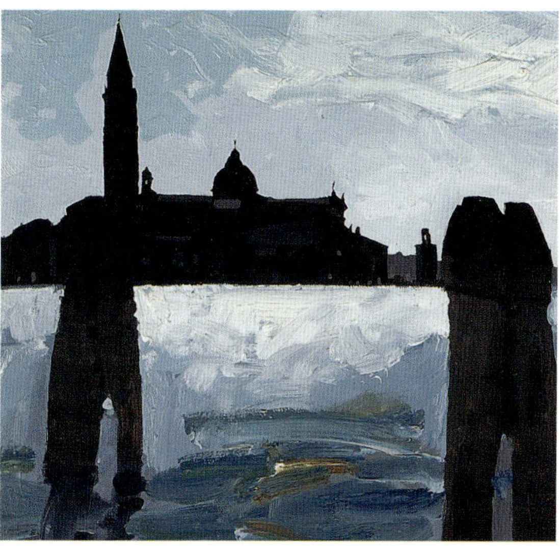

▲ This image is composed in a similar way with the addition of the *bricola* or navigation posts positioned approximately one-third of the way in from the right- and left-hand sides.

USING THUMBNAILS

A subject's compositional possibilities are many. Using your viewfinder or fingers to create a frame will give some idea of the possibilities. However, these alternatives need to be pinned down—the answer is to make a series of small sketches that explore different configurations. These drawings are known as thumbnails. Thumbnails can be of any size but, by definition, should be just large enough to show essential information. Thumbnails can be made using a monochromatic medium; however, bear in mind that color plays an important part in any composition.

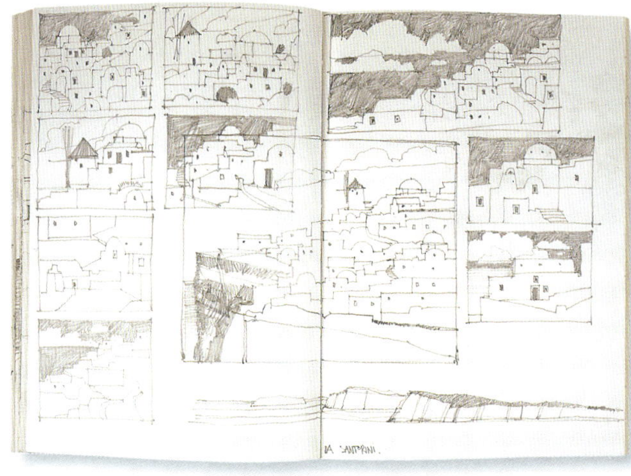

▲ This sketchbook spread shows thumbnail sketches that try to make compositional sense of the clusters of buildings in a Greek village.

LEADING THE EYE

The attention of the viewer should travel around the image, but ultimately the eye should arrive at the focal point. This can be achieved in a number of different ways. Perhaps the most obvious method is to create a pathway that leads the eye toward the desired position; this is known as a lead-in. In a landscape painting, this could literally be a path, a track, a road, a river, or a fence that the eye has a natural tendency to follow. In a portrait or figure painting, the lead-in might be formed by drapery or the pattern on a fabric. Alternatively, it might be provided by the linear characteristics of a piece of furniture. The important area can also be indicated by framing. In landscapes, this might be achieved by using the overhanging branches of a tree, the arches of a bridge, or the space between two buildings. In portraiture, the frame might be achieved using a doorway or window. An alternative way of drawing attention would be to use an eye-catching color or texture.

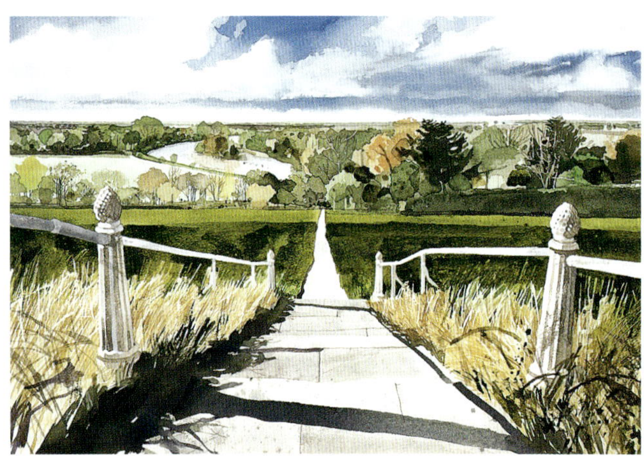

▲ Here the eye is led into the image both by the pathway that runs downhill toward the river and by the handrails that run on either side.

CREATING DEPTH

The primary method of achieving depth is the use of perspective. However, there are other means you can use to leave clues as to the spatial arrangement. One way is to crop your subject. If you use the edge of the support to cut through the subject, it will appear close to you. If you can see all of your subject, it will appear farther away. Another way of suggesting depth is by overlapping objects with the object seen in its entirety appearing the closest.

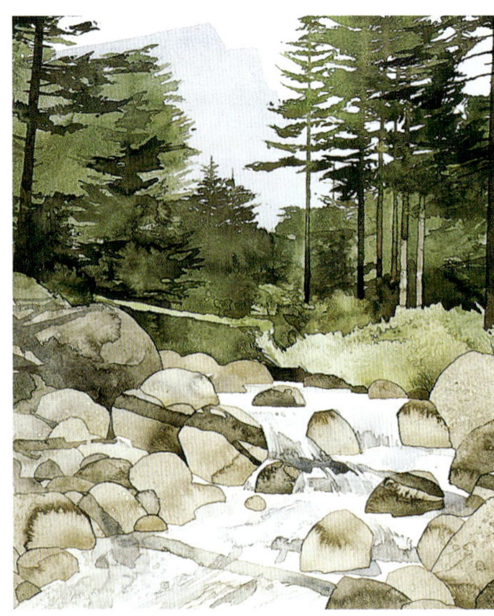

◀ In this image, the artist overlaps the bolders and trees, creating the impression of distance.

AERIAL PERSPECTIVE

In landscape painting, the illusion of depth is created primarily by using *aerial perspective*. If you look closely at the landscape, you will notice several things. First, the landscape in the distance looks cooler, with the colors appearing to be more blue. Colors in the foreground are warmer, with noticeable reds and warm browns. Second, tonal contrast is greatly reduced in the distance, while closer strong darks and bright highlights give a full tonal scale to things. Detail and texture is less evident in the distance. Last, objects seen in the distance are smaller than objects seen close-up. Artists often exaggerate these phenomena to increase spatial awareness.

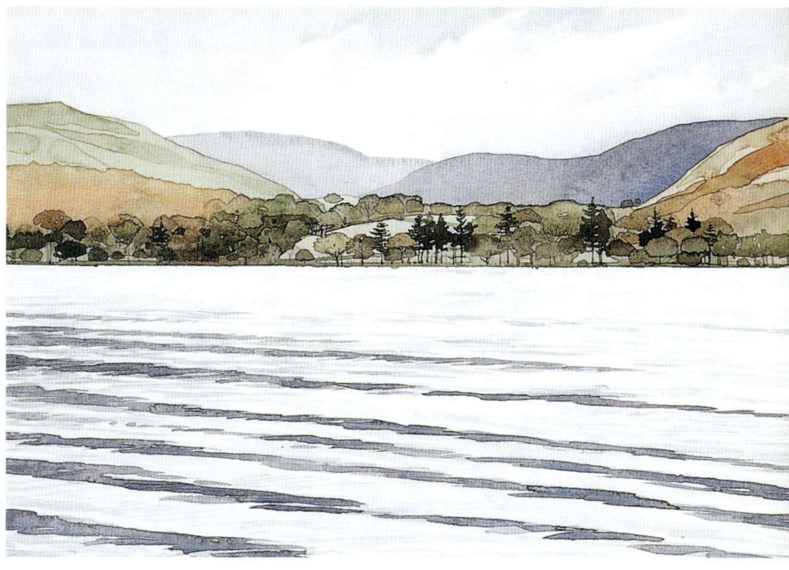

▲ By using the principles of aerial or atmospheric perspective, your landscape images will have greater depth.

LINEAR PERSPECTIVE

Linear perspective is less tangible and, in many cases, less noticeable than aerial perspective. *Linear perspective* creates the illusion of three-dimensional depth on a two-dimensional surface.

The primary rule of linear perspective states that all parallel lines on a plain will converge into a *vanishing point* as the plain recedes. This vanishing point is positioned on the *horizon line*, also known as the "eye level," since it always runs across the field of vision at eye level regardless of the viewer's position. All perspective lines that originate above the eye level run down to meet the vanishing point, while all perspective lines that originate below the eye level run up to meet the vanishing point.

Linear perspective, although associated with buildings or objects that have a distinctly geometric shape, can be utilized when drawing anything—including the human figure. This is done by working with a simple cube- or boxlike structure into which the shape of the body can be correctly orientated; this is especially useful when dealing with foreshortening.

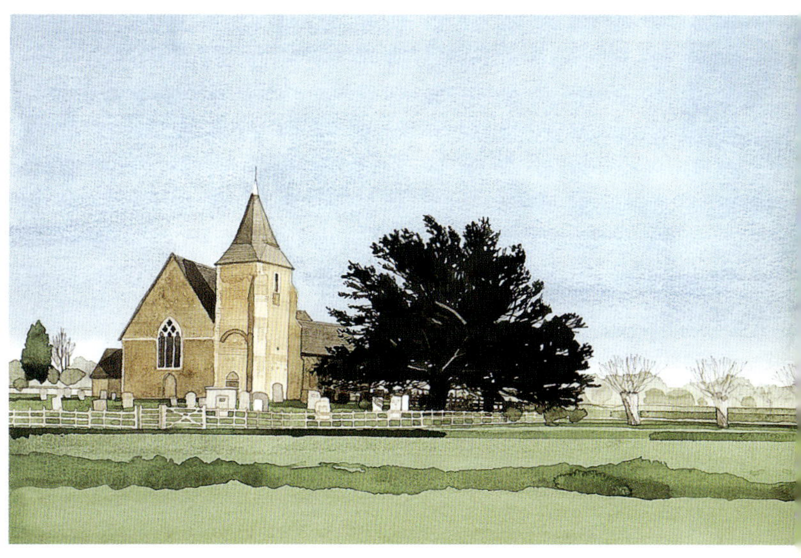

▲ In this image of a country church, the underlying perspective is not at first obvious.

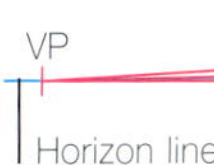

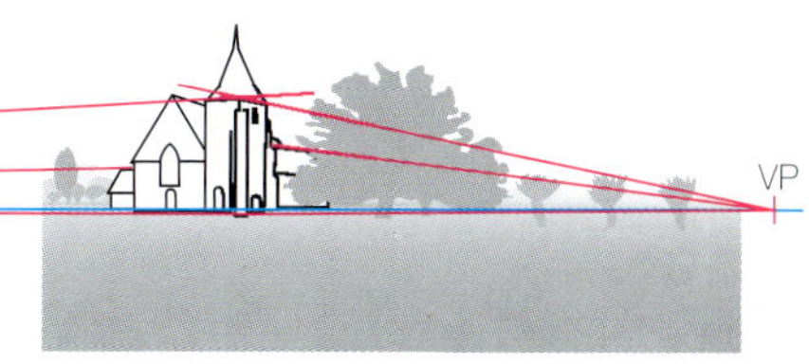

COLOR AND TONE

Color and tone are essential components of most paintings, and to produce successful images, you will need to learn how to handle both with a degree of confidence.

COLOR

The most important device for helping you understand color is the *color wheel.* This shows the colors in the visible spectrum in one continuous progression. In terms of pigment, red, yellow, and blue are the three primary colors and cannot be made by mixing other colors together. Mix together any two primary colors, and you will create the three secondary colors: orange, green, and violet. Mixing together a primary color and the secondary immediately next to it results in the six tertiary colors: red-orange, yellow-orange, yellow-green, blue-green, blue-violet, and red-violet. Adjusting the proportion of color in the mixes results in a wide range of subtle variations.

COLOR TEMPERATURES

All colors are described as being either warm or cool when seen in the form of a color wheel. Red, orange, and yellow are warm while green, blue, and violet are cool. However, it is not that simple, as all colors have warm and cool variants. Cadmium red light is considered to be a warm red because it leans toward yellow, which is also considered to be warm; whereas alizarin crimson is considered to be a cool red because it has a blue bias, and blue is considered to be a cool color. The knowledge of color "temperature" is important because warm colors tend to advance whereas cool colors recede, and this is an important consideration when giving the illusion of depth.

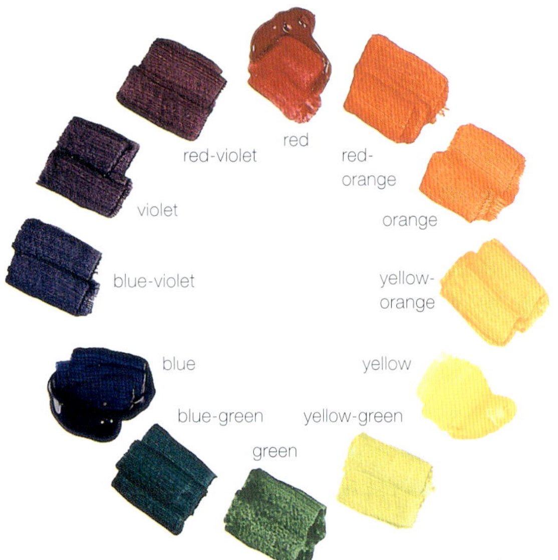

▲ The color wheel shows the three primary colors, the three mixed secondary colors, and the six mixed tertiary colors.

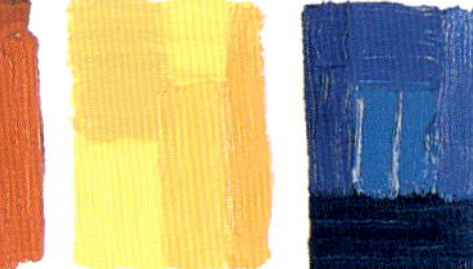

▶ Primary colors are manufactured and can be purchased in a range of warm and cool variations.

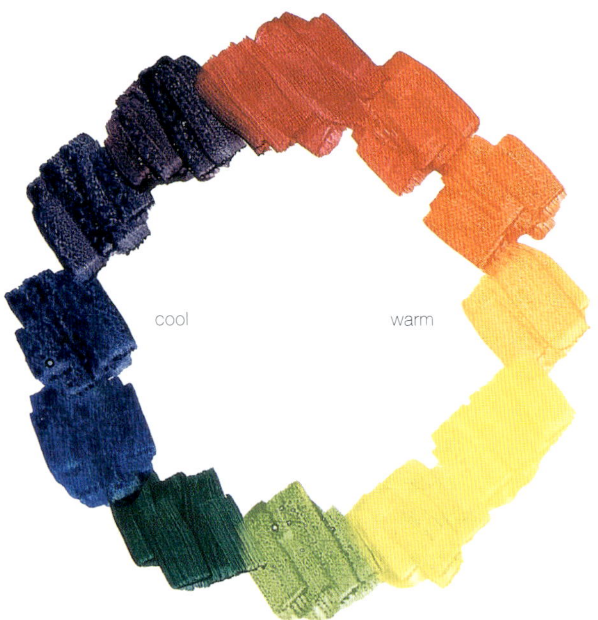

▶ The color wheel is divided into a "warm" and a "cool" side, with red, orange, and yellow considered warm, and green, blue, and violet considered cool.

COMPLEMENTARY COLORS

Those colors that fall opposite one another across the color wheel are also known as complementary pairs and have a very special relationship. When complementary colors of a similar intensity are placed next to each other they have the effect of intensifying or brightening each other. This is caused by an effect known as "simultaneous contrast"; however, if you mix two complementary colors together physically, they have the effect of first subduing each other and, as more is mixed, of canceling each other out. This is known as "neutralizing" and results in a range of beautiful grays and browns that are extremely useful colors.

It can be seen that—in theory, at least—it would be possible to mix every color from the primary colors red, yellow, and blue. But in reality, there are many different reds, yellows, and blues, and different combinations will make slightly different secondary and tertiary mixes. It is for this reason that most artists choose to work with a color range that includes at least one warm and one cool variant of each primary.

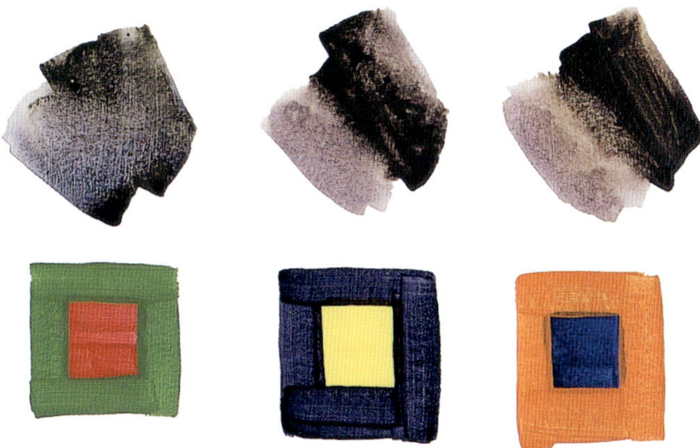

▲ Colors falling opposite one another on the wheel are complementary, and when placed next to one another they appear much brighter. However, when mixed together, they cancel each other out, resulting in a range of neutral gray and brown mixes.

TONE

Tone (also called "value") describes the relative lightness or darkness of a subject and helps describe its form. The more a surface faces the light source, the lighter it will appear to be. Conversely, the more a surface faces away from the light source, the darker it will appear. Tone can be difficult to assess since color, texture, and pattern all serve to obscure it. Squinting your eyes can help to simplify the perceived tonal range because it cuts down the midtones and exaggerates the lights and the darks. The minimum number of tones needed to see form are three: white, black, and one midtone. This results in an image that is strong in contrast and is the type of image seen in very bright light. In subdued light, the tonal range is wider, with more emphasis on the midtones.

Color plays an important part in tone. It is a relatively easy task to assess tone in terms of black, white, and gray, but when color is introduced, the subject becomes a little more complex. All colors have an equivalent or distinct tonal value that is most evident when looking at a black and white photograph. When looking at the photograph, what becomes immediately evident is that colors that are completely different are in fact tonally identical. Being able to judge and mix these tones correctly makes a convincing and successful representation.

▼ **TONAL VALUE CHART**

To make a tonal value chart, divide a sheet of watercolor paper into 10 even squares and number them 1 to 10. Leave the first square white. Paint the second square in a very light tone of your chosen color (burnt umber is shown here), and gradually darken the following squares until number 10 is as dark as possible (you may need two coats for this).

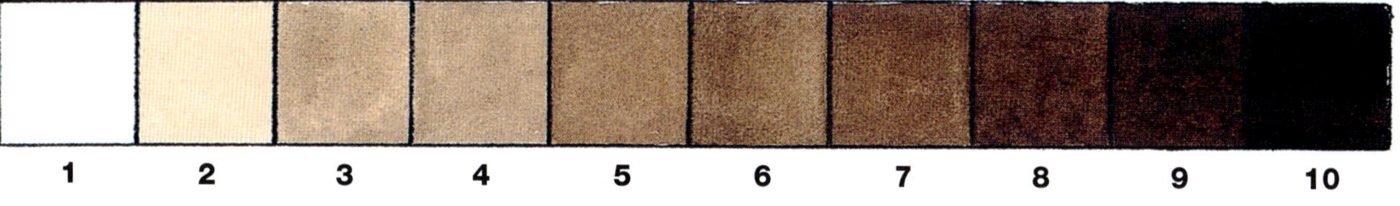

PLANNING THE WORK

Preparatory work might include reference photographs, exploratory drawings, visual and written notes on colors and tone, thumbnail sketches that explore compositional alternatives, and sketches that work out any complex perspective issues.

PRODUCING A WORKING DRAWING

A popular way to start your painting is to produce what is known as a working drawing. This is often made so that it is the same size as the intended painting. The drawing can be as involved or as simple as you wish, but its purpose should be to pull together all the important elements featured in the finished work. The main elements of this drawing can then be transferred onto the support, and provide a guide for the subsequent applications of paint.

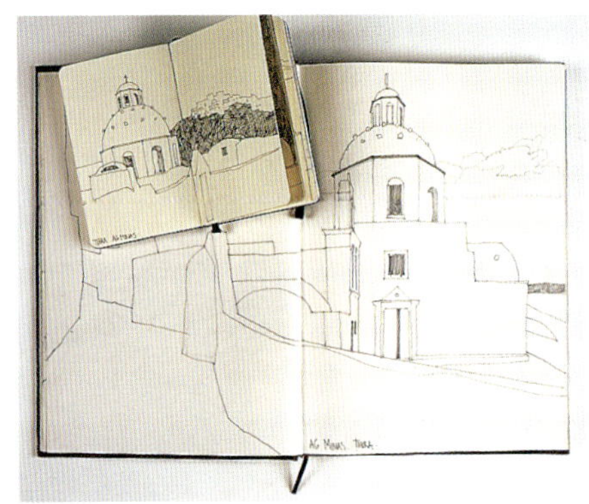

◀ Assemble any preparatory drawings, sketches, and other reference material.

TRANSFERRING THE DRAWING

If you are confident, then the drawing can be copied without using any aids. However, many prefer to copy the drawing precisely (either by using a tracing or by making a grid of squares that covers the drawing) and then making an equivalent grid of squares on the painting support. The image is then transferred a square at a time. The grid method is very useful, as it enables you to enlarge or reduce an image simply by adjusting the size of the squares on the support so that they are larger or smaller than the grid of squares on the working drawing.

The drawing on the support can be made in any drawing or water-based media you wish. If using a soft pigmented drawing tool, you may find that it is a good idea to fix it either using spray fixative or by brushing it over with a 50/50 mixture of water and matte medium. This may make the drawing slightly less distinct, but if it is brushed on lightly using a large brush, the mixture will not remove the drawing completely.

1

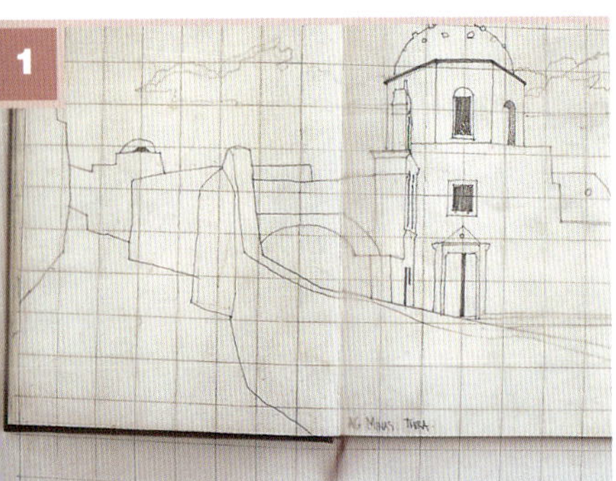

STEP 1 If a drawing is to be transferred, using the grid method will result in a perfect copy.

2

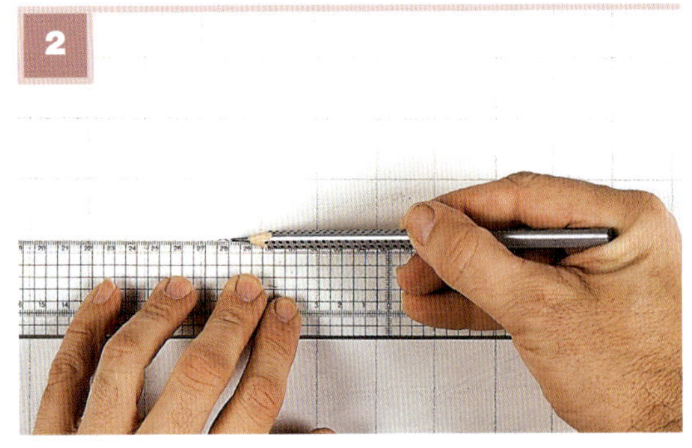

STEP 2 To transfer the drawing, the support will need to be gridded.

3

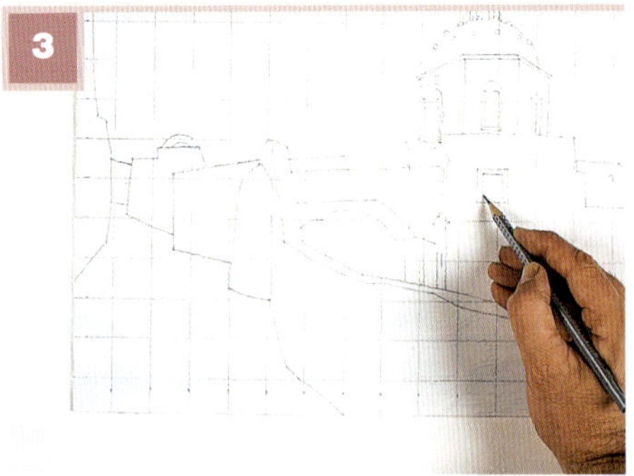

STEP 3 Transfer the drawing carefully, square by square.

CREATING A COLORED GROUND

If you have decided to work on a colored ground, you can add color to the gesso primer, or you can apply a colored wash over the support prior to making the drawing. However, if you did neither of these, you will have to establish the ground. This is achieved by applying the desired color over the drawing. Do not make the color too dark or apply the paint too thickly or you will simply obliterate your drawing. If you are working on paper using thin washes of color, then your choice of drawing materials is quite important, since the washes of color may not cover up the drawing. In such instances, the drawing needs to be made using a material that will disappear easily beneath the layers of wash, and experience shows that graphite is a good choice.

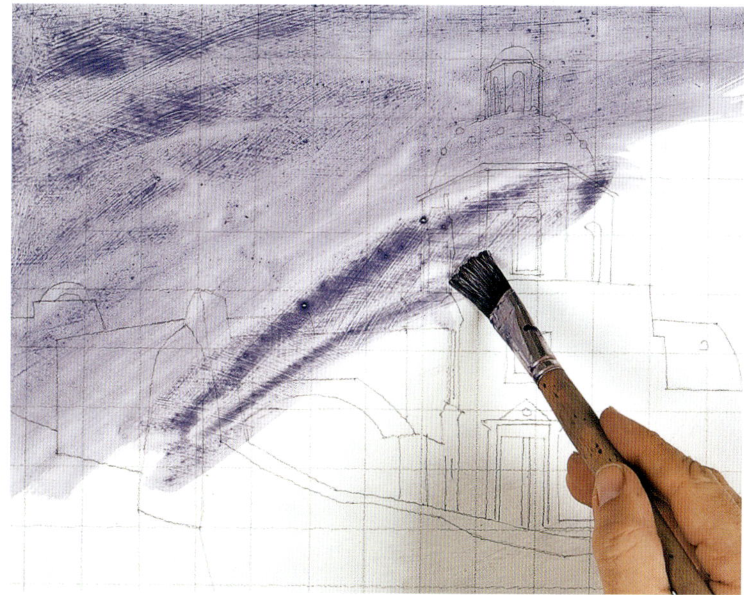

▲ Once the drawing has been transferred, a colored ground can be applied, but take care not to make this so dark that it obliterates your drawing.

UNDERPAINTING

You are now ready to begin painting. If you are using watercolor wash techniques, you will be working light to dark using thin washes of color on (more than likely) a white support. By definition, these washes will be thin, so an early building up of paint should not be a problem. However, when the intention is to produce a work that ultimately uses thicker layers of paint, use thin paint for any initial blocking in or underpainting. A buildup of thick paint can be a drawback since acrylic paint once dry cannot be removed.

Although working with an underpainting is not always necessary, it has several advantages. First, if working on a white ground rather than on a toned ground, the underpainting subdues the harshness of the support color, making it easier to assess the correct color and tone of subsequently applied paint layers. Acrylic paint does have good covering power, but some colors and mixes can lack opacity, and working over an underpainting will increase the color depth. Working with an underpainting also enables you to make decisions about composition and tone, and leaves you free to concentrate on decisions about precise color, brushwork, and how to represent texture at a later date. An underpainting allows you to check the look of the piece before you have spent too long working on it, and, because of the fast drying time of thin acrylic paint, thicker applications can be applied almost immediately. Remember to allow each layer of paint to dry before applying more. This will keep your colors and brushwork looking fresh and the colors clean. If you do wish to work wet into wet or plan to blend colors together, use a retarding medium. Make full use of acrylic mediums and additives as you work. They are intended to help you realize the full potential of the material and contribute enormously to how the piece will look and how the paint will handle.

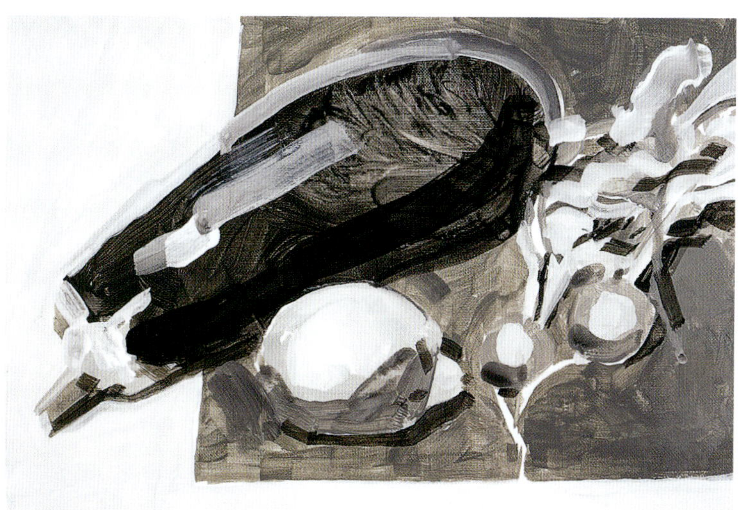

▲ If you intend to produce a work that uses thick layers of paint, make your initial blocking in or underpainting using thin paint.

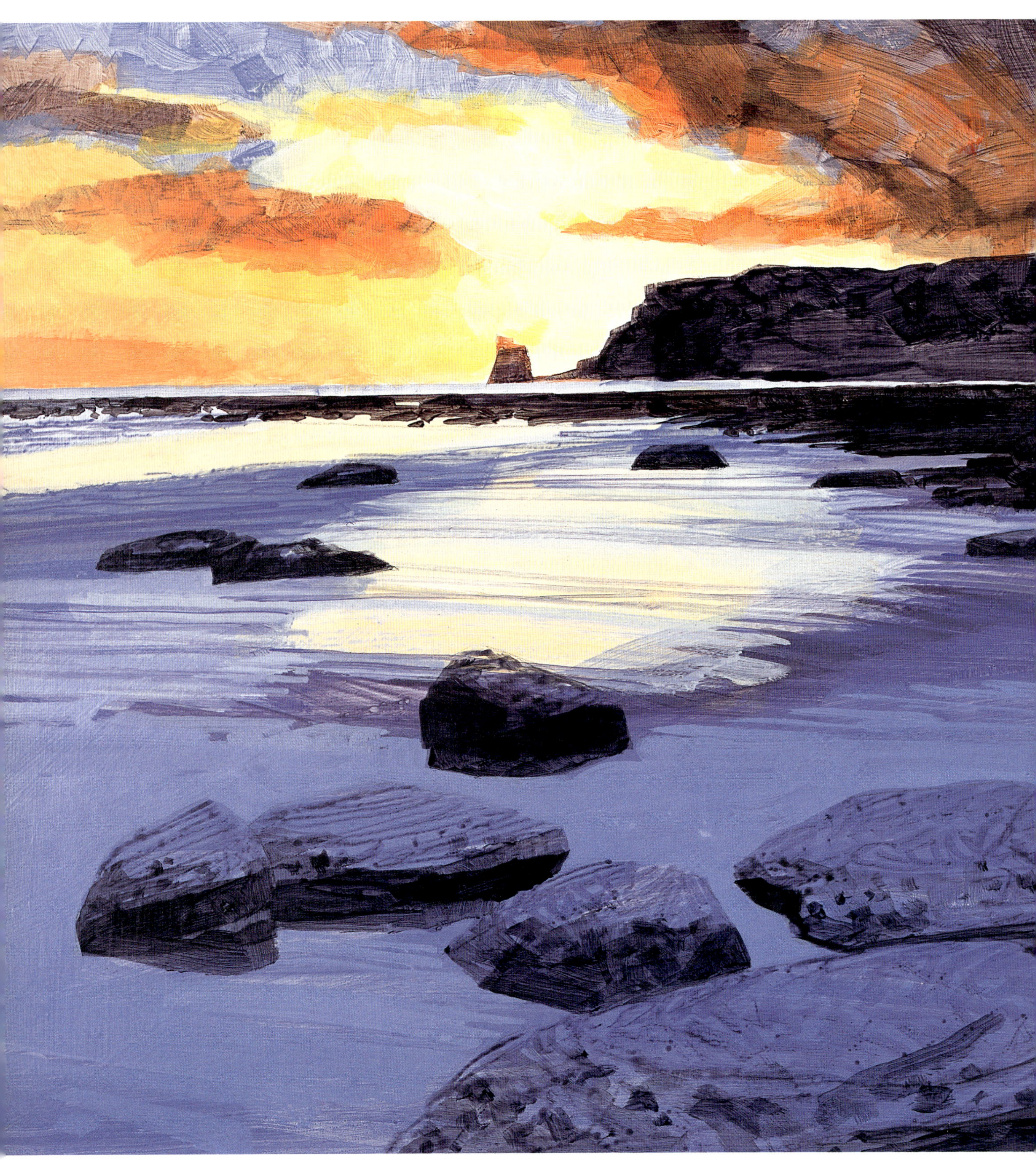

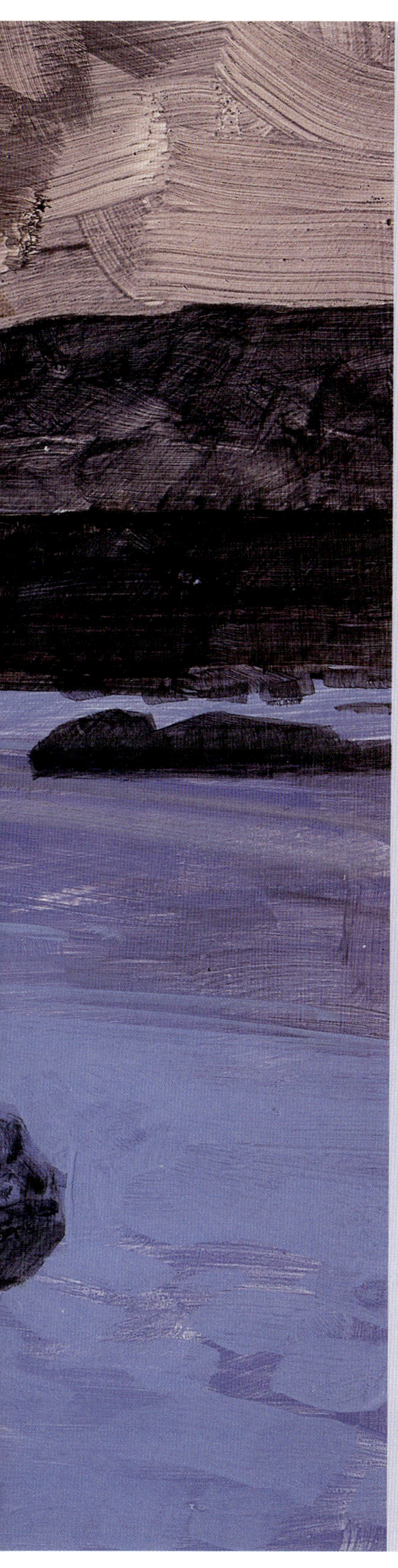

PART TWO

TECHNIQUES

Acrylic paint can reproduce practically all other types of paint, including watercolor, tempera, and gouache. Acrylic paint is also the perfect partner for mixed-media work using graphite, pastel, chalk, ink, or collage. Work through these techniques and you will be equipped to use acrylic in any form.

BASIC TECHNIQUES

Some knowledge of the basic techniques combined with practical experience will help you to gain confidence.

BLENDING

To create graded tones or to make one color gradually change into another, blend applications of wet paint into one another. The quick-drying nature of acrylic paint can make blending more difficult than with traditional oil paint. When using acrylic painting mediums and thick impasto paint, the paint will stay workable for longer; but if you have a large area to blend, it could easily become unworkable before you have finished. Manufacturers have recognized this problem and supply retarding mediums that, when added to the paint, prevent it from drying out too quickly. Alternatively, artists sometimes use a fine spray to apply a mist of water onto the paint. This can be a difficult technique to master, as the water mixes with the paint and can become thinner than was intended.

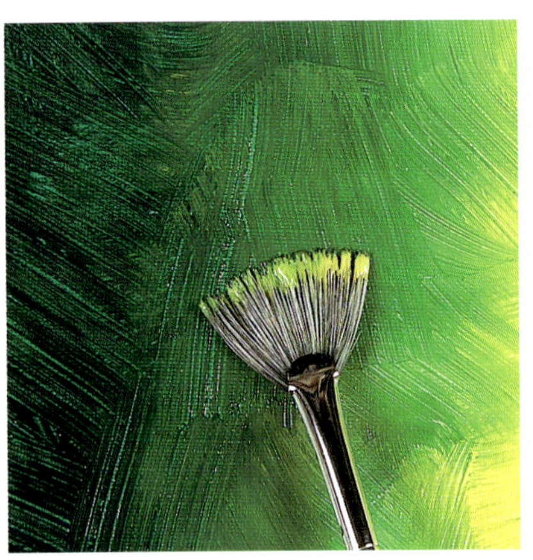

FAN BLENDER

The fan blender brush was invented for this very blending process. It is available in several sizes in both bristle and synthetic fiber variations. If you wish, you can begin the blending using a flat brush. Once the rough blending has been completed, use the fan blender to complete the process. Use a series of crisscrossing strokes to pull the colors together. Clean the brush periodically, but do not rinse in water until you have completed the area.

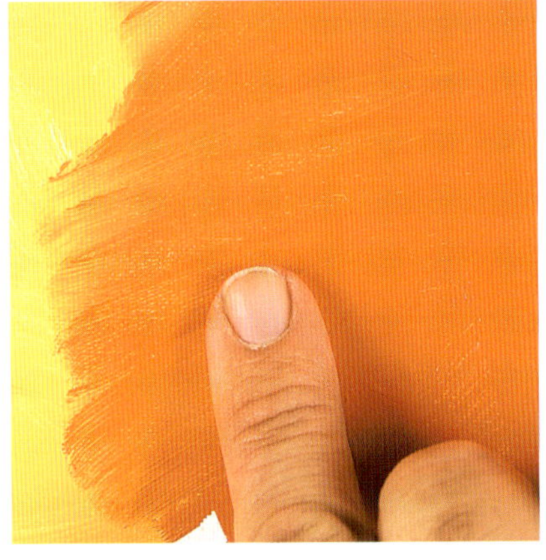

FINGER BLENDING

A useful and quick way to loosely blend an area is to use a finger instead of a brush. Apply the paint so that the two colors to be blended almost touch; then run the finger through the paint, rubbing and blending the two colors together. This is a very quick way of working and only useful for rough blending or for pushing together two relatively small areas of color.

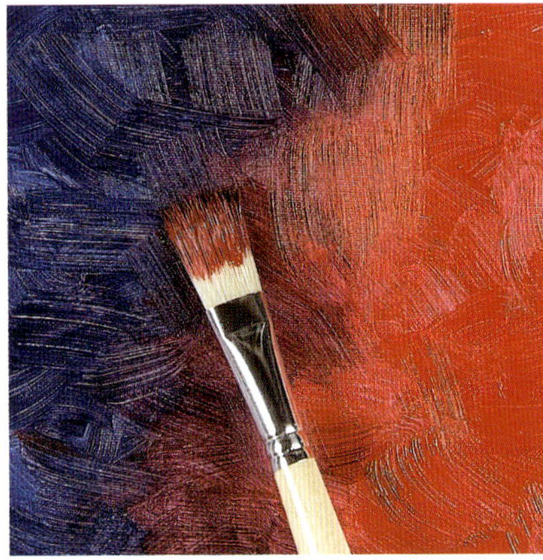

BRUSH BLENDING

Flat brushes are best for blending. Blend the area loosely at first, gradually pulling and pushing the colors together using a series of multidirectional strokes. As paint builds up on the brush, you will find that you are transporting paint to where it is not needed, and the blending process becomes increasingly difficult. Clean the brush by wiping off the paint using a paper towel or a rag, but do not wet the brush by rinsing it in water. Wetting the brush means that, when you return to continue the blending process, the water left on the brush will mix with the paint, thinning it slightly and making it look different than the thicker paint in the surrounding area.

BRUSHMARKS

The primary and most important tool for applying paint is the brush. As we have mentioned in the section on brushes and other tools (see page 20) there are many different sizes and shapes available, all of which make a series of different marks.

Some brushes are far more useful than others, whereas some have special uses and may be used only occasionally. While much can be done with a single brush, more can be achieved if you have a selection. The abrasive action of rough-textured supports gradually wear down the brush fibers, and this often results in a brush "tailoring" itself to a specific use. These brushes then become favored for a time—that is, until they wear too much and become unusable. However, never throw an old brush away, because at some point you will find a use for it.

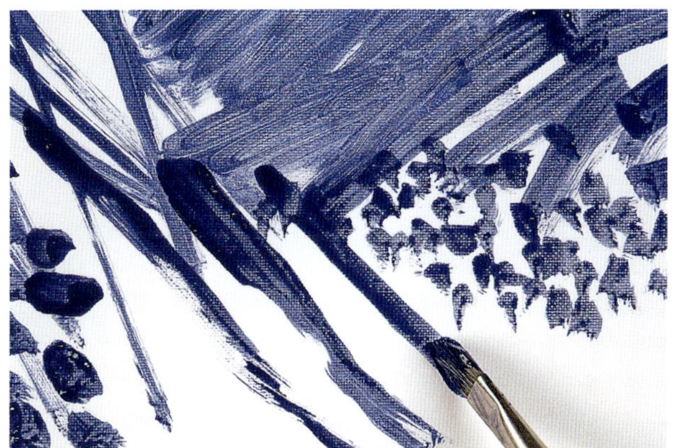

FILBERT BRUSHES

The rounded end of the flat filbert brush enables it to do most of the work of both the flat and the round brush. It is good for detail and looser work but not as good for applying flat areas of paint or fine blending. The brush comes into its own when applying paint using fluid, expressive brushwork and for scrubbing and scumbling paint to create the illusion of texture. Filberts in many ways resemble and behave like well-used, worn flat brushes.

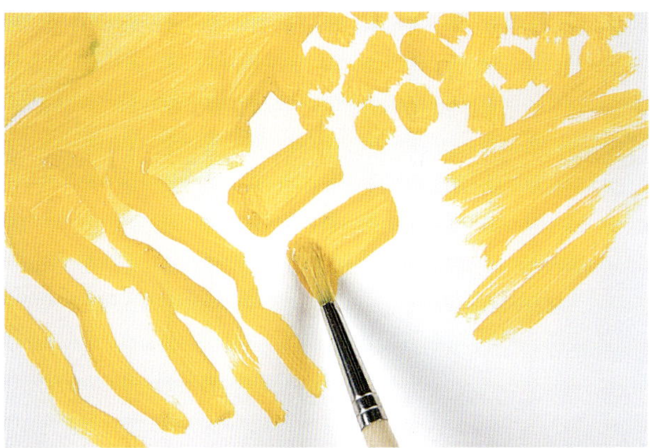

ROUND BRUSHES

Round brushes made from hair or synthetic fibers are often more pointed than round brushes made from bristle, and this makes them far more useful for painting details. Round bristle brushes were once more popular than they are now. Used on their side, a wide stroke can be made; but pull along their width, and the stroke will be only as wide as the bristles are arranged. Apply more pressure, and the bristles will splay to create a wider stroke. Round brushes are useful for applying blobs or dabs of color and for loosely sketching out the main structure and elements of the image. Round brushes are not good for applying flat areas of paint.

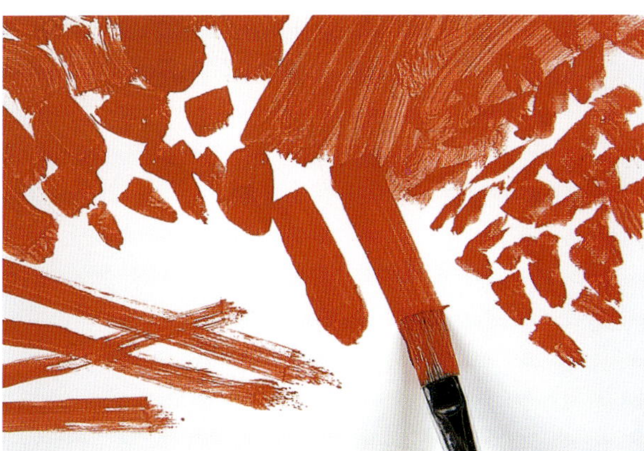

FLAT BRUSHES

Flat brushes are very adaptable. They can deliver paint in a uniformly flat manner over a large area, and they can be used for blending colors and tones together. Used on the edge, thin linear marks can be made, and the corner of the wedge-shaped tip can be used to paint details or add very small dabs of paint. Used with impasto applications, flat bristle brushes deliver the paint in long or short fluid strokes that can be made to follow the contours of the subject being painted. Large flat brushes can be used to quickly block in very large areas.

DRYBRUSH

The *drybrush* technique can be used with both transparent or opaque paint, but it works better when used with thin, fluid paint rather than with thick paint.

Even done properly, drybrushing can be tedious, but is very controllable and capable of achieving fine results. Although the technique can be applied on an unpainted support, it is usual to work on a previously painted surface since using drybrush techniques to actually cover an area can take forever. Drybrush technique is used to create texture and to model form.

USING A BRUSH

To drybrush, almost all the paint needs to be removed from the brush fibers or bristles. Any type of brush can be used, but flat soft bristle brushes and round soft brushes tend to work best. The brush is loaded with paint in the normal way, and the brush is then wiped on a rag or paper towel to remove most of the paint. The fingers splay the brush fibers, separating them out. The small amount of paint still left on the brush fibers is enough to create a mark. Leave too much paint on the brush, and the mark will look like a straightforward brushstroke and the open, linear quality of the mark will be lost. Use too little paint, and the stroke will hardly be visible.

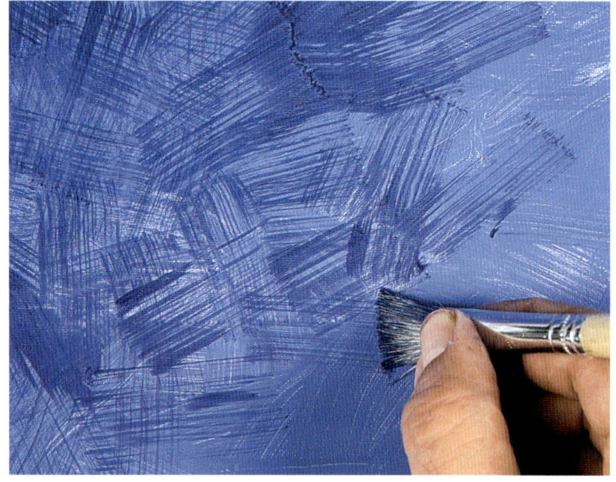

LOOSE SCRUBBING

Scrubbing is similar to *scumbling* (see "Scumbling and Broken Color," page 40). Unlike delicate drybrush, which shows up the individual hair fibers, scrubbing simply distributes the paint over the support surface in a semitransparent film. The technique is faster to do than the previous two methods and is best done with thick paint and a brush with stiff bristles. As before, the bulk of the paint needs to be removed from the brush fibers, but the delivery can be more forceful and follows more of a scrubbing action than an actual stroke.

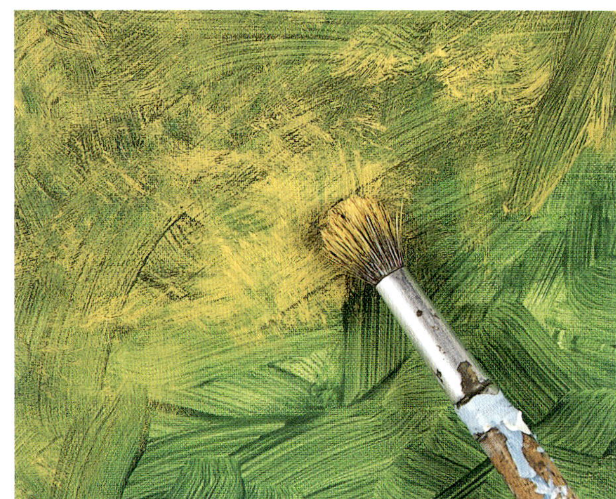

USING A FAN BLENDER

Although not designed with drybrush in mind, fan blenders make the perfect tool for the job. The brush is designed so that the fibers remain permanently splayed. As with an ordinary brush, take care to not overload the brush with too much paint. A useful trick, and one that seems to allow just enough paint onto the brush fibers, is to soak a rag or paper towel in the desired color and then wipe the brush over the rag, coating the fibers with just the right amount of paint.

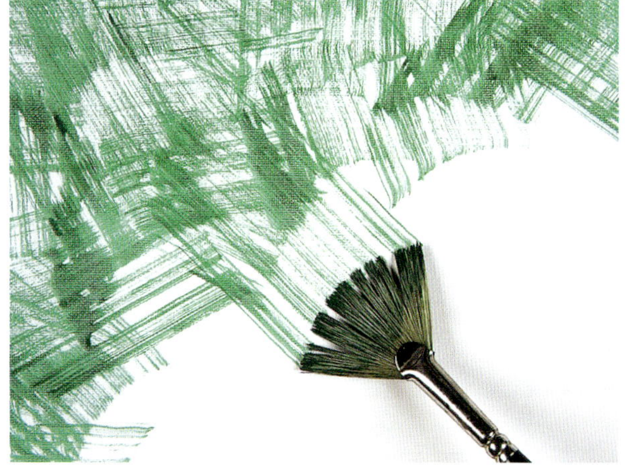

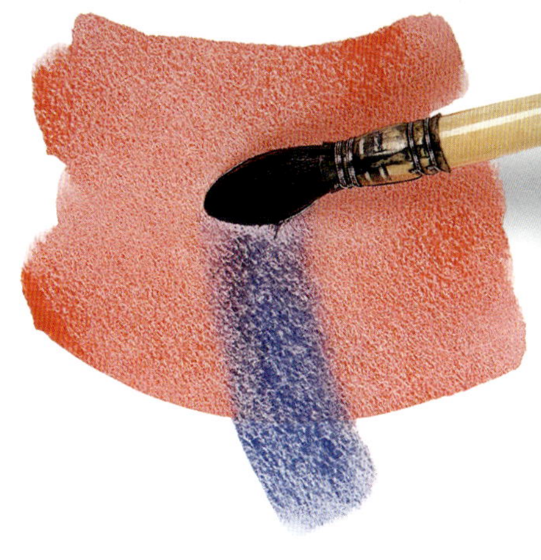

WATERCOLOR

Acrylic paint can be used in the same way as watercolor—without white paint. Water is added to create thin semitransparent washes.

Color and tone are made lighter by adding more water and made darker by adding more pigment. When mixing dark or intense colors, care needs to be taken not to add so much paint that the liquid's semitransparent consistency is lost and the paint becomes too thick and opaque.

WASHES

Paint thinned with water and applied in a semitransparent layer is known as a wash. In watercolor painting, washes are built up one over the other, each wash altering the one beneath. Washes can be flat or graded, so they become lighter or darker. Alternatively, washes can be made that change from one color to another. To make a flat wash, mix up plenty of the desired color. Tilt the support slightly so that when you make your brushstroke, the paint puddles slightly along the bottom edge of the stroke. Load the brush again with paint and make another stroke so that it slightly overlaps the first. The paint collects along the bottom of this stroke. Continue until the area is covered. To make a graded wash, proceed in the same way, adding a little more water into the mix after each stroke. To make a variegated wash, simply change the color at any given point. Alternatively, gradually add a different color into the mix a little at a time after each stroke of the brush.

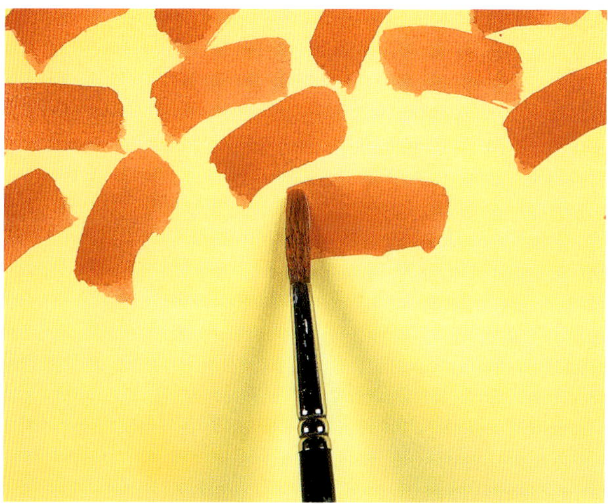

WET ON DRY

Paint applied onto a previously applied wash that has been allowed to dry is known as wet on dry. With wet-on-dry techniques, the paint does not spread but stays where it is put and retains the shape of the brushmark. Paint applied in this way has a crisp, hard edge, and wet-on-dry techniques are used to pull a painting together and bring elements into sharp focus. Previously applied colors can be altered and modified by applying different colored washes over them. For instance, a yellow wash could be made orange by applying a red wash over it.

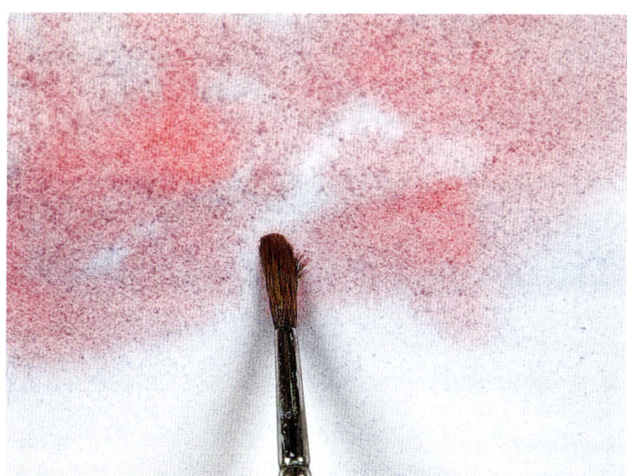

WET ON WET

If you apply wet paint onto a previously applied wash that is still wet, the newly introduced paint will push and spread into that wash, blending with it to create soft amorphous shapes. The degree and speed with which the paint spreads is determined by how wet the initial wash is. If the wash is only slightly damp, the spread will be slow and limited. If the wash is very wet, the newly introduced paint will spread quickly and over a wider area. Wet-into-wet washes can be difficult to control, but the effects that are possible really show up the beauty of the watercolor technique. In practice, wet-into-wet washes are invariably used in tandem with washes that are termed wet on dry.

STIPPLING

Color and tone can be built up by using a network of small dots or dashes, a process known as "stippling." Using this technique rather than actual brushstrokes builds a surface that sparkles with a jewel-like quality.

The important thing to remember when stippling is to stick to a dabbing action and avoid making strokes, or the effect will be compromised. There is a certain advantage in using acrylic paint because it dries quickly, making it possible to work back and forth over a given area in a short space of time.

ROUGH STIPPLING

Stippling does not always need to be done neatly using small blobs of color. Rough stippling can be done using a large round brush, preferably one that has seen better days. The dabbing action is the same, but the bristles deliver the paint in a far looser pattern. The technique resembles scumbling (see Scumbling and Broken Color, page 43), and it can be an ideal way of applying a loose texture over an otherwise uninteresting, flat area of previously applied color. This technique is also popular with landscape artists for representing foliage.

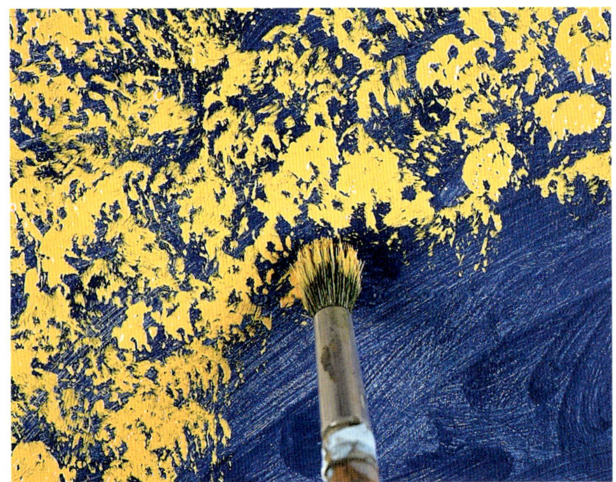

STIPPLED DOTS

This process is the same as that used by the *pointillists*, who used small dabs of color grouped in such a way that they mixed optically on the support. Although a slow process, the use of relatively fluid paint and the quick-drying properties of acrylic paint make it far quicker than when done with oil paint—and when it's done carefully, beautiful color combinations can be achieved. Each dot should remain separate from the one next to it, so work in layers and allow each layer to dry before applying the next. The technique is easier and faster if done using an old, "blunt" round brush rather than one that has a point.

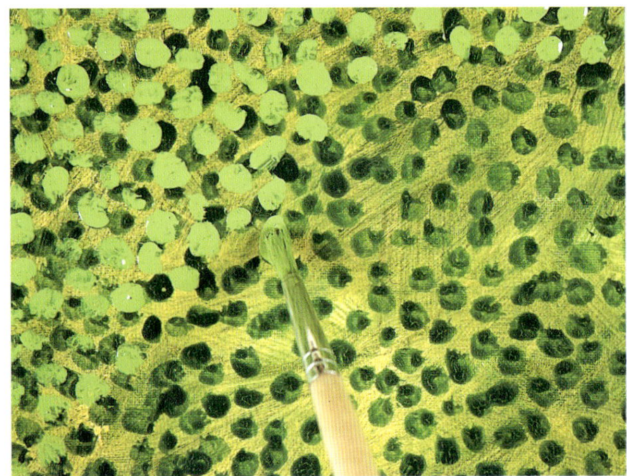

STIPPLING WITH THE SIDE OF THE BRUSH

The stippling technique can be used with other shaped brushes using the tips, the side, or the edge. The important thing is to make sure the action that delivers the paint is a dabbing action rather than an actual stroke. Here, the flat side of a large flat decorator's brush has been "dabbed" briefly into the paint before being dabbed onto the support. The pattern left is more linear due to the length of the bristles. This technique would be good for painting grass.

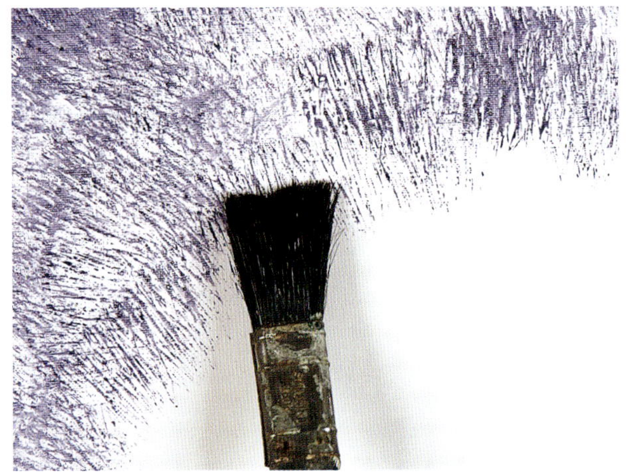

GLAZING

Glazing is a classic oil painting technique that takes time because each layer of glaze needs to dry thoroughly before the next is applied.

Due to the speed with which acrylic paint dries, results can now be achieved in a fraction of the time. The principle is not unlike the watercolor wash technique (see page 37); like that technique, thin transparent layers of paint are laid one over the other, each altering the color or tone of the one beneath. Color combinations that have been achieved using glazing techniques tend to be very rich and clear. You can mix your glazes using water, but thinning with a gloss medium will give much better results; this medium increases the transparency of the paint and intensifies the brilliance of the colors.

GLAZING OVER IMPASTO AND OPAQUE PAINT

Glazes can be applied to good effect over paint previously applied using other techniques, such as impasto (see page 42). When applied over impasto work, the fluid nature of the glaze makes it settle in the lower areas of paint, making the color look deeper; at the same time, it runs off the peaks and ridges, making these areas appear lighter. Glazes can also be used to modify those areas of a painting that appear to be either too warm or too cool. A single colored glaze can also be used over the entire finished painting to unify and harmonize the colors.

GLAZING OVER COLOR

Here, a red glaze is brushed over a yellow and a blue swatch. The true color of the glaze can be seen in the white area that separates the swatches: seen against the yellow, the red glaze becomes a deep orange; seen against the blue, it becomes violet. Dark colors are usually glazed over light colors, although you can modify dark colors by glazing light over dark, as seen here. To achieve bright glazes, avoid mixing in white and, where possible, avoid using those colors that naturally are excessively opaque. You will notice that because acrylic mediums are slightly milky when wet, the true brilliance of the colors becomes apparent only when the glazes are completely dry.

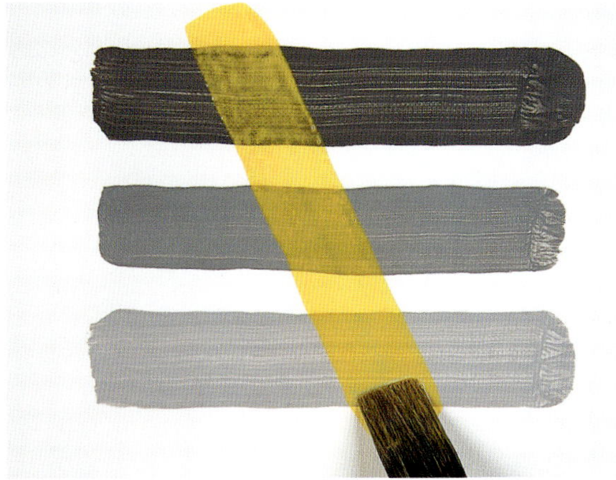

GLAZING OVER A TONAL UNDERPAINTING

A traditional technique is to apply the colored glazes over a tonal underpainting that has been painted using black and white. This underpainting is known as a "grisaille." When using this technique, it is important to make sure that the glazes are applied using those colors that are naturally lighter first, and those colors that are naturally much darker last; otherwise the effects of the gray underpainting could easily be lost.

SPONGING

Sponges should be a part of every artist's toolbox. They can be used in a number of ways, not only to apply paint but also to remove it.

Natural sponges are perhaps the most widely used, but manufactured sponges are useful too. Natural sponges are found in different sizes and textures. Smaller sponges are perhaps more useful than larger sponges, since they are far more easily managed, and even a small sponge can hold a surprisingly large amount of paint. Both manufacured sponges and natural sponges can be torn or cut into smaller sizes.

APPLYING FLAT AREAS OF PAINT

A sponge soaked in relatively thin, fluid paint can be used to cover large areas very quickly, and, with practice, the application can be reasonably flat. When using thin, fluid paint, mix a quantity of paint in a container. Mix more than you think you will need, since even a small sponge will soak up a large quantity of paint. Wet the sponge first, and squeeze it dry; then use it to soak up the paint. As you apply the paint, squeeze the sponge gently to release the paint. But take care not to squeeze too hard, or you will end up with a puddle. Whereas thin paint is soaked up into the sponge fibers, thick paint only sits on the sponge surface.

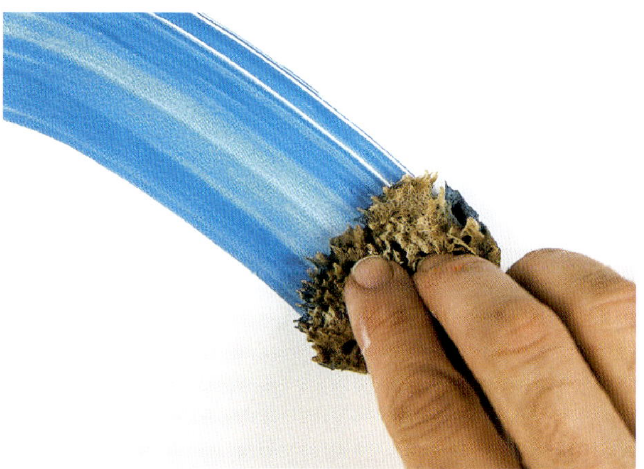

MANUFACTURED SPONGES

Manufactured sponges are made from foam and have an even, mechanical surface pattern that, when used for making printed marks, can look too regular. However, sponges are inexpensive and interesting effects can be made by cutting the sponge up into small sections and using these to print with. As with natural sponges, turning the sponge as you work will add variety, keep the marks interesting, and avoid repetition.

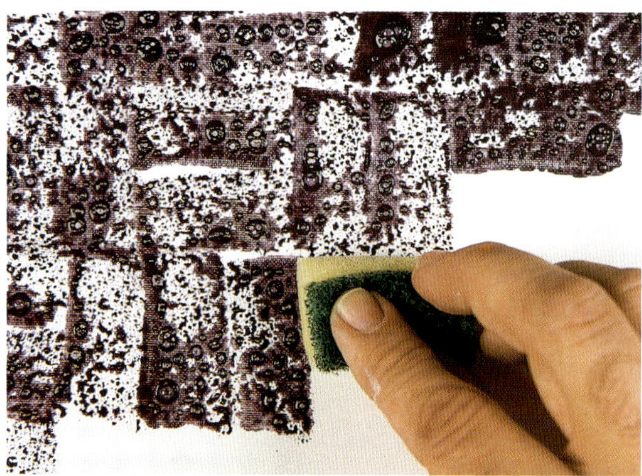

CREATING TEXTURE AND BROKEN COLOR

If the sponge is simply dipped in the paint (rather than used to soak it up) and then applied to the support surface in a dabbing action (rather than pulled across its surface), a print of the sponge texture is left. These prints can be built up to create textures or areas of broken color. Allowing the paint to dry and then reworking the area results in a complex, interesting surface texture that would be difficult to achieve by other means. As you use the sponge, keep turning it so that the printed pattern left by its surface changes constantly.

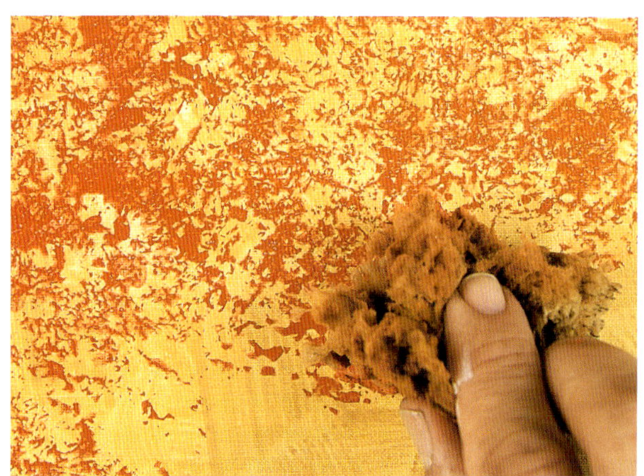

SPATTERING

Flicking and spattering paint or water onto the support is a good way of creating a range of effects. The technique is usually used together with masking techniques to protect those areas where the spatter or splashes of paint are not required.

As a general rule, short bristle brushes loaded with thickish paint create a fine spray, whereas soft fiber brushes loaded with thin, fluid paint create larger blobs. The brush loaded with paint is either tapped with the finger to release the paint or the finger is pulled over the bristles bending them backward, so that when they are released, they spring forward and release the paint toward the support. Many artists utilize old toothbrushes and shaving brushes, and brushes intended for decorating and home improvements.

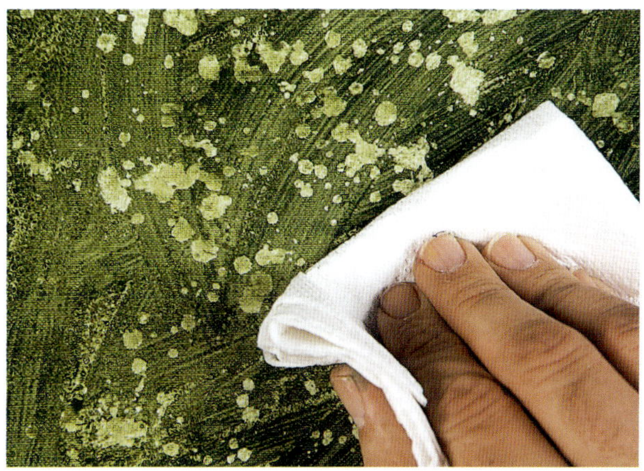

SPATTERING WATER

An interesting effect can be achieved by applying paint to the support and allowing it to dry slightly but not completely. Before it is completely dry, clean water is spattered onto the area, which is then left to dry further. Once dry, a clean paper towel can be used to blot up the spatters of water that prevented the underlying paintwork from drying. The paint will be lifted off with the water, creating a mottled effect. As before, this process could be repeated several times to create a complex surface that would be impossible to achieve using other means.

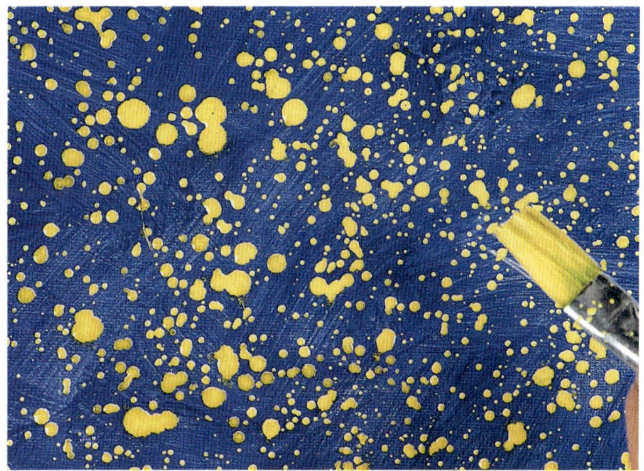

SPATTERING PAINT ONTO A DRY SURFACE

Thick or thin paint spattered onto a dry surface and allowed to dry will retain the blob-like shape that it makes as it lands on the support. However, if you put down too dense a layer at any one time, the layers will run together and merge where they touch, and the spatter-like effect can be lost. The solution is to lay down an area of spattered marks, allow that to dry, and then repeat the process using the same color. Alternatively, the color of each spattered layer of paint can be altered, creating a complex multicolored surface. By using natural colors, this process would be ideal for representing a pebble beach. Directional spattering is achieved by flicking the paint onto the support from an angle.

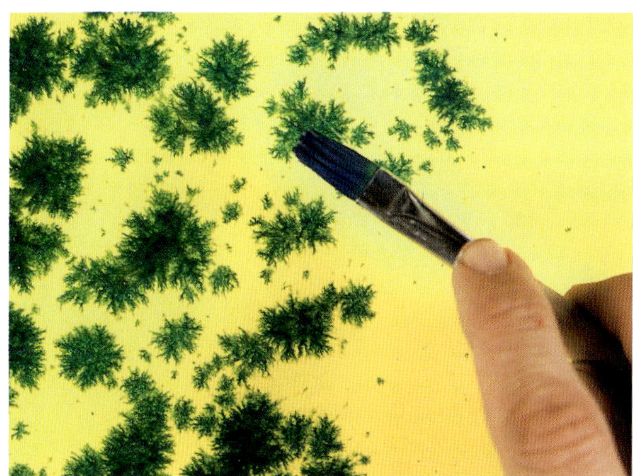

SPATTERING PAINT ONTO A WET SURFACE

Paint that is spattered onto a wet surface tends to spread, creating an amorphous irregular shape. The degree of spread depends on the fluidity of the paint being spattered and the wetness of the surface onto which this is spattered. If allowed to dry, the process can be repeated by rewetting the area with clean water and spattering again. Alternatively, a richly colored surface is made if several different colors are all spattered into one another while the surface is still wet.

BRUSH IMPASTO TECHNIQUES

The word *impasto* is derived from the Italian word for dough, and it describes the technique of applying the paint so thickly that the marks of the tool used to apply it remain visible and become an important part of the finished image.

Impasto paint can be applied using a brush or knife, and it is often applied straight from the tube onto the support. Acrylic paint straight from the tube is usually of about the right consistency for impasto work, but it can be thickened further by adding a heavy gel medium.

DIRECTIONAL STROKES

When using impasto techniques, the rough-textured surface left by the brushstrokes or knife marks really makes its presence felt and, in some instances, seems to become as important as the image itself. One of the most pleasing aspects of working with thick paint is the way in which the brushstrokes can be made to actually follow the contours of the object or subject being painted, which has the added effect of leading your eye in the direction of the strokes and helps you almost "feel" the shapes. This also lends a very tactile feeling to the piece and makes you almost want to run your fingers over the work.

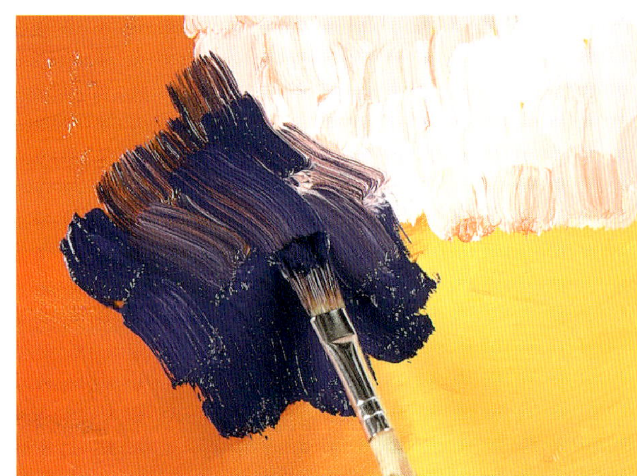

BUILDING UP PAINTWORK

Using thick applications of paint in the initial stages of a painting can be counterproductive. This is especially true when working in acrylic as, unlike oil paint, acrylic dries quickly and cannot be scraped off. The answer is to work over a thinly applied underpainting. This can be made in monochrome or color, but the important thing is that the paintwork should not be too thick. Once you are happy with the image, it can be repainted using the underpainting as a guide but with thicker applications of paint.

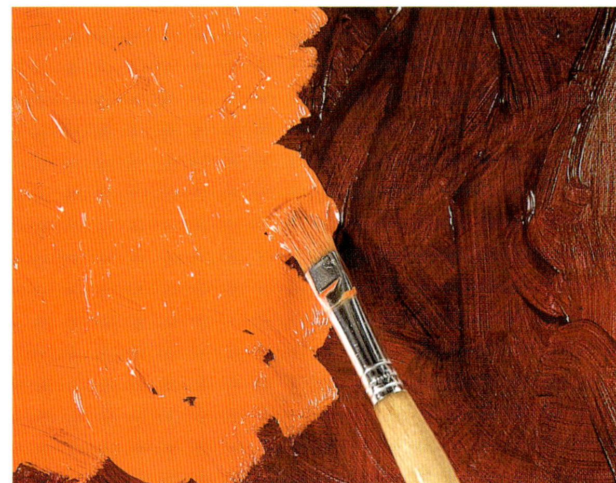

WORKING INTO WET PAINT

One of the main attractions of impasto is the way in which brushmarks remain visible. This is possible because the paint is applied at a stiffer consistency than might normally be used. The introduction of other colors into a still-wet surface is also a characteristic that can easily be lost, as the acrylic paint can dry so quickly that it prevents the artist from going back and reworking an area. The solution is to introduce a retarding medium into the mixes to help slow down the drying time. Better still, use the relatively new acrylic paints; when used as a thick impasto, they can take up to several weeks to dry.

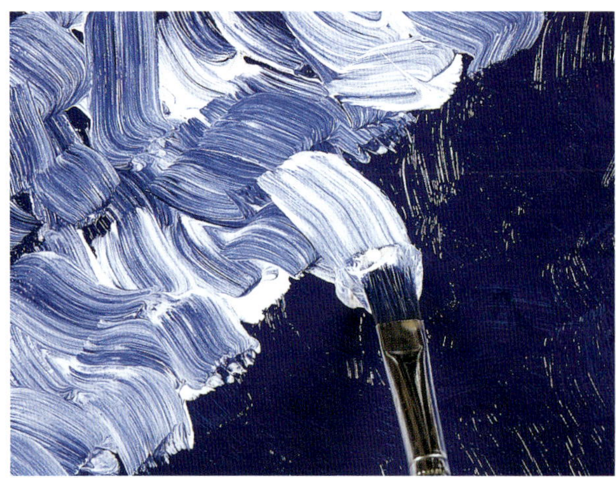

SCUMBLING AND BROKEN COLOR

In nature, areas of color are seldom completely flat, and very subtle and often not-so-subtle variations of color can occur in surprisingly small areas.

Even when color is relatively flat, as in a bright, clear blue sky, painting it in that way can result in a large uninspired area of flat paintwork—far better to paint the sky in such a way that there is some subtle variation. There are two ways of achieving these effects in paint: scumbling and broken color. Both can be achieved using colors that are very close in hue and tone so that the effects are subtle. Alternatively, you could use very different colors that will mix optically when viewed from a distance. Dark colors can be scumbled over light, and light colors can be scumbled over dark.

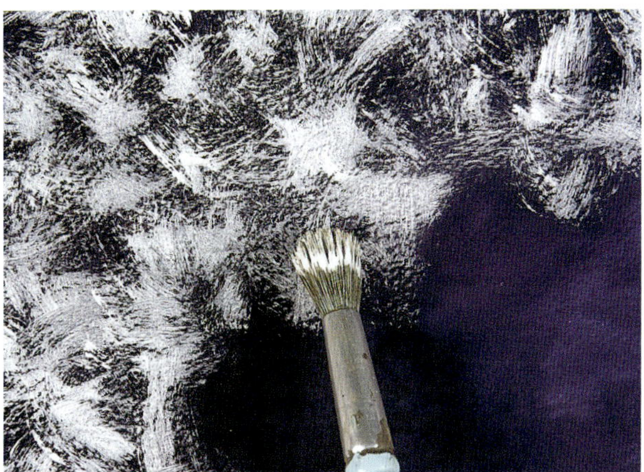

SCUMBLING WITH A BRUSH

When scumbling one color over another, the base color needs to be completely dry. The idea is to scrub the color being scumbled over the area so that the color beneath shows through in places. Actual brushmarks are best avoided, so it is far better to scrub or use the side of the brush in a rolling action when applying the paint. Round brushes are better than flat ones for scumbling, and the older the brush, the better. Use paint that is stiff or of a high viscosity rather than loose fluid paint, which spreads far too easily. Support texture also plays a part, and scumbling is especially successful when carried out on rough canvas.

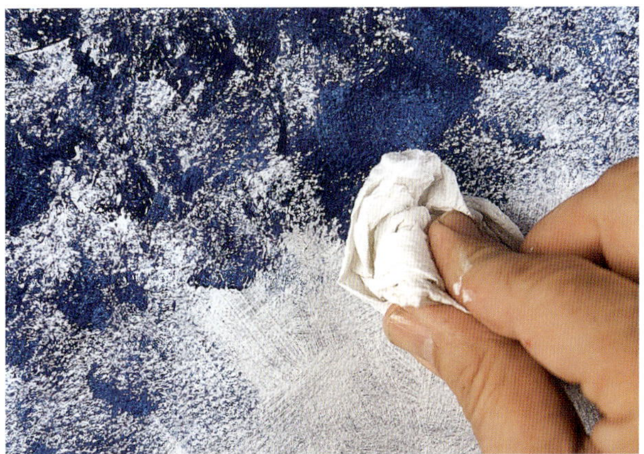

SCUMBLING WITH A RAG

Scumbling can be done in exactly the same way using a rag, and it can often be an easier task to get an even coverage using this technique than when using a brush. When scumbling, the paint—although thick—is applied in a thin layer and so dries very quickly. Adding a little retarding medium into your mixes will keep the paint workable for longer. Any number of layers can be scumbled one over the other, but remember to allow each one to dry before applying the next, or the effect will be lost.

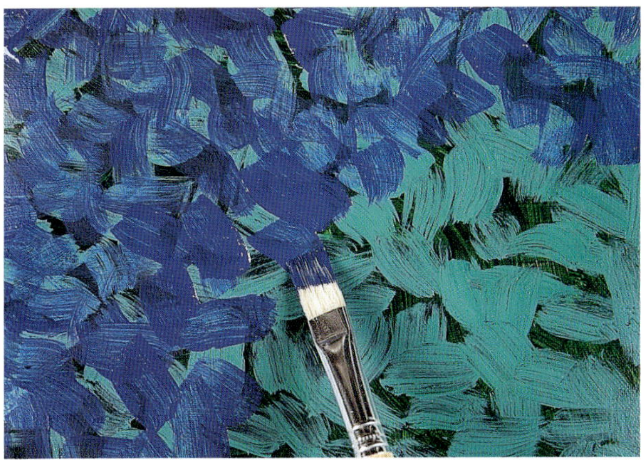

BROKEN COLOR

Broken color is similar in effect to scumbling but is usually made using actual brushstrokes, although broken color effects can also be achieved using sponges or by spattering. As with scumbling, layers of color are built up, and each layer allows the layers beneath to show through. Broken color techniques are often used in paintings that are made over a colored ground. In the finished image, this colored ground, which has been allowed to show in places, helps to create an overall color harmony. As with scumbling, the layers are built up wet onto dry.

ADVANCED TECHNIQUES

Although the term "advanced" is used for the following techniques, none of them is really difficult, but each requires a little practice.

MASKING

There are several ways to mask your painting, and the one you use will depend on what you are working with and what effect you are trying to achieve.

Masking techniques are used for two distinctly different purposes. The first is to prevent paint from getting onto an area where it is not wanted. This might happen when blocking in an area using loose expressive brushstrokes or when using techniques that can be difficult to control, such as spattering. Masking techniques can also be used to give a distinct edge to an area of paint, which would be difficult to achieve using a brush or a painting knife.

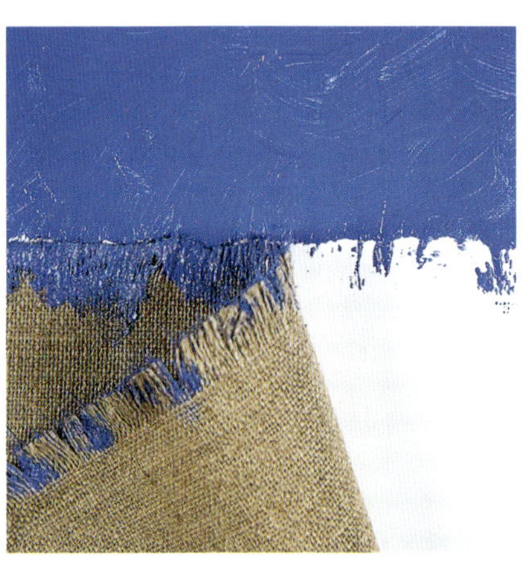

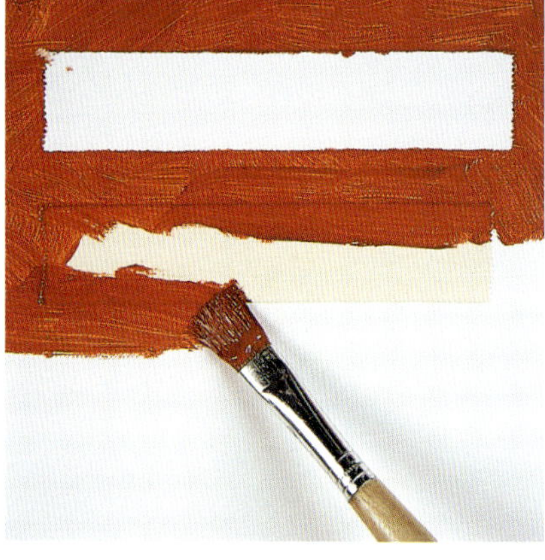

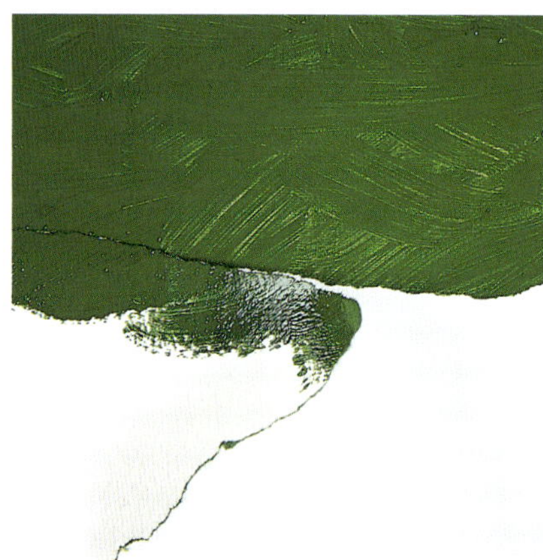

FABRIC MASKS

Cut and torn fabric can be used in the same way as one would use paper; however, only very thin fabrics can be torn. Thicker fabrics need to be cut, but then fibers can be pulled away from the cut edge to open it up and create a broken edge. Remnants of canvas are particularly good for this. Fabric masks are best used with thicker paint, as thin, fluid paint tends to soak into the edge of the fabric and can spoil the desired effect.

MASKING TAPE

Masking tape is familiar to most and is available in a range of different widths. It can be used on both paper board and canvas. When using paper, take care not to tear the surface when the tape is removed. The traditional use for masking tape is to make painting straight lines a quick and easy exercise; however, it can be used in several other ways too. Very thin masking tape can be made to follow a curve; if you do not have thin masking tape then place a strip of masking tape onto a cutting board or sheet of glass or plastic and cut it into thin strips using a craft knife. Masking tape can also be torn to give an interesting edge. Whatever way you use the tape, make sure that it is securely attached to the support, and always work away from the tape to prevent paint from being pushed underneath it.

PAPER MASKS

Masks can also be made using paper. If you are masking out a large area prior to applying some energetic paintwork, you could use newspaper secured around the edges using masking tape. Use the tape first to follow the required contour; then use the paper to mask out the area fully. Paper can also be used to mask out straight edges, or it can be torn to give a unique edge quality. Thicker watercolor and Indian Khadi papers tear particularly well, and if you are understandably reluctant to tear up your expensive papers, keep all your failed pictures for this very purpose. As with tape, always work away from the mask to prevent paint from being pushed beneath it.

KNIFE PAINTING

Although thin paint can often be applied with a knife with excellent results, it is more commonly associated with thick impasto work.

When paint is applied as impasto using a brush, the brushstrokes are very noticeable. When thick paint is applied using a knife, the effect is much smoother and can appear to lack character. It is possible to make a wide range of marks when using a single brush, but the same is not true of the painting knife; you will find it beneficial to equip yourself with a range of knives of different shapes and sizes. Thick paint of a smooth and creamy consistency handles well and will take quite easily to smooth or textured supports. Heavy gel medium added to the paint will add body.

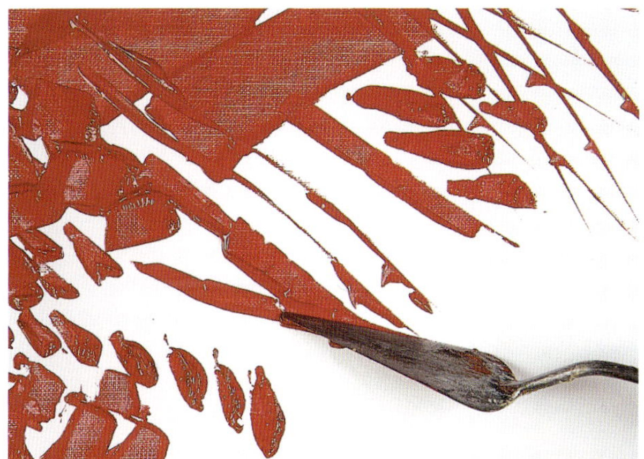

MAKING MARKS

Each shape of knife is capable of making a limited range of marks. The potential of the tool is greatly increased if you have several different shapes and sizes. The large trowel-shaped knife used here will deliver broad areas of paint using the full flat area of the blade or small dabs of color if only the pointed end is used. The very edge of the blade can be used to make very thin long marks while applying the paint, but turning the blade as you work produces a line that will vary in thickness.

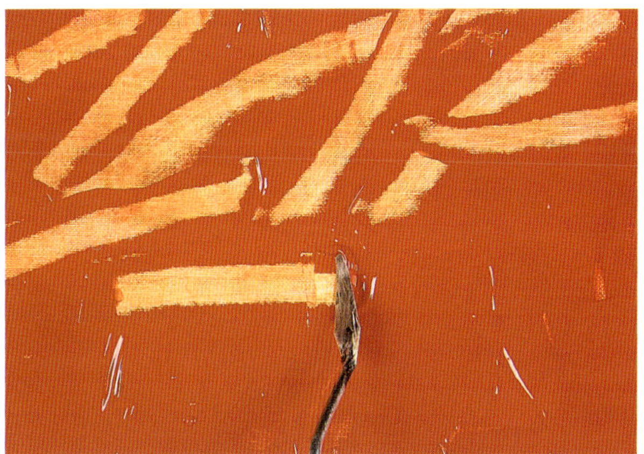

REMOVING PAINT

It is as easy to remove paint with a painting knife as it is to apply it, and removing paint is an important and effective way of creating a number of effects. Apart from removing areas of paint to facilitate correcting mistakes, paint is also removed to create textures or to allow the texture of the support or a previously applied color to show through. Even thick applications of acrylic paint allow only a limited window of opportunity during which the paint can be manipulated, and it is a good idea to introduce a slow-drying additive to increase the time that the paint remains "open." Alternatively, use the new type of acrylic paint that is slow to dry.

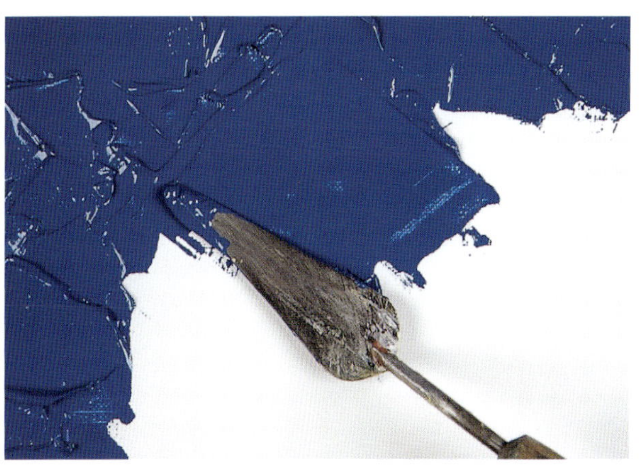

APPLYING PAINT

Paint can be mixed on a palette and transferred to the support using the painting knife. If the color is correct it can be applied to the support straight from the tube. The flat blade of the knife spreads the paint smoothly, leaving a slightly raised edge around each mark that catches the light and creates interesting shadows. When using acrylic paint with the knife, take care to let each layer dry thoroughly before applying additional layers. Thick paint can form a skin as it dries, and if fresh paint is applied before the previous layer is fully cured, the skin that has formed on the lower layer can be broken and could spoil the appearance of the paint surface.

SGRAFFITO

The word *sgraffito* comes from the Italian word *graffiare*, meaning "to scratch." It refers to the technique of scratching through one layer of paint to reveal the layer of paint or the support beneath.

Sgraffito techniques can be done through wet or dry paint, although with acrylic paint, they are easier to do while the paint is still wet. You can use sharp knives, painting knives, the wooden handle of your brush, bits of wood, or the sharp broken edge of an expired credit card—in fact, you can use anything that is sharp enough to cut through the paint.

SCRATCHING AND SCRAPING

Over a wide area, good results can be achieved by scraping off wet paint using the edge of a card or a palette knife. No matter how hard you scrape, a thin layer of paint will always be left behind clinging to the texture of the support. On dry paint used on a nonflexible support, sandpaper can create excellent effects. However, this will work only on thin applications of paint and should be attempted only when the paint is completely dry.

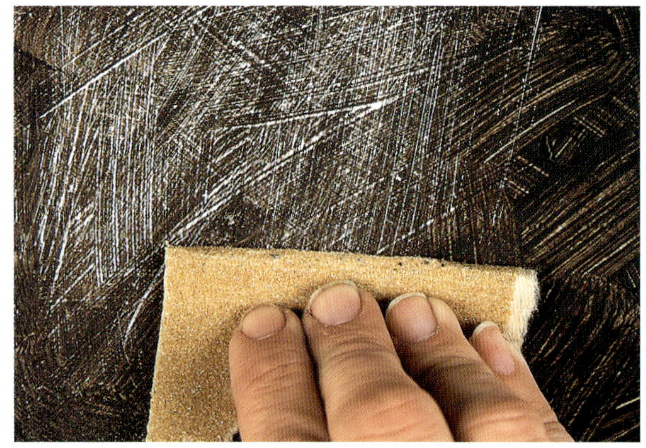

SGRAFFITO THROUGH WET PAINT

On flexible supports, such as canvas, and using relatively thick applications of paint, you will find it easier to make any scratching effects while the paint is still wet. Here, the wooden handle of the brush used to apply the yellow paint has been used to scratch through the paint and reveal the red underpainting. To build up this type of effect, you will need to allow each layer to dry before applying a fresh layer of paint and then scratching into that.

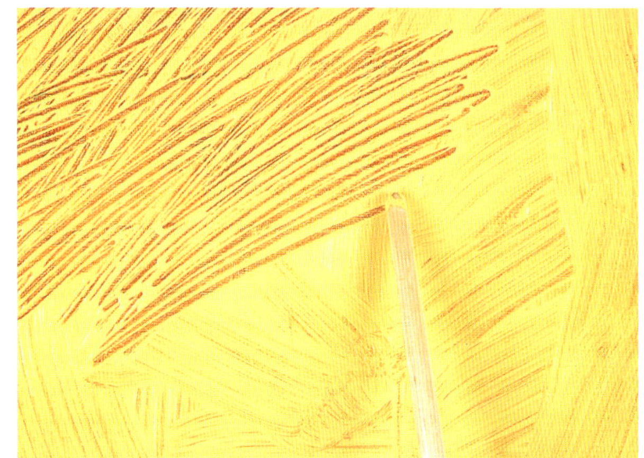

SGRAFFITO THROUGH DRY PAINT

On nonflexible supports, such as board and stretched paper, it is possible to create sgraffito effects through relatively thin dry paint. On a board prepared with gesso and thin paint, a sharp blade can easily scratch through the paint to reveal the support beneath. However, if two or more layers of paint have been used and the aim is to scratch through the top layer to reveal the one beneath, the task becomes more difficult, as it is easy to scratch right through all the layers down to the support. The answer in these cases is to scratch through the wet paint, as before.

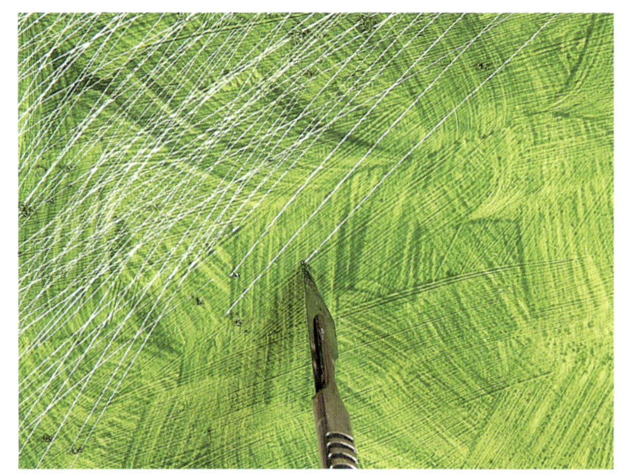

TEXTURE AND MODELING PASTE

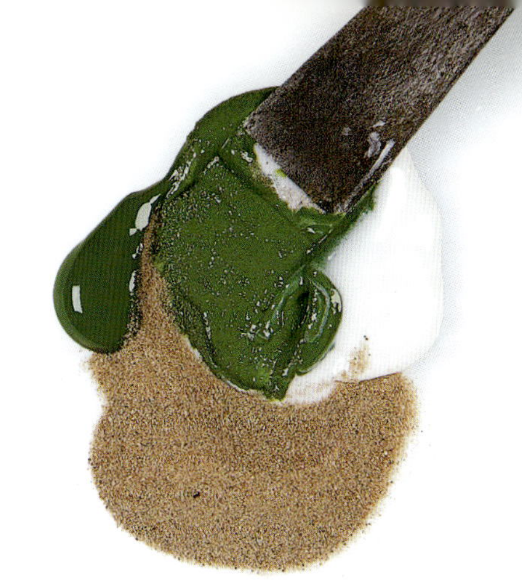

Acrylic paint manufacturers have created a range of texture pastes that can either be mixed with the paint and applied to the support or applied to the support and painted over once they have dried.

Texture can be added and used simply to provide interest or to imitate those textures seen in reality. To this end, several are available that contain various additives. These include resin sand, glass beads, small opaque flakes, blended fibers, black lava, and pumice. All of these pastes are best applied using painting or mixing knives, as they can very quickly ruin brushes. If you do use them with brushes, wash them thoroughly afterward, to make sure all traces of the pastes are removed.

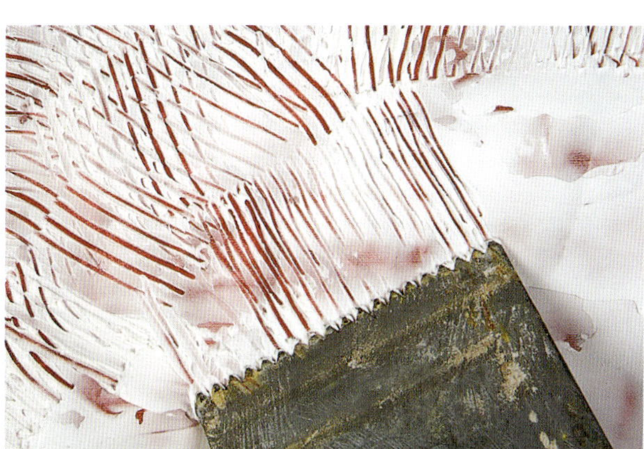

MODELING PASTES

Modeling pastes are slightly different from texture pastes in that they dry to a very hard finish. The pastes can be applied very thickly, but they can be very heavy, so it's best to use them on stable supports such as MDF. Thick applications are best built up in layers, and any cracks that become apparent can be filled with more paste. Modeling pastes are best painted once dry.

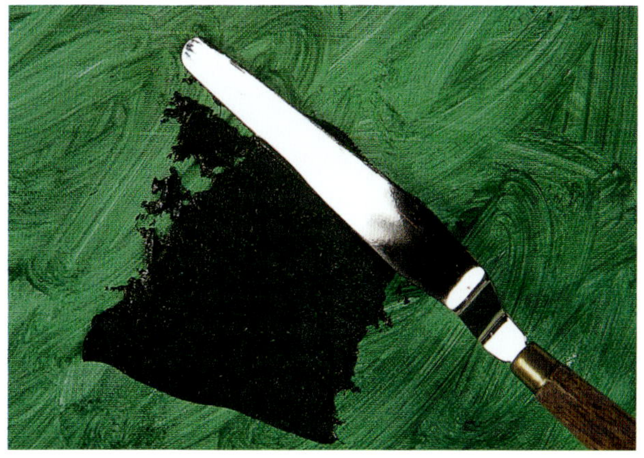

APPLYING PASTES MIXED WITH PAINT

All of the pastes can be mixed with paint prior to being applied, and this is best done using a painting or palette knife. The thickness of the paste together with paint extends the drying time slightly; but if you want the option of working into the paste or removing it and redistributing it onto the support several times, you should add a retarding medium. The gels can be thinned using water and "brushed" or spread out so that the actual texture material within the paste is less dense.

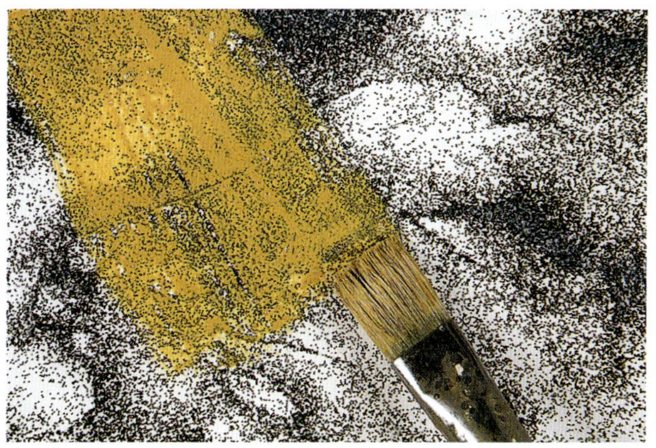

APPLYING PASTES BEFORE APPLYING PAINT

Texture pastes can be used straight from the container and spread onto the support using a brush or knife. They can be thinned first with water or used thick, straight from their container. Before applying paint, allow the pastes to dry thoroughly, a process that can be accelerated by positioning the support somewhere warm or by using a hair dryer. Remember to use relatively thin, fluid paint over the paste, as using thick applications will simply obliterate the texture.

PRINTING AND IMPRINTING

Printing and imprinting are other techniques you can use with acrylic paint. Adding a retarding medium will keep the paint workable longer and prevent it from drying before you have finished printing.

If the paint is too thin and fluid, imprinting or impressing techniques will not work. When using printing techniques, the consistency of the paint depends on the type of material being printed. The answer is to experiment until satisfactory results are achieved.

PRINTING

When printing, rather than pressing an object into the paint, paint is applied to the surface of an object that is in turn pressed onto the support so that an image of that object is left behind. When mixing the paint to be used for printing, it should not be too fluid, as this can lead to an indistinct smudged image. It is always sound advice to test the mix by making a trial print onto a support similar to the one being used for the actual painting. Here, crumpled silver foil is used to create a random textural effect.

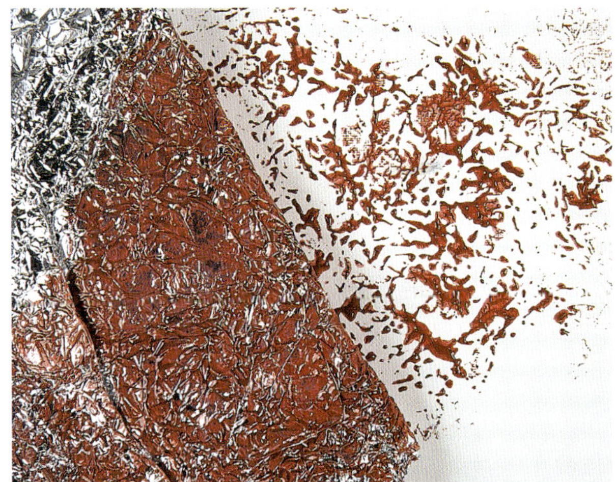

IMPRINTING

When imprinting, the object to be used is pushed into the wet paint in order to make an impression that remains visible once the object is removed. The thickness and consistency of the paint is important. When imprinting textured fabric onto a smooth surface, such as a gesso-prepared board, the paint can be relatively fluid, or it can be stiff but then brushed out to create a relatively thin film. The impressions of larger objects, such as pieces of wood or coins, tend to be clearer and more satisfactory when imprinted in a thick impasto.

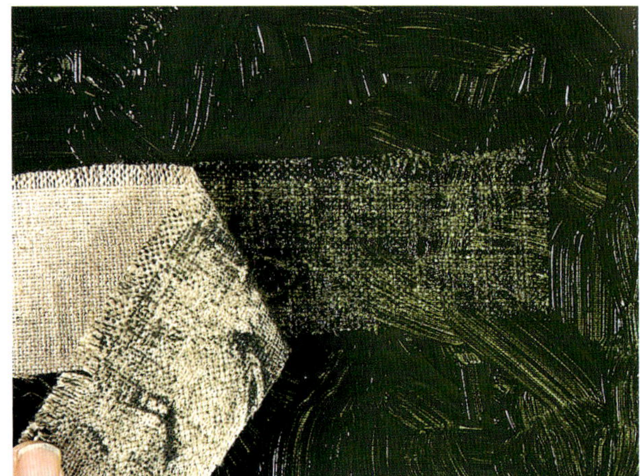

EFFECTS

Both imprinting and printing techniques can be used either to create textural effects or to create imagery of the actual objects being used. Here a coil of string has been dipped in paint and then laid onto the support. This technique could quite easily be used to represent the coils of rope on the deck of a fishing boat. Alternatively, you can use real leaves to make a print of leaves in the foreground of a landscape. The purpose here is to help create marks and imagery that have a unique quality and would be difficult to make using the traditional brush or knife. The trick is to introduce these effects into your work without them looking obvious and contrived.

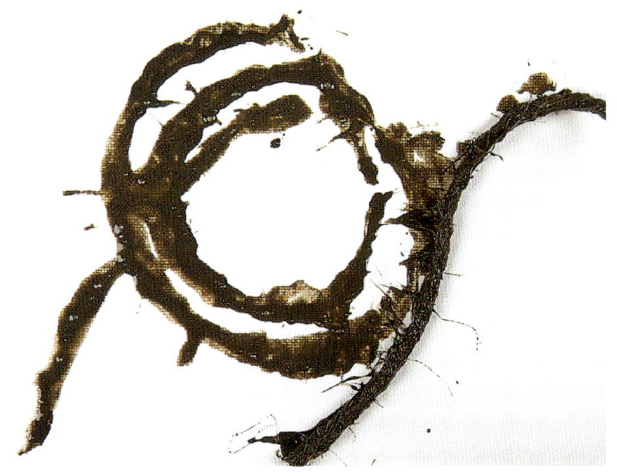

MIXED MEDIA

The qualities and characteristics of acrylic paint and acrylic mediums make it possibly the most ideal material to use as a basis for mixed media work. Acrylic paint is perfect for underpainting prior to working in oils, as well as mixing easily with other water-based painting materials, such as watercolor and gouache. Acrylic mediums also mix physically with drawing materials, such as charcoal, chalks, and pastel. The adhesive qualities of acrylic increase its potential, making it perfect for use with collage.

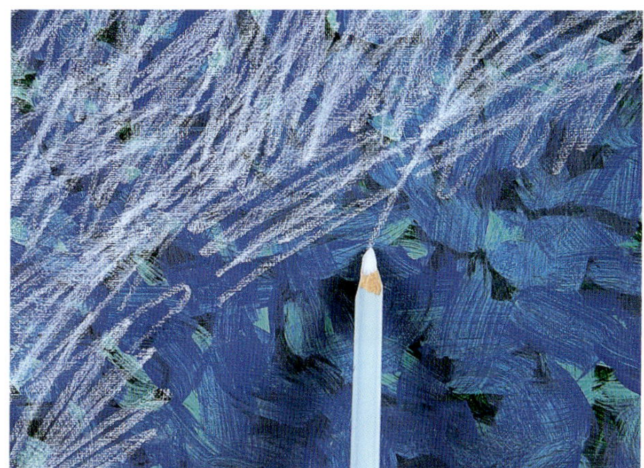

WORKING OVER PAINTWORK

While still wet, acrylic paint can be worked with drawing materials. But perhaps the best results are achieved once the paint is dry. Drawing materials can then be applied in layers over the dry paint surface to create complex and interesting textural effects. Texture pastes mixed into the paint will provide a subtle texture, or tooth, that provides a responsive surface that pastel and chalks will take to easily.

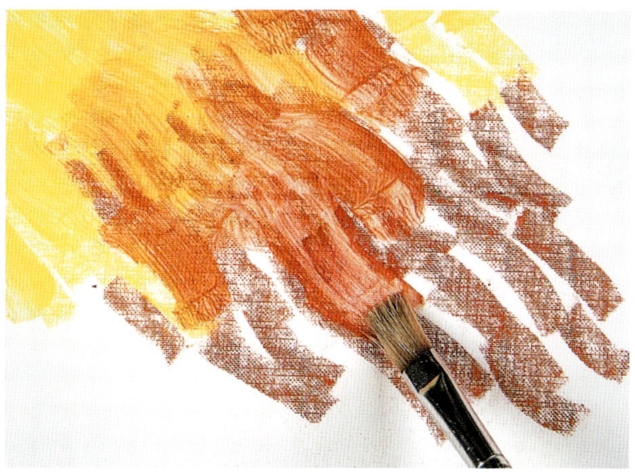

USING ACRYLIC MEDIUMS

Acrylic matt and gloss mediums mix perfectly with dry pigment drawing materials, such as charcoal, graphite, chalks, and pastels; and in doing so the mediums literally turn them into acrylic paint. Here, red and yellow hard pastel marks are worked into with matte medium. The matte medium mixes with the pastel, which is little more than pigment held together with a gum binder. This can then be spread over the support and will become as permanent as acrylic paint, once dry. This technique is especially useful in preparing a tonal or color underpainting where the image can be sketched in first, utilizing drawing techniques before being worked into with the medium.

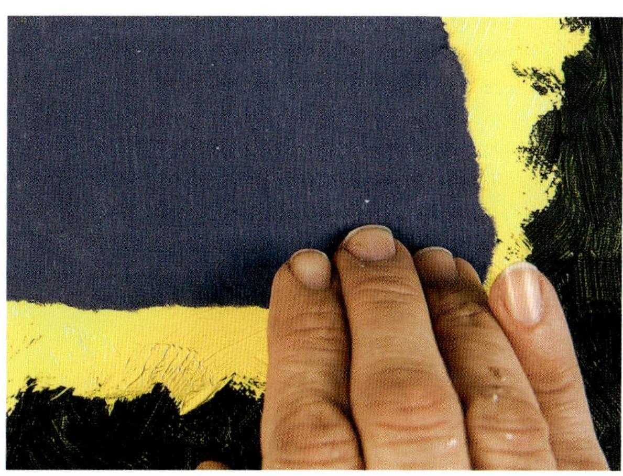

COLLAGE

The adhesive qualities of acrylic paint and acrylic mediums invite the introduction of collage. Even relatively bulky objects can be attached to the image by using a heavy gel medium or a modeling paste. Here, a dark blue heavy paper is fixed to the support by pressing it into wet acrylic paint. Acrylic mediums, although a milky color when wet, dry clear and can be used to secure paper and card without the worry that the adhesive medium might get on the side that is to be seen. In fact, once the piece has been finished, a coat of medium over the entire work acts as a protective varnish.

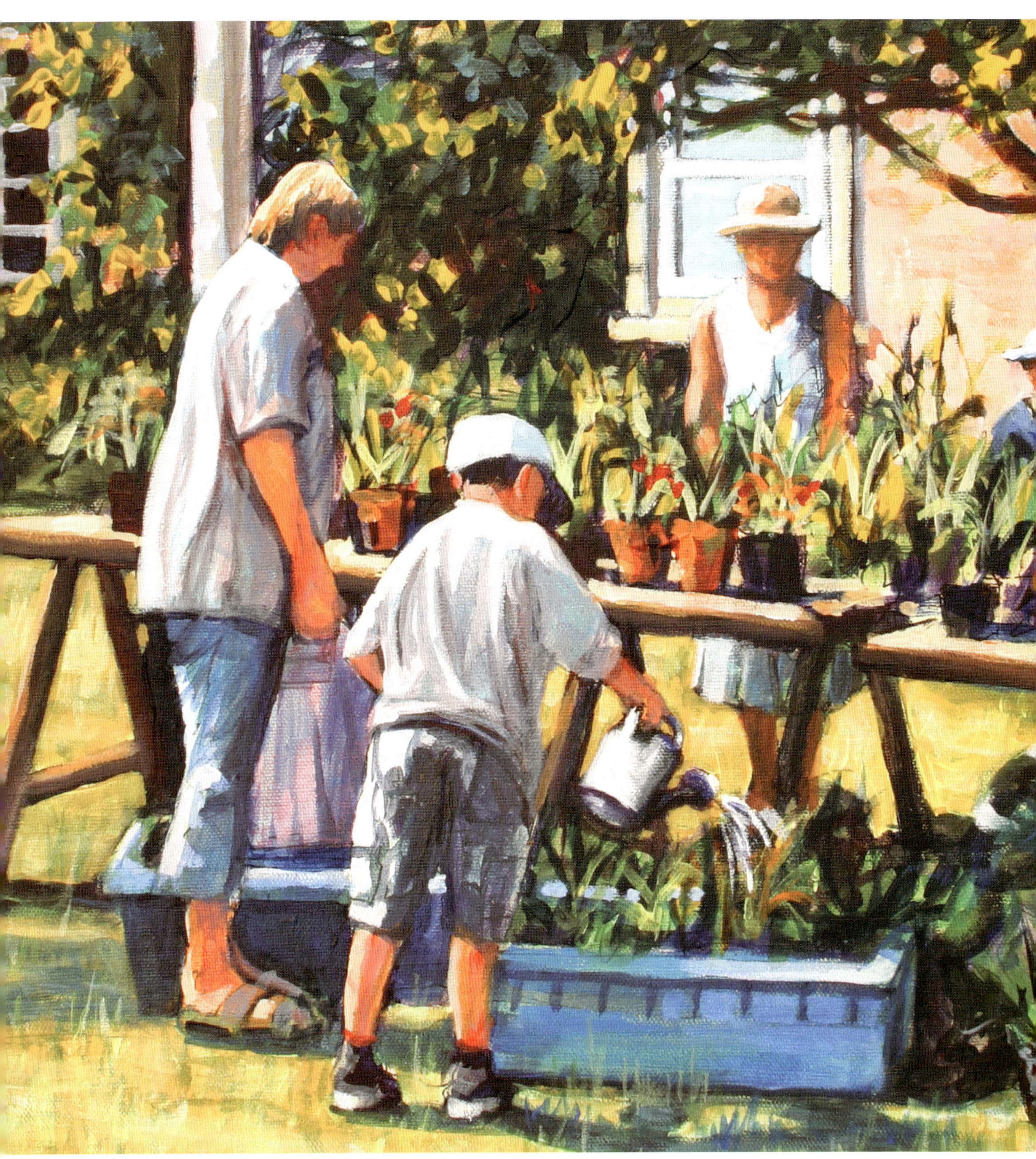

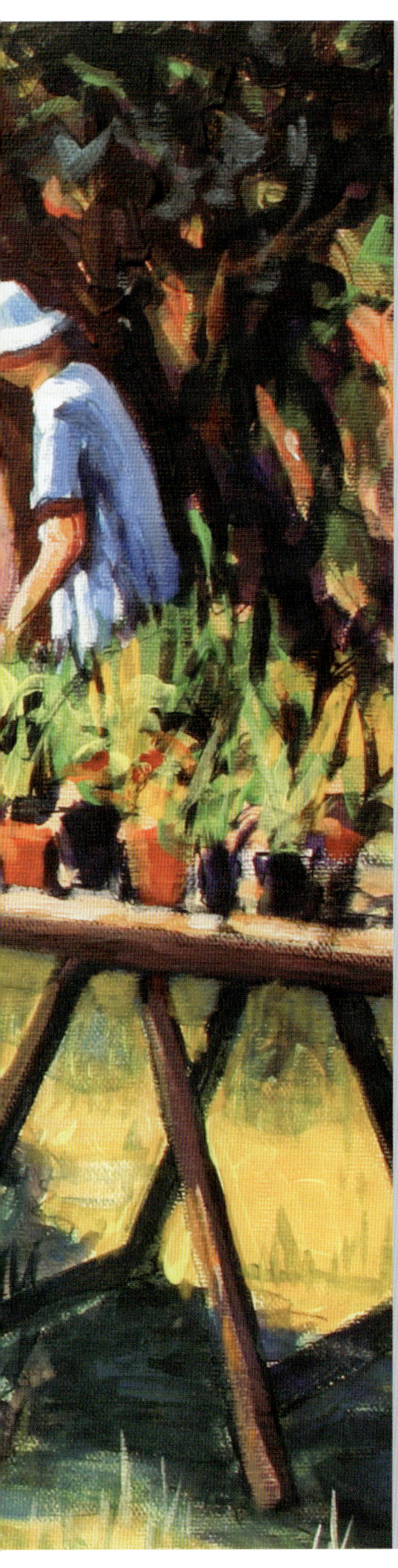

PART THREE

EXPLORING THEMES

The qualities of acrylic paint make it the ideal material for producing images regardless of subject or style. Whether you work in the studio or on location, paint portraits or landscapes, acrylic paint is the perfect all-purpose medium.

THIN OPAQUE PAINT IN LAYERS

by IAN SIDAWAY

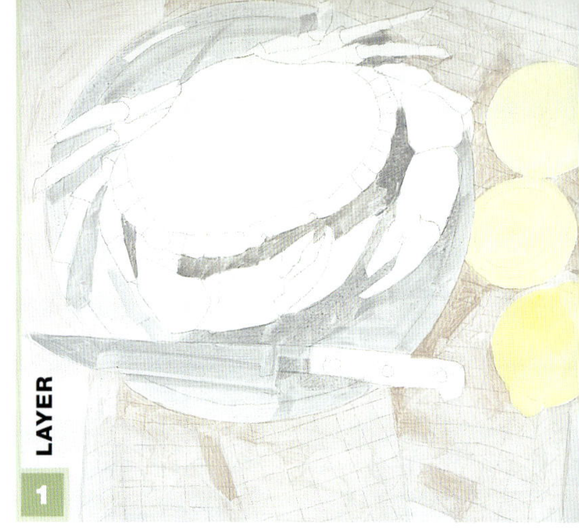

The fast drying time of acrylic paint makes it the perfect painting material for building up an image using layers. Unlike with oil paint, there is no lengthy wait for each layer to dry before it becomes possible to apply the next. Thin layers of acrylic paint dry in minutes and a painting that could take days if made in oil can be completed in hours with acrylic. Working in thin layers enables you to alter color tones and shapes, pushing and pulling the image until a satisfactory result is achieved with no discernable build-up of paint. What in effect happens is that the initial layers act as an underpainting that is then consolidated by overworking. Mistakes are easily painted over and alterations made using opaque paint, while semi-opaque paint layers are used to add depth and texture.

1 ESTABLISHING THE LIGHT TONES

A light pencil drawing acts as a guide. The lighter colors and tones are blocked in first using a 10mm flat soft-fiber brush. Light gray for the plate is made using titanium white and ivory black. Cadmium red light is added to this for the napkin color, and a mix of Cadmium yellow light and white provides the base color for the lemons.

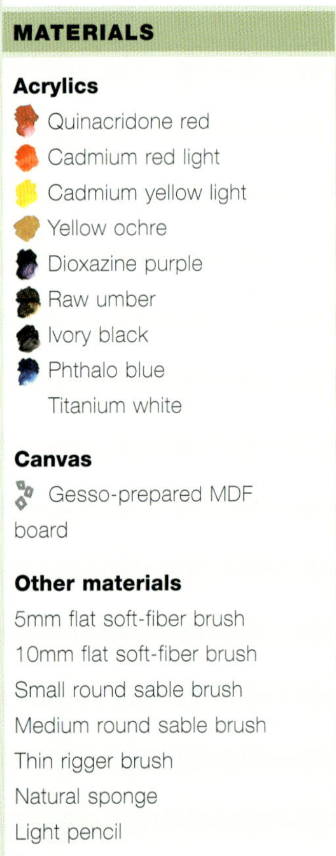

MATERIALS

Acrylics
- Quinacridone red
- Cadmium red light
- Cadmium yellow light
- Yellow ochre
- Dioxazine purple
- Raw umber
- Ivory black
- Phthalo blue
- Titanium white

Canvas
- Gesso-prepared MDF board

Other materials
- 5mm flat soft-fiber brush
- 10mm flat soft-fiber brush
- Small round sable brush
- Medium round sable brush
- Thin rigger brush
- Natural sponge
- Light pencil
- Paper

Cut around the light areas of the plate.

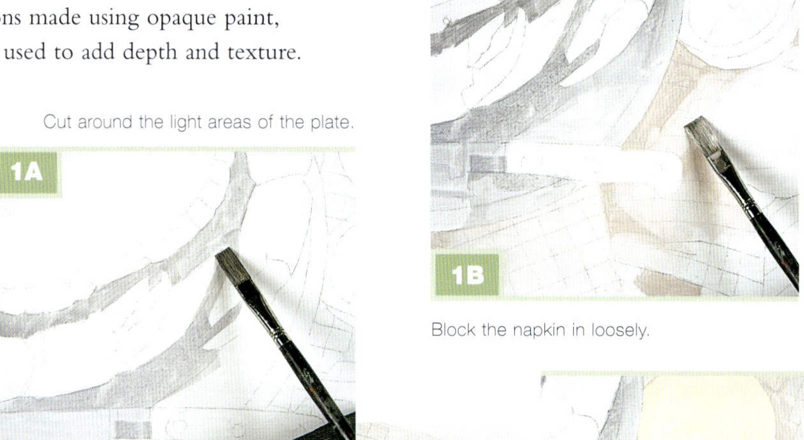

Block the napkin in loosely.

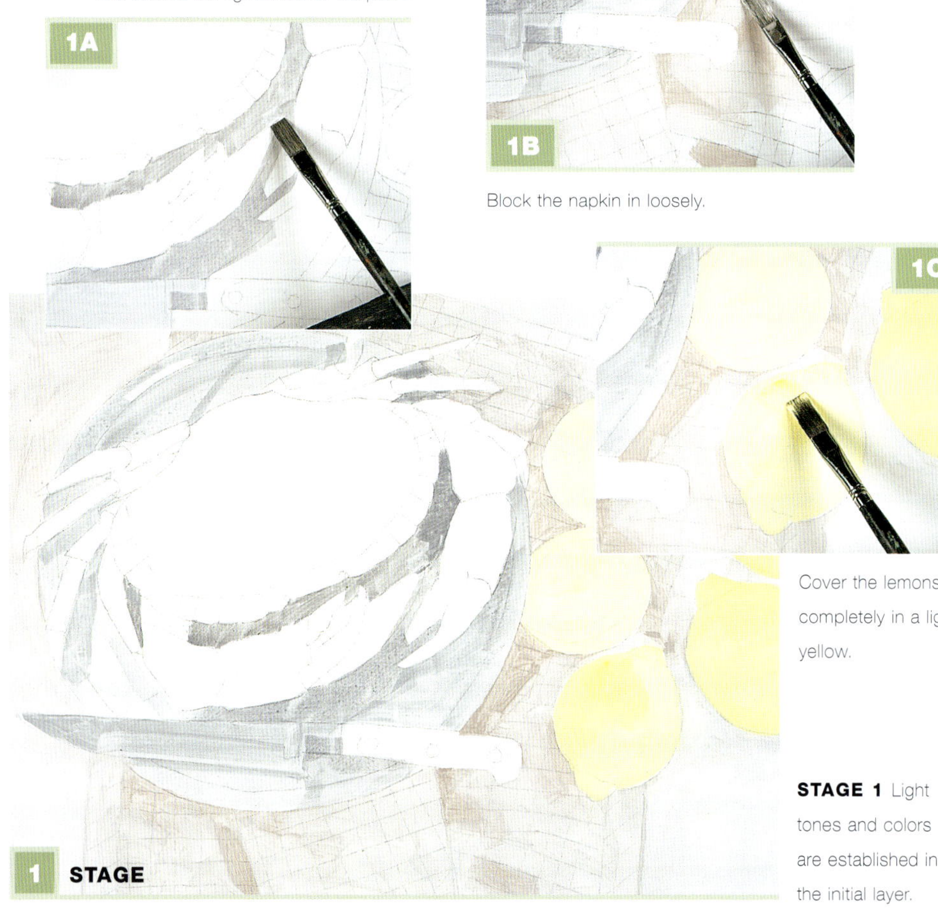

Cover the lemons completely in a light yellow.

STAGE 1 Light tones and colors are established in the initial layer.

2 ESTABLISHING THE MIDTONES

A smaller 5mm flat soft-fiber brush is used to start establishing the midtones. These consist of a range of grays made using white, black, and raw umber for the knife. Phthalo blue and black is used for the edge of the plate. Yellow ochre, cadmium red light, and white are used for the crab and cadmium yellow light, cadmium red light, and white for the lemons.

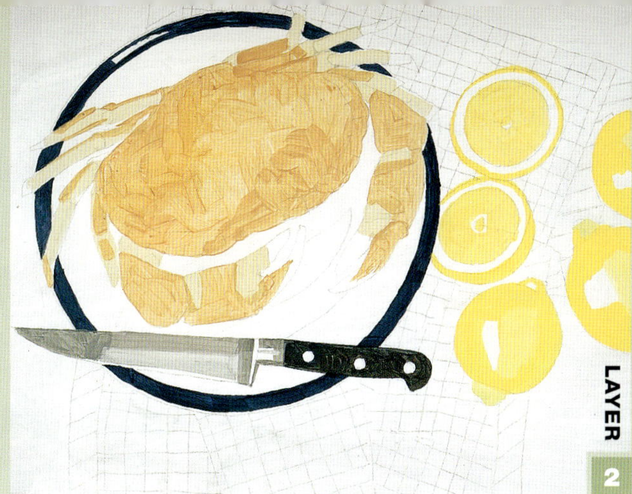

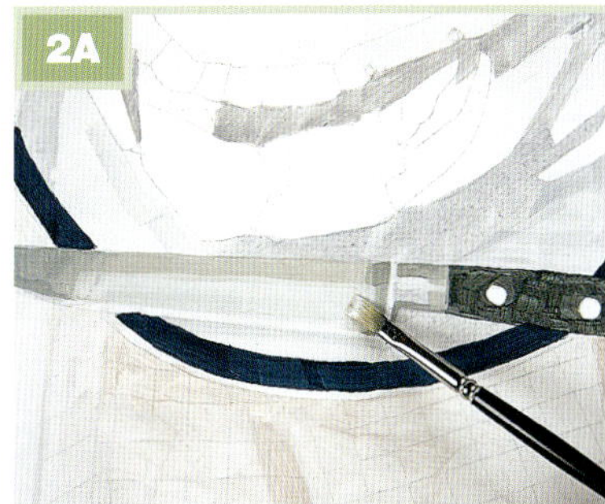

Use precise strokes to paint in the line around the plate and the handle and blade of the knife.

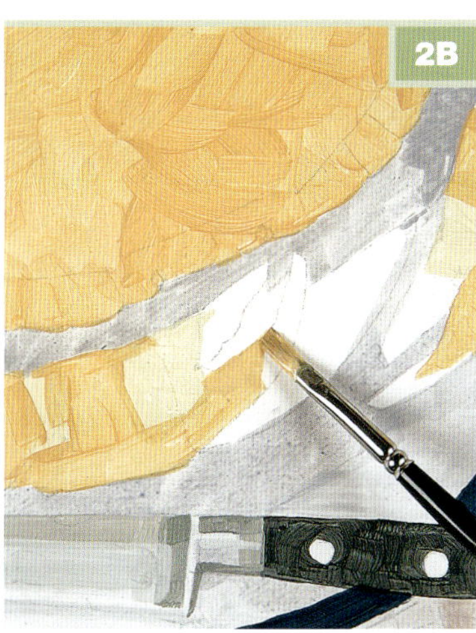

Use the larger flat brush for the crab's shell and the smaller brush to paint the legs and the claws.

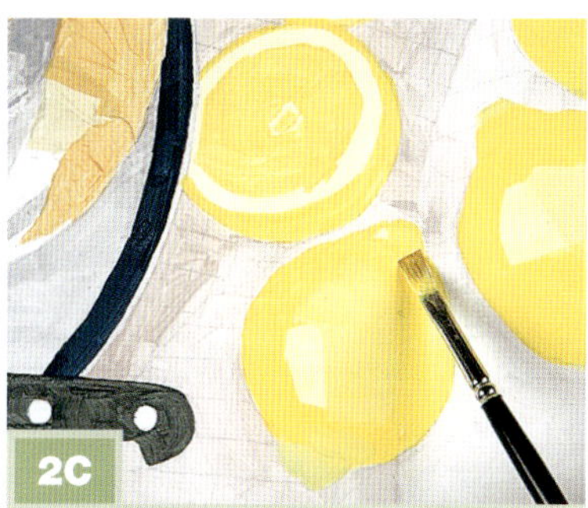

Paint around the lighter areas on the lemons, leaving the areas themselves uncovered.

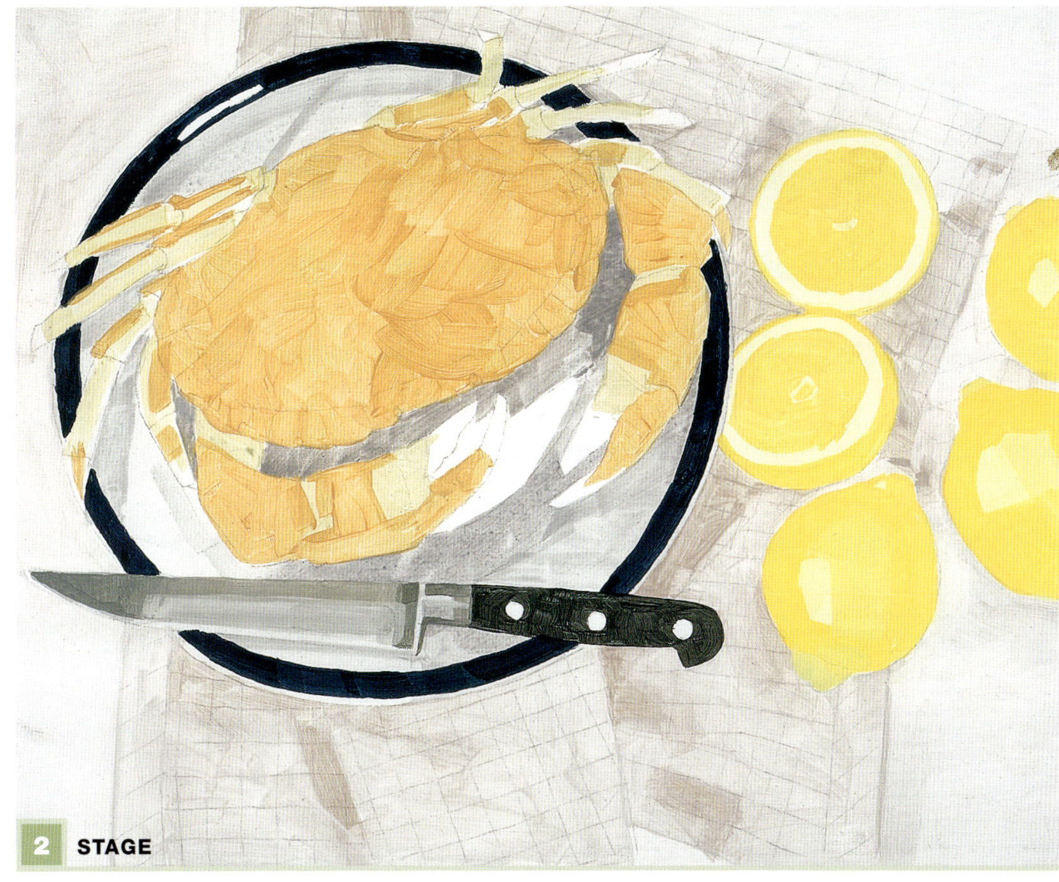

STAGE 2 Most of the support has now been covered with paint.

3 DARK TONES AND COLORS

Cadmium red light, dioxazine purple, raw umber, and white create the colors for the crab. The grays on the knife are consolidated and the colors of the lemons developed.

LAYER 3

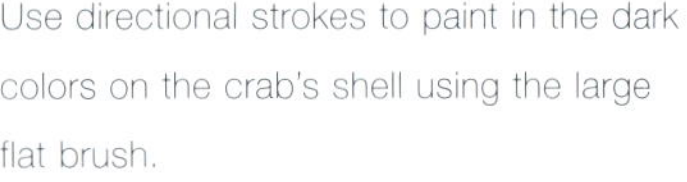

3A

Use directional strokes to paint in the dark colors on the crab's shell using the large flat brush.

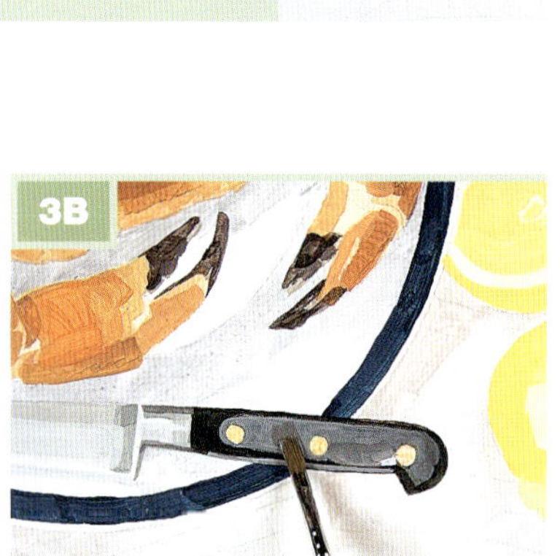

3B

Use careful brushwork on the knife blade and handle.

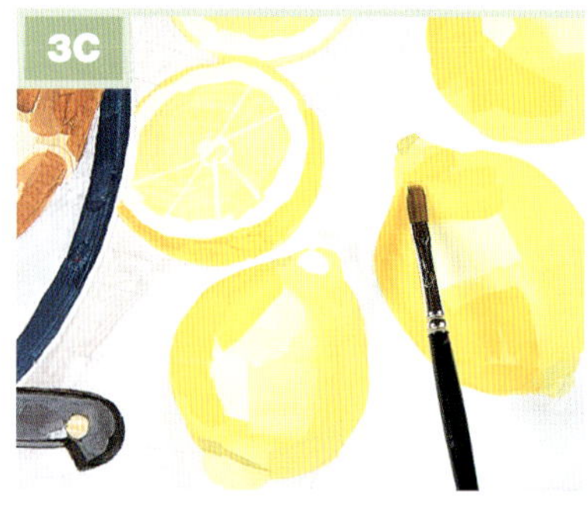

3C

Use a range of yellows to suggest the form of each lemon.

3 STAGE

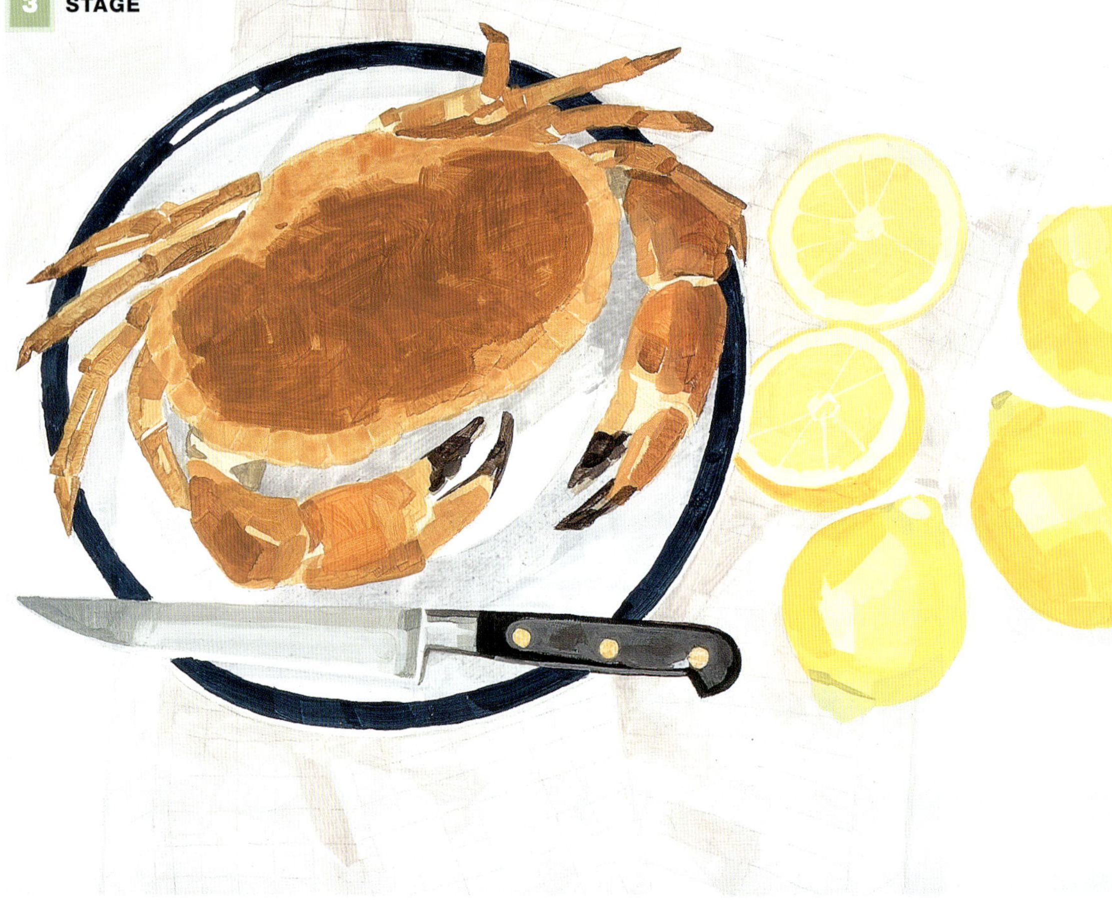

STAGE 3 The forms become more evident as the darker tones and colors are established.

4 CONSOLIDATING THE FORMS

Colors are reapplied to consolidate and deepen those colors already applied. Crumpled paper is used to dab paint onto the back of the crab and stippled light yellow paint is used to suggest the pitted texture of the lemon skin.

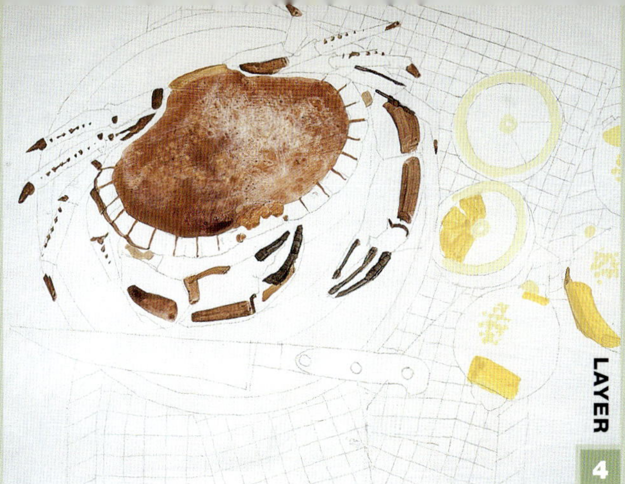

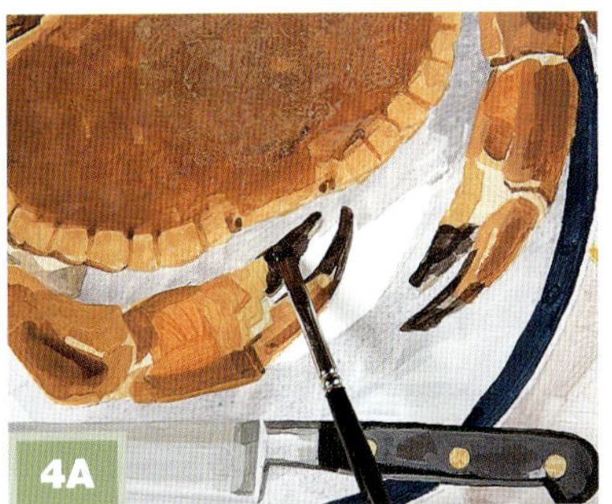

Carefully apply directional strokes to darken the ends of the crab's claws.

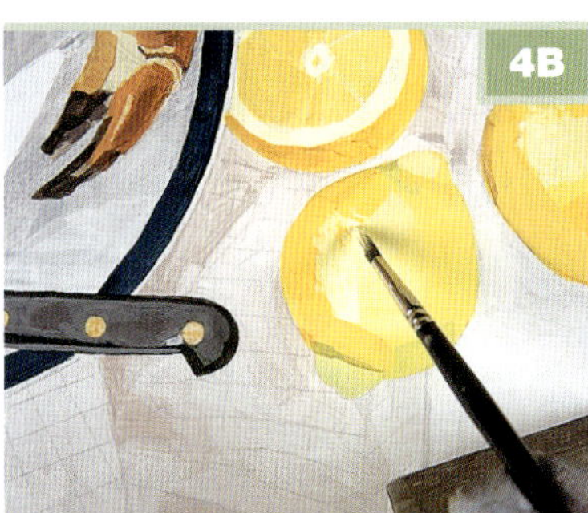

Use the stippling technique to give the skin of the lemons a pitted appearance.

STAGE 4 As texture is applied, the image begins to look more realistic.

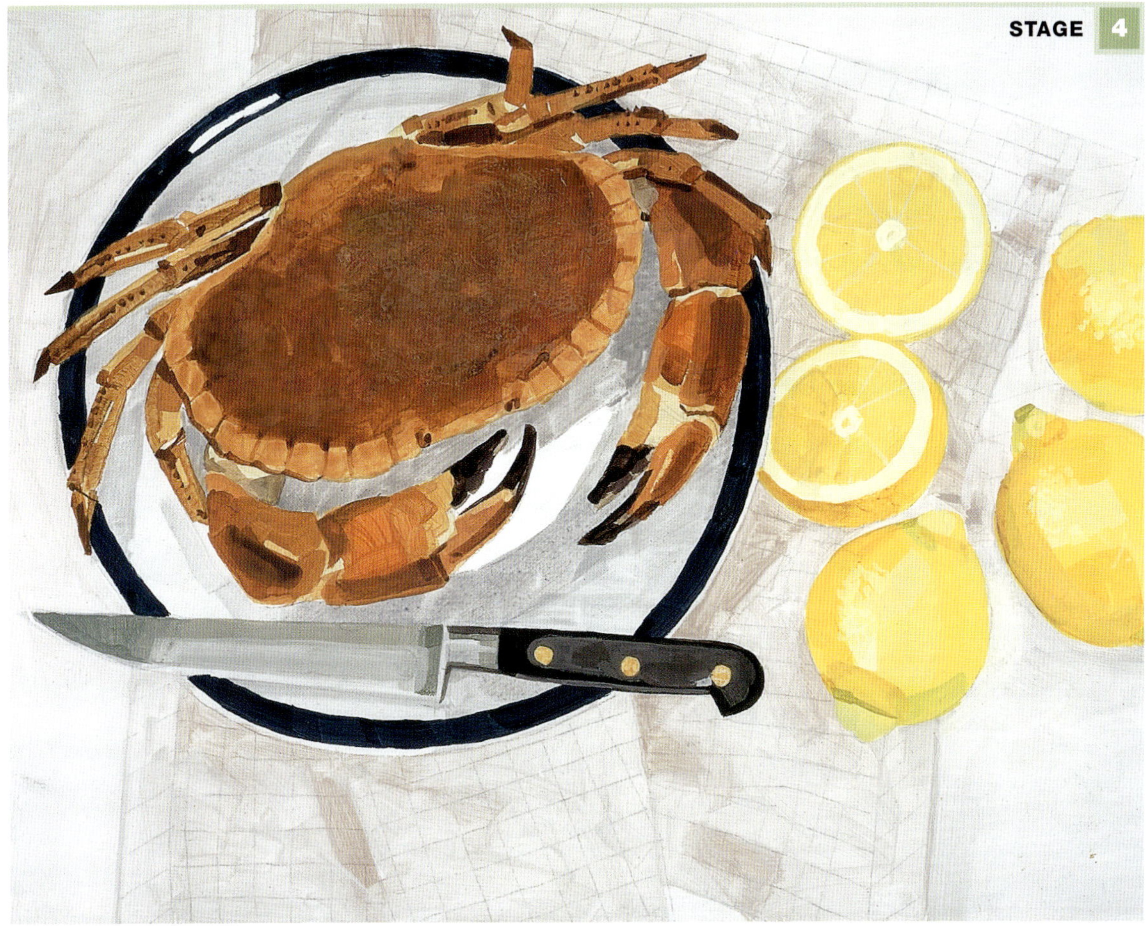

5 ADDING TEXTURE

The barbs and textural patterning on the back of the crab are painted next using a combination of brushwork and sponging. The natural sponge used to create the textural effect has the perfect surface pattern for this.

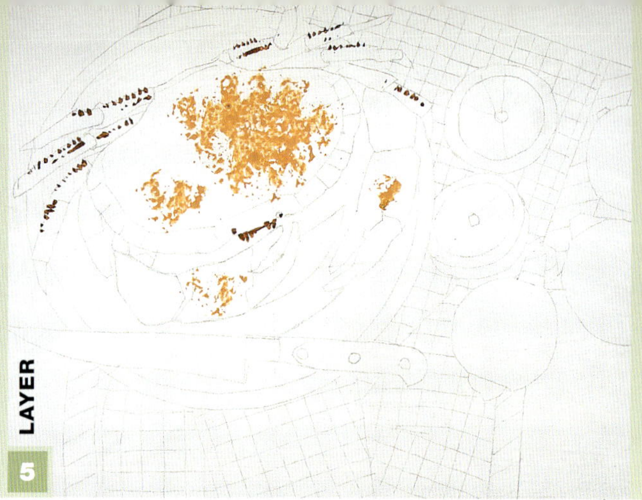

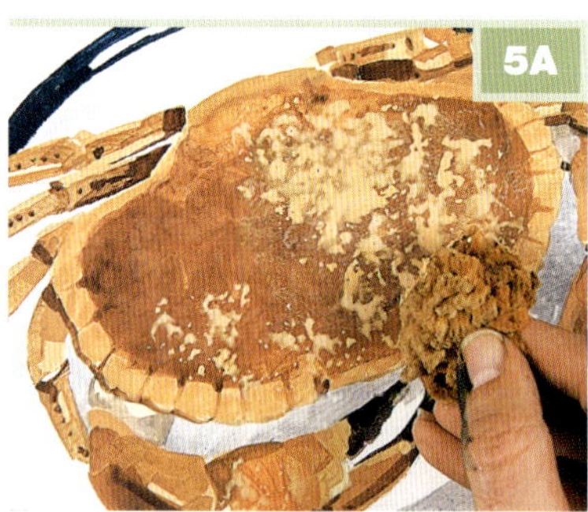

Dip the sponge into relatively fluid paint and apply where required, turning the sponge with each application to vary the pattern.

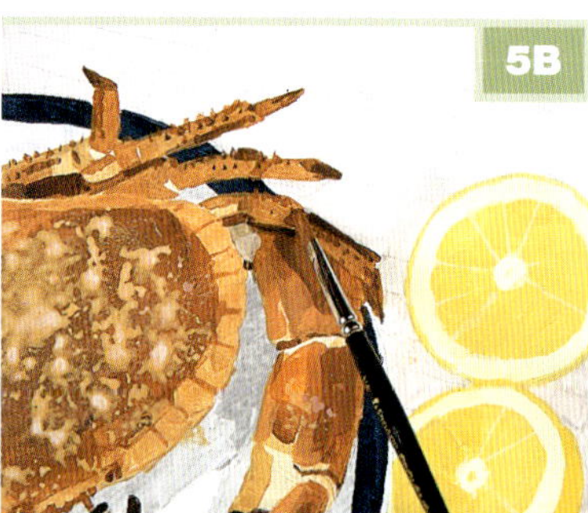

Use the corner of the small flat brush to flick in the fine barbs.

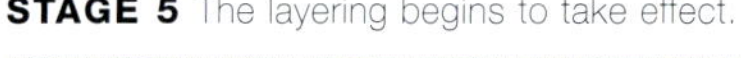

STAGE 5 The layering begins to take effect.

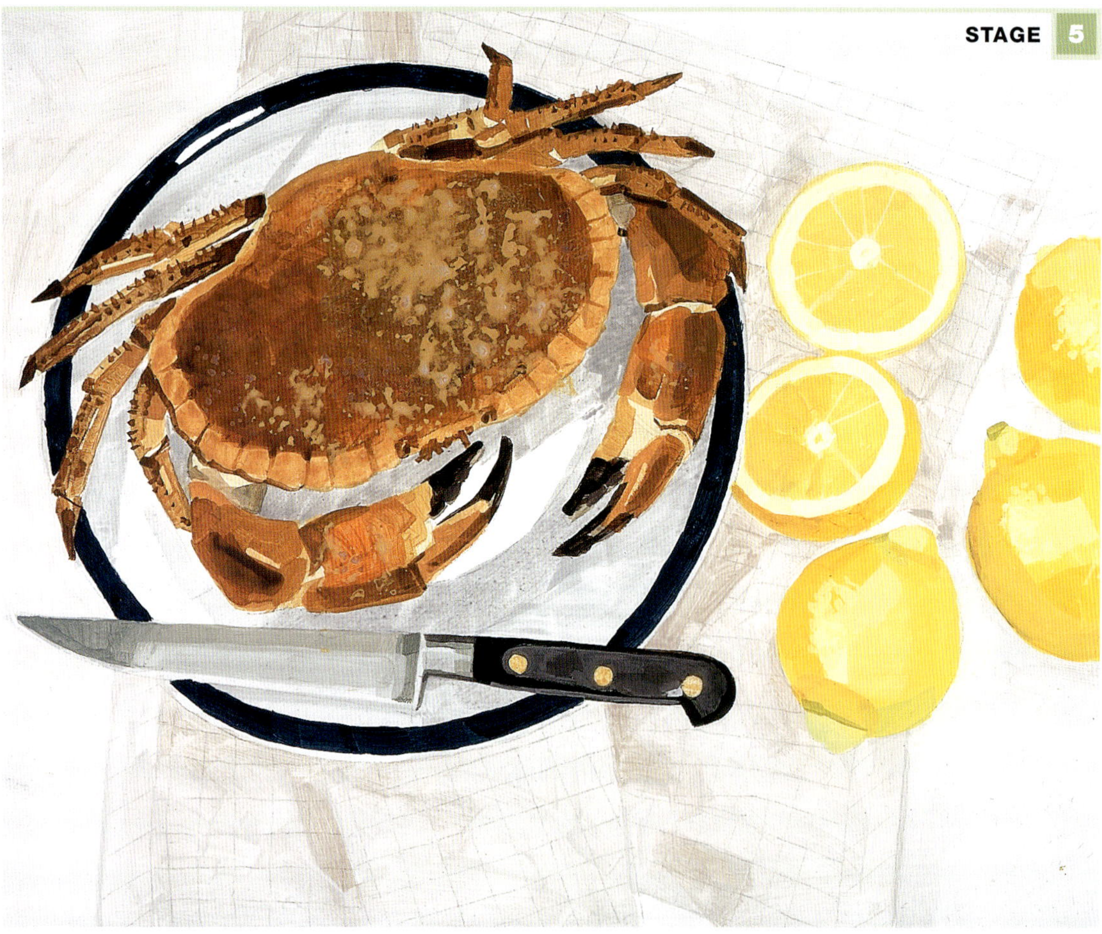

6 ADDING THE FABRIC PATTERN

The fabric patterns are painted in carefully once the underpainting is in place. The direction and angle of the patterns suggest how the cloths are crumpled and folded. Mixes of cadmium red and quinacridone red are applied using both a small and medium round sable brush. The reflections on the plate are repainted using a range of light grays.

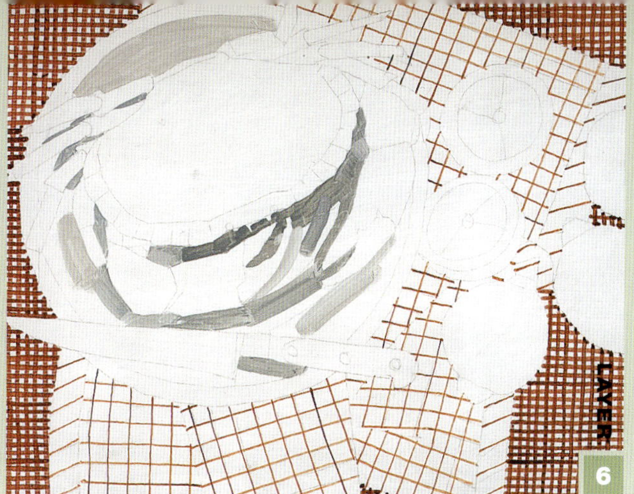

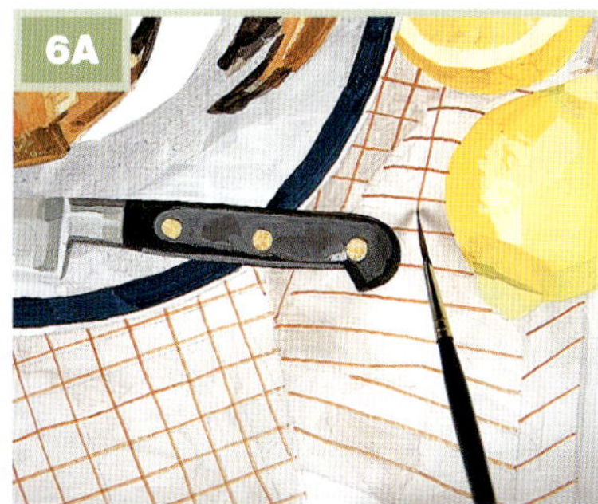

Use a thin rigger brush to describe the thin linear pattern.

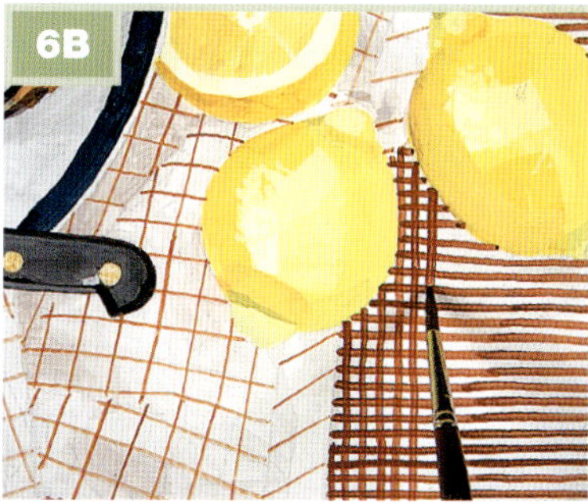

Paint the tablecloth to create a network of small white squares.

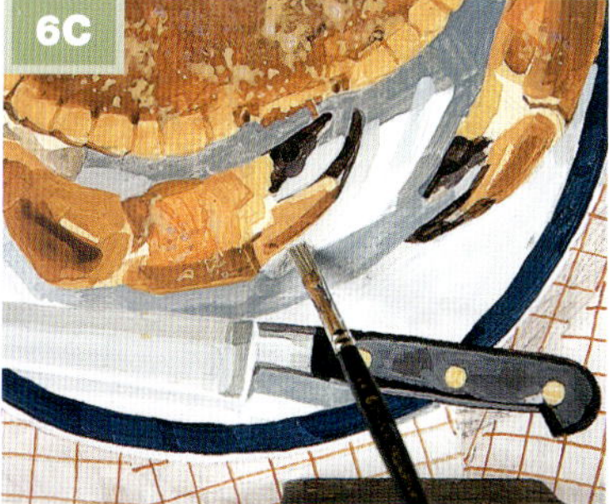

Use the small flat brush to flick in the light reflections.

STAGE 6 The pattern on the fabric brings the whole image to life.

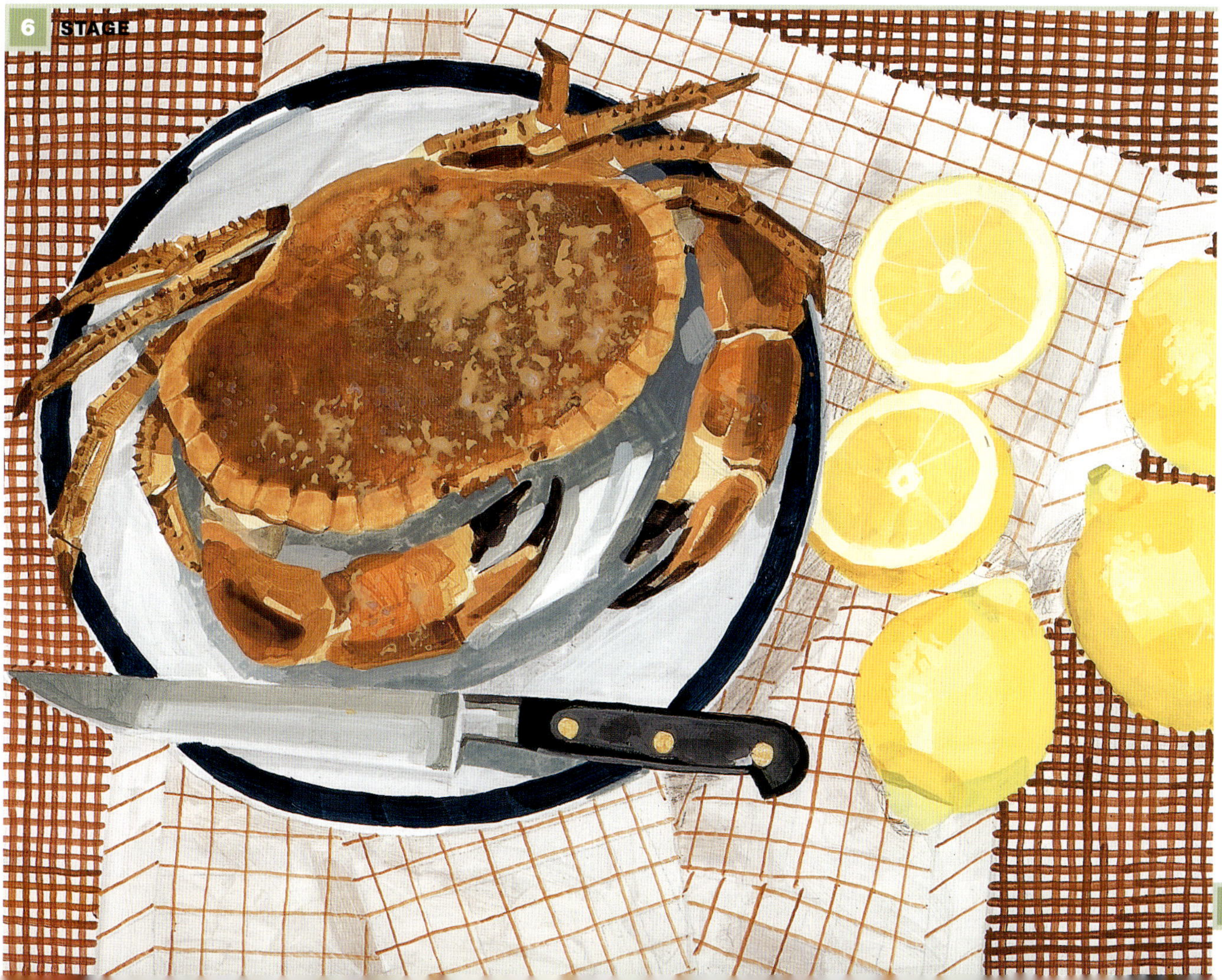

6 STAGE

LAYER 1

COMPOSITION

by FREDA ANDERSON

Composition is an important part of any picture-making process. Many artists use composition in an intuitive way, naturally creating arrangements that are pleasing and compositionally sound. Several devices have evolved which help the process, including the rule of thirds, which is used here. The picture area is divided horizontally into three equal rows and vertically into three equal columns. Important elements are distributed on or about the intersecting lines. This technique is simple and it works.

1 ARRANGING THE SPACE

Stick charcoal is used to sketch out the main elements of the image. These are arranged on the grid of lines that have been previously drawn.

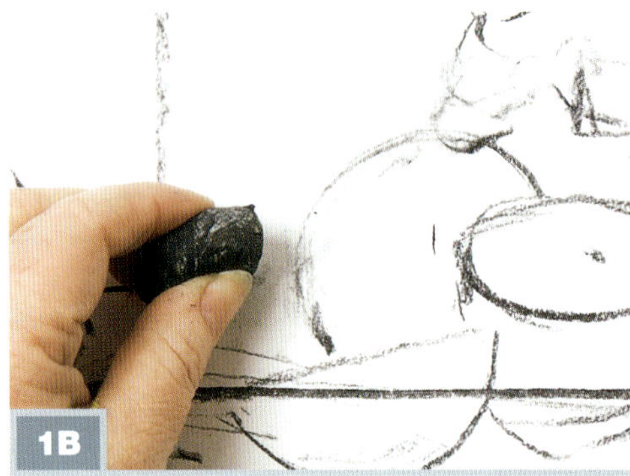

1B

Erase and reposition these elements as required.

Loosely position the main elements.

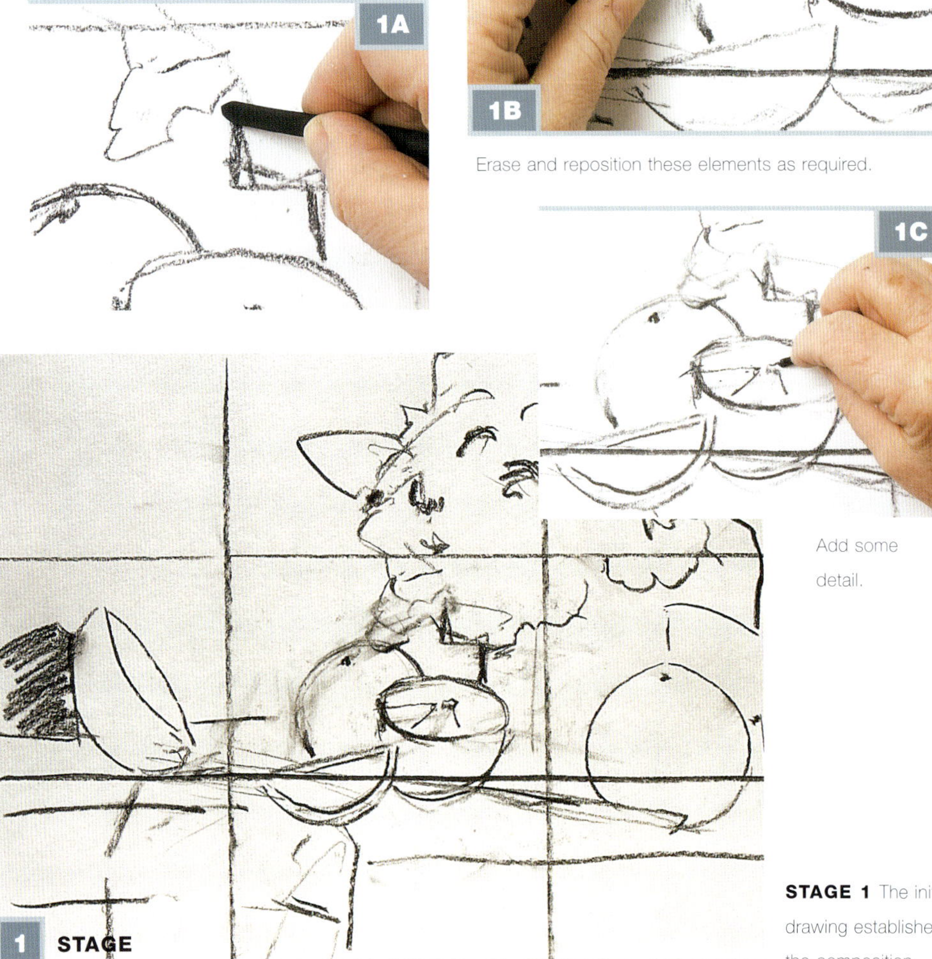

1A

1C

Add some detail.

1 STAGE

STAGE 1 The initial drawing establishes the composition.

MATERIALS

Acrylics

- Titanium white
- Dioxazine purple
- Phthalo blue
- Ultramarine blue
- Indigo
- Cadmium yellow
- Lemon yellow
- Naples yellow
- Burnt umber
- Yellow Ochre

Canvas

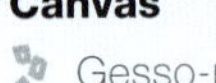

- Gesso-prepared board

Other materials

- #4 flat brush
- #8 flat brush
- #1 round brush
- Stick charcoal
- Eraser
- Water

2 CREATING THE TONAL DRAWING

This artist works in two distinctive stages. First, the drawing is used to describe the tonal arrangement. This acts as a precise guide for the subsequent painting.

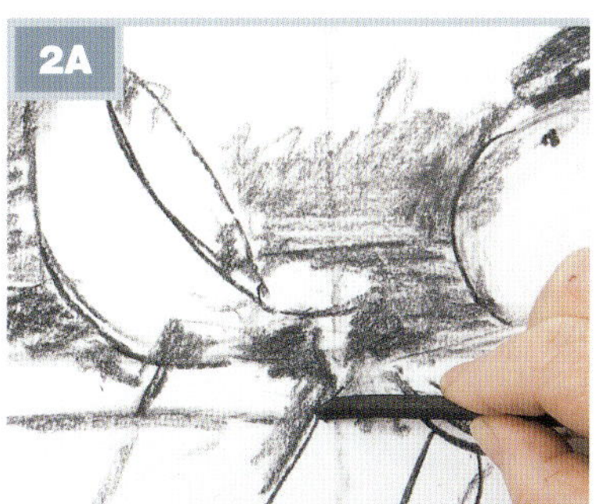

First, loosely apply the tone.

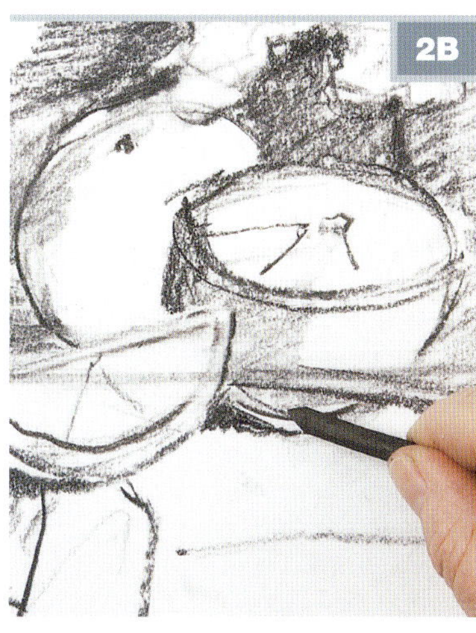

Gradually build up and modify the tonal values.

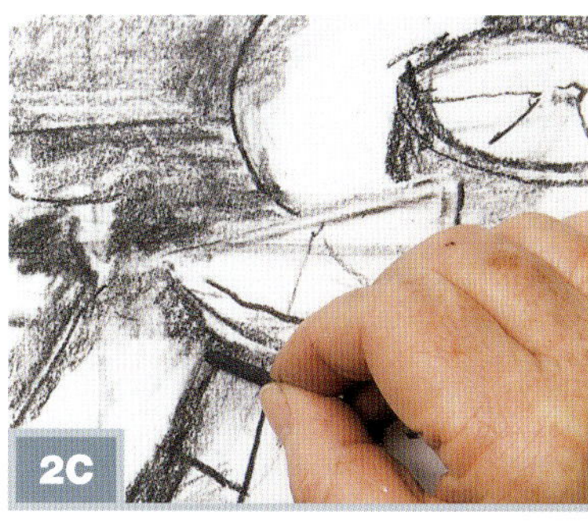

Add some detail.

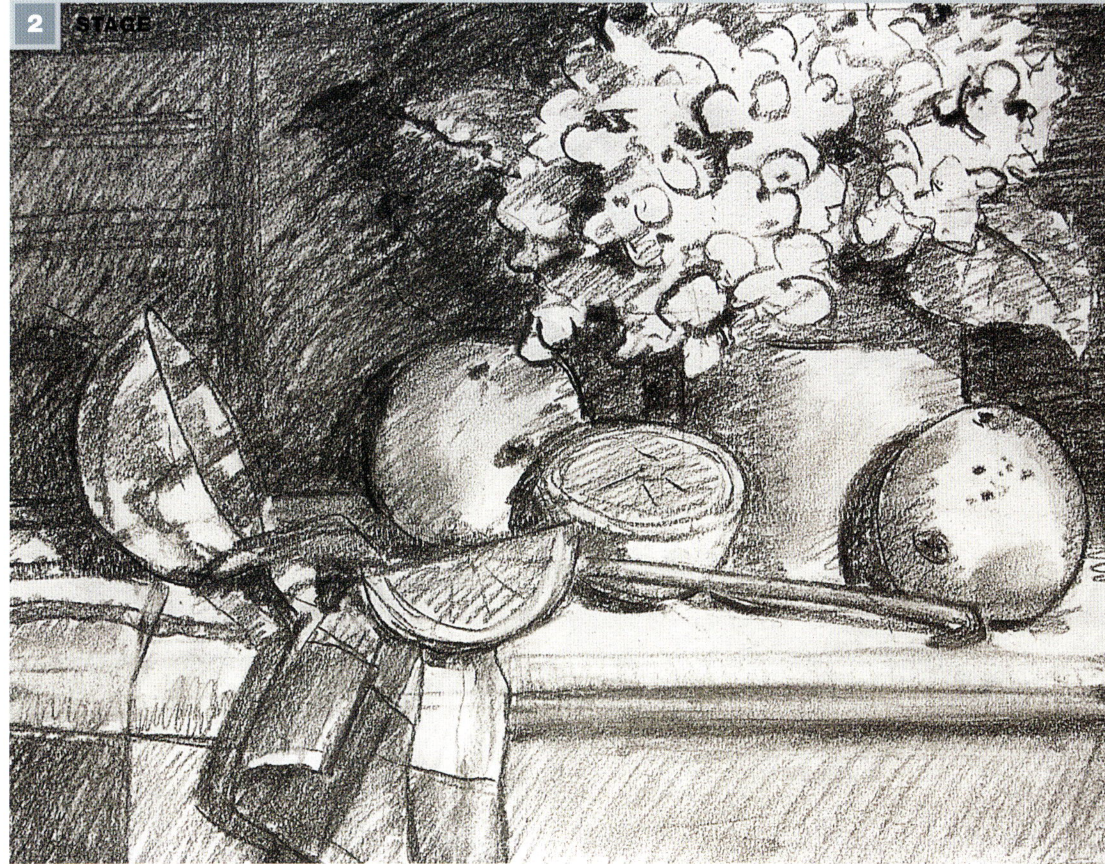

STAGE 2 This tonal drawing acts as a guide to the tonal underpainting.

3 THE IMAGE OUTLINE

Once the faint charcoal trace of the image has been positioned, the trace is removed and the lines are redrawn using acrylic paint.

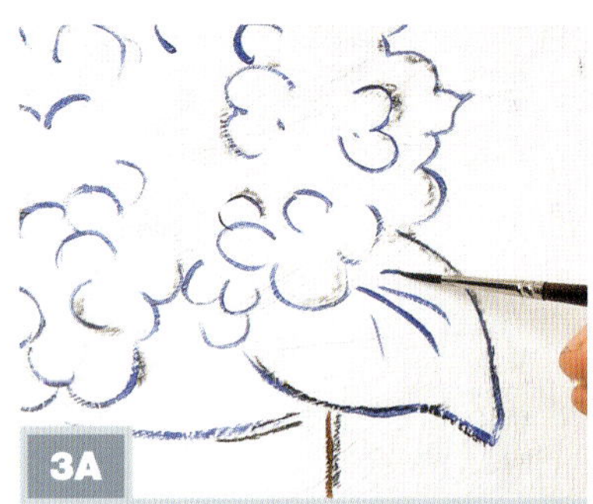

Apply ultramarine blue with a small #1 round brush.

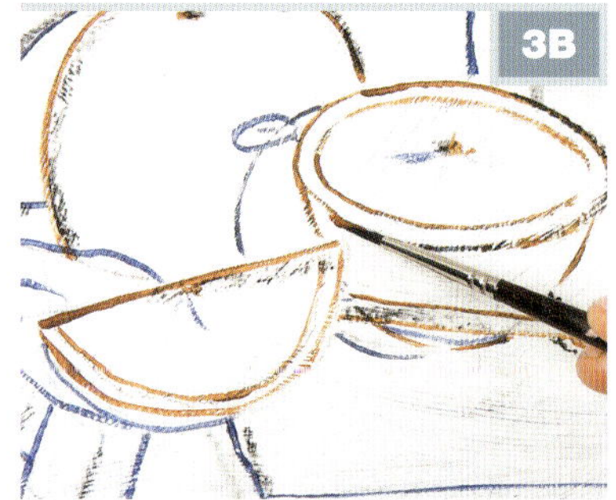

Use burnt umber to paint the oranges and the ladle.

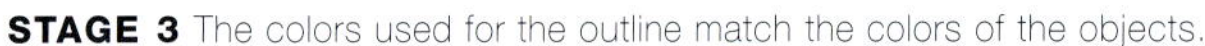
STAGE 3 The colors used for the outline match the colors of the objects.

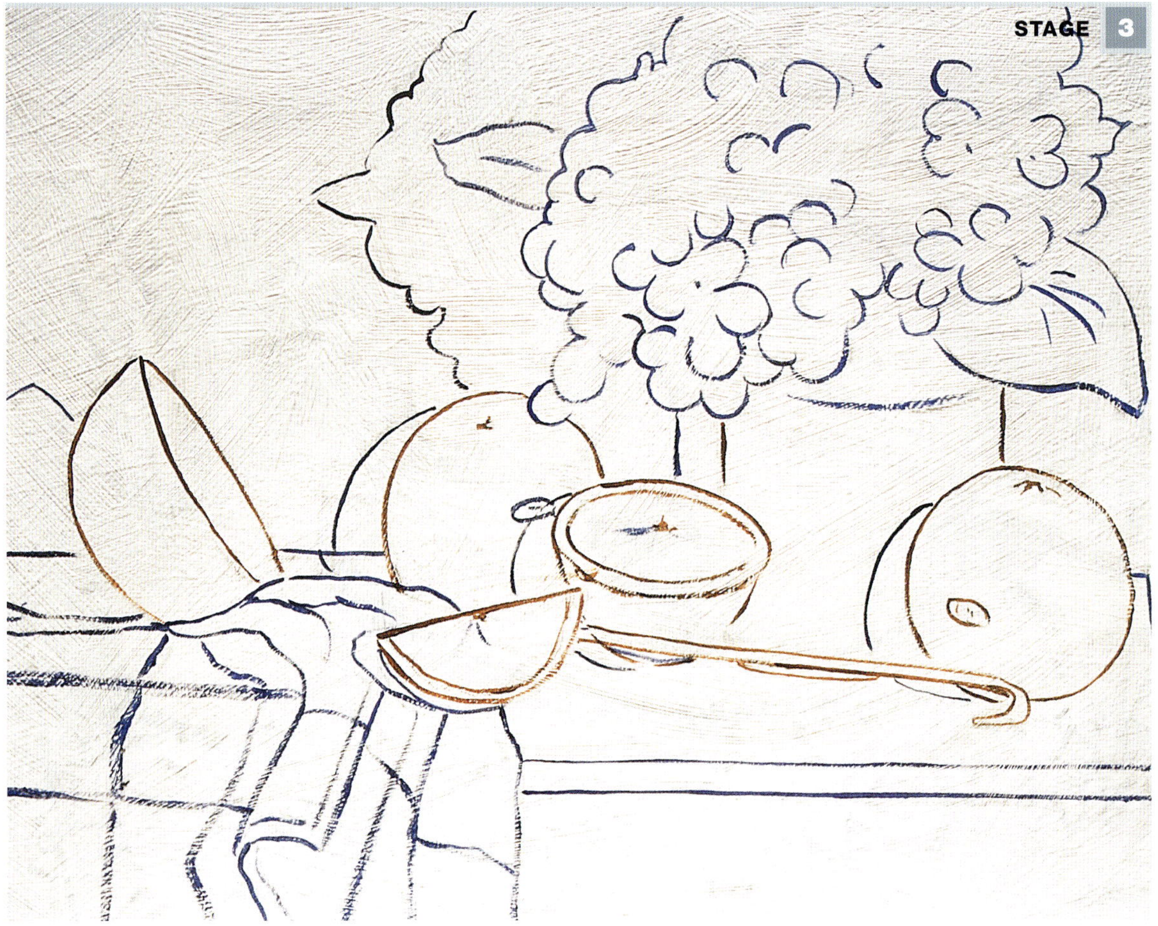

4 THE TONAL UNDERPAINTING

A tonal underpainting is now made using the outlined drawing as a guide. Ultramarine blue and burnt umber mixes are used, applied with a #8 flat brush.

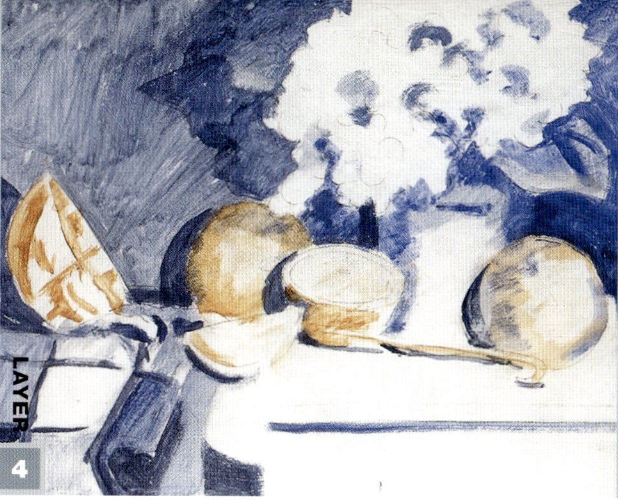

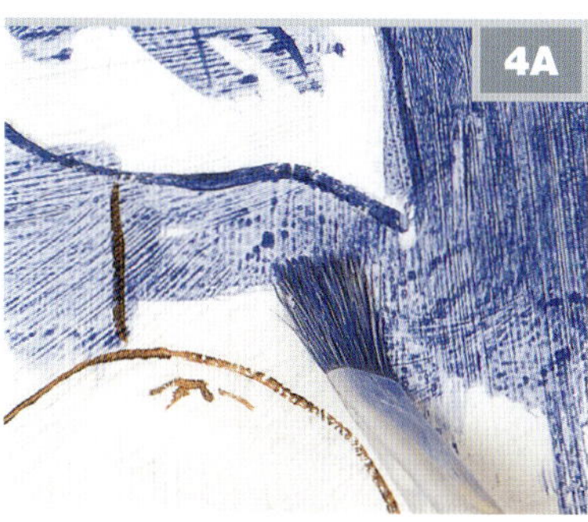

Apply the ultramarine blue in a thin layer.

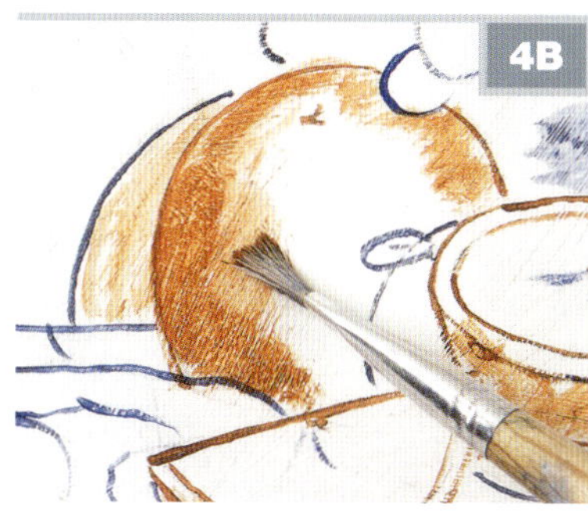

Use burnt umber mixes on the oranges and the copper ladle.

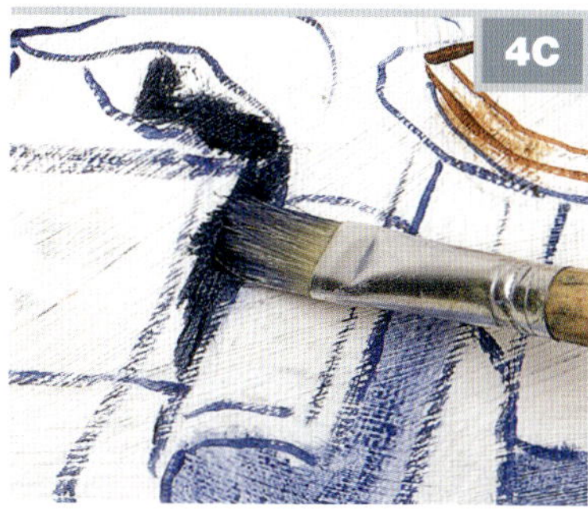

Mix the two colors together to produce a deep blue-gray.

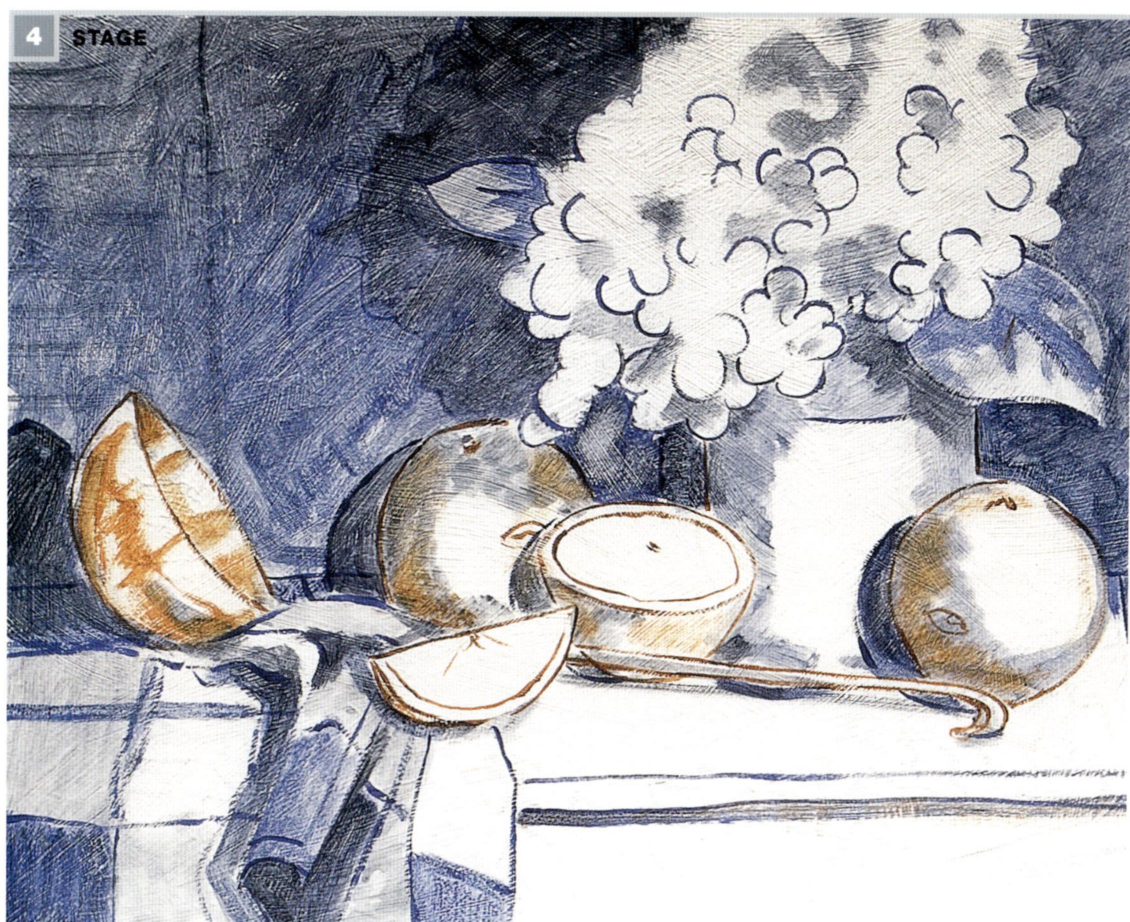

STAGE 4 The tonal underdrawing forms the base for subsequent applications of color.

5 ESTABLISHING THE COLORS

Cadmium and lemon yellow mixes darkened with burnt umber are applied to the fruit. A similar range of colors is used on the copper ladle, which also reflects the color of the fruit. Phthalocyanine blue, indigo, and dioxazine purple is worked into the hydrangea flowers. Yellow ochre is applied to the whole of the background.

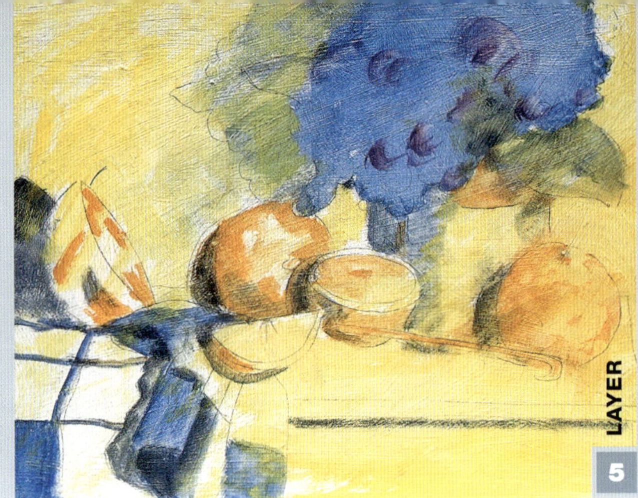

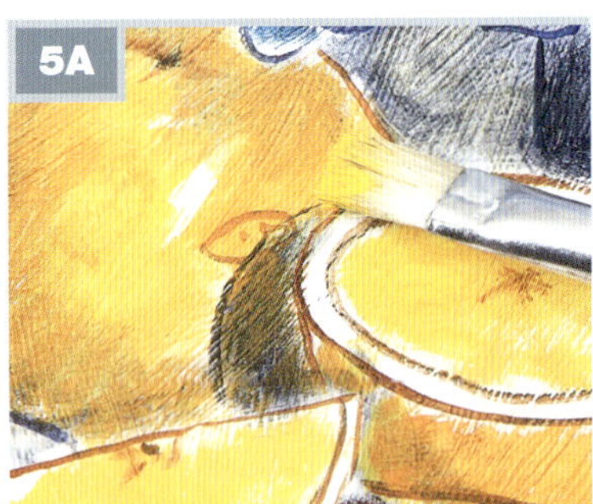

Keep the mixes relatively thin to allow previous applications of paint to be seen.

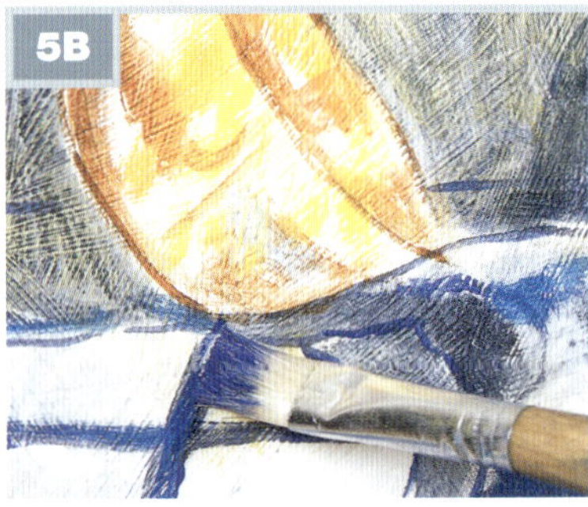

Use ultramarine blue to strengthen the pattern on the cloth.

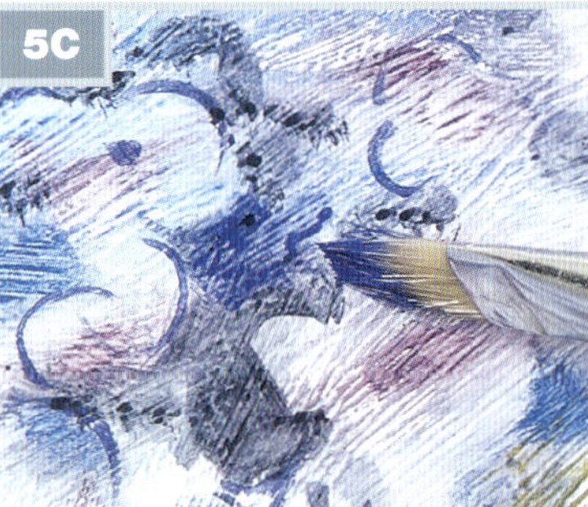

Use dark blues to paint the negative spaces around the individual flower heads.

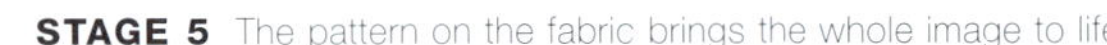

STAGE 5 The pattern on the fabric brings the whole image to life.

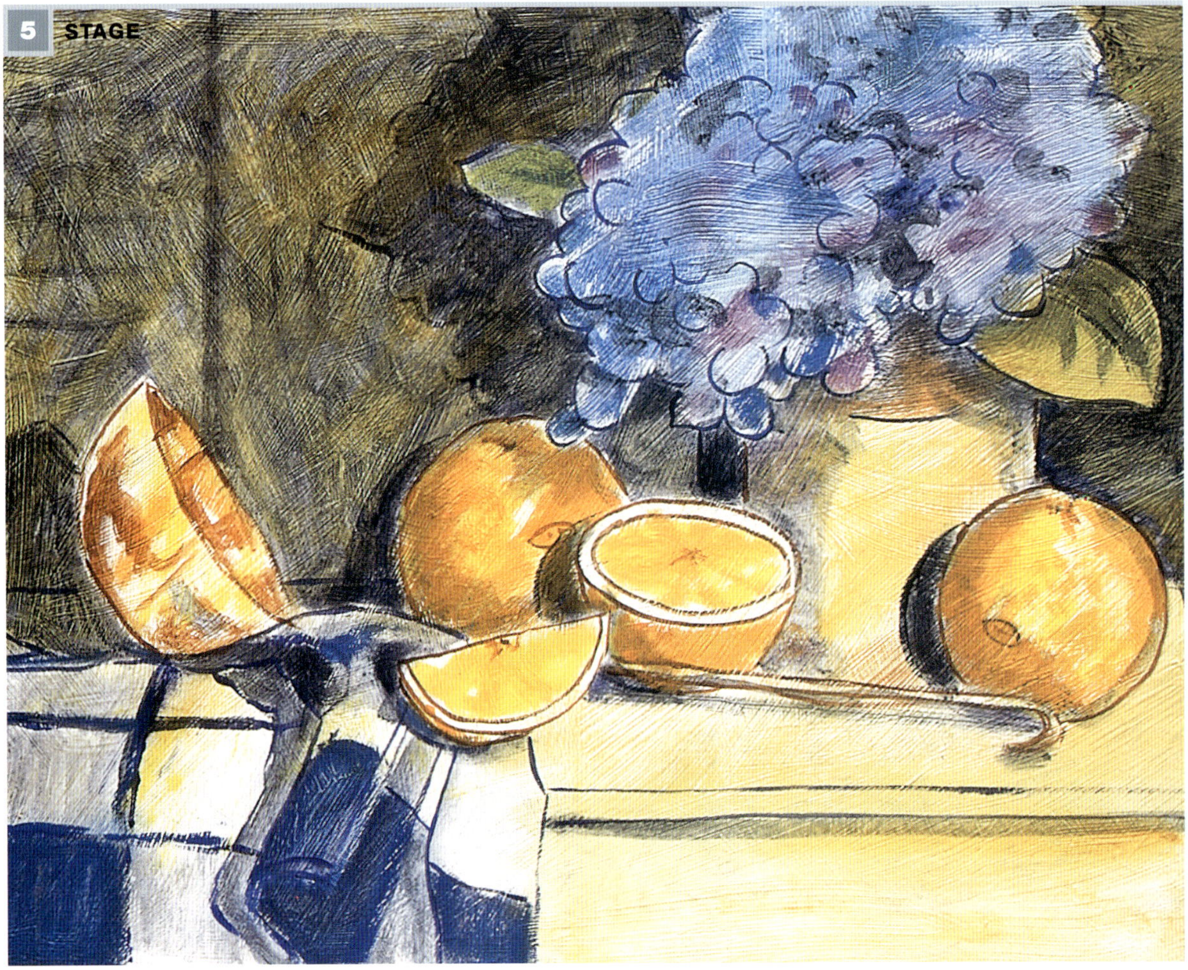

5 STAGE

6 ADDING THE DETAILS

Colors are strengthened, highlights added, and the areas of the thin yellow ochre wash applied in the previous stage are worked over using a mix of titanium white and Naples yellow.

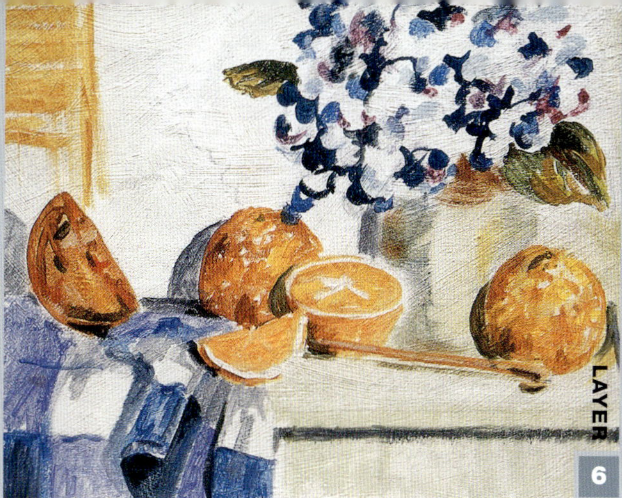

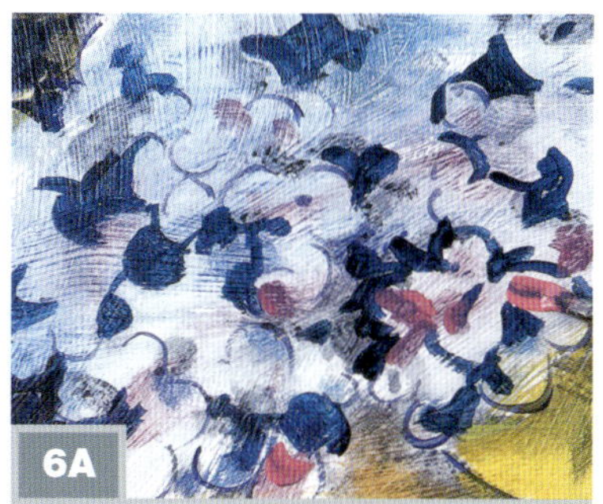

Work dioxazine purple and white into the flower heads using a #4 flat brush.

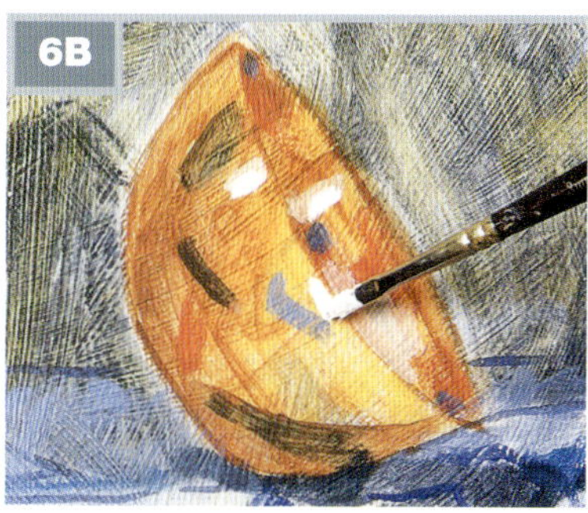

Apply white highlights to the ladle.

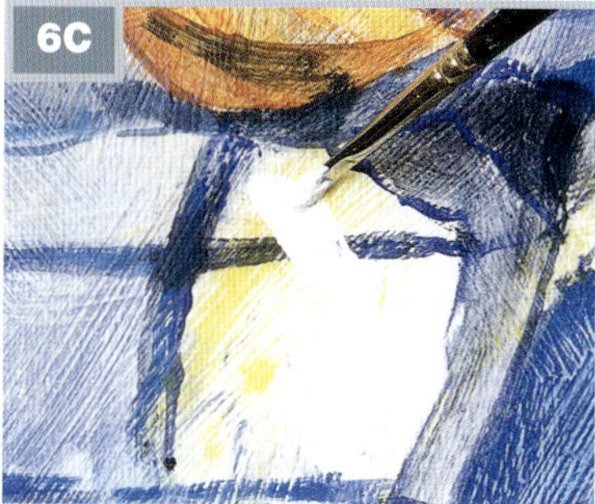

Lighten the white panels on the cloth.

STAGE 6 The tonal underpainting gives depth to the color.

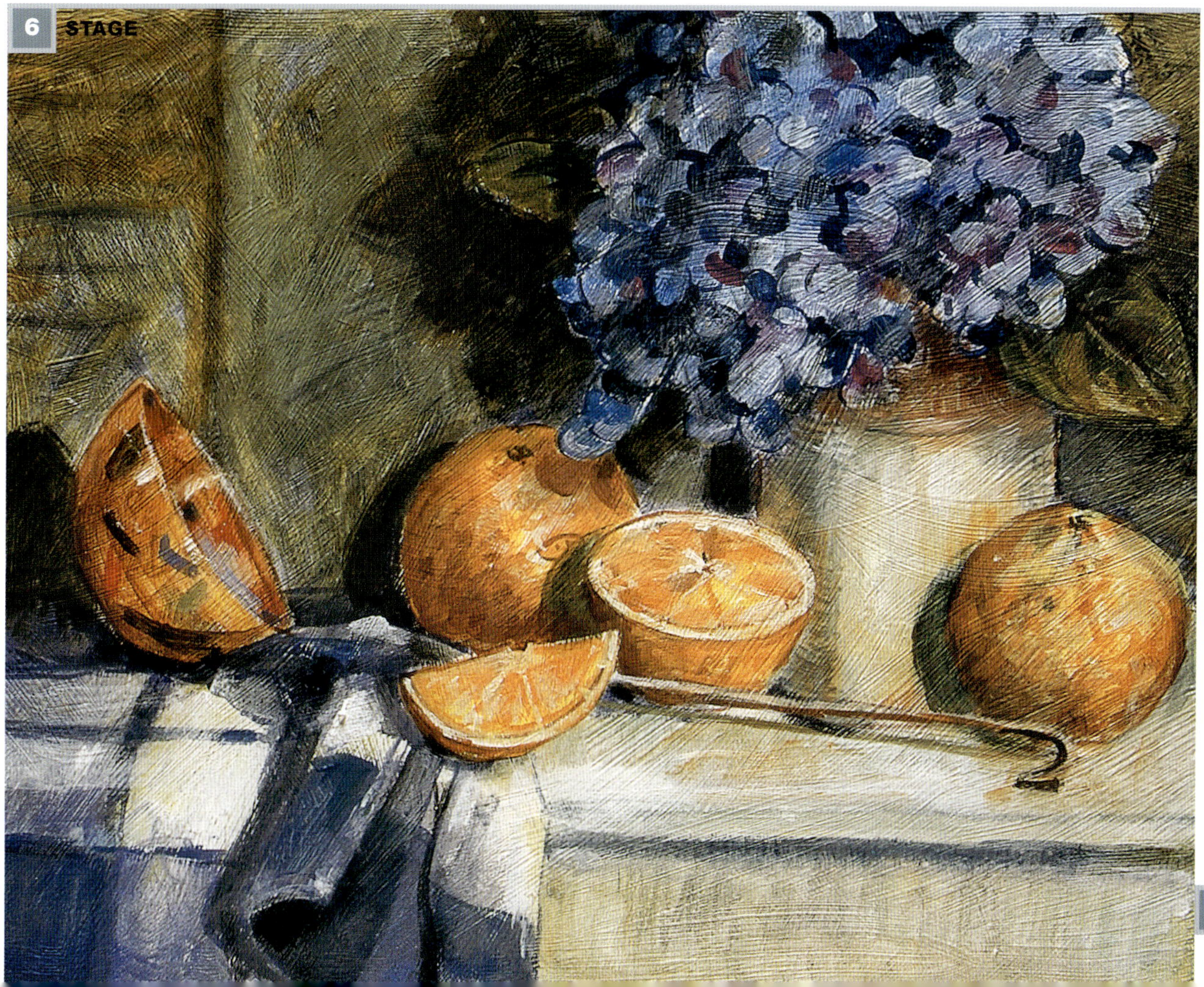

6 STAGE

GLAZING

by FREDA ANDERSON

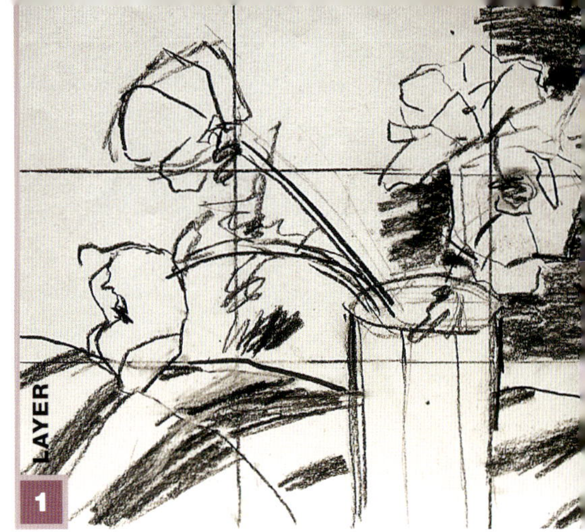

Glazing is a traditional technique that is ideal for painting flowers. Traditionally, thin semitransparent washes of color, not unlike those used in watercolor, are applied over a tonal underpainting. The underpainting describes the form and is allowed to be seen through the thin colored glazes. Acrylic is an ideal medium for glazing because the glazes need to be applied wet on dry, and thin acrylic paint dries very quickly. This artist always begins her work by producing an elaborate tonal drawing and then uses her own version of glazing.

1 WORKING OUT THE COMPOSITION

The composition is based on *the rule of thirds* (see page 25). Charcoal is used to draw in the main elements.

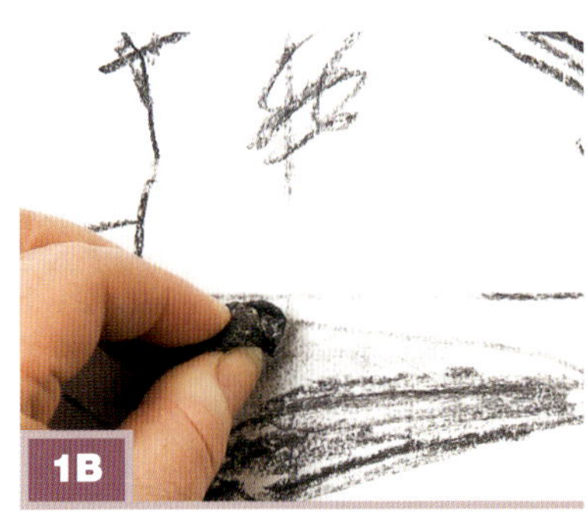

Alter the drawing as needed.

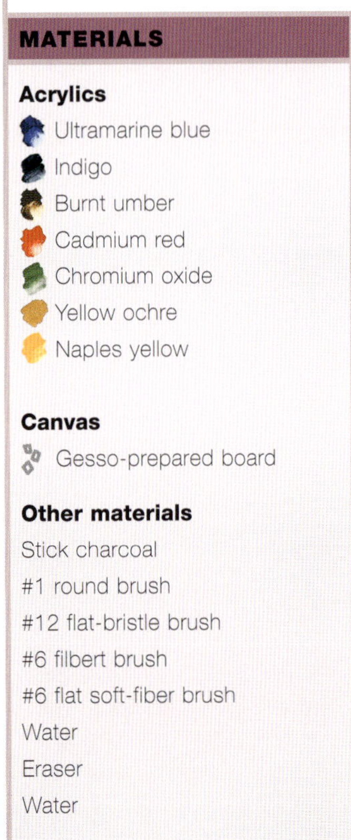

MATERIALS

Acrylics
- Ultramarine blue
- Indigo
- Burnt umber
- Cadmium red
- Chromium oxide
- Yellow ochre
- Naples yellow

Canvas
- Gesso-prepared board

Other materials
- Stick charcoal
- #1 round brush
- #12 flat-bristle brush
- #6 filbert brush
- #6 flat soft-fiber brush
- Water
- Eraser
- Water

Use simple line work to establish the composition.

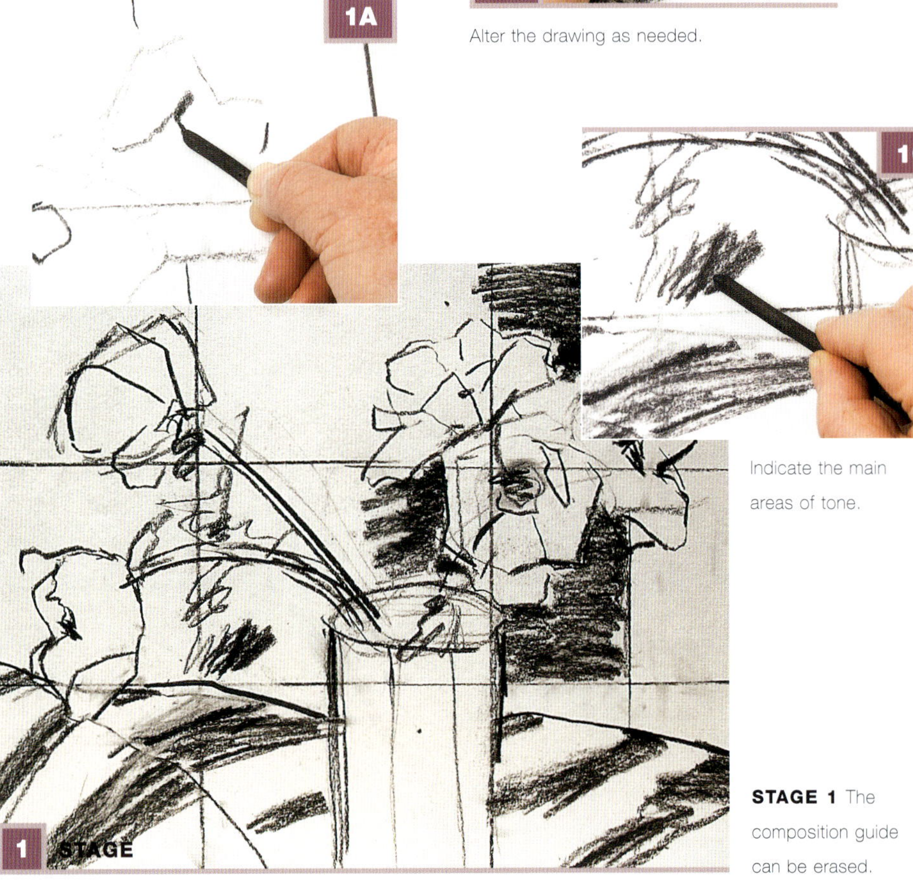

Indicate the main areas of tone.

STAGE 1 The composition guide can be erased.

2 THE TONAL DRAWING

Once the artist is happy with the composition and the position of the elements, tone is added. Charcoal is built up steadily until the correct depth and scale of tone is achieved.

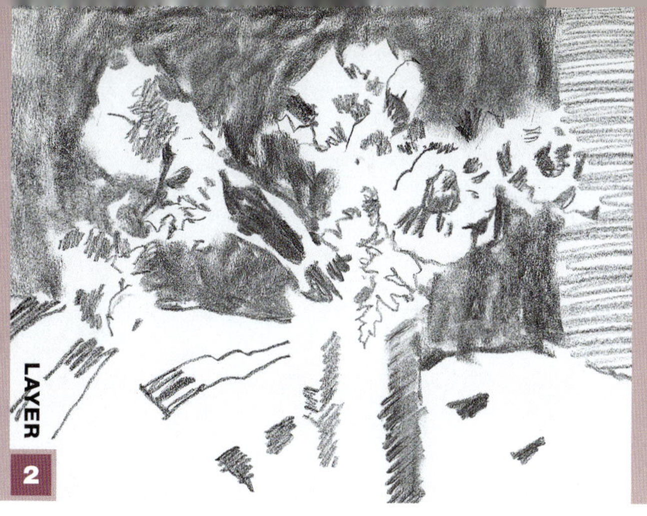

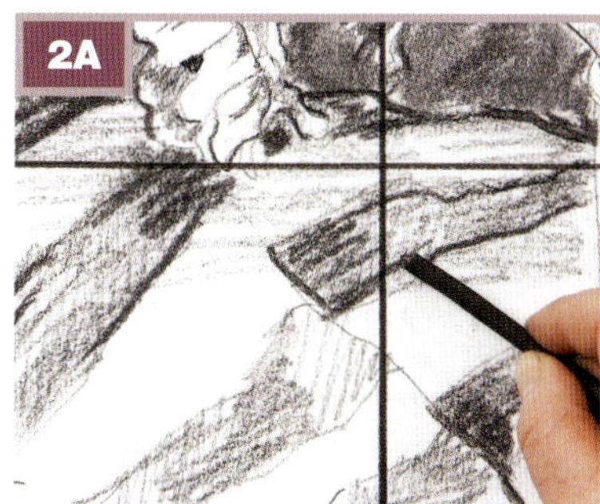

Scribble dark tone onto the cloth pattern.

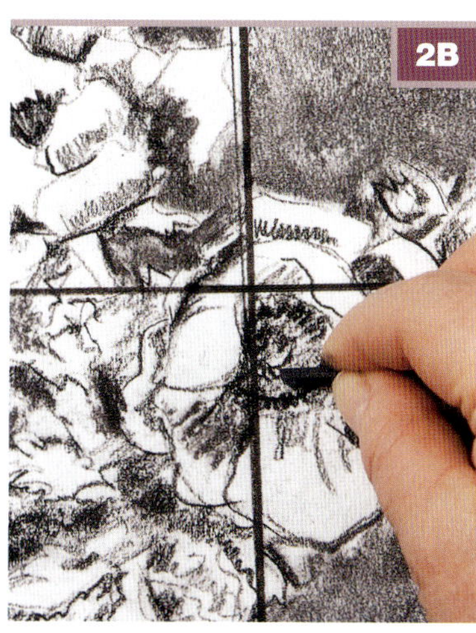

Add details to the flowers.

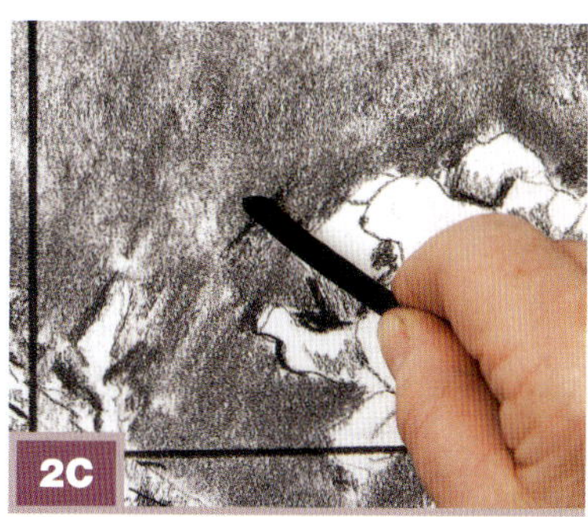

Apply a tone across the background.

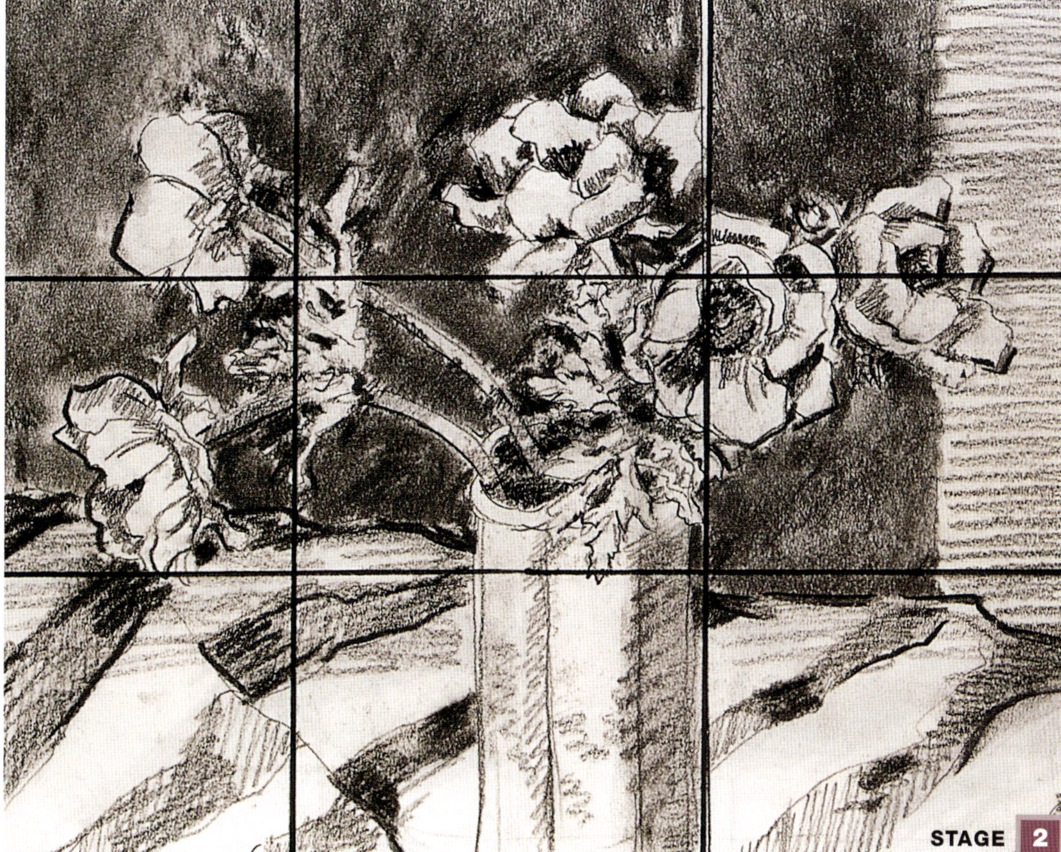

STAGE 2 Apply charcoal tones in layers.

3 TRANSFERRING THE DRAWING

Once the composition and tone have been established, the artist transfers the drawing onto a gesso-prepared board. This is done by using a simple tracing.

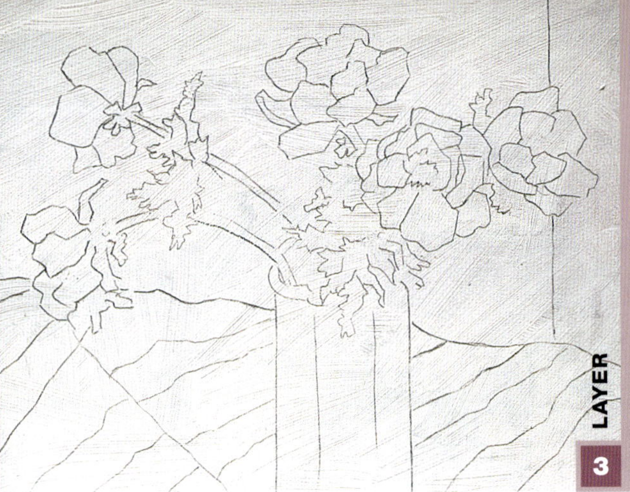

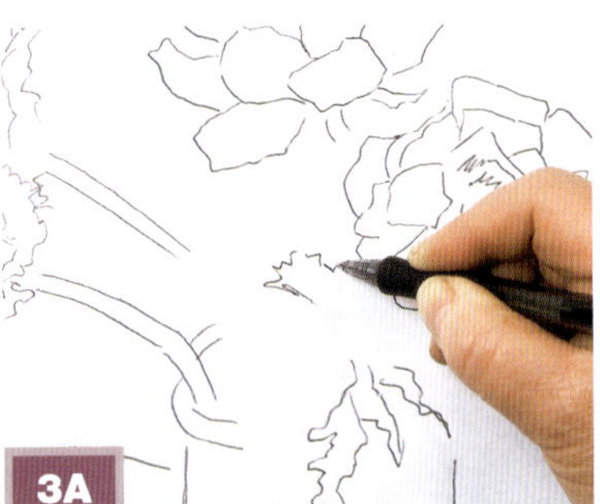

Use a pen to trace the completed charcoal drawing onto a sheet of thin paper.

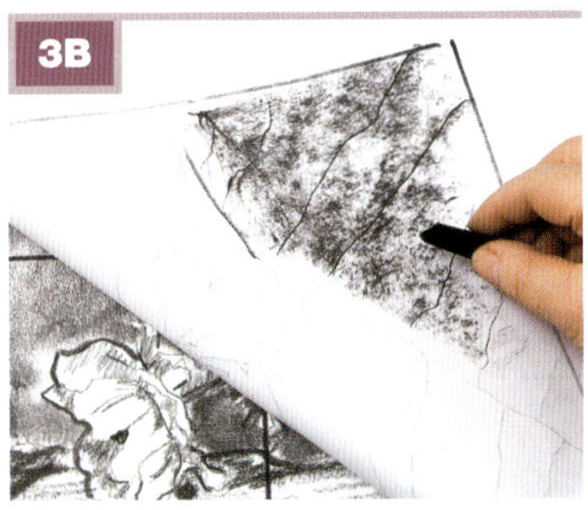

Cover the back of the paper in charcoal.

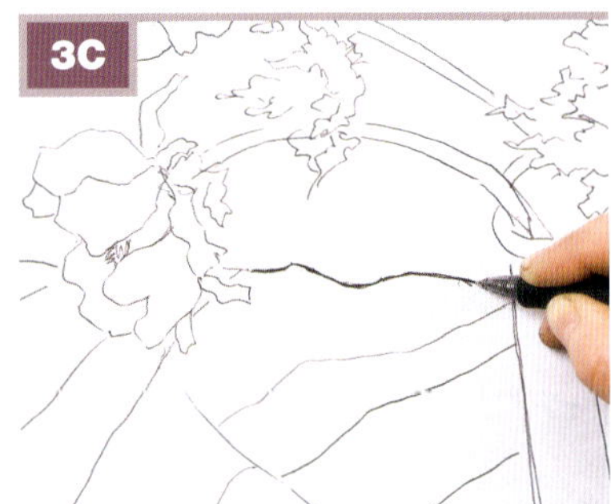

Place the paper on the prepared board and transfer the image by redrawing it on the tracing.

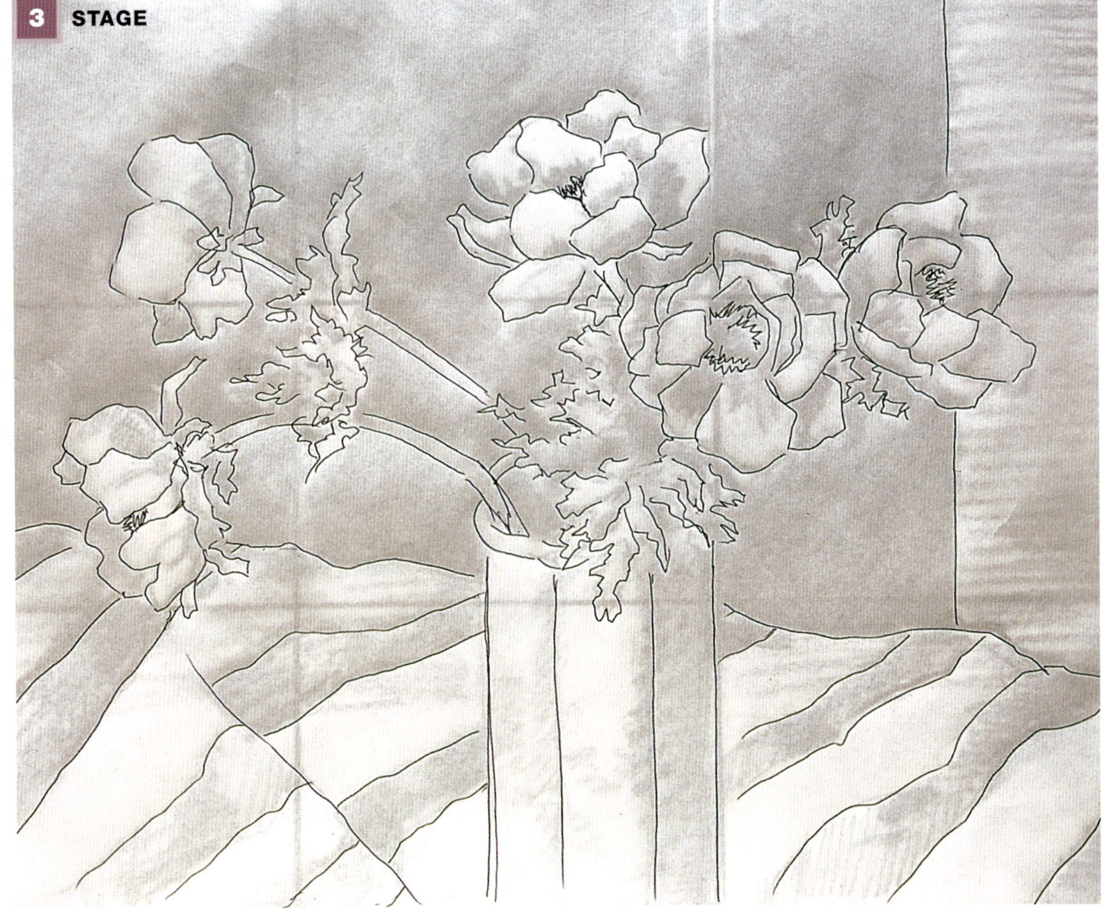

STAGE 3 Avoid too much tracing detail.

4 STRENGTHENING THE LINE

The transferred charcoal drawing is delicate and easily smudged, but this can be fixed by strengthening the line. Use a fine #1 round brush to paint an ultramarine blue line onto the drawing.

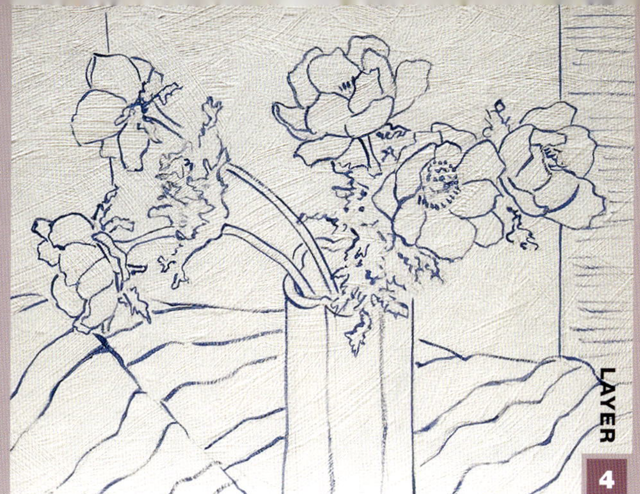

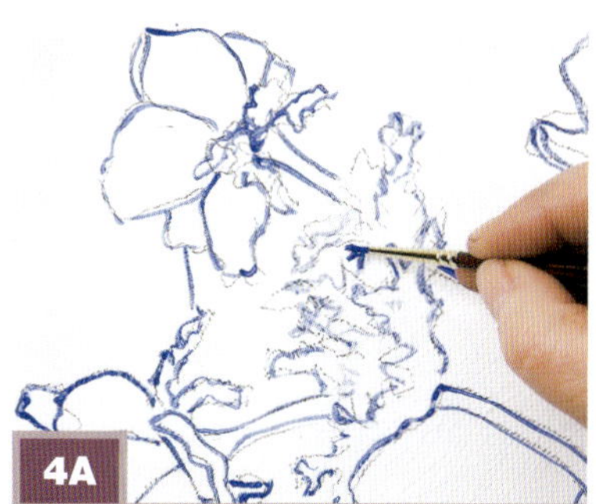

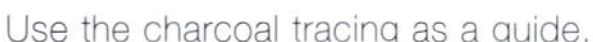

Use the charcoal tracing as a guide.

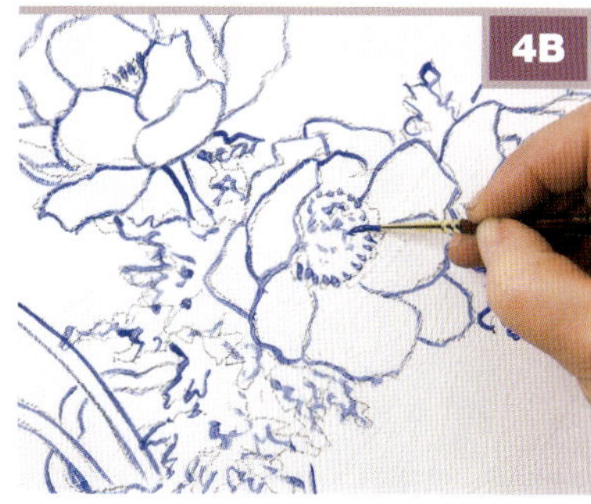

Add details to the flowers.

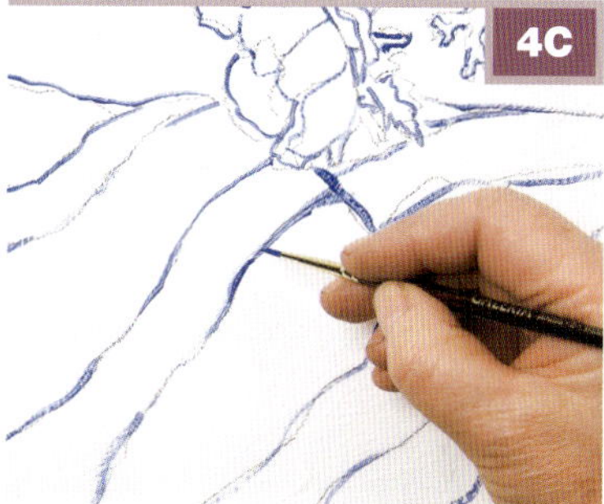

Draw the pattern on the cloth.

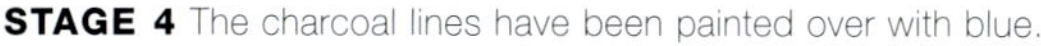

STAGE 4 The charcoal lines have been painted over with blue.

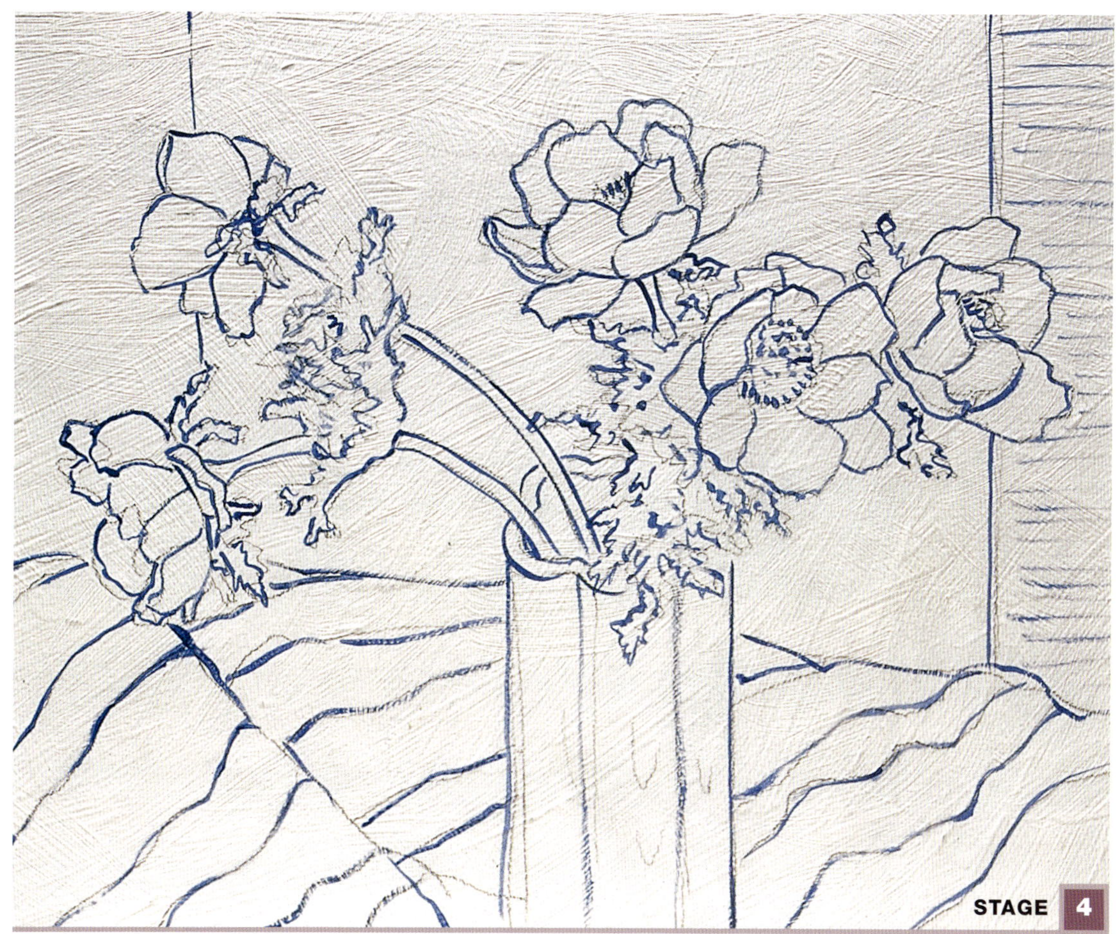

5 THE MONOCHROMATIC UNDERPAINTING

The monochromatic underpainting is made using thin mixes of ultramarine blue and indigo. No white paint is used; the colors appear lighter because they are mixed with more water. The paint is applied to the background using a medium #12 flat-bristle brush and to the flowers using a small #6 filbert brush.

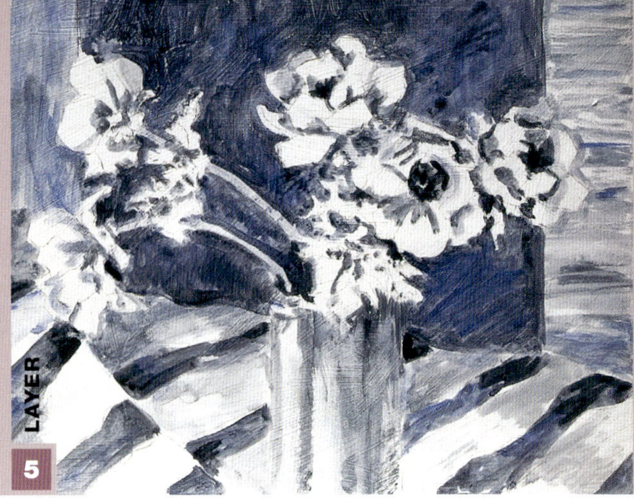

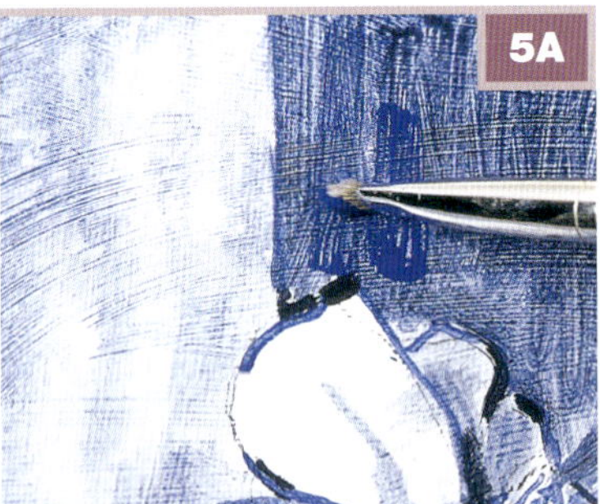

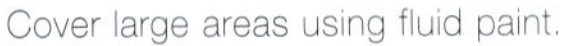
Cover large areas using fluid paint.

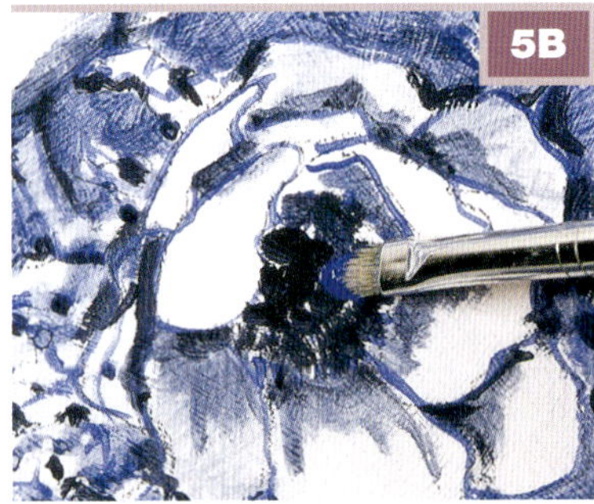

Add details to the flowers.

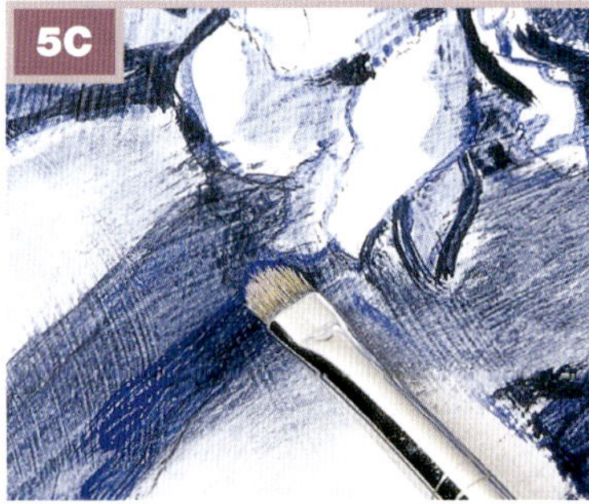

Vary the shape of the pattern to show the shape and folds of the cloth.

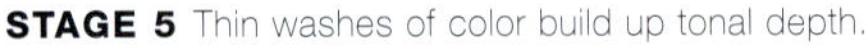
STAGE 5 Thin washes of color build up tonal depth.

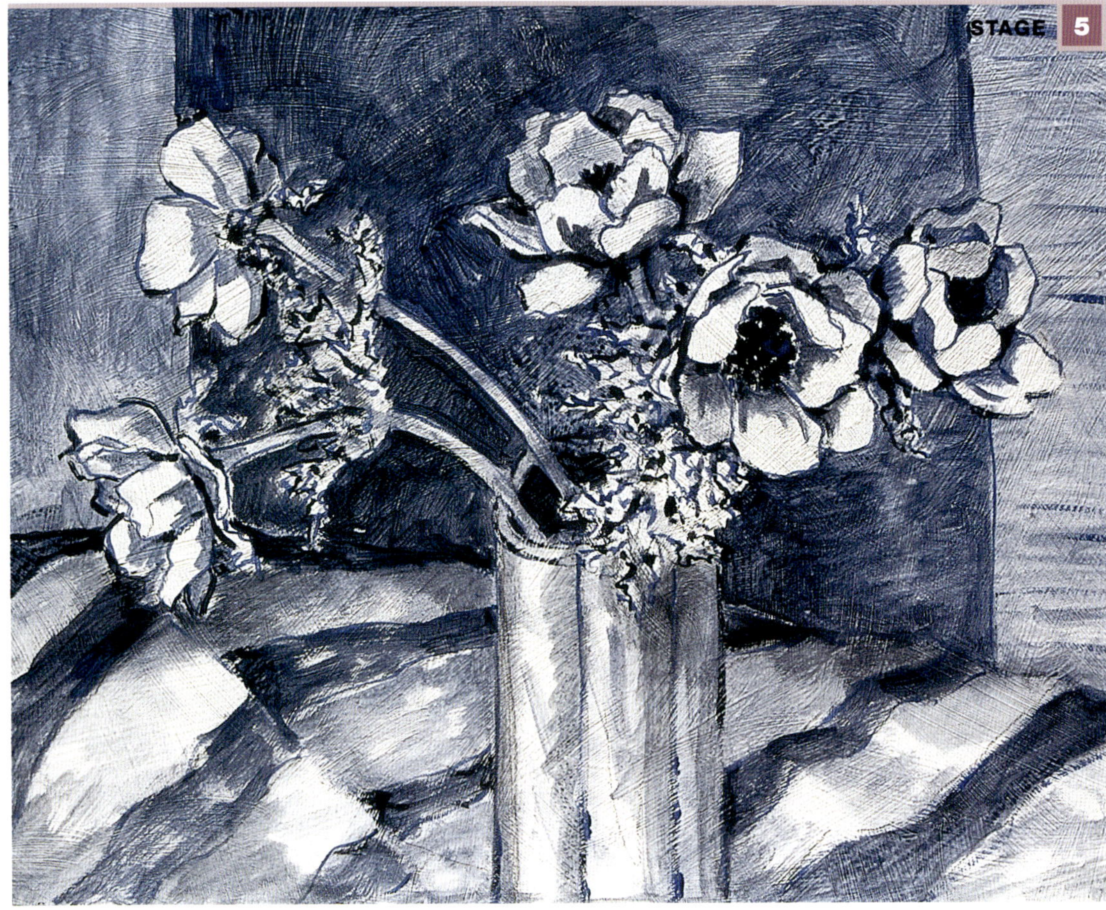

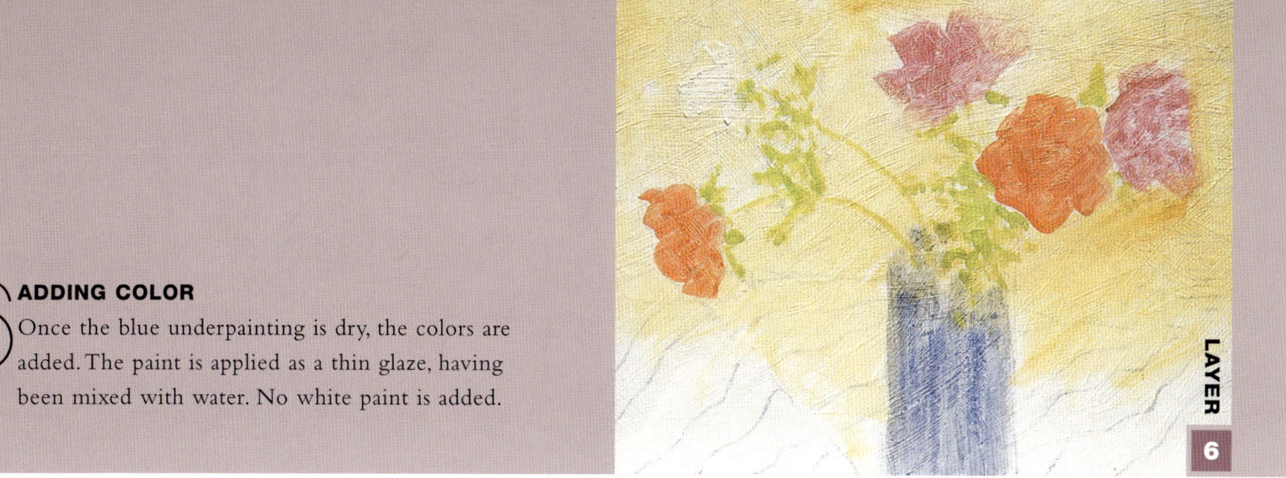

6 ADDING COLOR

Once the blue underpainting is dry, the colors are added. The paint is applied as a thin glaze, having been mixed with water. No white paint is added.

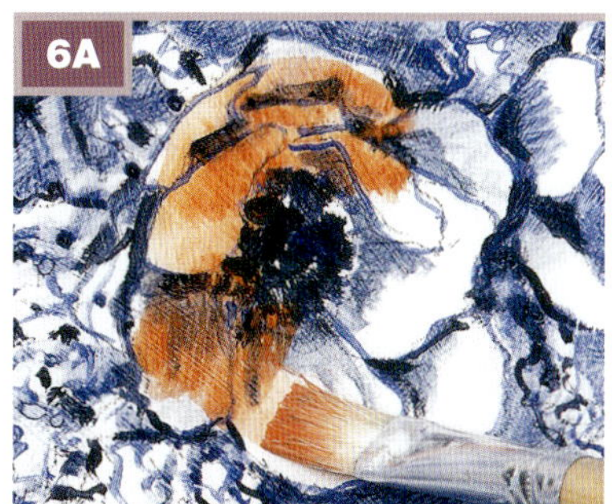

Use the large flat brush to apply cadmium red to the flower heads.

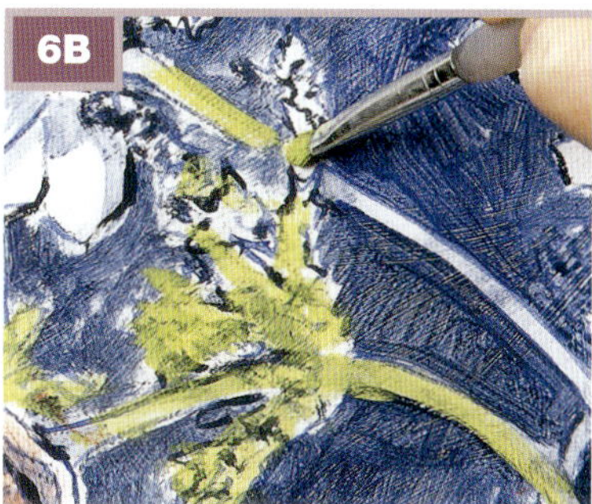

Apply chromium oxide to the leaves and stems.

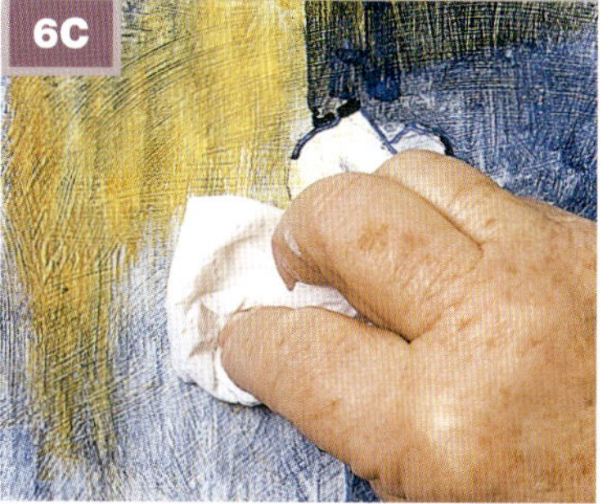

Apply a thin mixture of yellow ochre and Naples yellow to the background and distribute the paint using a rag.

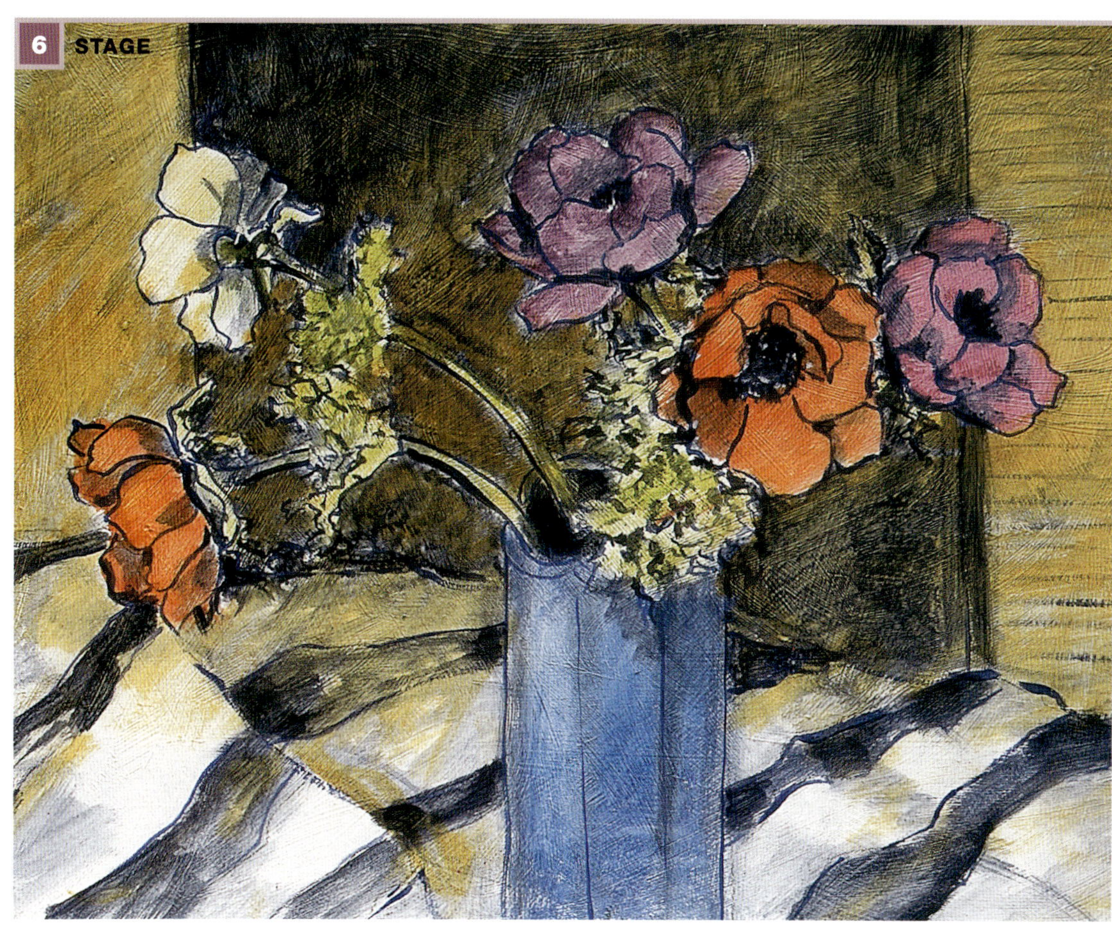

STAGE 6 The colored glazes are simple mixes.

7 PAINTING THE DARKS

A dark brown is mixed using burnt umber and indigo. This is used to darken the background and is carefully painted around the flower heads, foliage, and stems. More blue is added to the mix, and the stripes on the tablecloth are darkened.

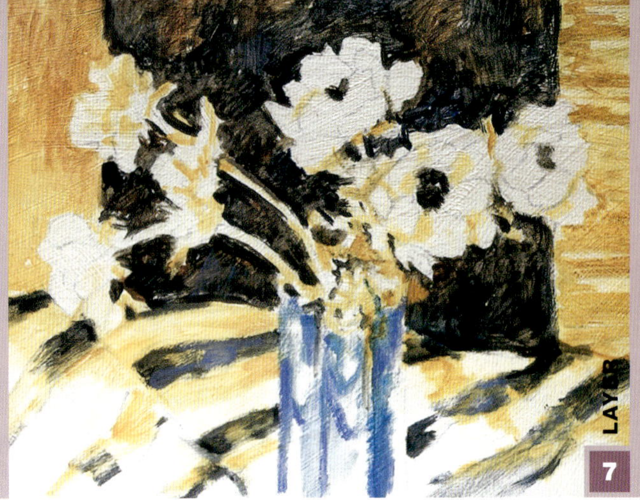

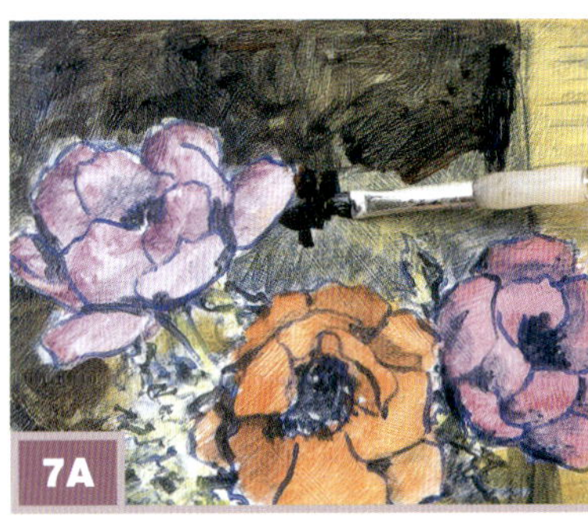

Carefully work around the flower heads, redefining their shapes.

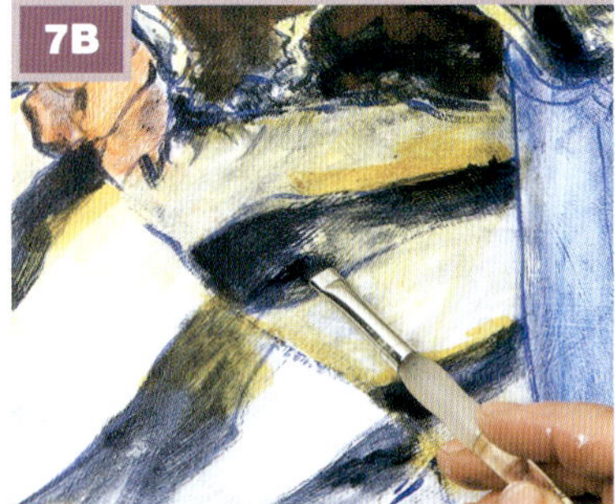

Darken the pattern on the cloth.

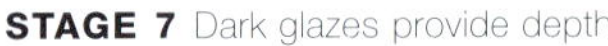

STAGE 7 Dark glazes provide depth.

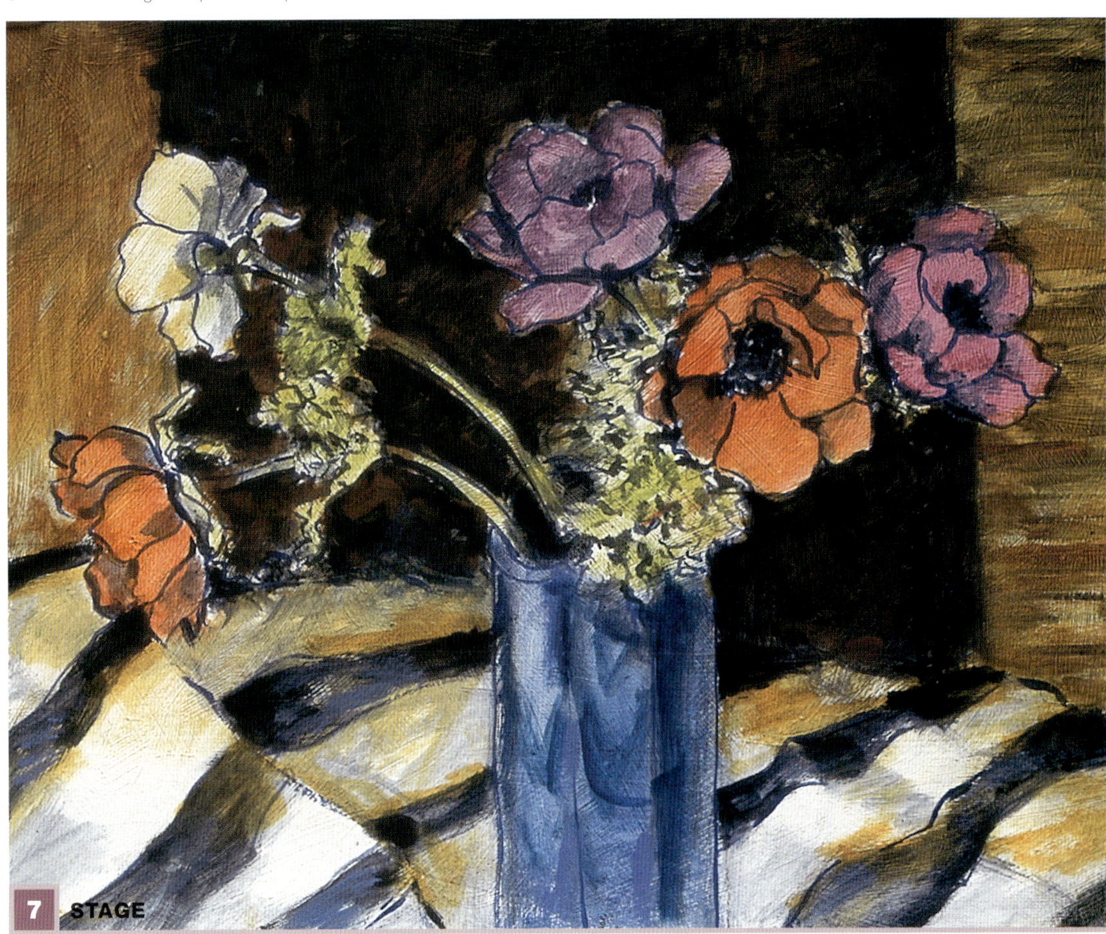

8 ADDING THE DETAILS

A gray mix is loosely scumbled over the entire background. The final step is to add the details that bring the image to life. These include adding reflections to the blue vase. The foliage is reworked using chromium oxide mixed with a little indigo, and the patterns on the flower petals are painted using unmixed color straight from the tube.

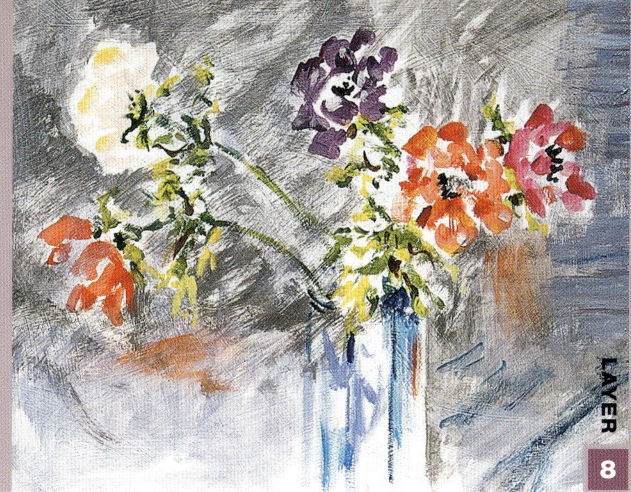

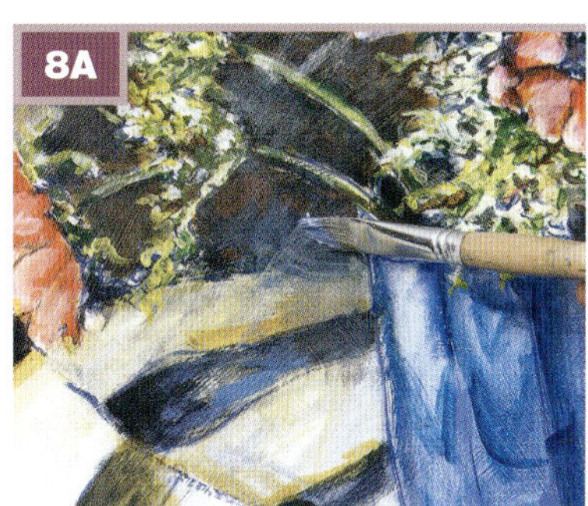

Use the large flat brush to apply the gray scumble.

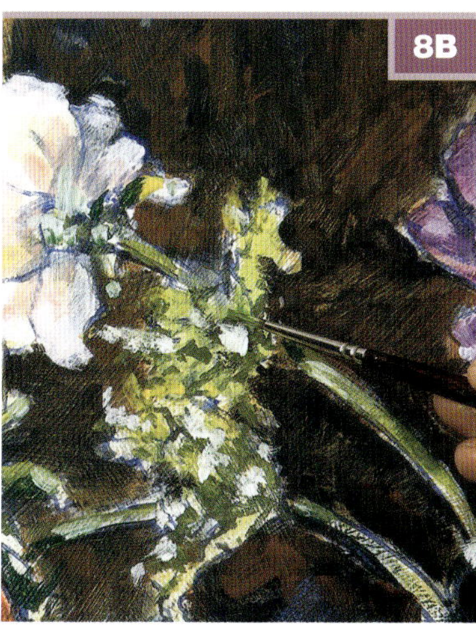

Use a #1 round brush to add a dark green to the anemone leaves.

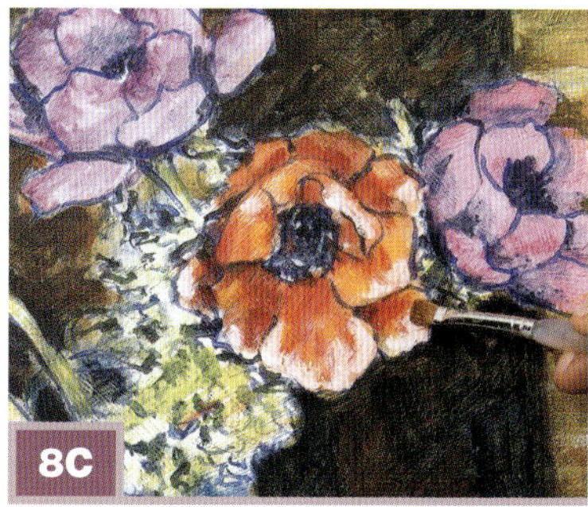

Add details to the flower petals using a #6 flat soft-fiber brush.

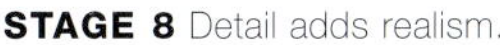

STAGE 8 Detail adds realism.

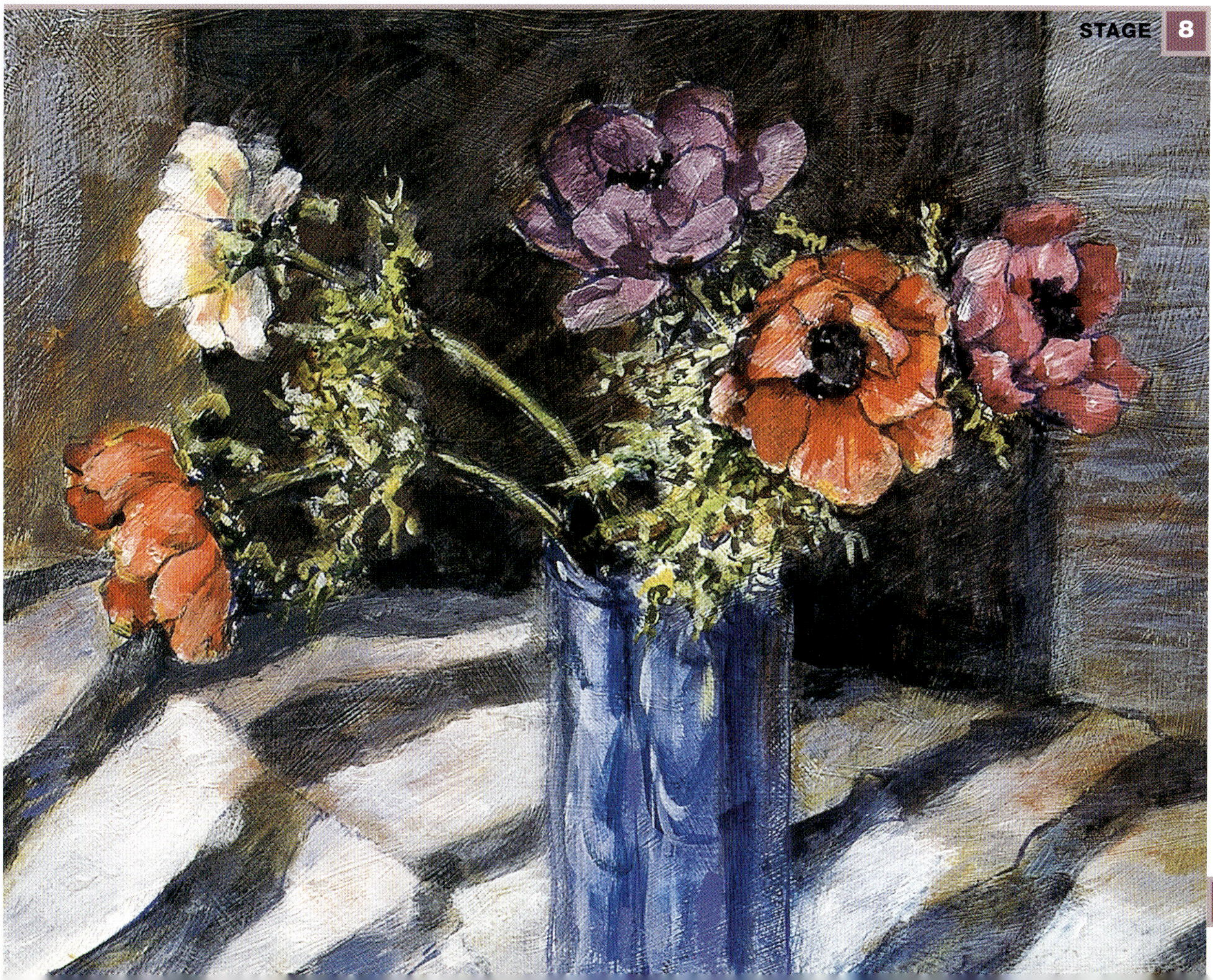

STAGE 8

PAINTED TEXTURES

by STEPHEN RIPPINGTON

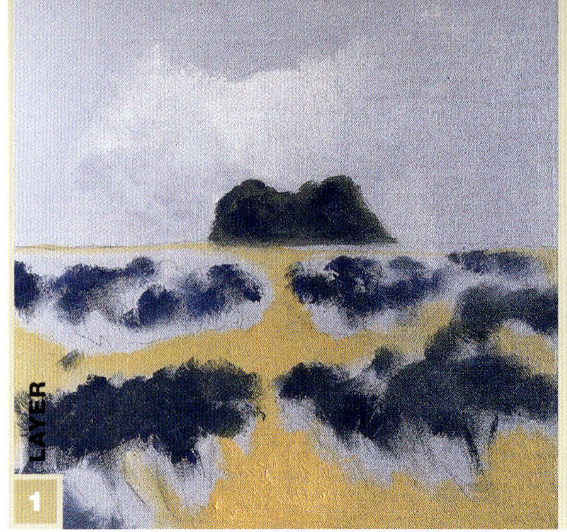

PAINTED TEXTURES

Texture describes the surface of a thing and can be represented in two distinctly different ways. Paint can be used to create an image of the texture, or it can be used so that its physicality replicates the appearance of the texture. This is often achieved by mixing various texture pastes into the paint. It is possible to create textural effects simply by applying the paint relatively thickly so that the brushmarks are raised from the surface. Here, both techniques are used together.

1 BLOCKING IN

The canvas has been prepared using a mix of light blue-violet and white. A light pencil drawing indicates the position of things. The areas between the gorse bushes are blocked in using a Naples yellow and white mix. Cobalt blue, yellow ochre, and white create a blue-gray for the base color of the bushes, and titanium white and light blue-violet are used for the clouds.

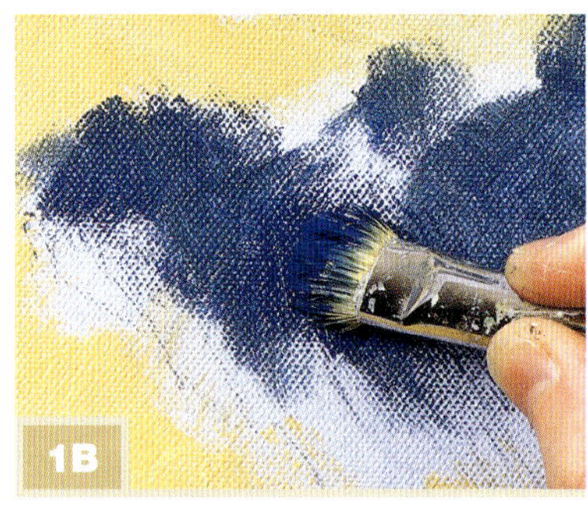

Use open brushwork.

MATERIALS

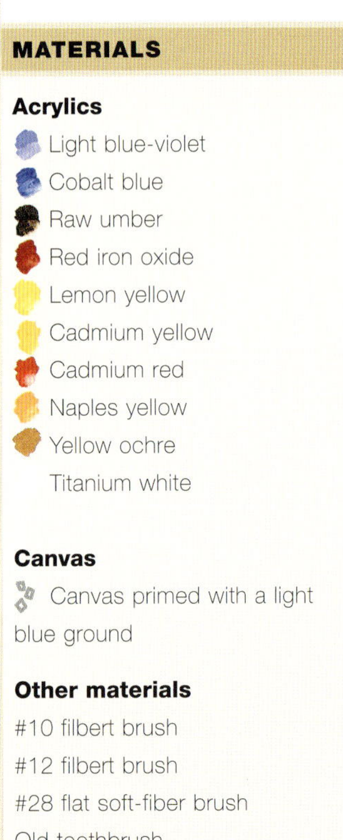

Acrylics

- Light blue-violet
- Cobalt blue
- Raw umber
- Red iron oxide
- Lemon yellow
- Cadmium yellow
- Cadmium red
- Naples yellow
- Yellow ochre
- Titanium white

Canvas

- Canvas primed with a light blue ground

Other materials

- #10 filbert brush
- #12 filbert brush
- #28 flat soft-fiber brush
- Old toothbrush
- Water
- Pencil

Apply the paint using a medium-sized #10 filbert brush.

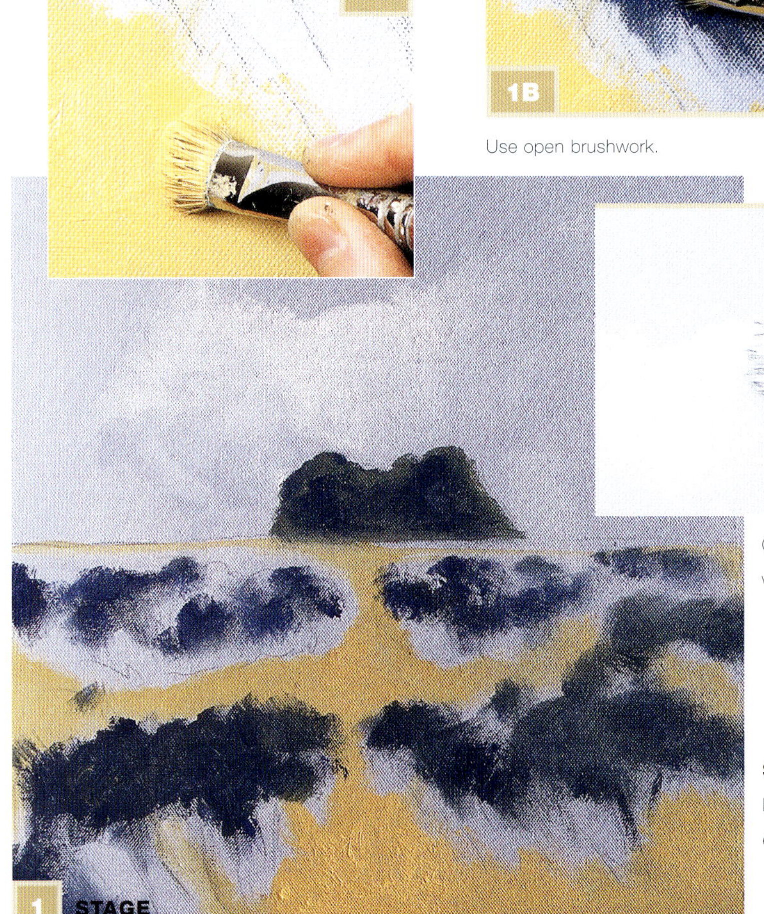

Create a broken edge when painting the cloud.

STAGE 1 Make the brushwork loose and expressive.

2 ADDING DEPTH

The gorse bushes are consolidated with the addition of a deep red made from red iron oxide and cobalt blue. The same mix is applied to the trees on the horizon. A deep orange, mixed using cadmium yellow and cadmium red, is applied between the bushes and more white is worked into the clouds.

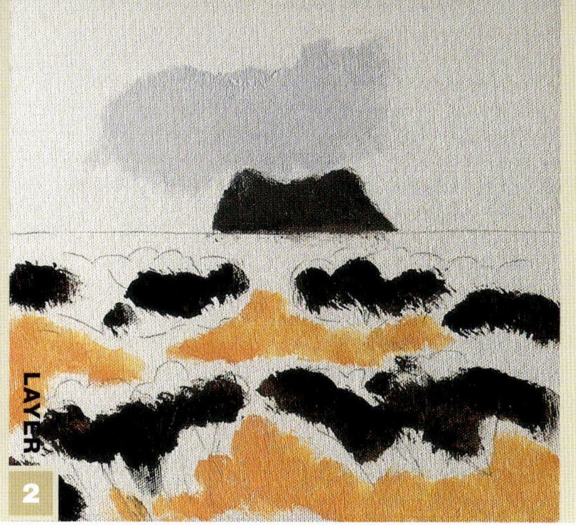

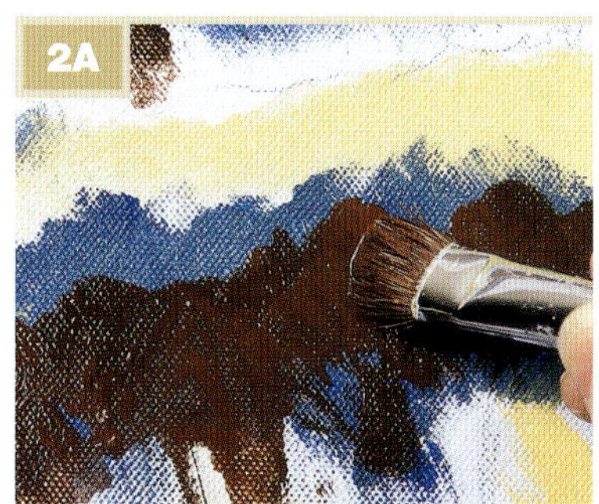

Consolidate the shape and density of the bushes.

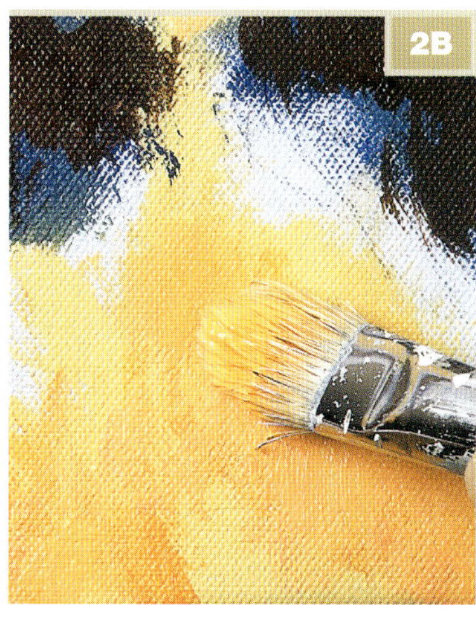

Intensify the color of the dry grass and bracken between the brushes.

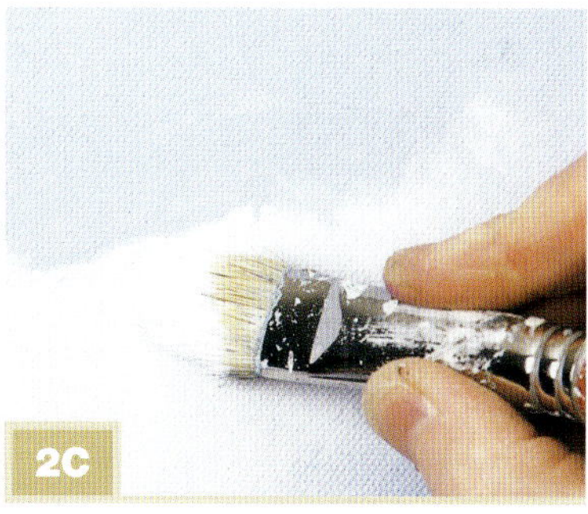

Apply the white paint using a stippling action.

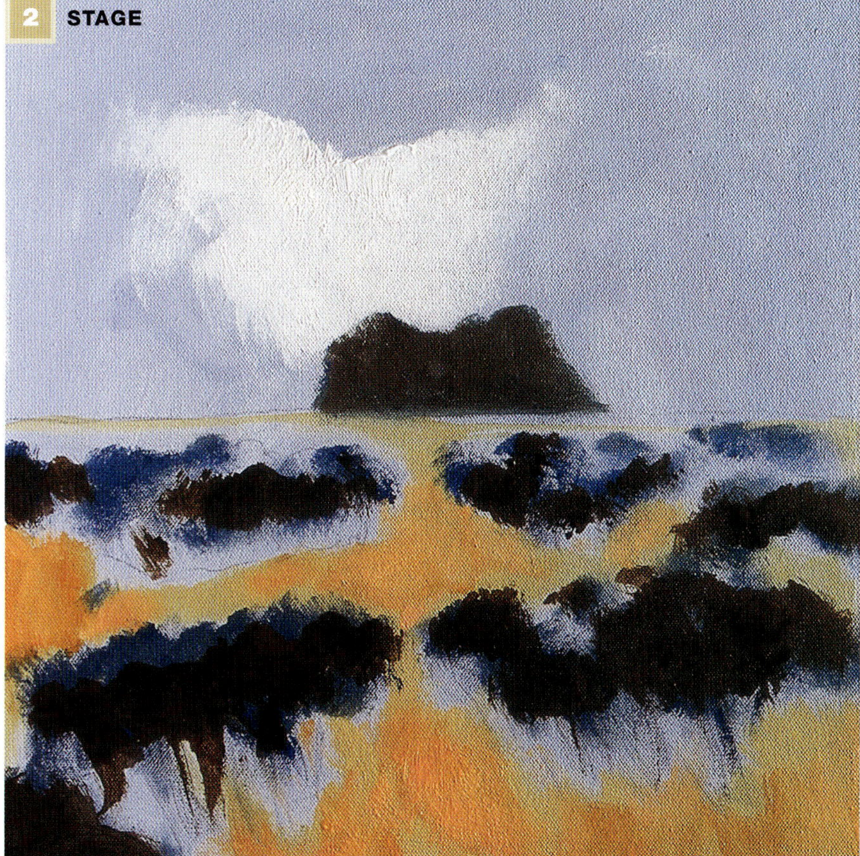

STAGE 2 Darker colors begin to add depth.

3 COLOR COMBINATIONS

The intricate color combinations seen around the gorse bushes are developed further by adding patches of green made by mixing lemon yellow with cobalt blue and adding white. Cadmium yellow straight from the tube is used for the flush of gorse flowers and a red iron oxide and Naples yellow mix is introduced into the lower part of each bush.

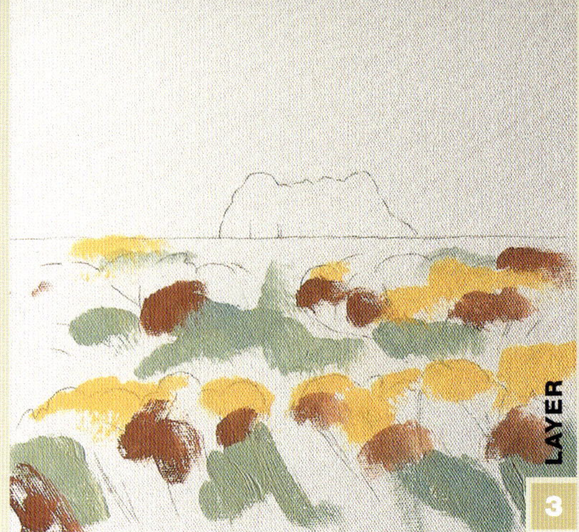

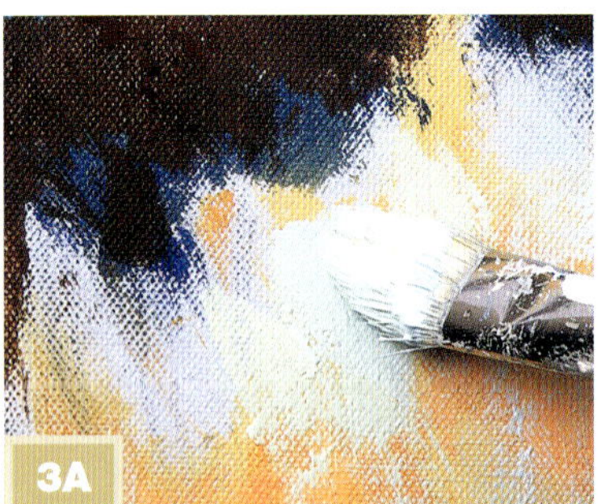

Apply the green using open, sparse brushstrokes.

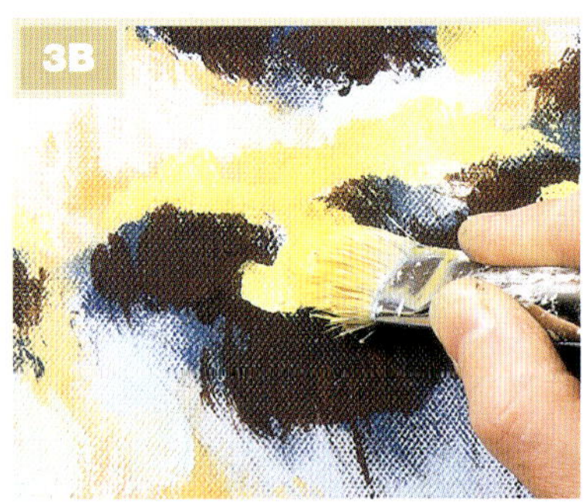

Apply yellow only to the tops of the bushes.

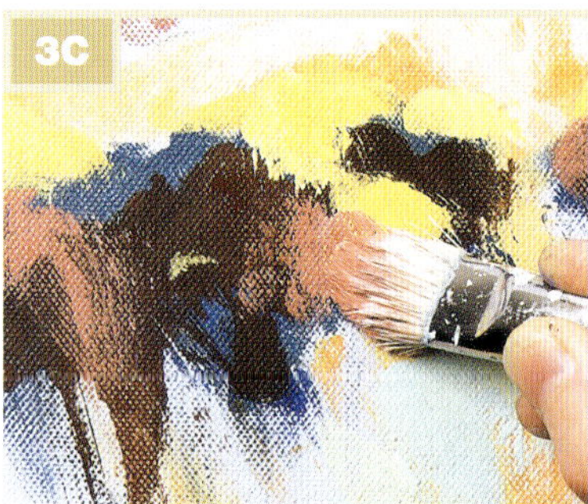

Apply the red so that the base color can be seen.

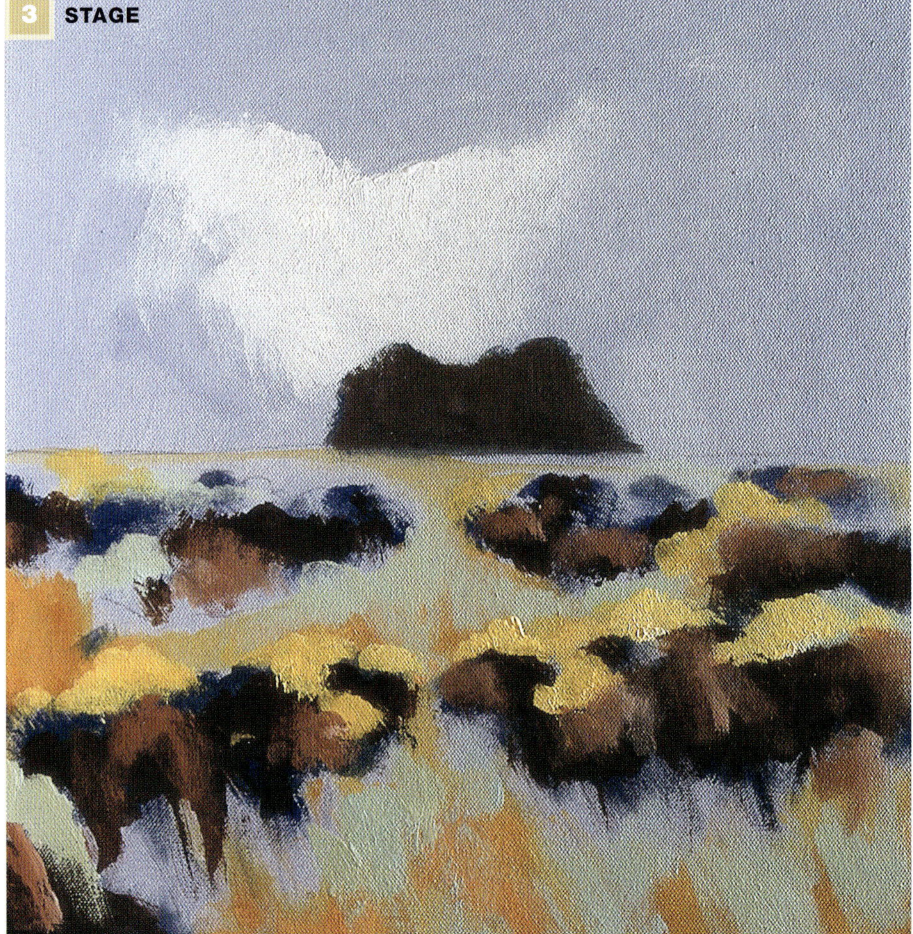

STAGE 3 Build up complex color combinations.

4 ADDING LIGHTS AND DARKS

The depth and intricate patterns of color continue to be built up with wet-on-dry applications of broken color. Cool blue mixed with cobalt blue and light blue-violet is applied to the distant trees, more green is worked into the bushes, and the trunks of the bushes are painted using a dark mix of cadmium red, cobalt blue, and raw umber.

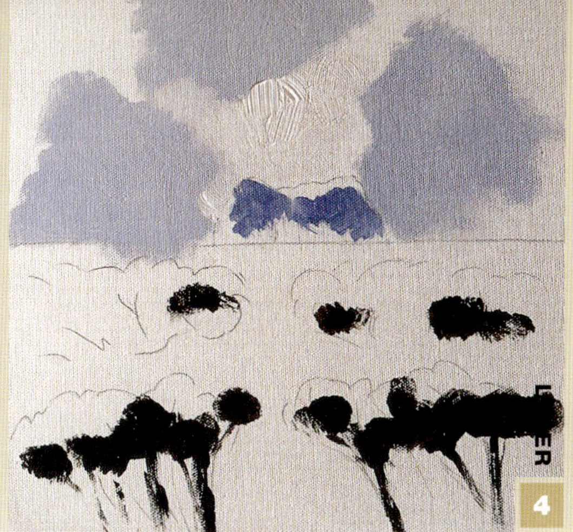

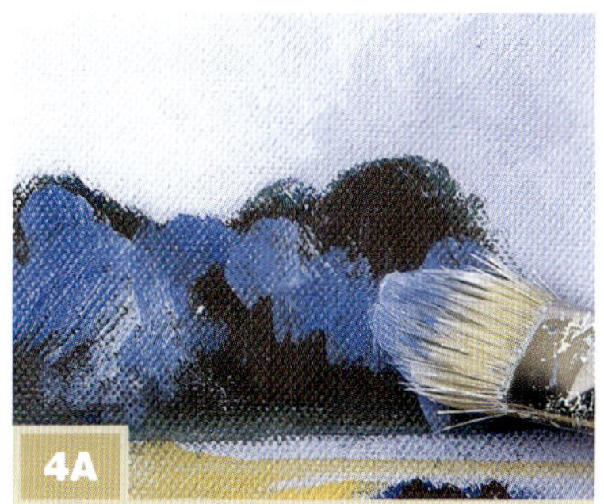

Apply the blue using short precise strokes.

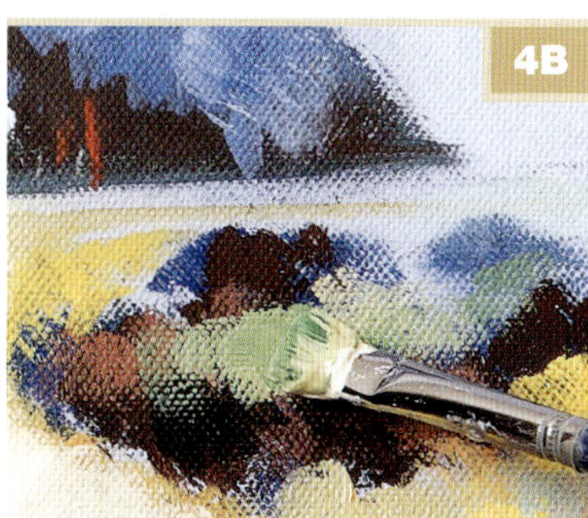

Use a smaller flat brush to create similar brushstrokes.

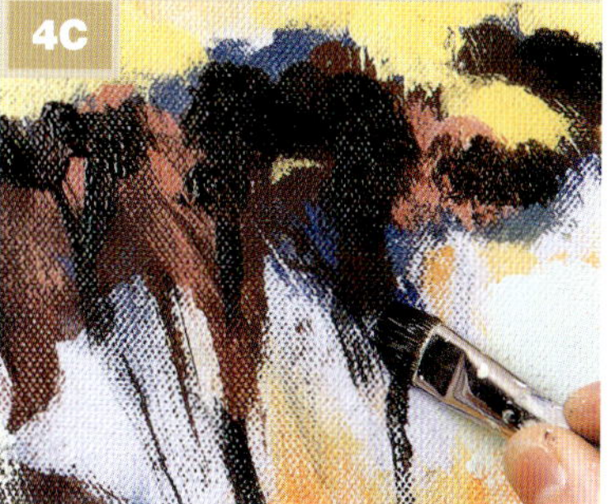

Allow the fluid paint to run down and create the trunks of the gorse bush.

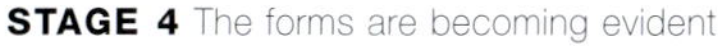

STAGE 4 The forms are becoming evident.

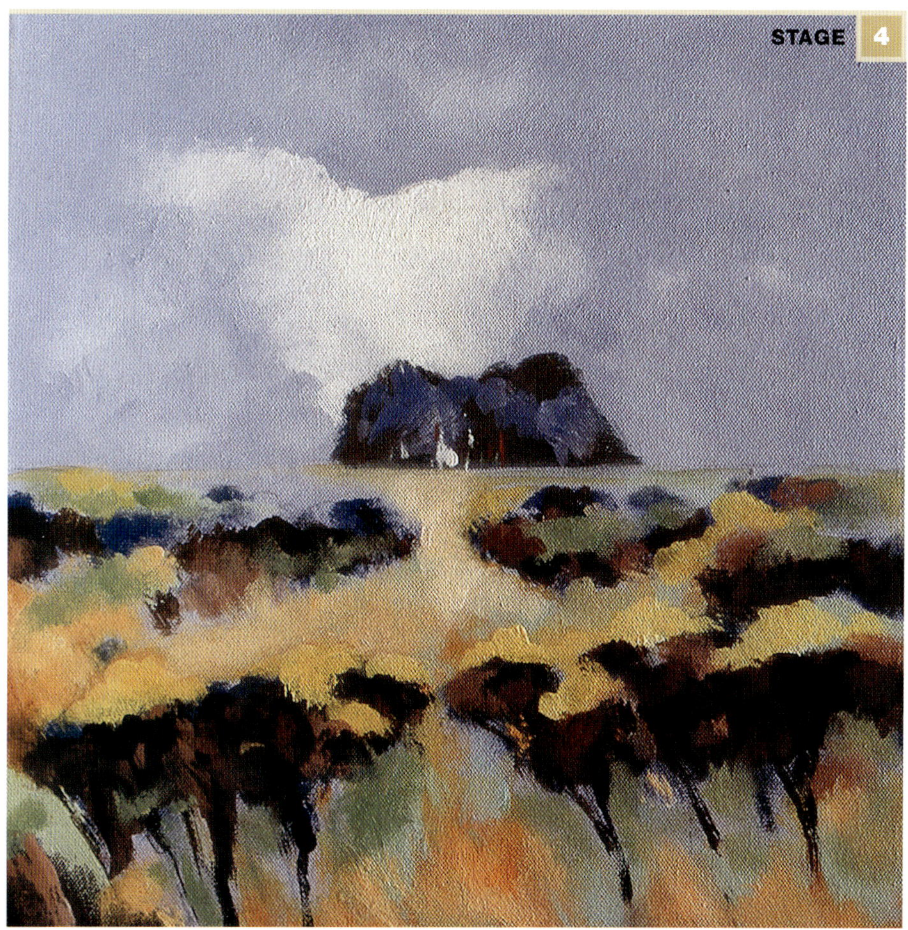

5 SUBTLE CHANGES

The colors and shapes continue to be altered and consolidated using increasingly thick paint. The paint is applied using short dabs and rough scumbles rather than in precise brushstrokes. The paint picks up on the texture created by previous applications of paint and the slight texture of the canvas.

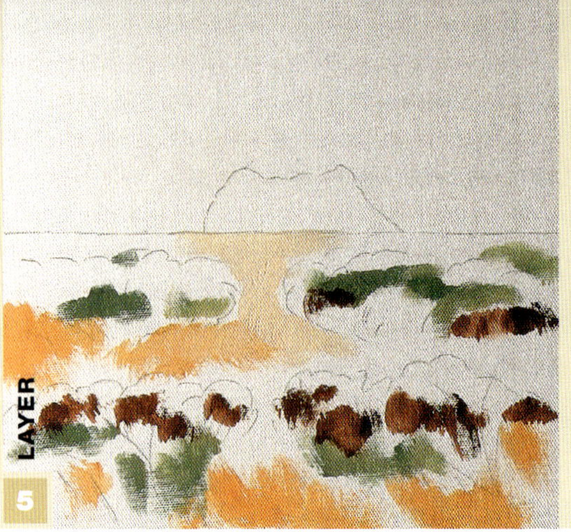

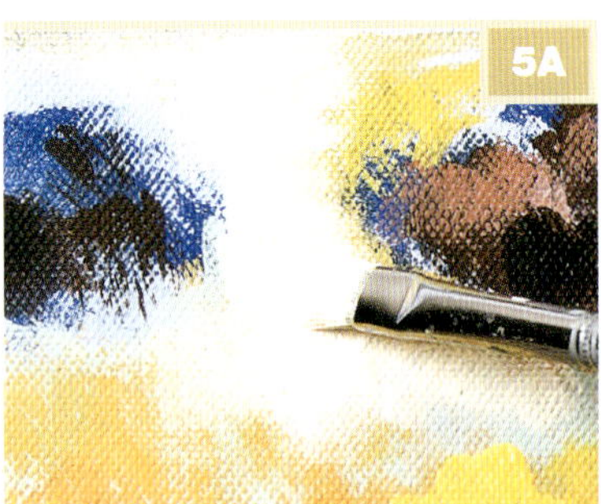

Use the smaller flat brush to carefully work the paint around the shape of each bush.

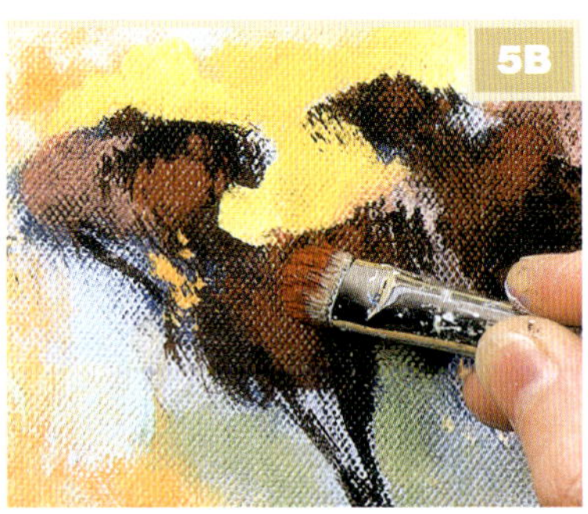

Warm mixes help the bushes appear closer.

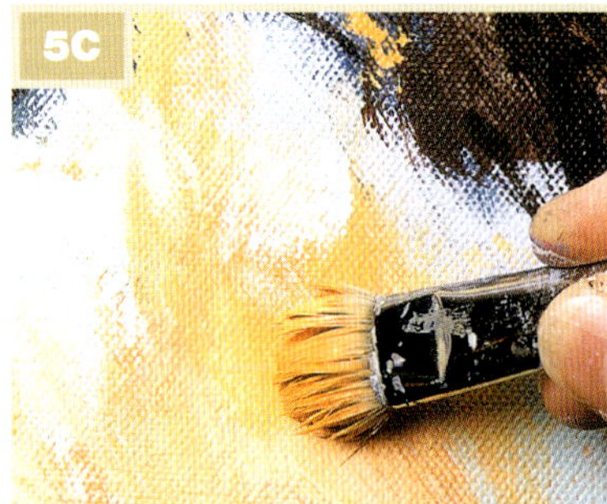

Use open bristles to help create the appearance of dry grass.

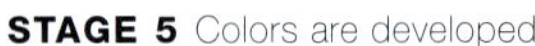

STAGE 5 Colors are developed.

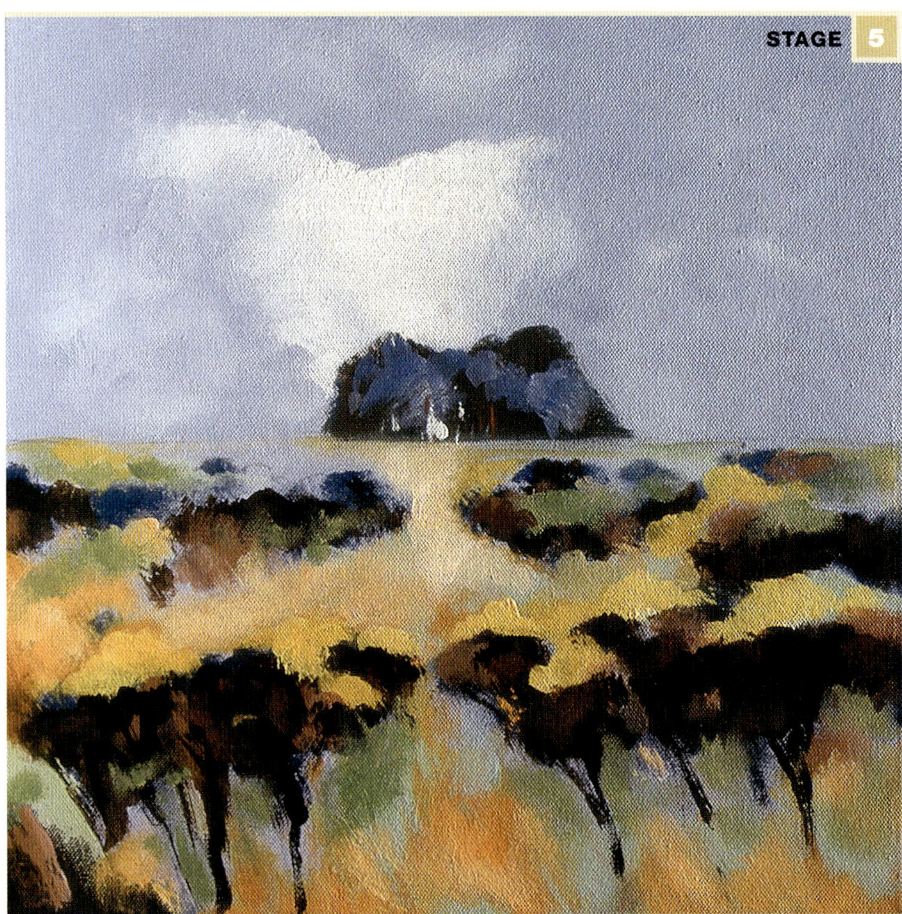

6 ADDING DETAIL

Once the paint is dry, work detailed and precise textural marks over the image. The scumbled layers of paint have created an interesting surface that matches the rough appearance of the subject. These marks are applied rapidly, often using a stippling action. The intention is not to cover up previously applied paint, but rather to add to the mosaic of marks.

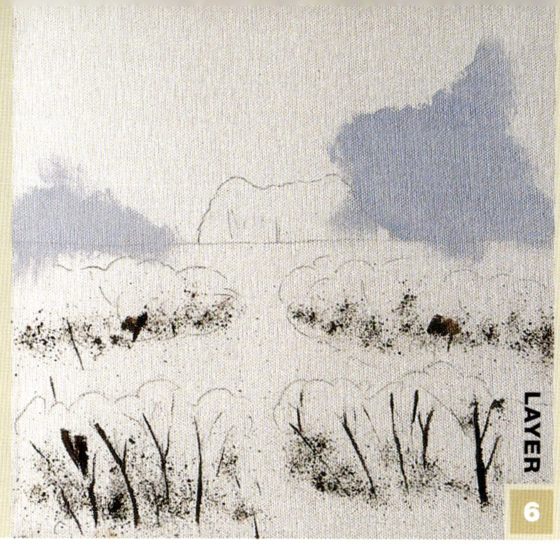

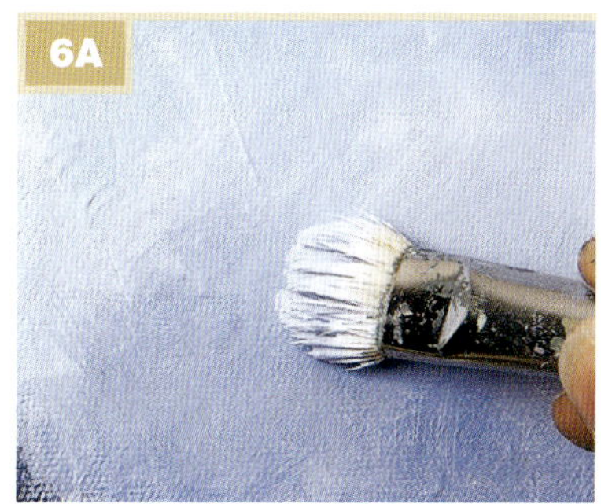

Use white and light blue-violet to soften the clouds.

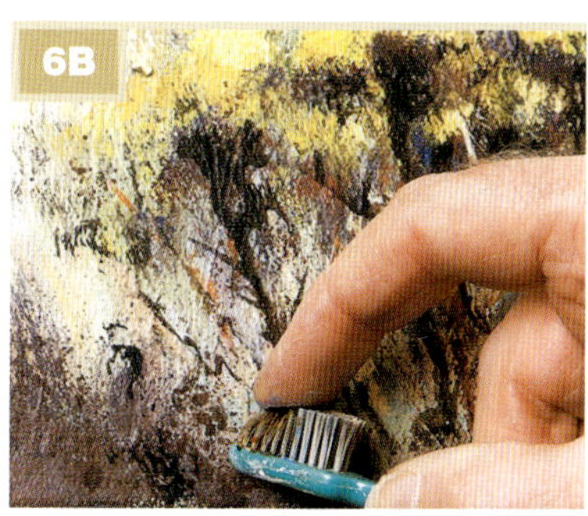

Spatter a range of the colors used in the painting over the area between the bushes.

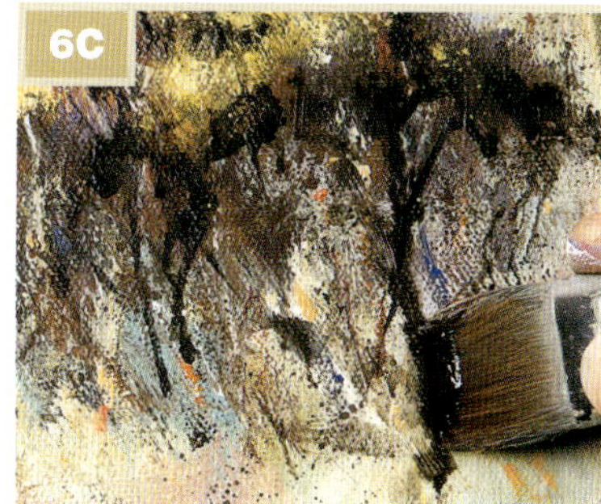

Use the edge of a large, soft, flat brush to consolidate the trunks and branches beneath each bush.

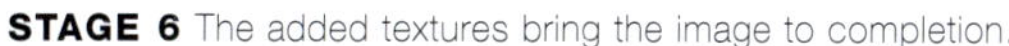

STAGE 6 The added textures bring the image to completion.

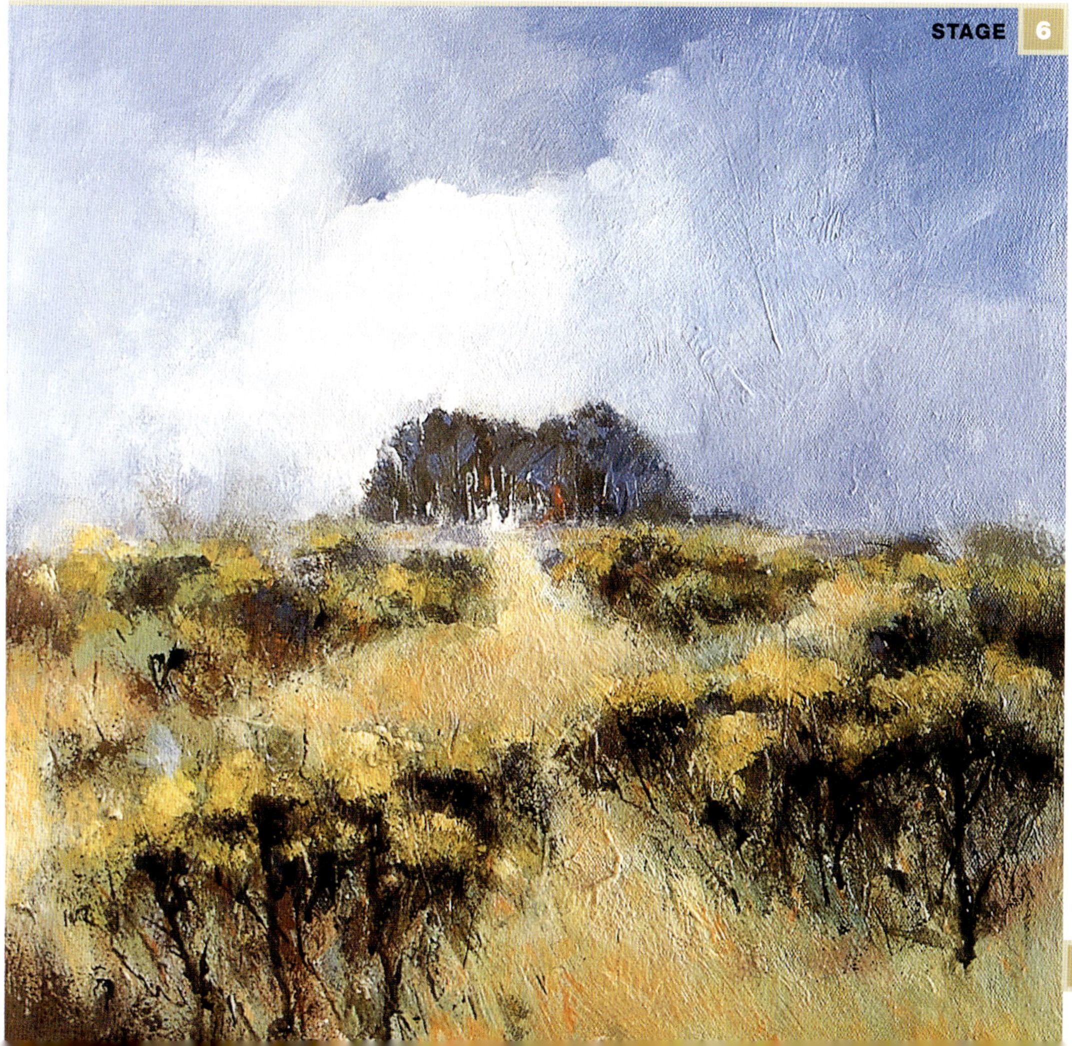

STAGE 6

USING AERIAL PERSPECTIVE

by TONY PAUL

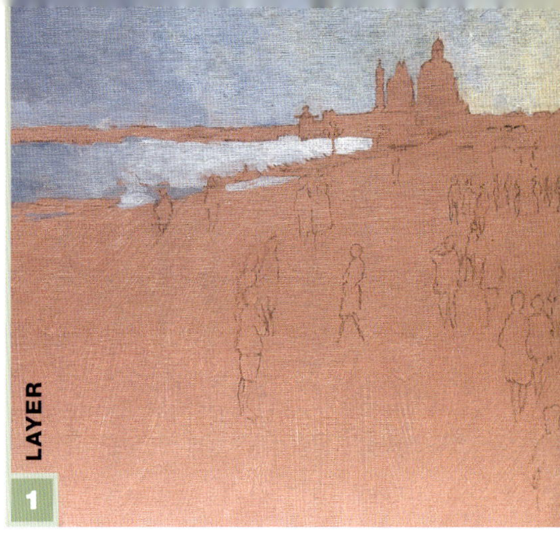

In order to create the illusion of space in a painting, artists use a technique known as "aerial perspective," which is surprisingly effective. The principles have been set out already in "Planning the Picture," page 24. The effect is easy to achieve and can be exaggerated although in reality aerial perspective effects are difficult to see. Depending on the subject, aerial perspective is sometimes linked with linear perspective, especially when the subject involves buildings or manmade structures.

1 ESTABLISHING THE LIGHTS

A pencil drawing keeps the painted image on track. The light sky and its reflection in the lagoon are painted first using a #10 flat synthetic-fiber brush. The colors are mixed using ultramarine blue, cerulean blue, Naples yellow, and titanium white. The sky is painted right to left, beginning with the lightest area first and gradually progressing across to the left-hand side.

MATERIALS

Acrylics

- Titanium white
- Cerulean blue
- Ultramarine blue
- Red iron oxide
- Naples yellow
- Burnt sienna
- Burnt umber

Canvas

- Canvas board prepared using gesso and an imprimatura mixed using white and red iron oxide.

Other materials

- #10 flat synthetic-fiber brush
- #4 flat brush
- #2 round brush
- Water

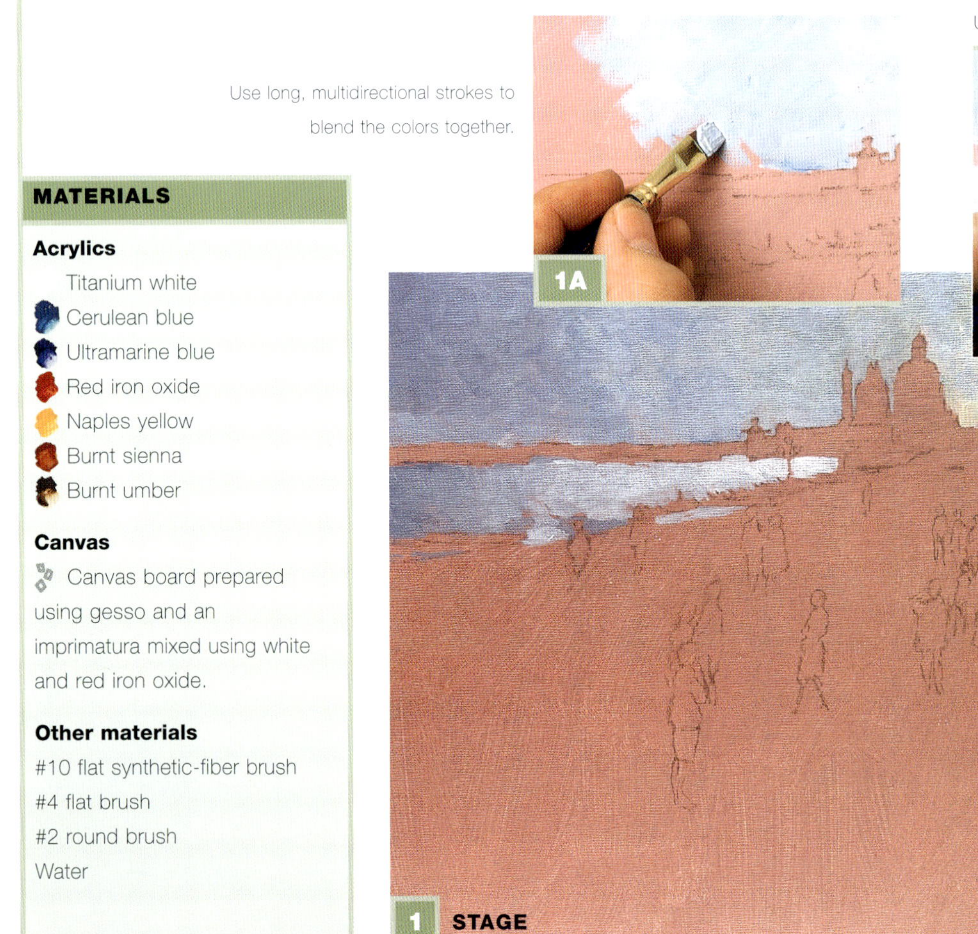

Use long, multidirectional strokes to blend the colors together.

Use the same colors for the lagoon.

STAGE 1
The light source has been established.

2 POSITIONING THE PEOPLE

The same flat synthetic-fiber brush is used with a mixture of burnt umber, burnt sienna, and a little added ultramarine blue to paint in the line of gondolas at the water's edge. The trees that can just be seen in the park behind the building on the right are painted. The figures seen in the distance are painted using a blue-gray made from ultramarine blue and burnt umber. This mixture is darkened slightly for the figures in the foreground.

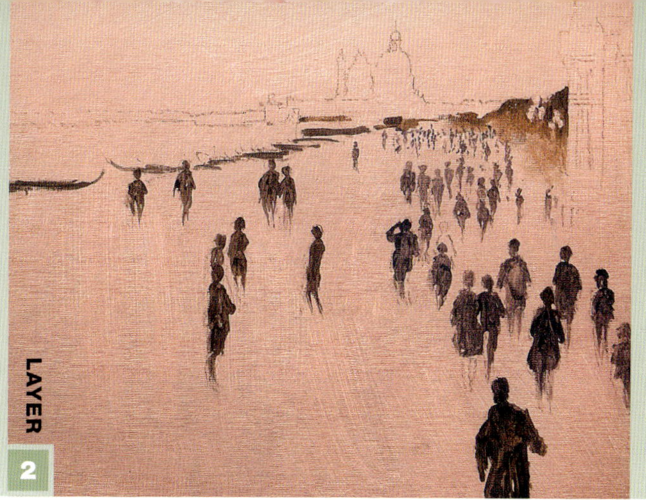

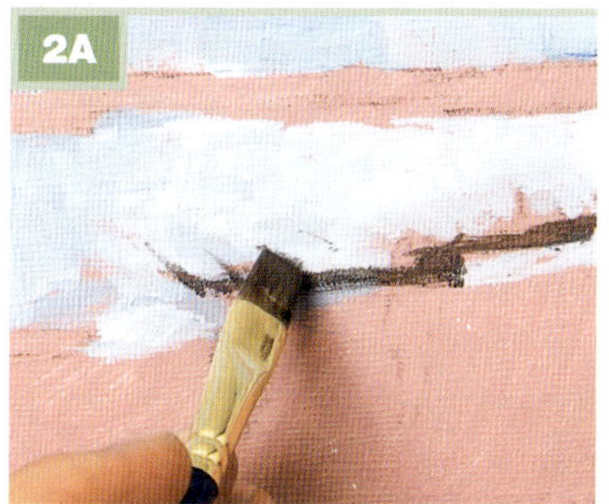

Utilize the shape of the flat brush to paint in the gondolas.

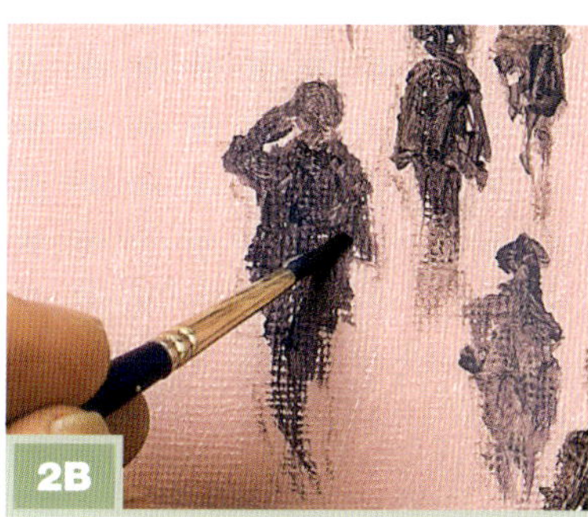

Define the figures in the foreground more clearly.

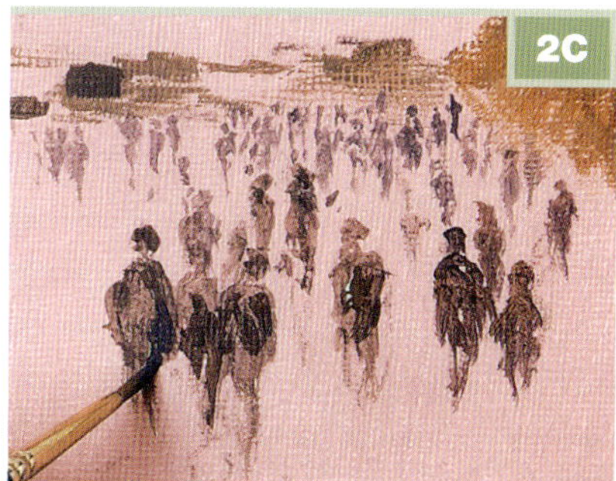

Use a small #2 round brush to paint the figures.

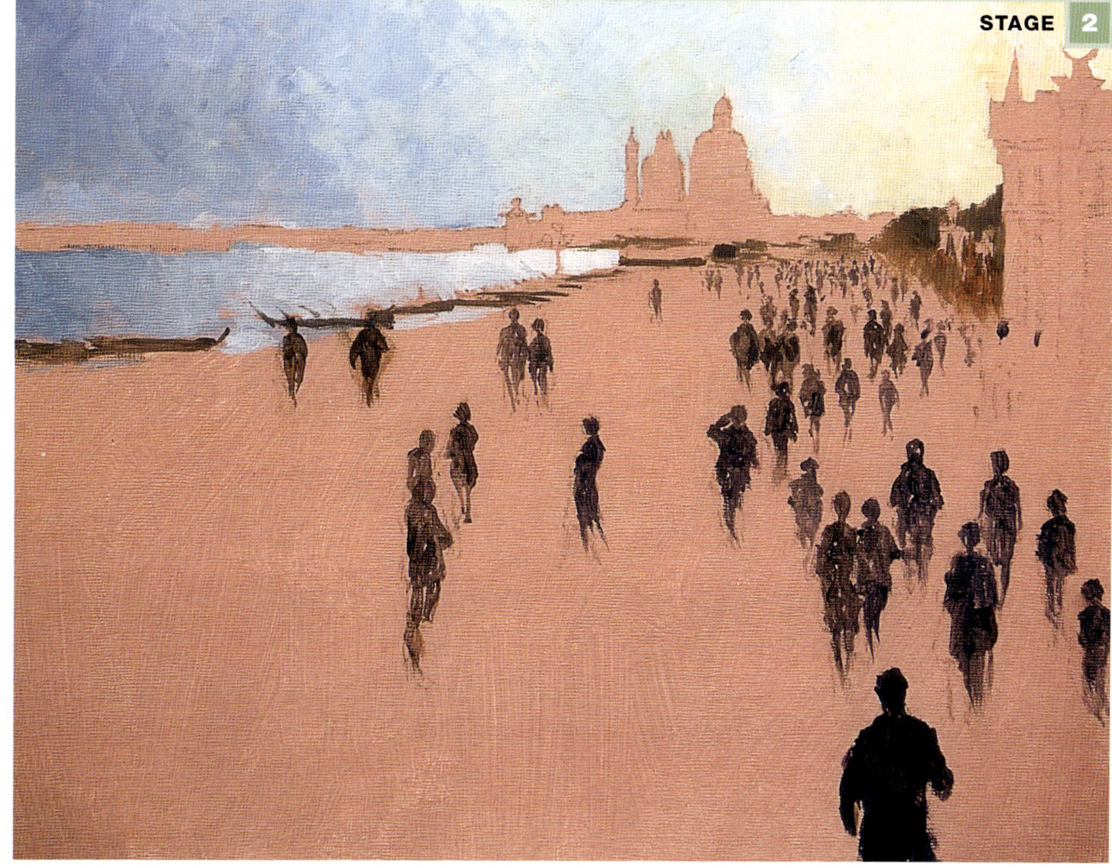

STAGE 2 The figures are painted in perspective.

3 PAINTING IN THE DISTANT BUILDINGS

Attention turns next to the row of buildings arranged against the distant horizon. The domed mass of S. Maria D. Salute and the Dogana are much closer to us. This is shown by making them darker than the row of buildings farther away behind the lagoon. Cerulean blue, ultramarine blue, and burnt umber mixes are used to make the range of grays.

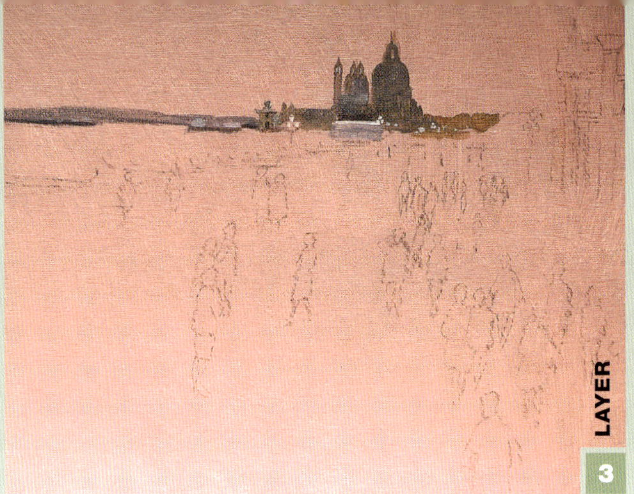

LAYER 3

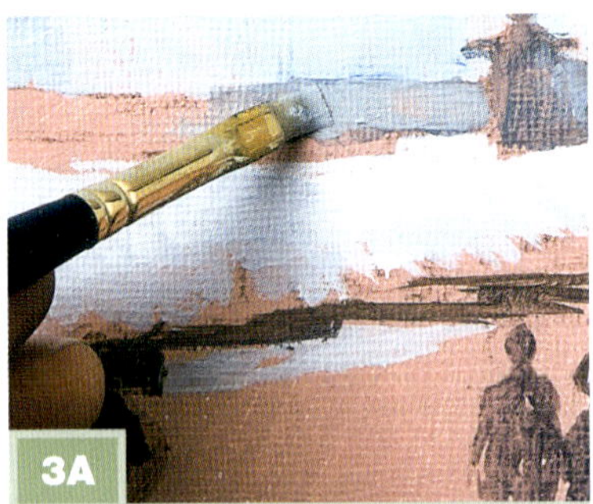

3A Paint in the buildings with simple, direct strokes using a #4 flat brush.

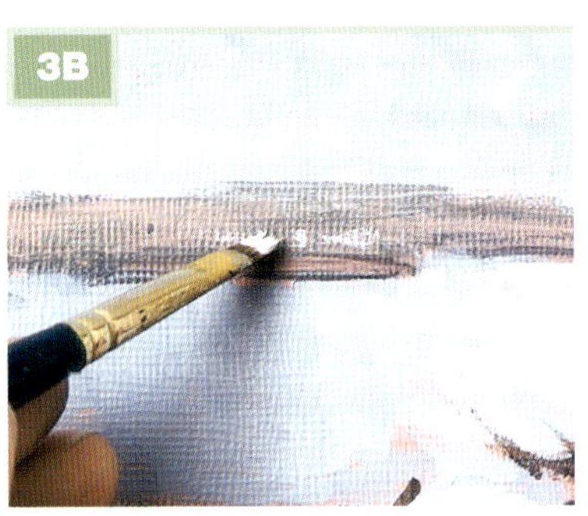

3B Use small dabs of light gray to suggest reflected sunlight.

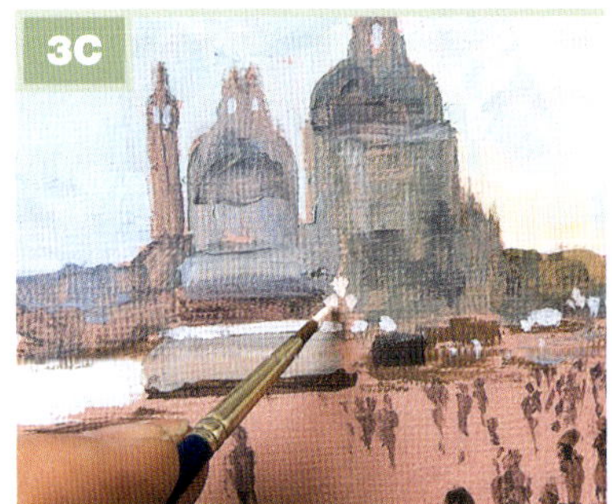

3C Paint the glass in the lamps using a #2 round brush.

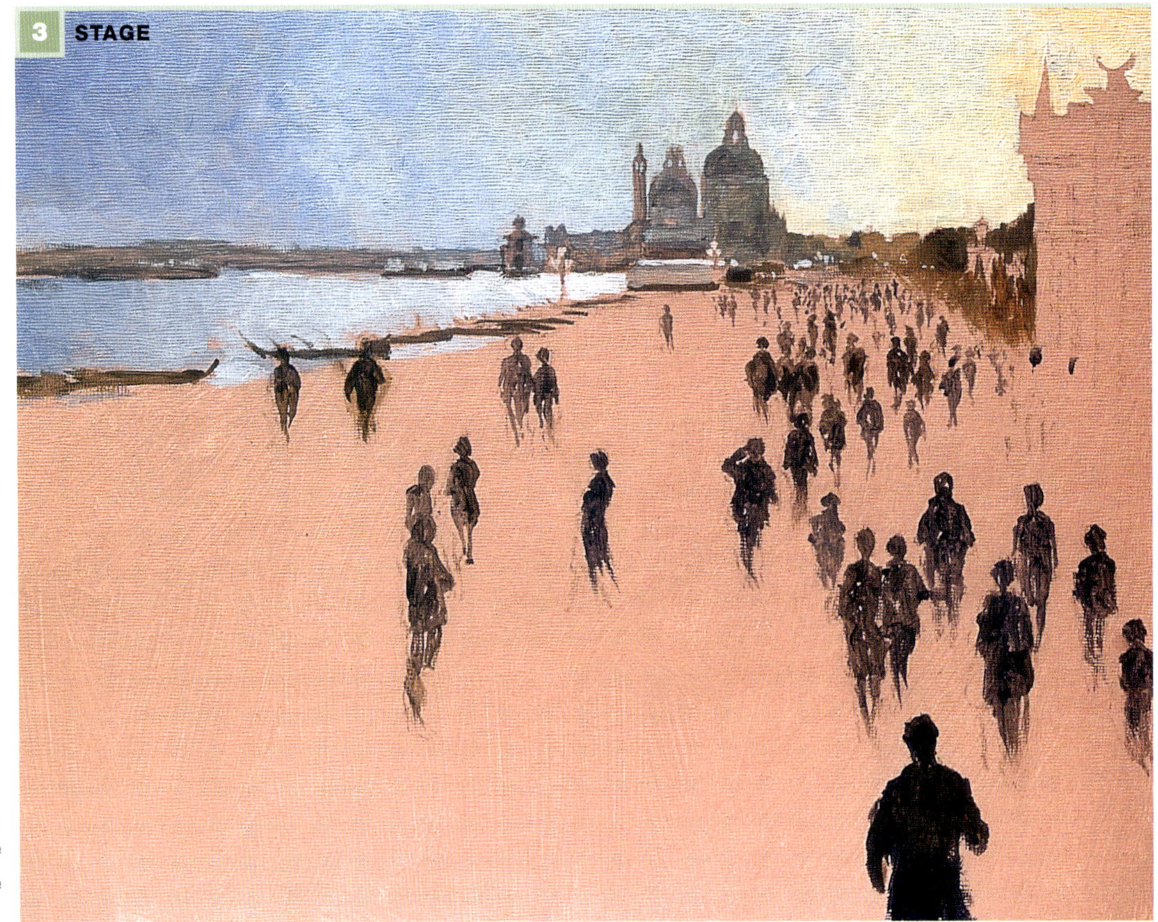

3 STAGE

STAGE 3 The aerial perspective is already evident.

4 ADDING THE BUILDINGS ON THE RIGHT

The building and the column seen on the extreme right are established along with the ornate lamp. The base of the building is left indistinct because it blends into the shadow cast across the cobbled foreground pavement. Similar mixes to those for the buildings in the distance are used. Add burnt umber for the column.

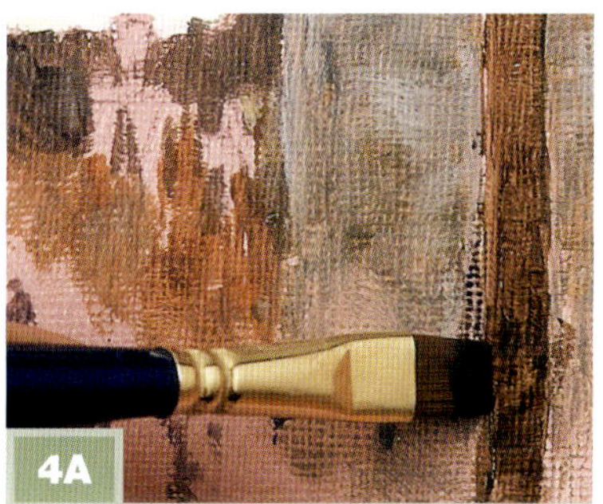

Use the #10 flat brush to paint in the building and the column.

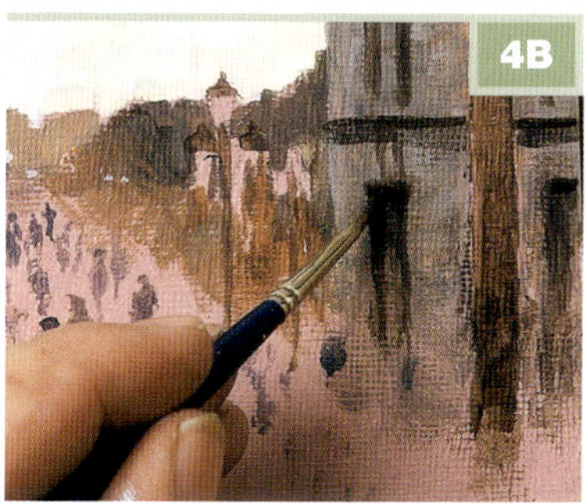

Use the #2 round to draw in the windows and the parapets.

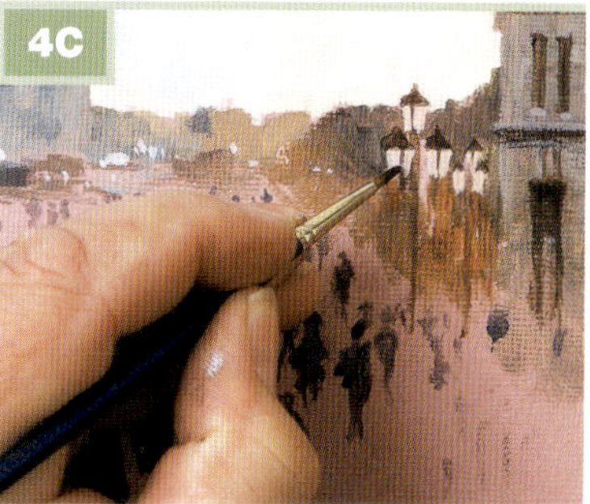

Add white to the glass in the lights.

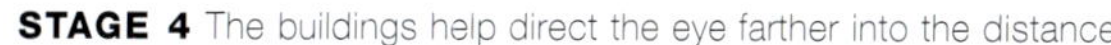

STAGE 4 The buildings help direct the eye farther into the distance.

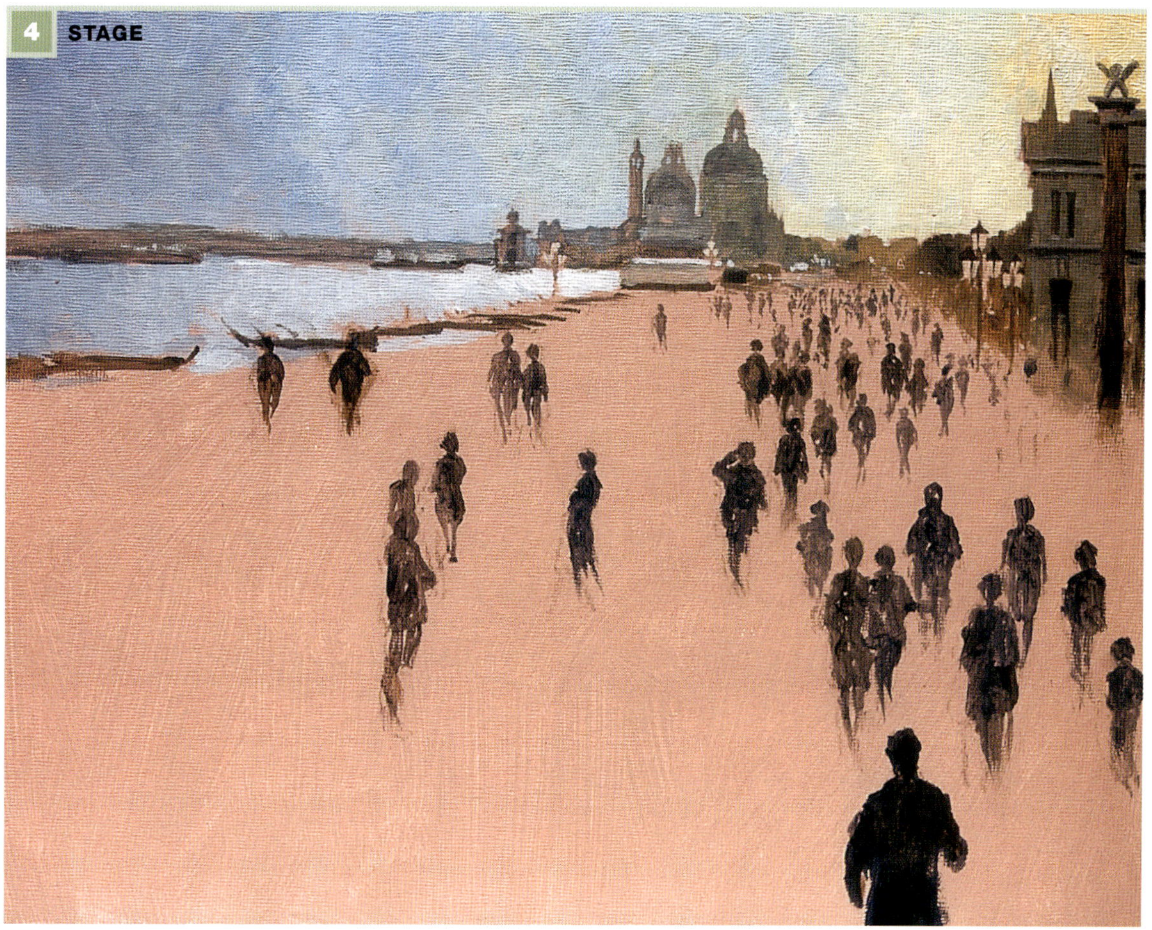

5 BLOCKING IN THE FOREGROUND

The broad pavement that runs along the water's edge is painted using a deep blue mixed from ultramarine with a little burnt umber and white. This immediately has the effect of grounding the figures and pulls the eye into the foreground.

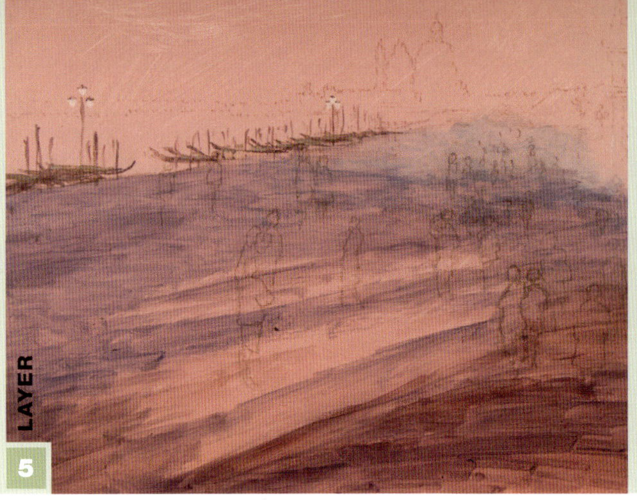
LAYER 5

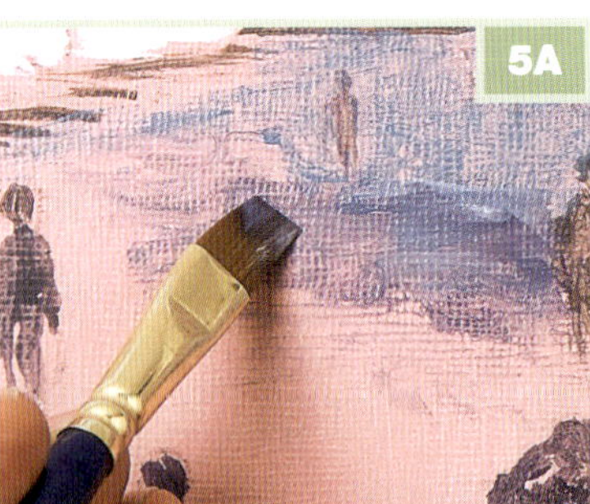
5A

Make the color lighter in tone in the middle ground.

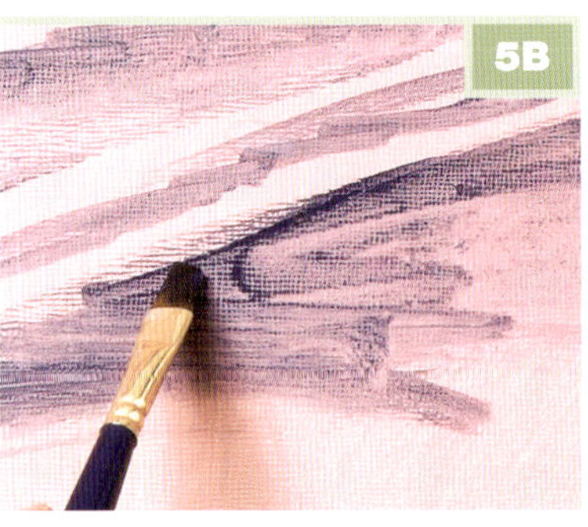
5B

Paint the dark blue-gray loosely across the foreground.

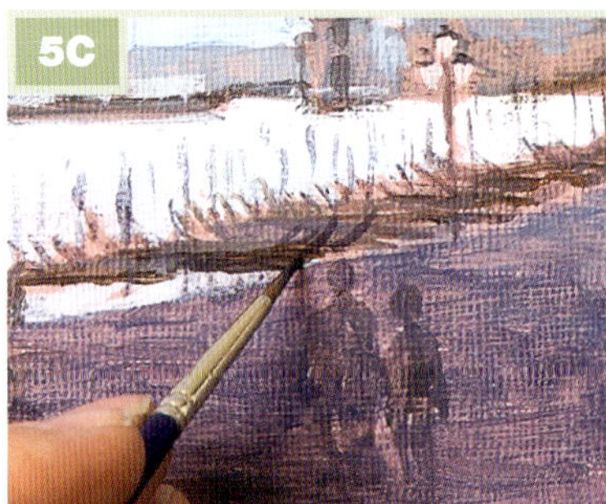
5C

Paint the mooring posts and gondolas using the small round brush.

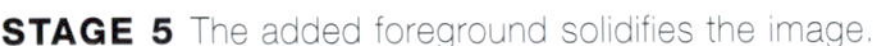
STAGE 5 The added foreground solidifies the image.

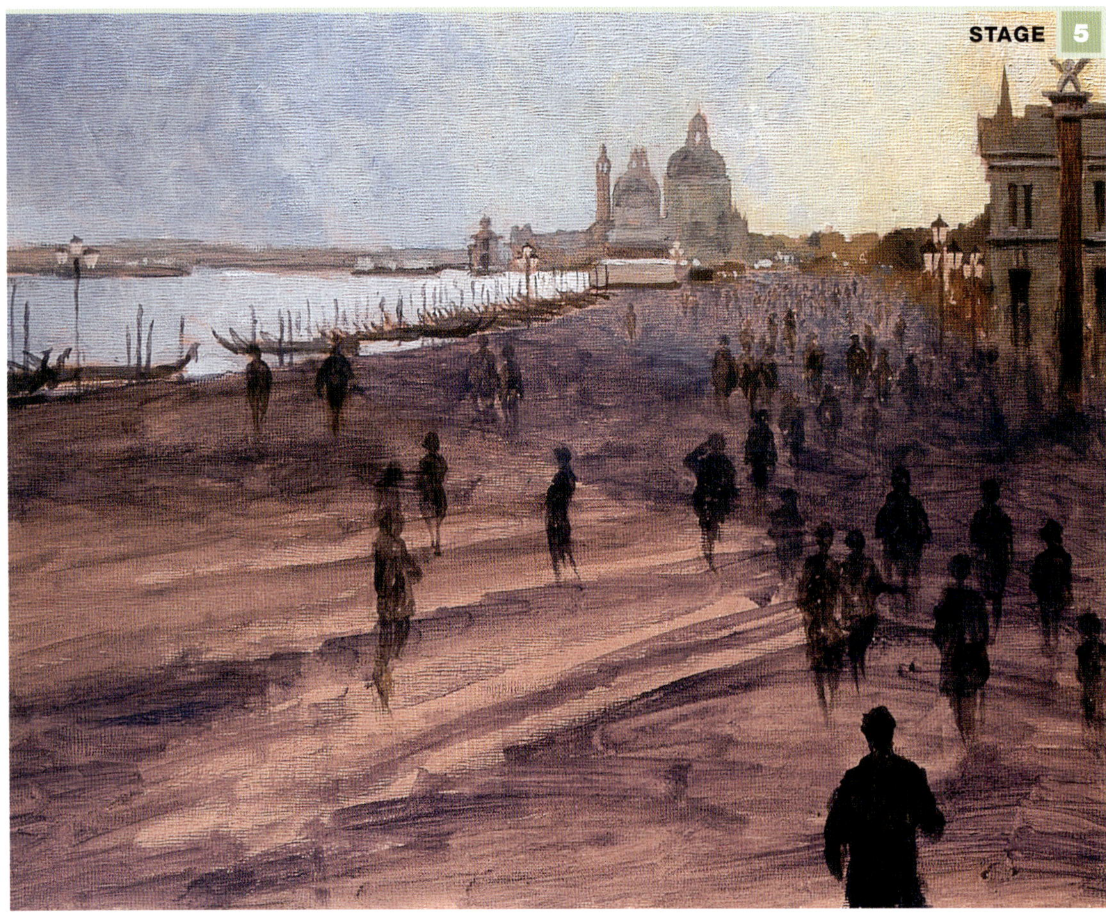
STAGE 5

6 FOREGROUND DETAILS

The figures closest to the viewer are reworked with detail and given a little modeling with the use of light and shade. This makes them appear closer. Red grays and orange mixes are worked across the foreground, creating a broken color effect where the light catches the pavement.

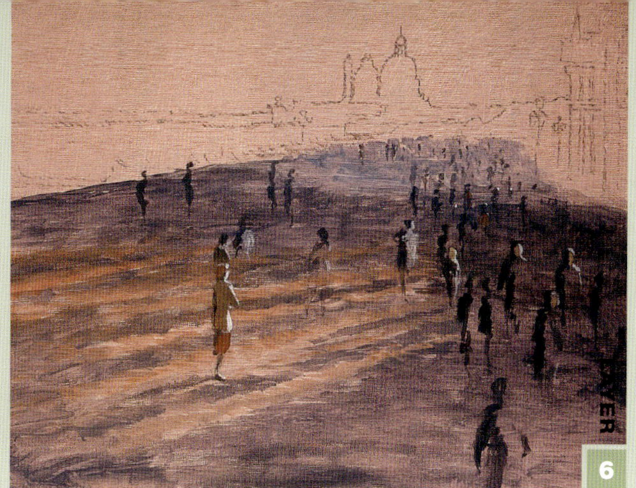

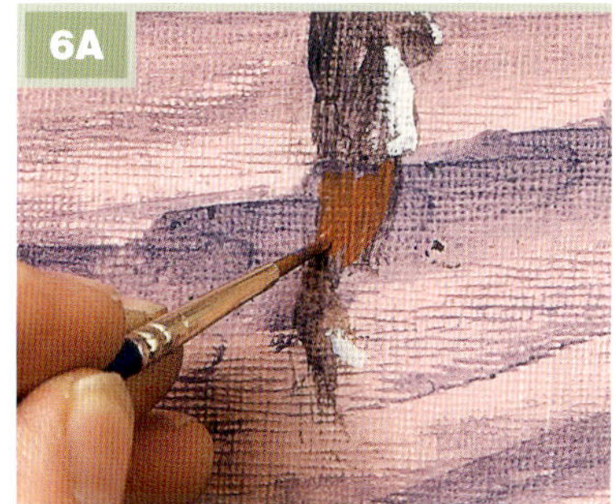

Use the small round brush to achieve detailing on the figures.

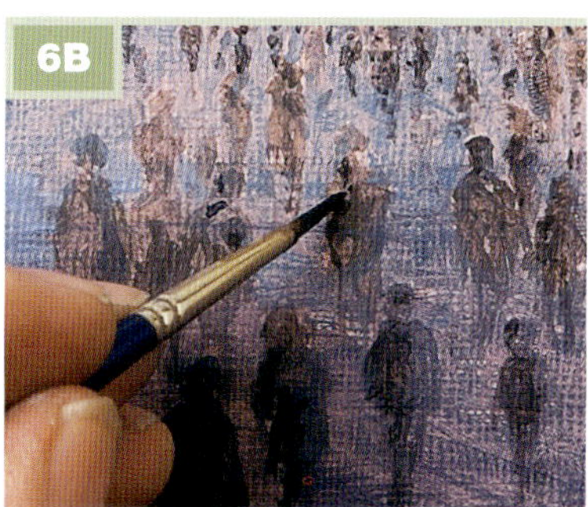

Darken the figures in the middle ground.

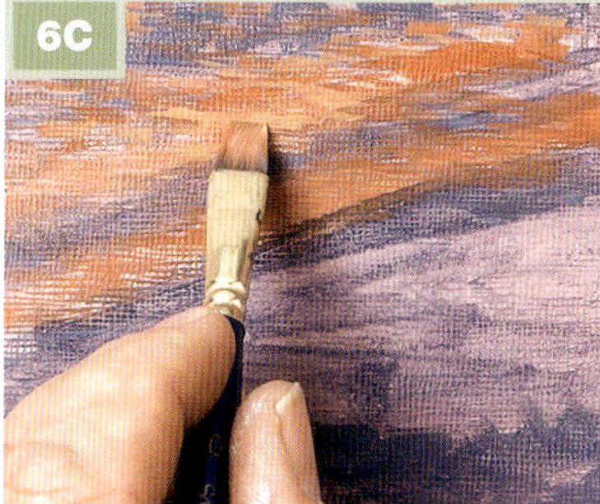

Use a large brush to paint in a mix of red iron oxide and Naples yellow for those areas not in shadow.

STAGE 6 Added detail makes the foreground advance.

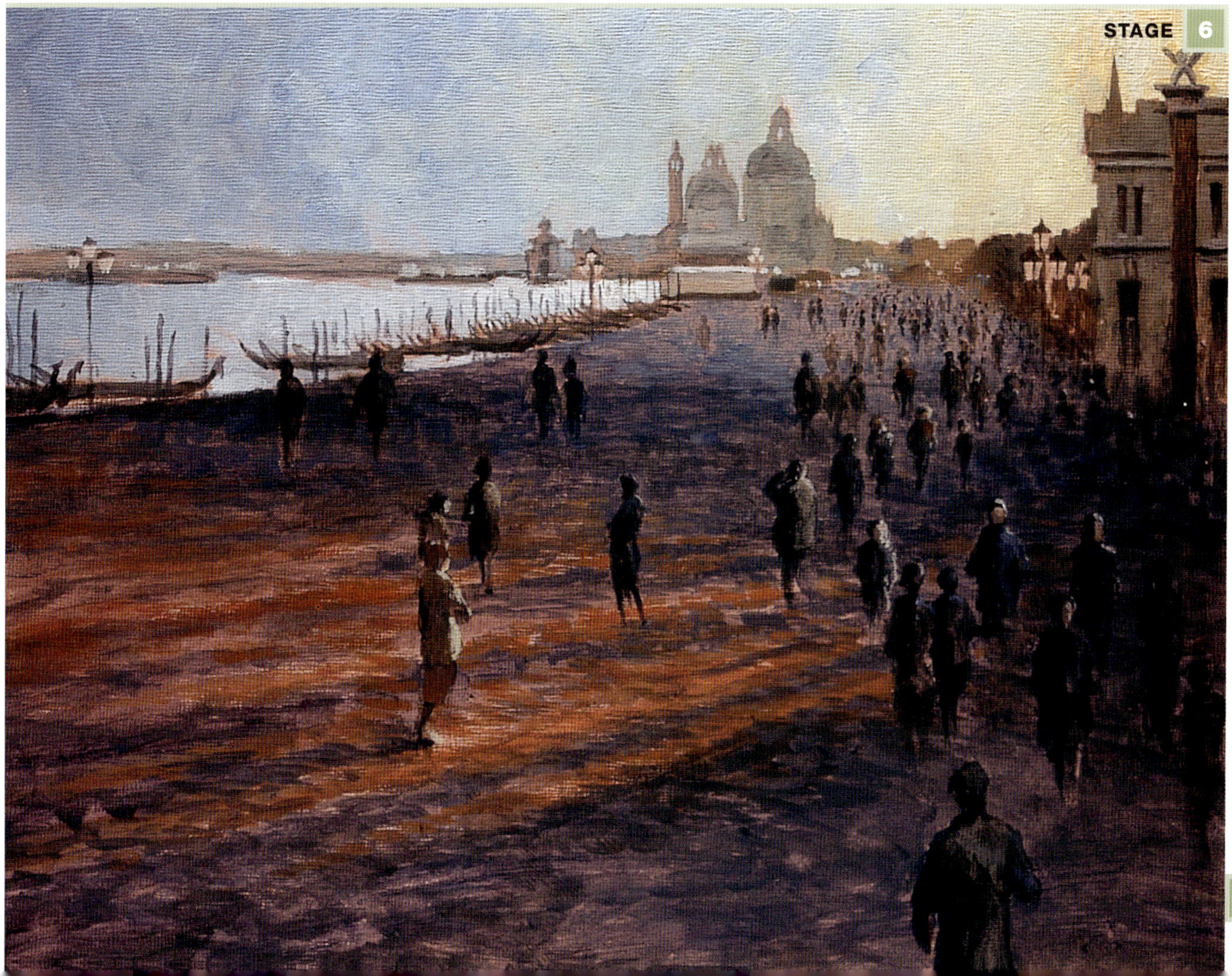

STAGE 6

CLOSED COMPOSITION

by TONY PAUL

LAYER 1

Composition can be expansive or closed with distinctly different results. Closed composition, illustrated here, draws the eye deep into the image. Notice how the artist uses a square support, receding street, and two artfully placed background figures—all of which combine to pull the viewer in.

1 ESTABLISHING THE LIGHTS

First draw the image in pencil. White mixed with a little raw umber and lemon yellow creates the light color for the sunlit wall, which is painted using the round brush. Using the flat brush, the same color is used above the arch. The crumbled plaster walls on the left of the image are established using raw sienna, cadmium red, and white. The walls on the right are painted with raw umber, burnt sienna, and white.

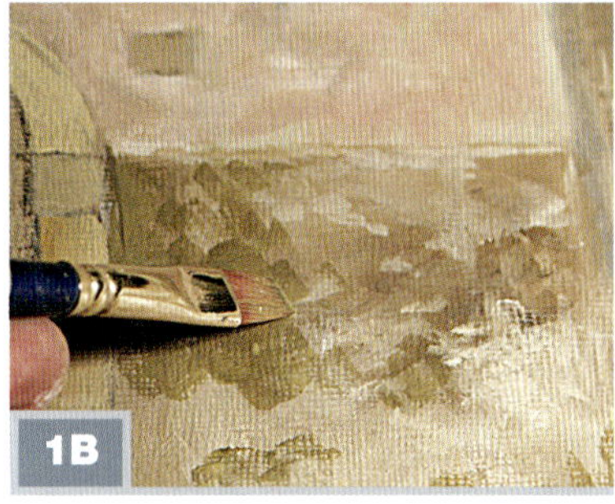

Suggest the crumbling plaster walls with loose brushwork.

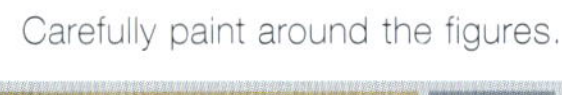

Carefully paint around the figures.

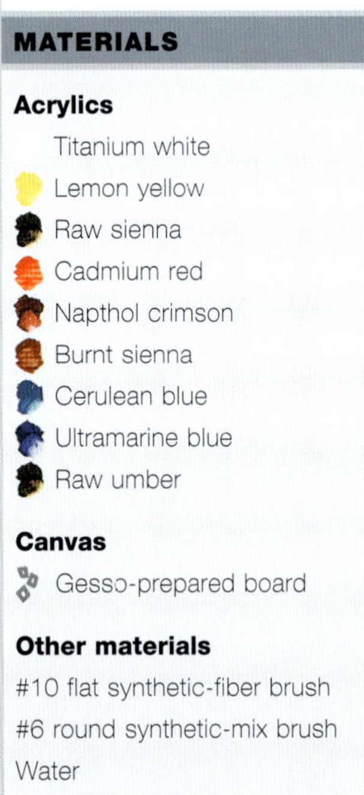

MATERIALS

Acrylics

- Titanium white
- Lemon yellow
- Raw sienna
- Cadmium red
- Napthol crimson
- Burnt sienna
- Cerulean blue
- Ultramarine blue
- Raw umber

Canvas

- Gesso-prepared board

Other materials

- #10 flat synthetic-fiber brush
- #6 round synthetic-mix brush
- Water

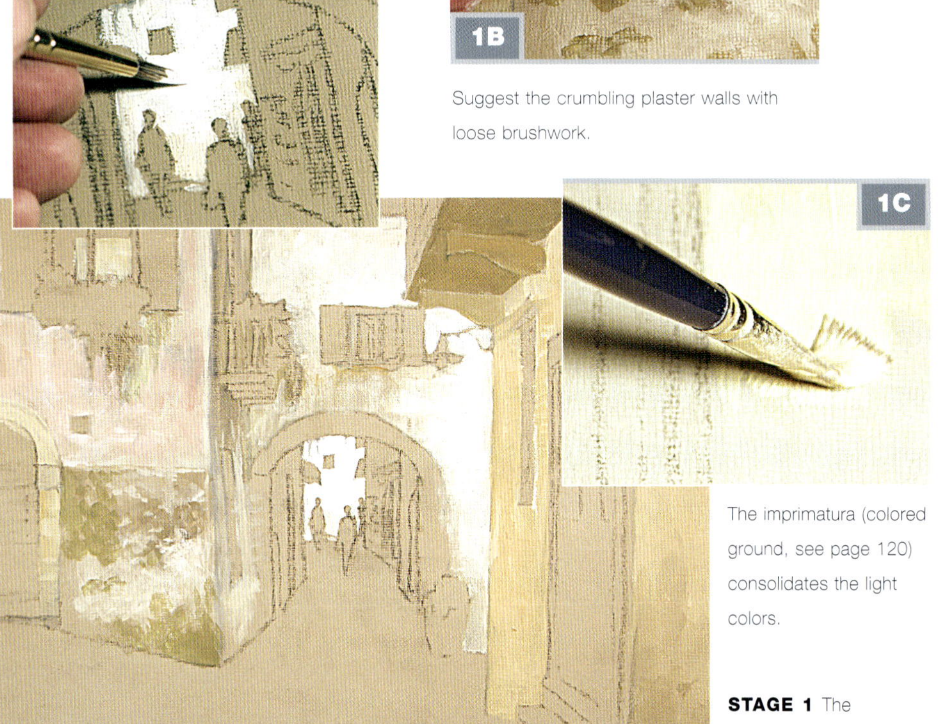

The imprimatura (colored ground, see page 120) consolidates the light colors.

STAGE 1 The lights are established.

2 PUTTING IN THE DARKS

By using a mix made from raw umber and ultramarine blue, the artist establishes the darks. These include the dark area beneath the arch, the doors and windows, the figures, and the shadows beneath the potted plants on the balconies.

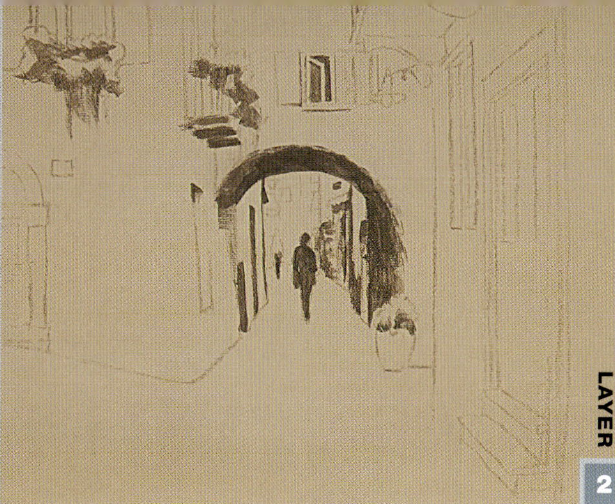

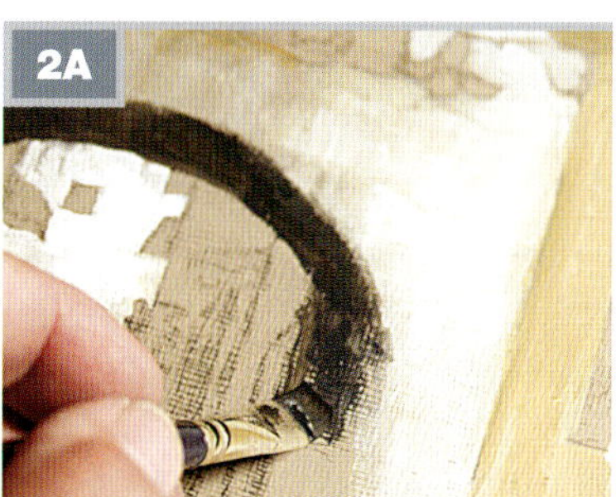

Paint beneath the arch using the flat brush.

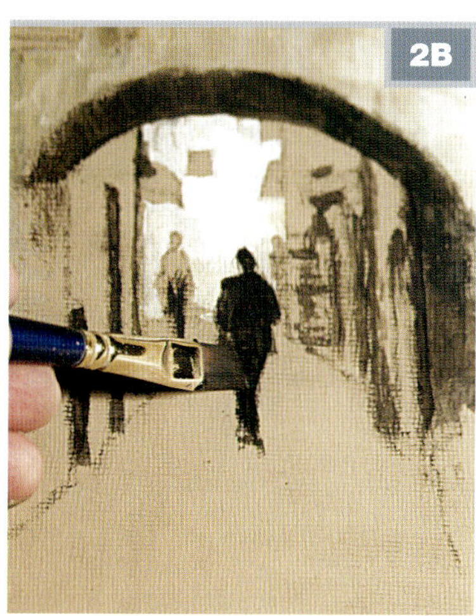

The shape of the brush aids the painting of the figure.

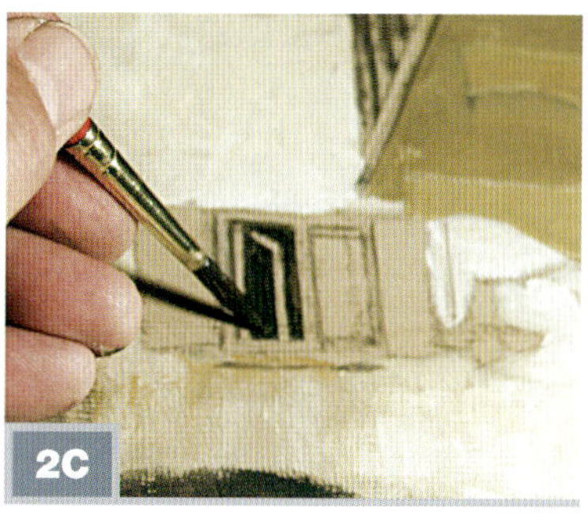

Use small round brush for small, precise areas.

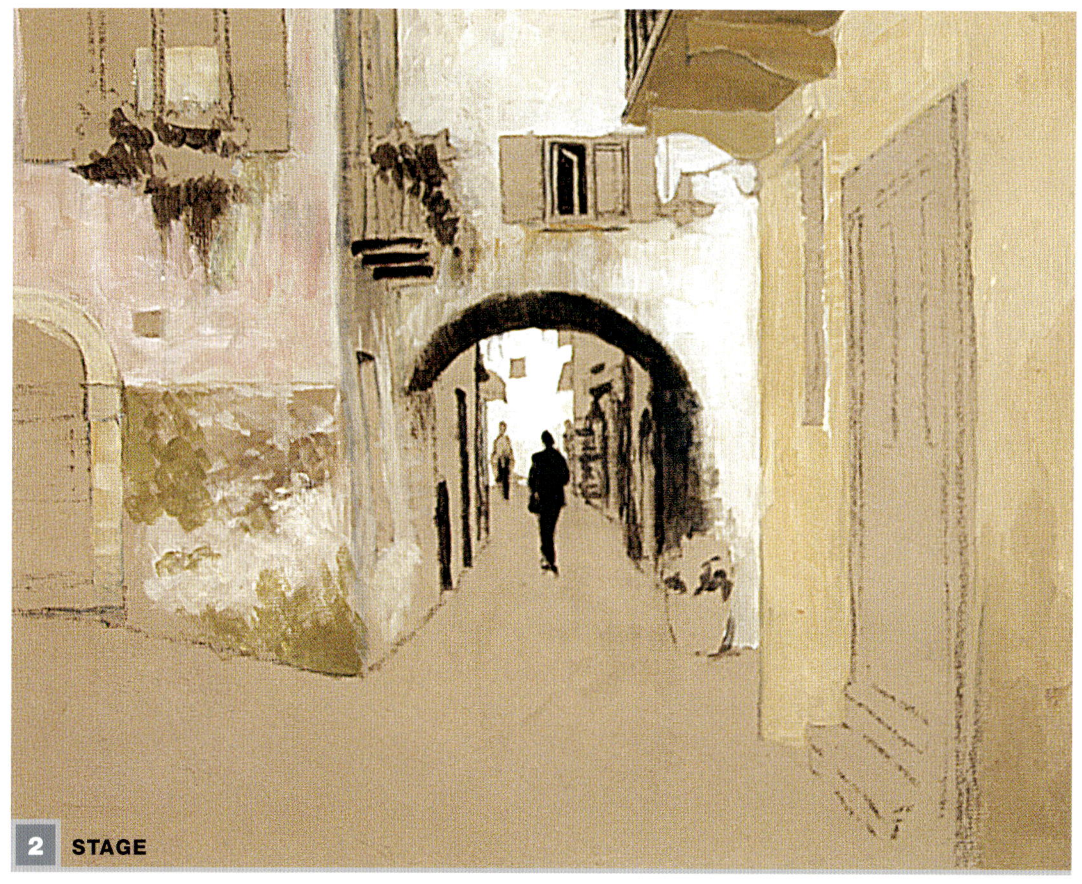

STAGE 2 The darks add depth.

3 PAINTING THE MID-TONES

Paint the mid-tones next. Use cerulean blue to create the cobblestone color. Where the cobblestones grow darker beneath the arch, add napthol crimson and ultramarine blue. Scrub a raw umber and ultramarine blue mix across the foreground before painting over it with more cobblestones. Darken the walls of the alley using a mid-tone of raw umber mixed with a little ultramarine blue.

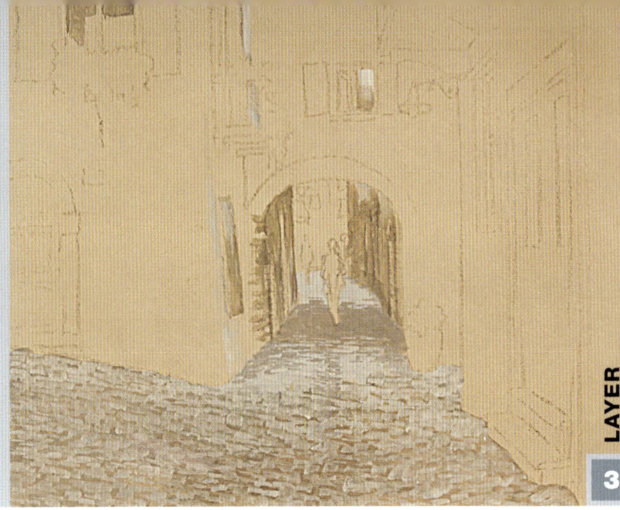

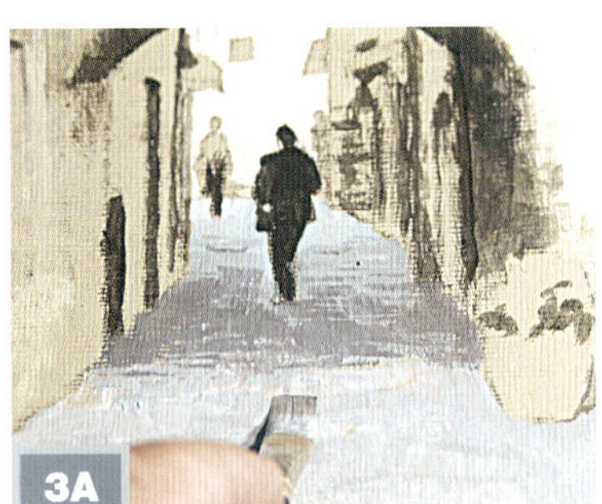

Use the corner of the flat brush for the cobblestones.

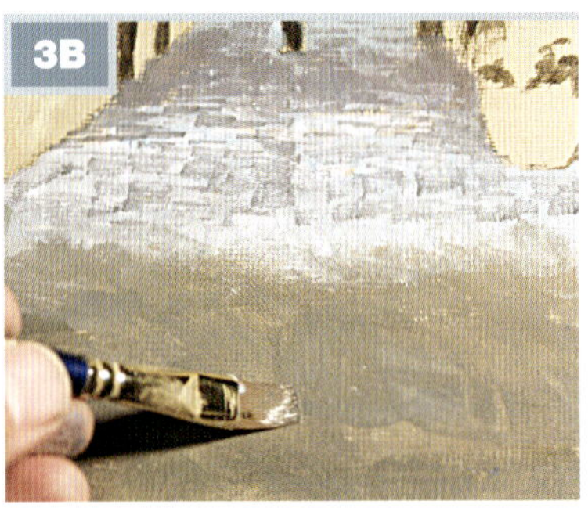

Allow the colored ground to read through.

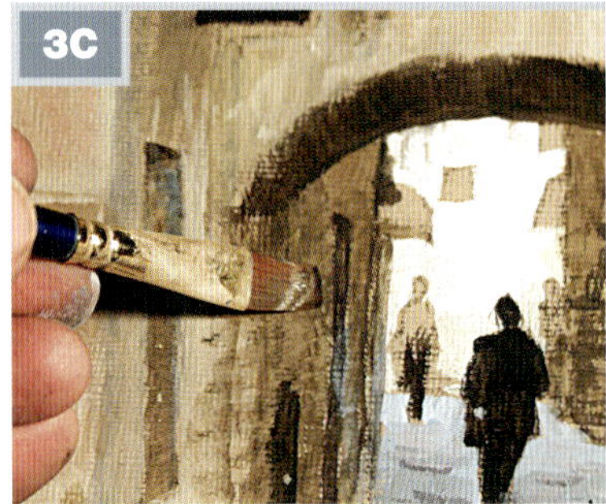

A fairly dry mix helps re-create the texture of the walls.

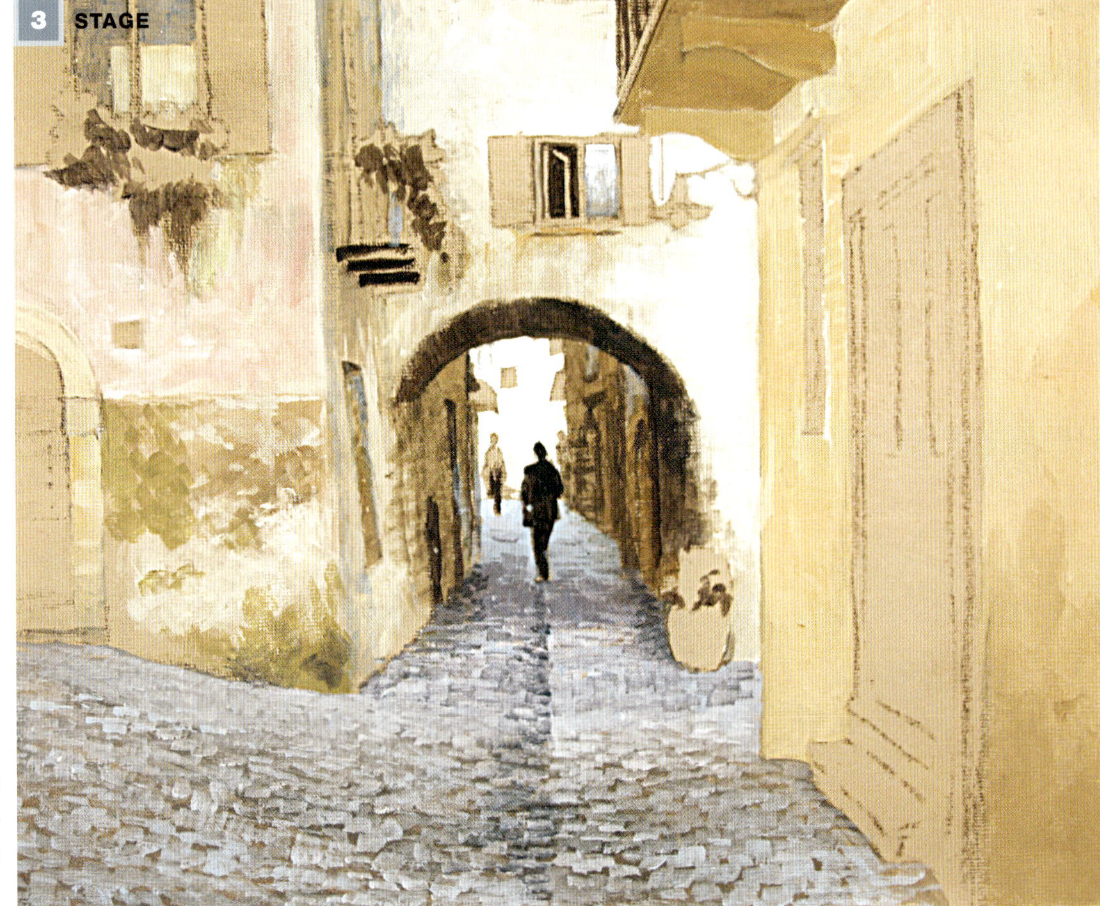

STAGE 3 The buildings become anchored to the road.

4 ADDING COLOR

The image changes dramatically as the warm color of the pots and the shutters are added. Make the color for these using mixes of white, raw umber, and burnt sienna. Note the difference between this color and the balcony timbers, which were painted using a mixture consisting of raw umber and ultramarine blue.

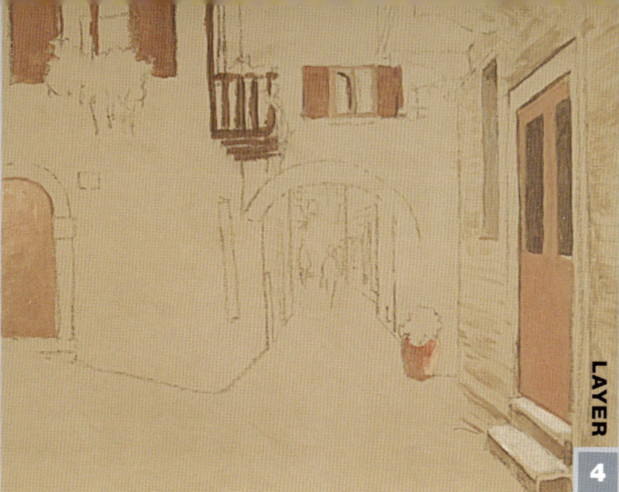

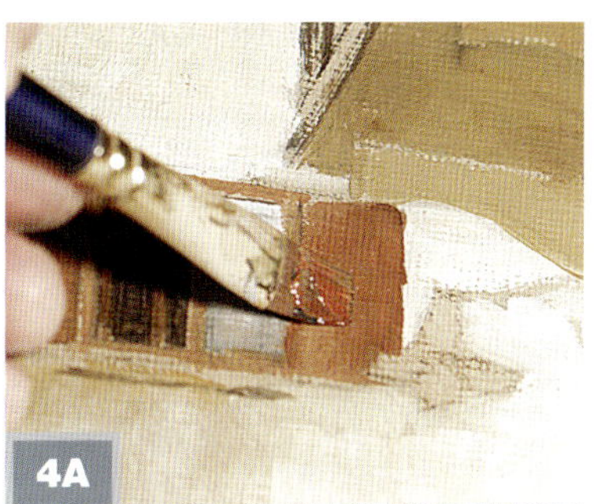

Create short, precise brushwork using the flat brush.

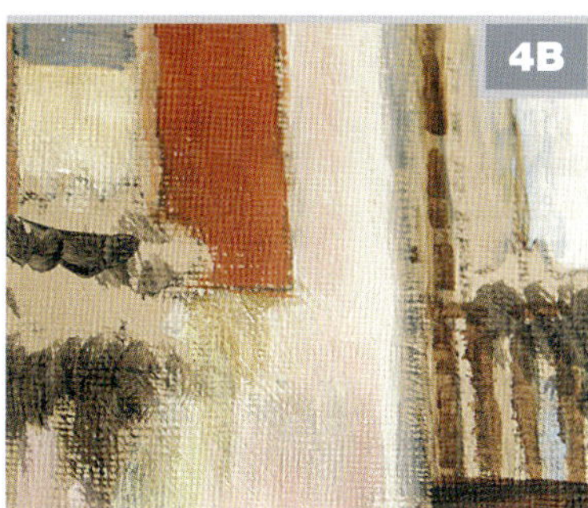

Paint the shutters a different color than the balcony timbers.

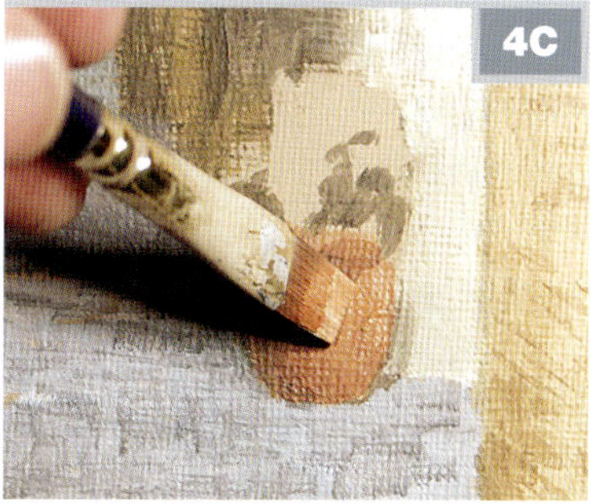

Paint the terracotta pots.

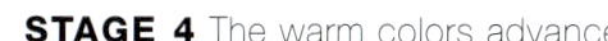

STAGE 4 The warm colors advance.

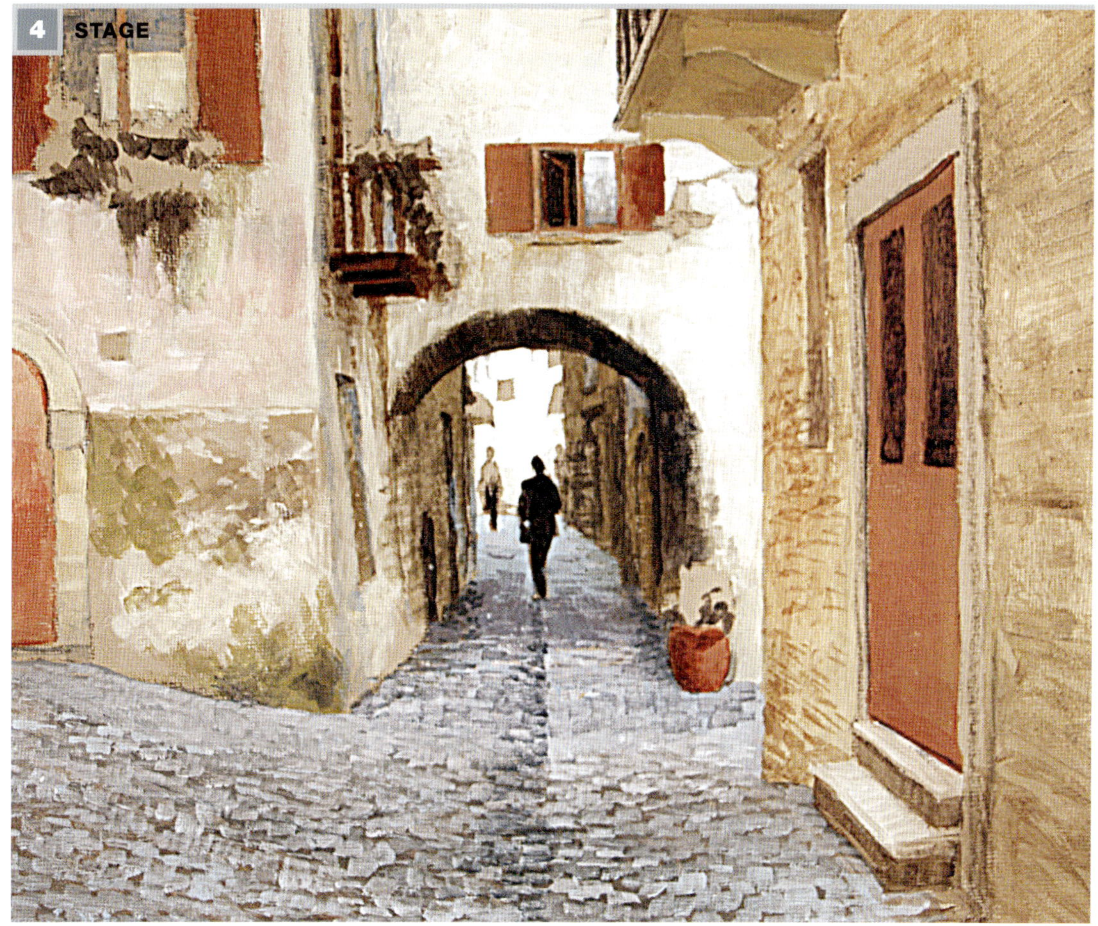

5 BRINGING THE IMAGE TO LIFE

Next paint the flowers in the pots on the balconies and in the alley. Paint the green foliage using mixes of ultramarine blue with lemon yellow and cerulean blue with lemon yellow. Use mixes of cadmium red, napthol crimson, and titanium white for the pink and red flowers.

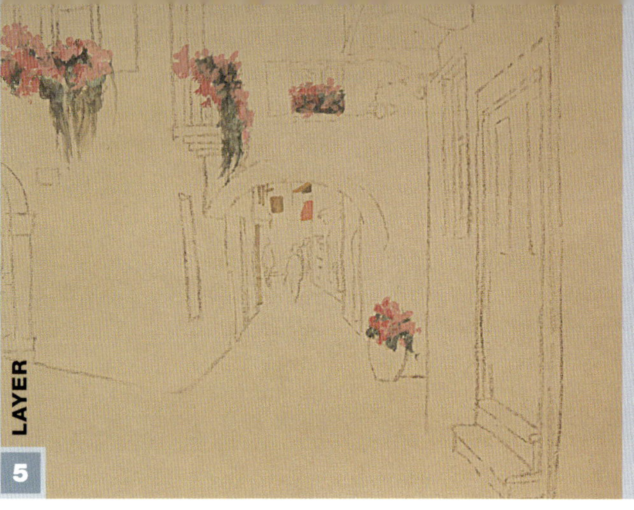

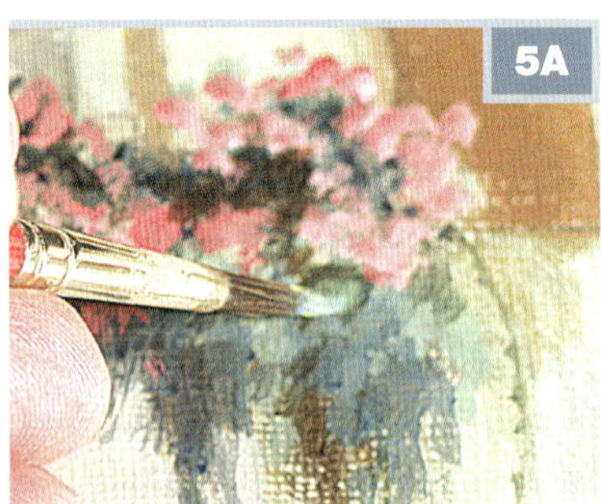

Add light green to the foliage with the small round brush.

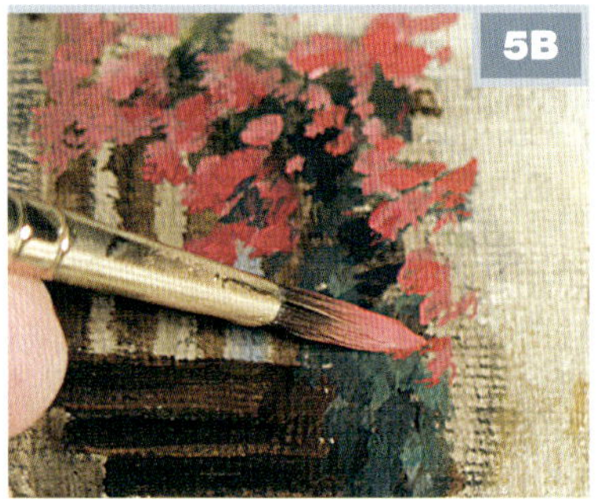

Add dark reds into the flower clusters.

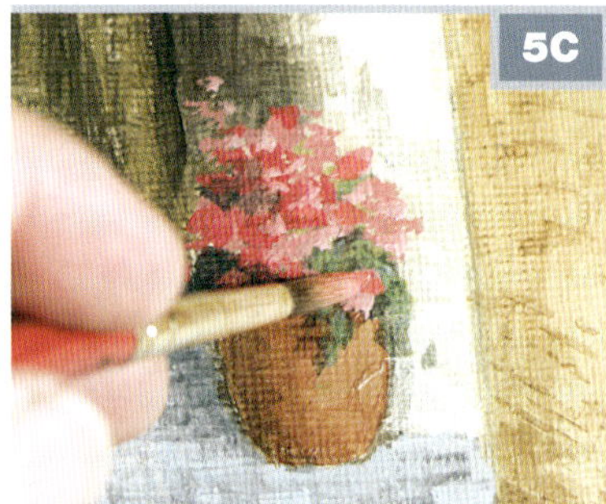

Apply the same treatment to the pot of flowers in the alleyway.

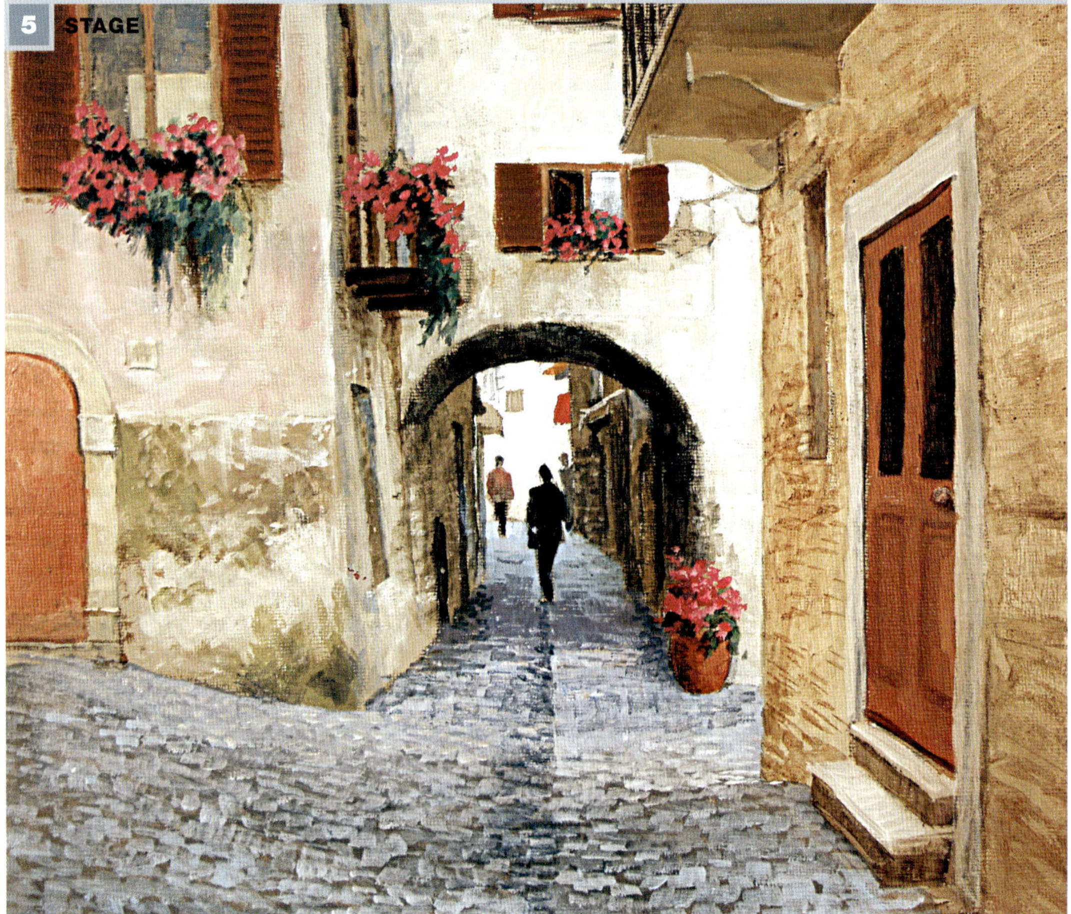

STAGE 5 The flowers add realism.

6 FINISHING THE IMAGE

Paint the final details using the small round brush: The red jacket worn by the far figure is cadmium red; the detailing on the wooden doors is burnt umber; the light on the wall, and the latticework on the door grill are white.

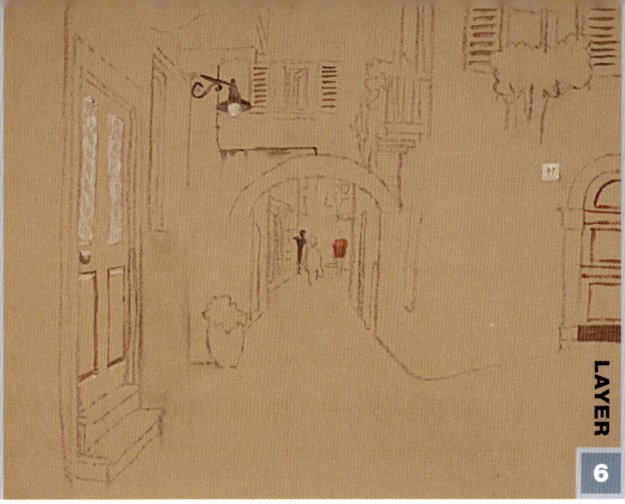

LAYER 6

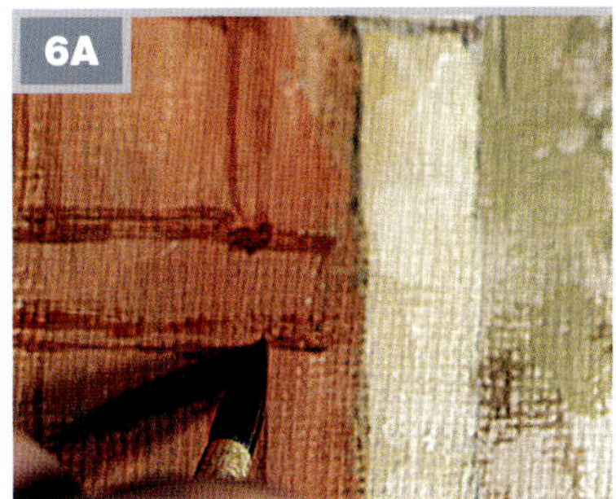

Use burnt umber for the door detail.

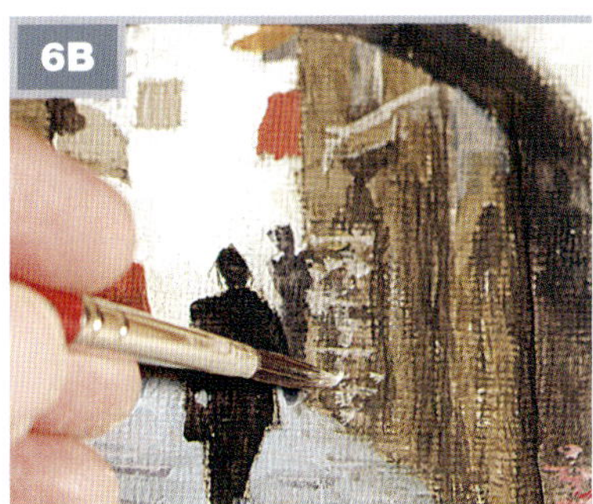

Details added to the brickwork.

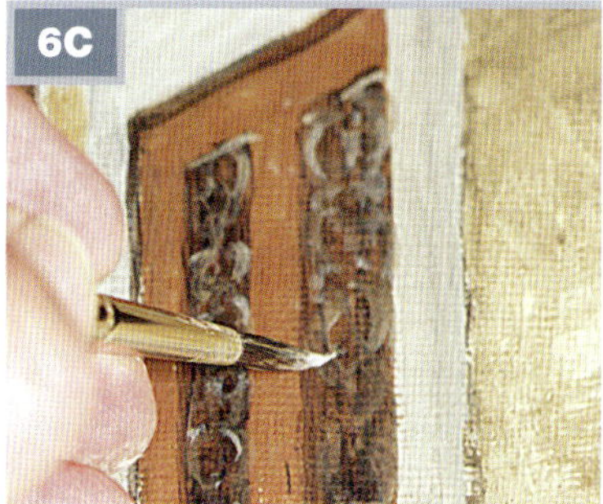

Pick out the ornamental latticework using white.

STAGE 6 The image is complete.

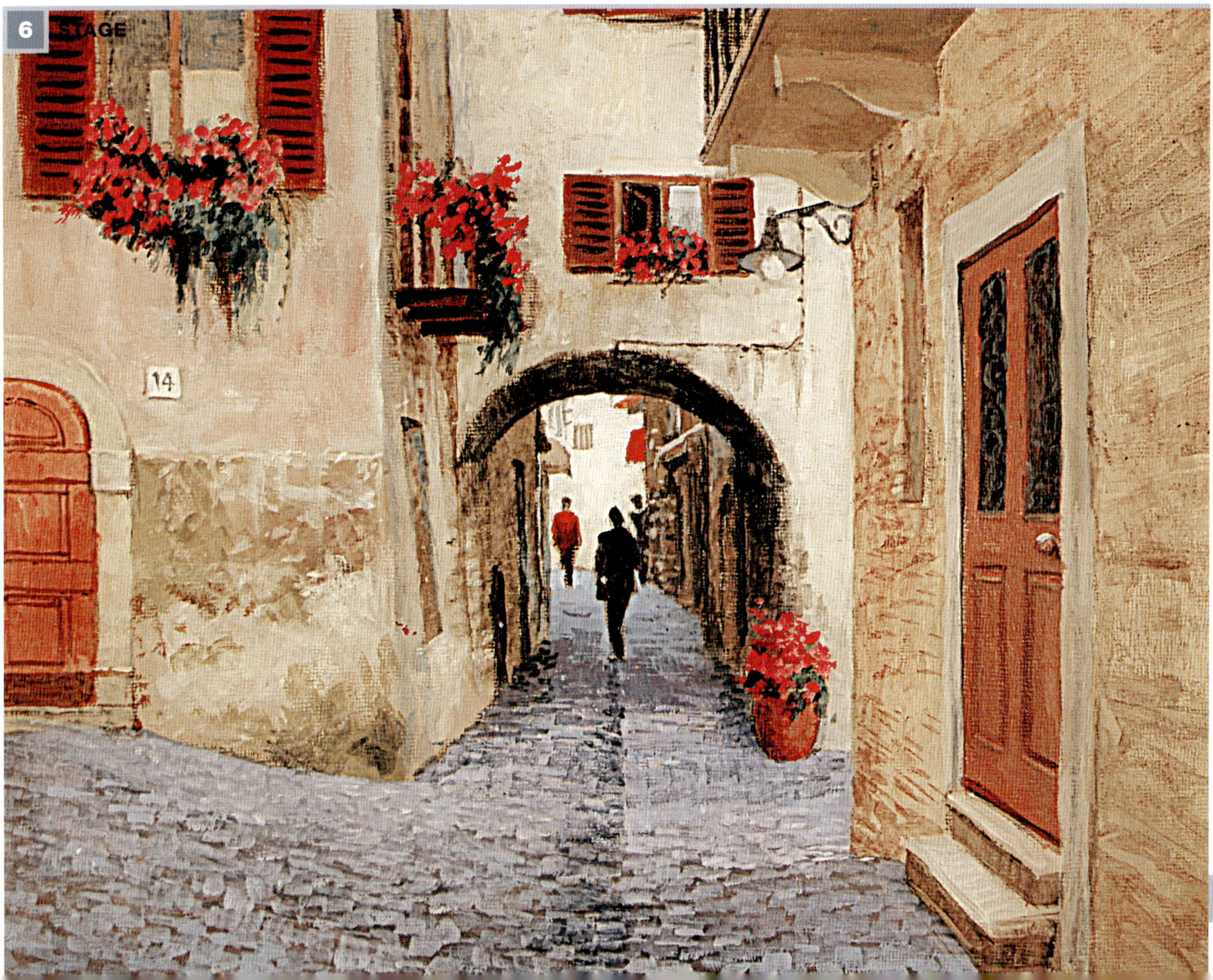

6 STAGE

REFLECTIONS

by IAN SIDAWAY

LAYER 1

The reflective quality of water varies depending on several factors. Water color is affected by tannins and minerals, water vegetation, the variable color of the sky, and disturbances at the water's surface. The colors and textures of the surrounding landscape can also influence reflective quality.

1 ESTABLISHING THE MOUNTAINS

Work washes of color into one another to establish the shape and base color of the mountains. Prepare mixes of acra crimson, ultramarine blue, yellow ochre, and titanium white. Use a large 1" (2.5 cm) flat soft-hair brush to work paint into the surface so that it dries unevenly and provides a variety of depths and color.

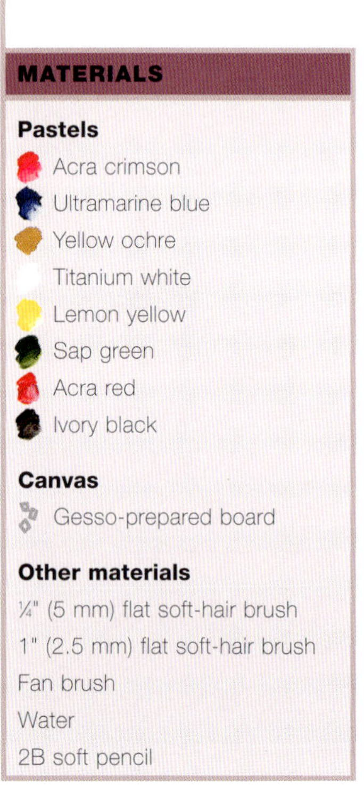

MATERIALS

Pastels

- Acra crimson
- Ultramarine blue
- Yellow ochre
- Titanium white
- Lemon yellow
- Sap green
- Acra red
- Ivory black

Canvas

- Gesso-prepared board

Other materials

¼" (5 mm) flat soft-hair brush
1" (2.5 mm) flat soft-hair brush
Fan brush
Water
2B soft pencil

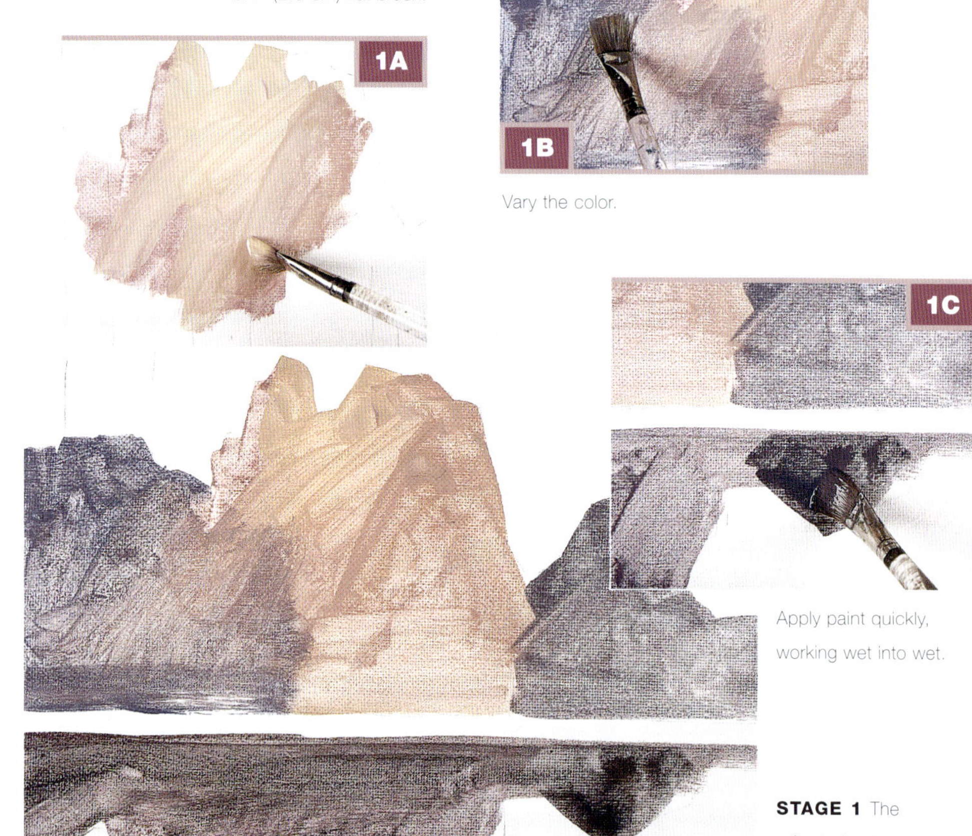

Fill in using loose brushwork and a 1" (2.5 cm) flat brush.

Vary the color.

Apply paint quickly, working wet into wet.

STAGE 1 The reflected color should appear slightly darker.

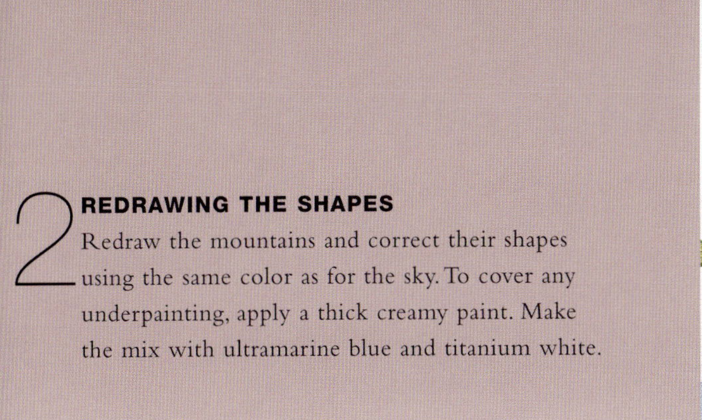

2 REDRAWING THE SHAPES

Redraw the mountains and correct their shapes using the same color as for the sky. To cover any underpainting, apply a thick creamy paint. Make the mix with ultramarine blue and titanium white.

LAYER 2

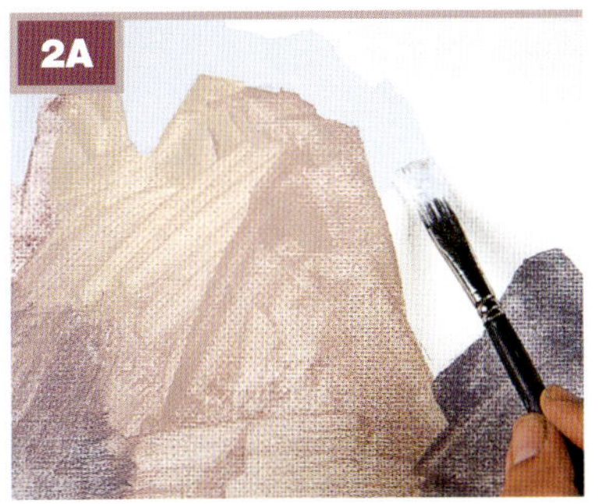

Use a ¼" (5 mm) flat brush to shape each mountain.

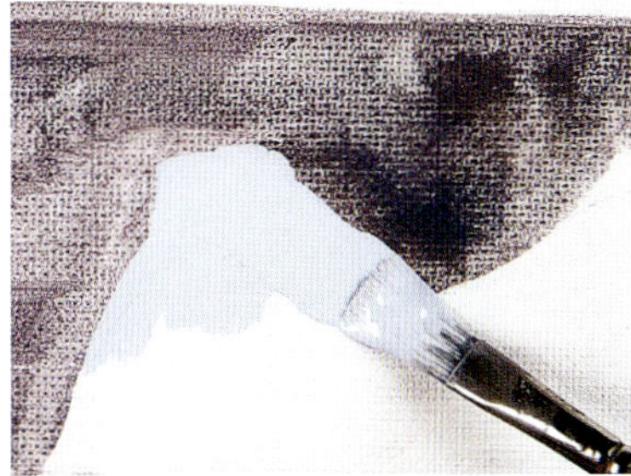

Do the same to the reflection, but darken the mix a little.

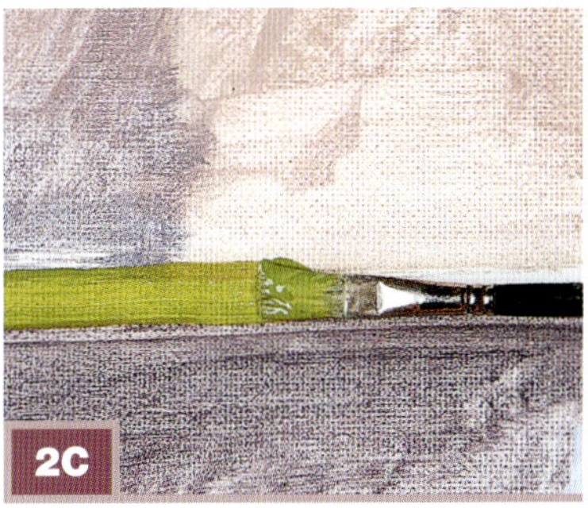

Use a lemon yellow and sap green mix for the strip of grass that separates the forest from the water.

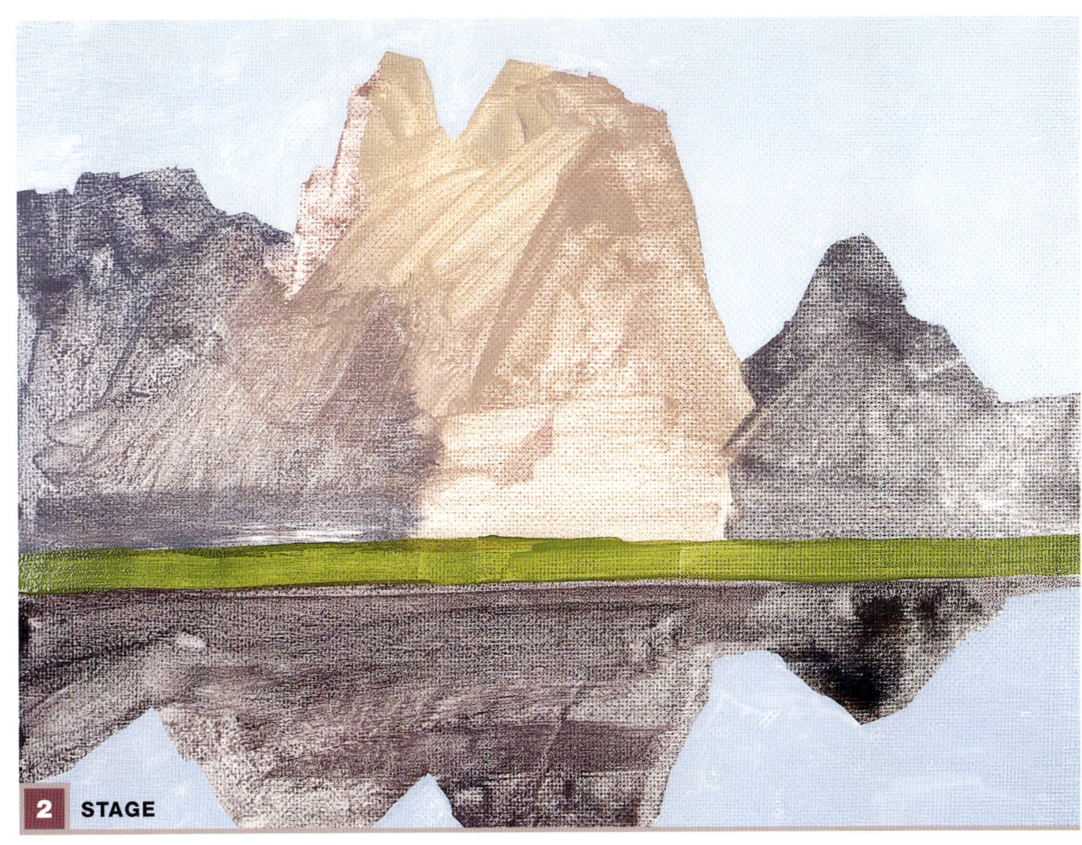

STAGE 2 The basic shapes of the image appear.

3 ESTABLISHING LIGHT AND SHADE

Use a darker mix of acra red, ultramarine blue, and yellow ochre to paint the shadows that fall across the mountains. Add more blue to emphasize the reflection. Paint the shadows on the grass with sap green mixed with a little of the shadow color used on the mountains.

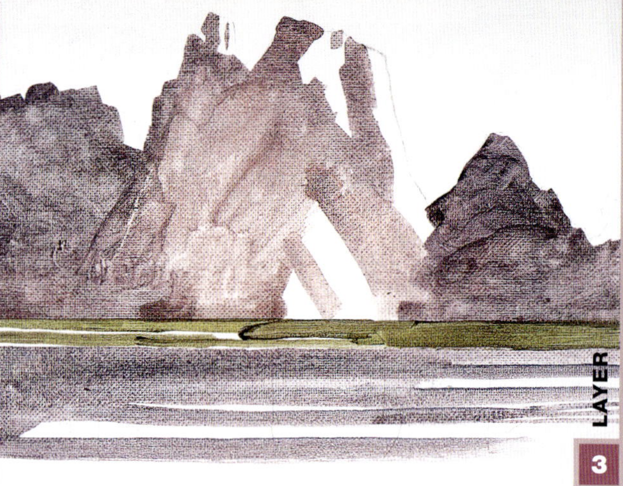

LAYER 3

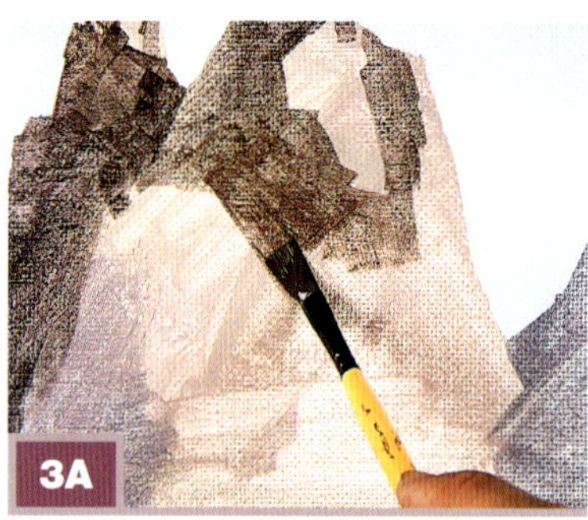

3A

Use a ¼" (2.5 cm) flat brush to sharpen the outline of the mountains.

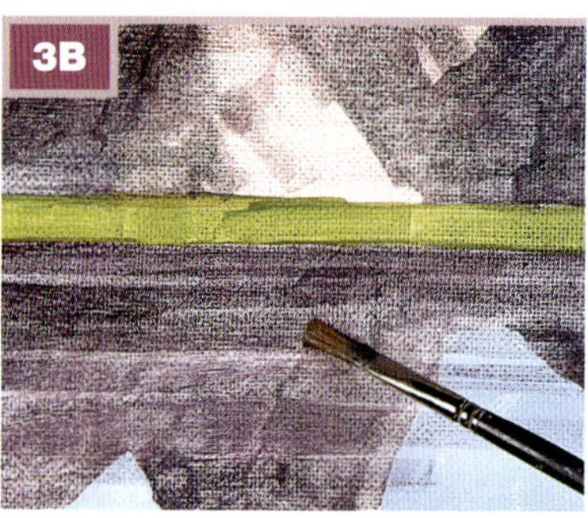

3B

Horizontal brushmarks indicate slight undulations on the water's surface.

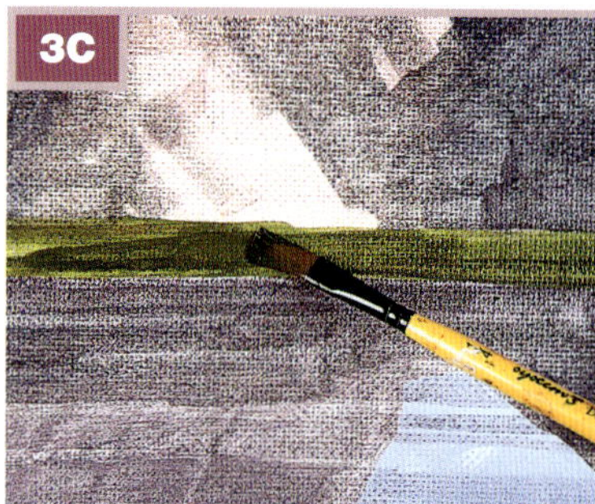

3C

Break up the uniform strip of green.

3 STAGE

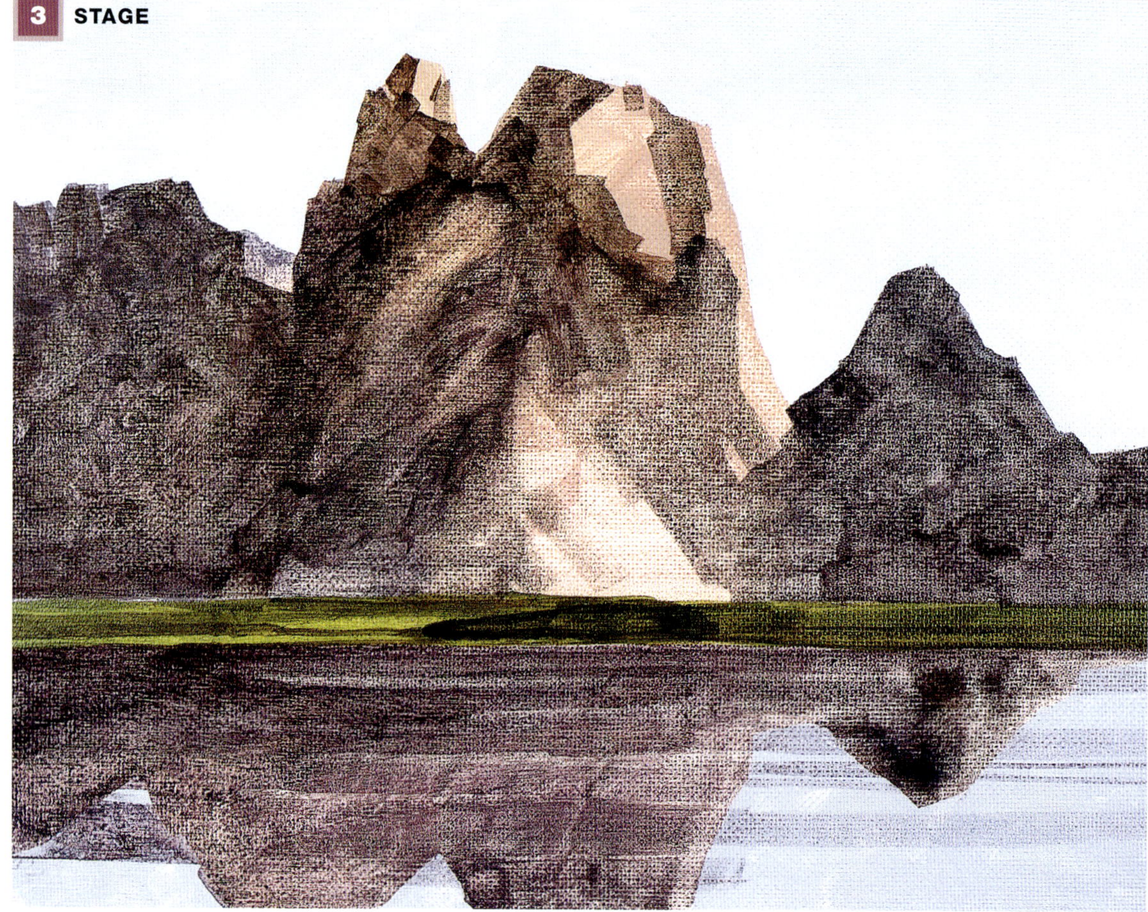

STAGE 3 The shape of each mountain now begins to emerge.

4 CONSOLIDATING THE COLORS

Before painting the trees, rework the color and detail on the side of the mountains using a blue-violet made with ultramarine blue and acra red. Paint a bright green strip along the water's edge, using masking tape to ensure clean lines. Make the bright green with sap green, yellow ochre, and titanium white.

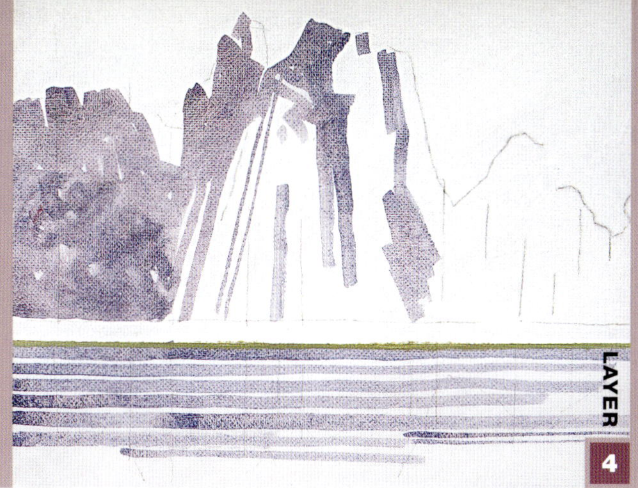

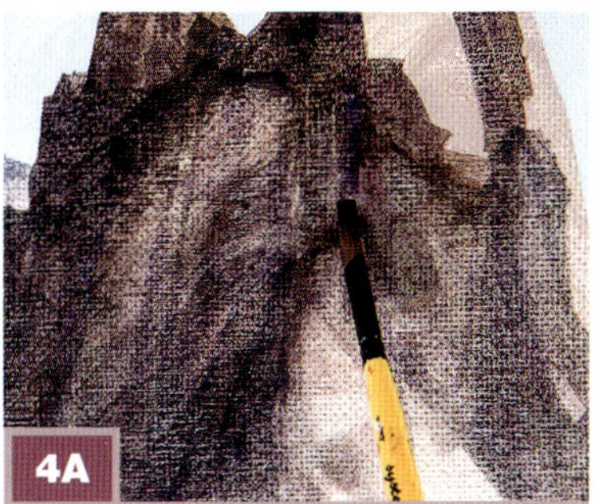

Use the shape of the small flat brush to paint the fissures of the rock face.

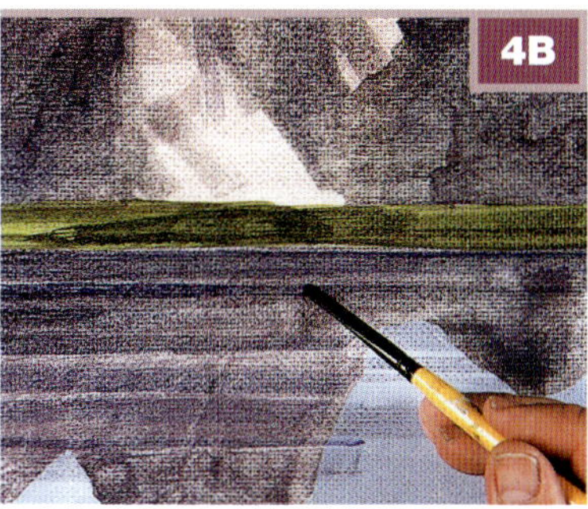

Paint thin lines in the same color to darken the ripples.

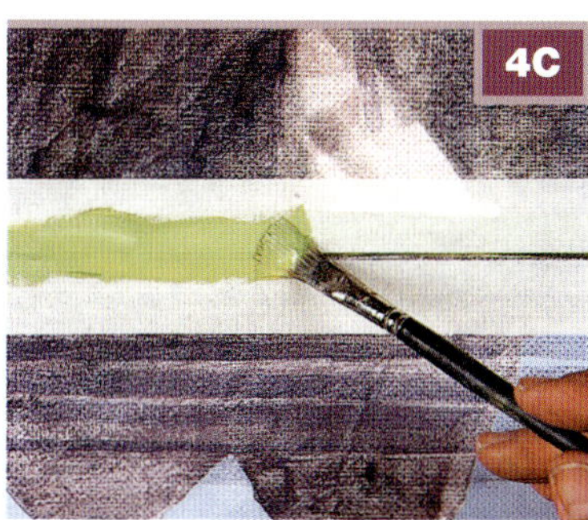

Masking tape creates a sharp edge.

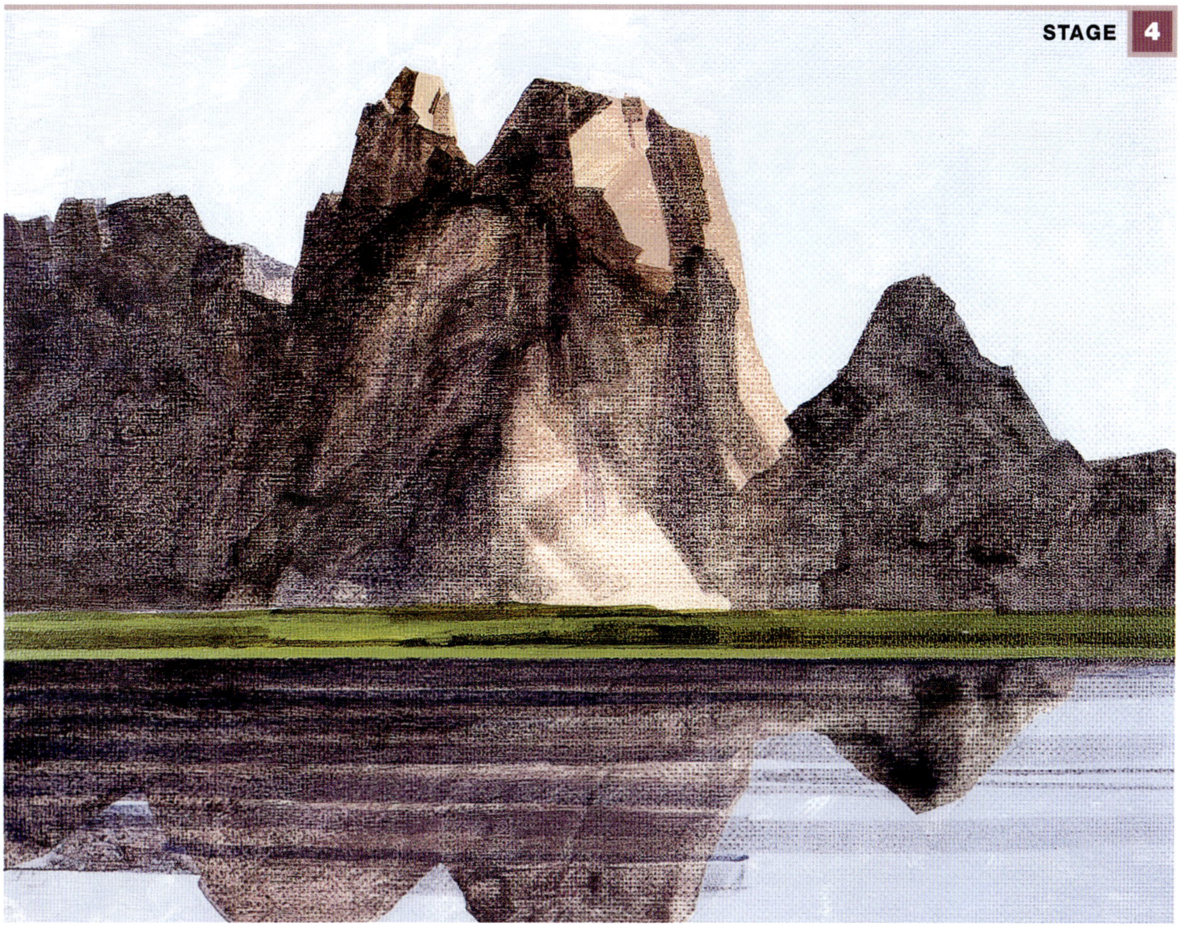

STAGE 4

STAGE 4 The complete underpainting awaits only detail.

5 ADDING DETAIL

Add the bank of trees. Use a small bristle fan brush and apply dark blue-green made with sap green, ivory black, and a little ultramarine blue. Add more blue to the mix for the reflection. Use a 2B soft pencil to draw fissures on the rock face.

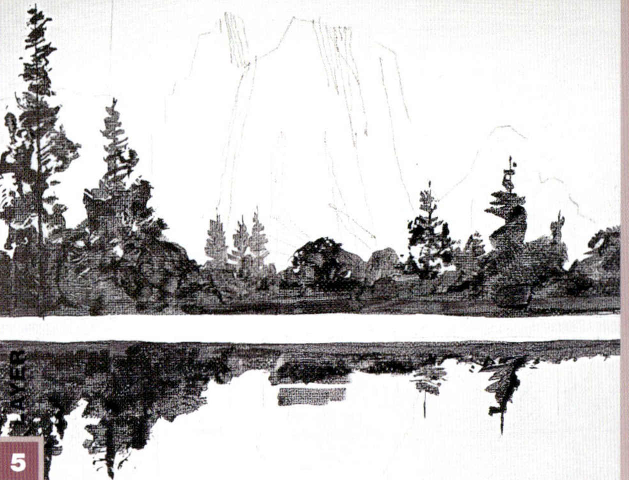

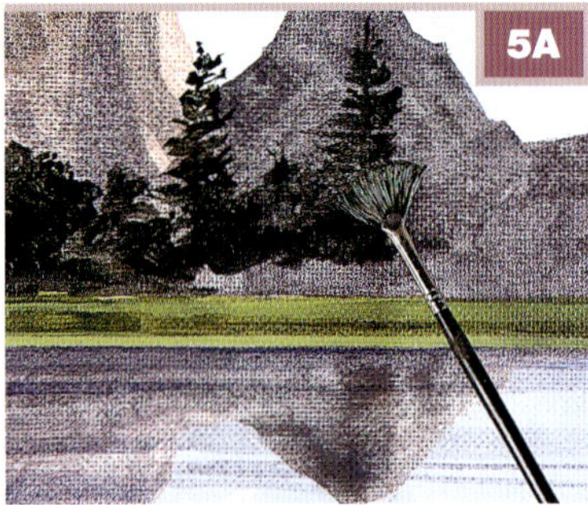

The shape of the fan brush makes it ideal for painting trees.

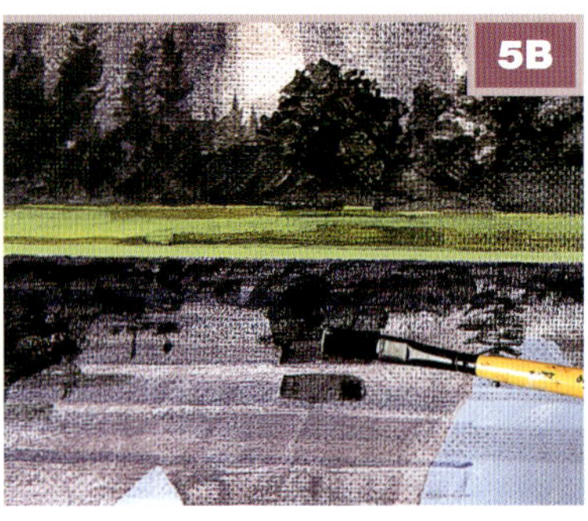

Allow lighter ripples to break up the reflection.

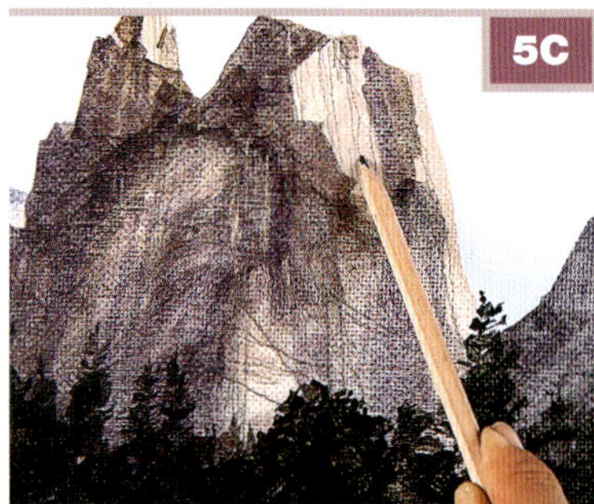

Lines create details on the mountainside.

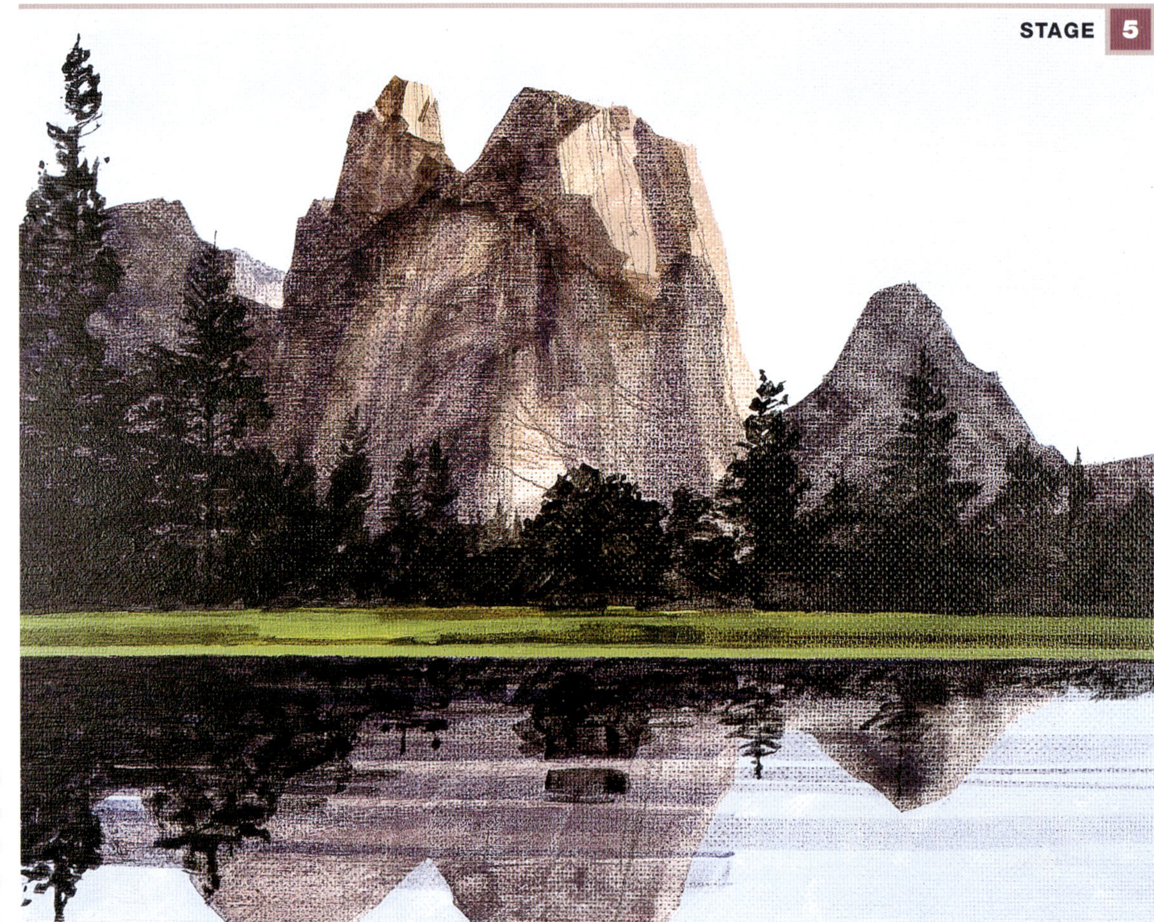

STAGE 5
Notice the light, dappled grass between the trees.

6 THE FINISHING TOUCHES

A few finishing touches complete the image. Paint the sky with a mix of titanium white and a little ultramarine blue. Use this mix to repaint the ripples in the water. Use a light orange made with white, acra red, and yellow ochre to add highlights to areas of the mountainside in the sun.

LAYER 6

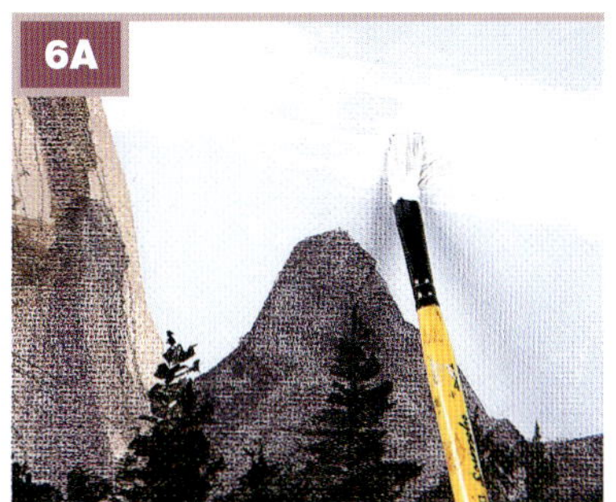

Drag the paint across the sky.

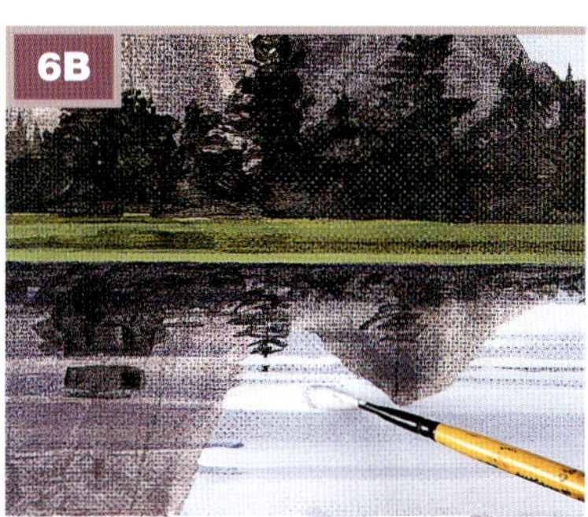

Suggest ripples with horizontal lines that vary in thickness.

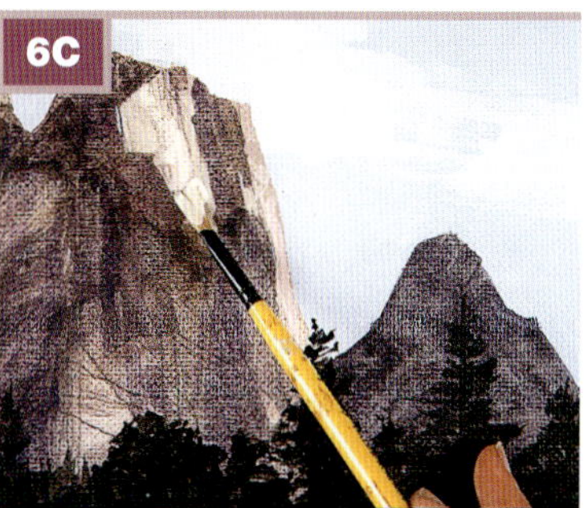

Add a few lighter touches to the rock face.

STAGE 6 Carefully applied details complete the image.

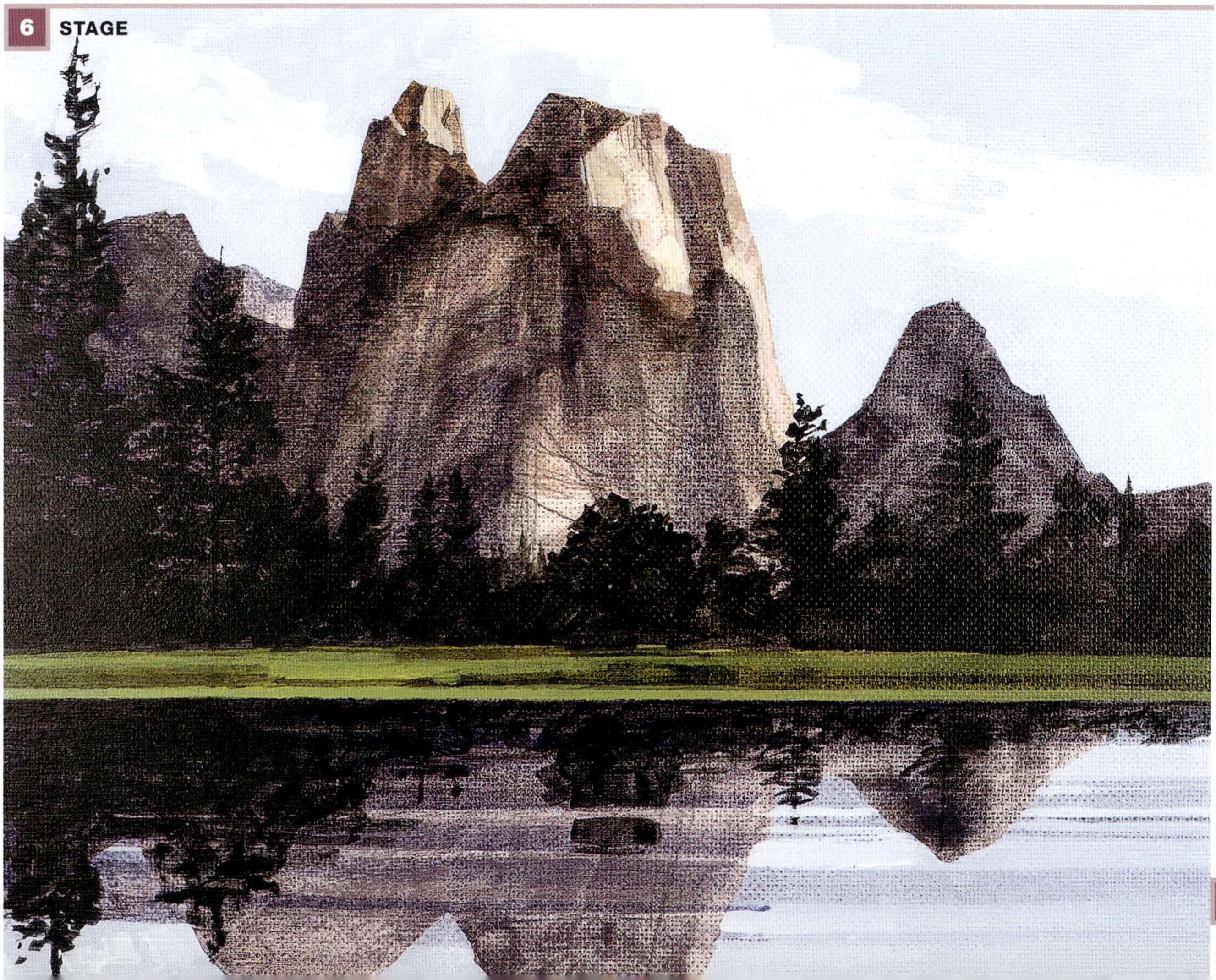

6 STAGE

PAINTING WATER

by STEPHEN RIPPINGTON

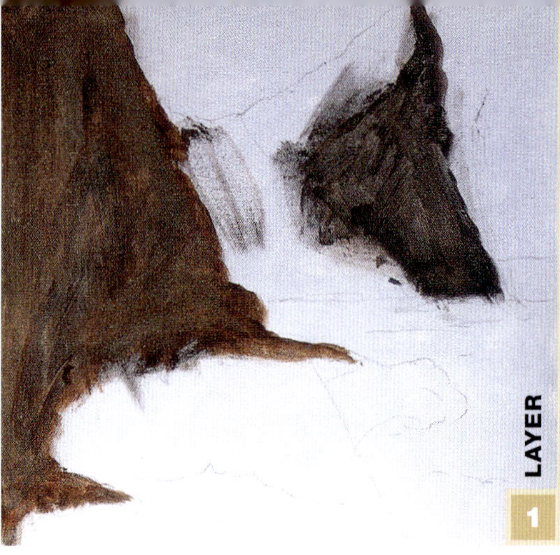

Water presents a particular challenge for the artist. Its movement, reflective qualities, and changing color can seem particularly illusive. Water is, however, very enjoyable to paint and provides an excuse to experiment with suitable techniques and expressive brushwork. Watercolor techniques that use thin paint are particularly suitable, as are glazing techniques. Here, the artist has chosen to use scumbled thick paint and spattering.

1 A SIMPLE BEGINNING

Burnt umber is thinned with water and scrubbed onto the support to represent the large rock mass to the left of the image. The rocky outcrop in the center of the image is painted in the same way, again using burnt umber, but this time with a little cobalt blue added to the mix.

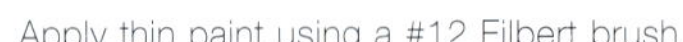
Apply thin paint using a #12 Filbert brush.

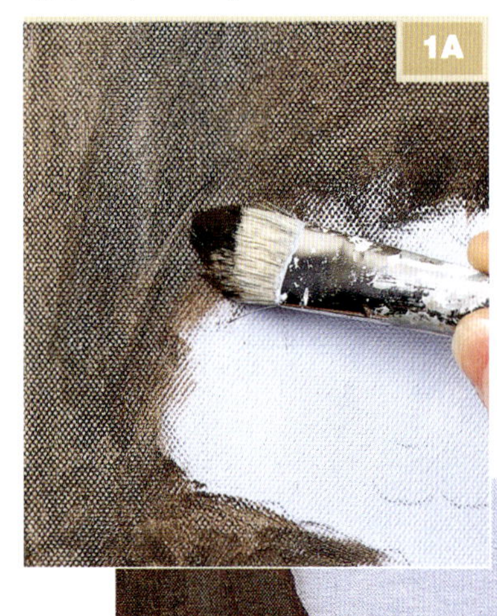

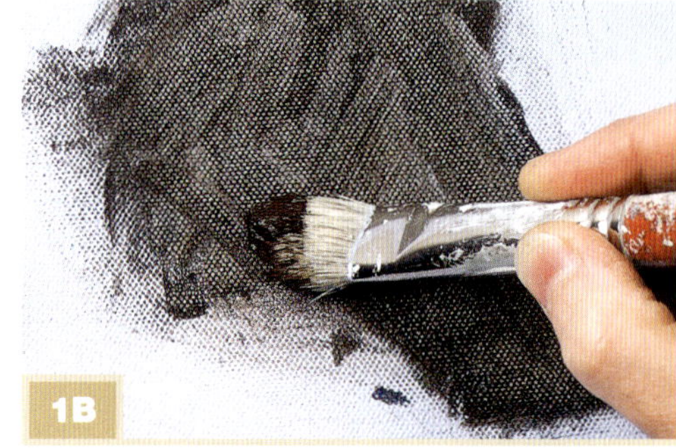

Add cobalt blue to slightly cool the brown.

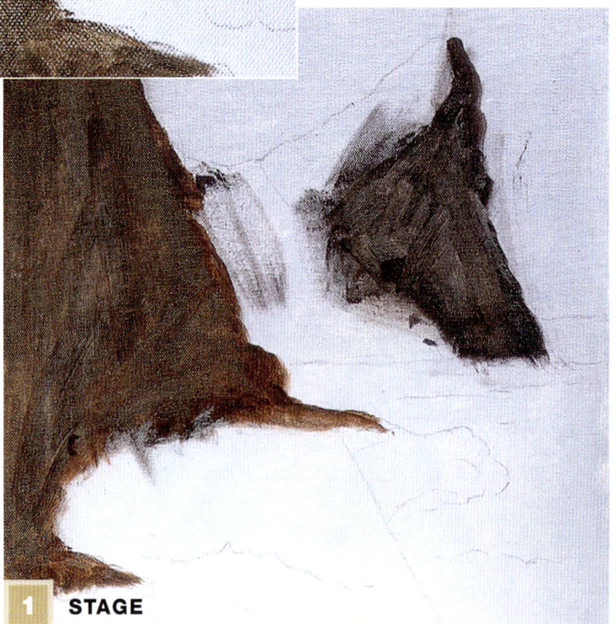

STAGE 1 The paint is applied loosely.

MATERIALS

Acrylics
- Naples yellow
- Yellow ochre
- Light blue violet
- Burnt umber
- Hooker's green dark
- Cobalt blue
- Red iron oxide
- Titanium white

Canvas
- Canvas primed with gesso and a light blue ground

Other materials
- #12 filbert brush
- #10 filbert brush
- Old toothbrush
- Water

2 ADDING COLOR

Begin to add color by working a mixture of Naples yellow across the area of sky. This is applied using relatively thick paint that is brushed out to allow the blue ground to show through as it nears the horizon. The mix is darkened with yellow ochre and used to block in the side of the central rocky outcrop.

LAYER 2

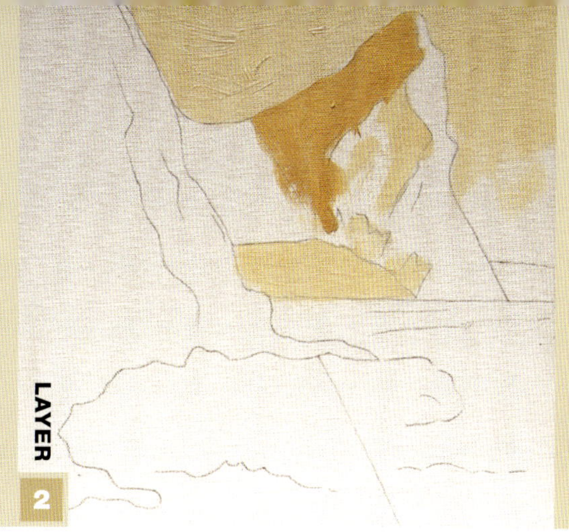

2A

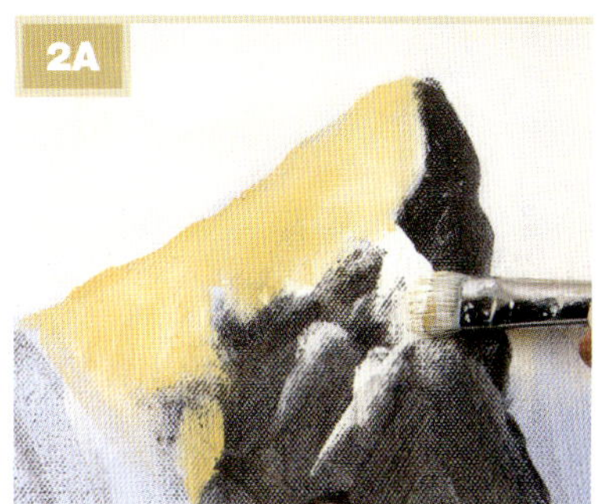

Pull some of the sky color over the central rocks.

2B

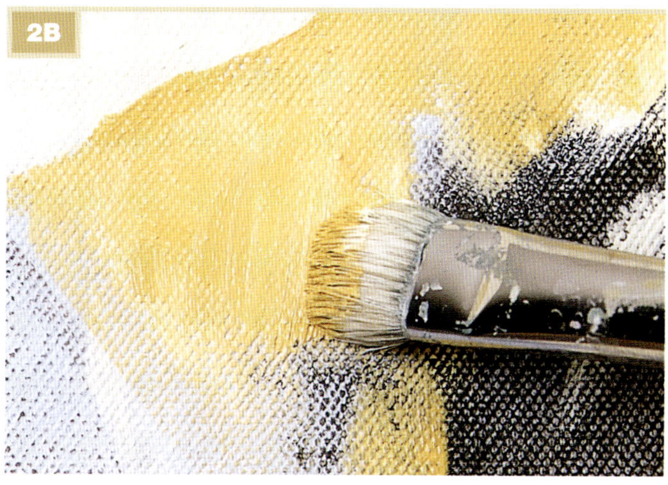

Use relatively opaque applications of paint.

STAGE 2

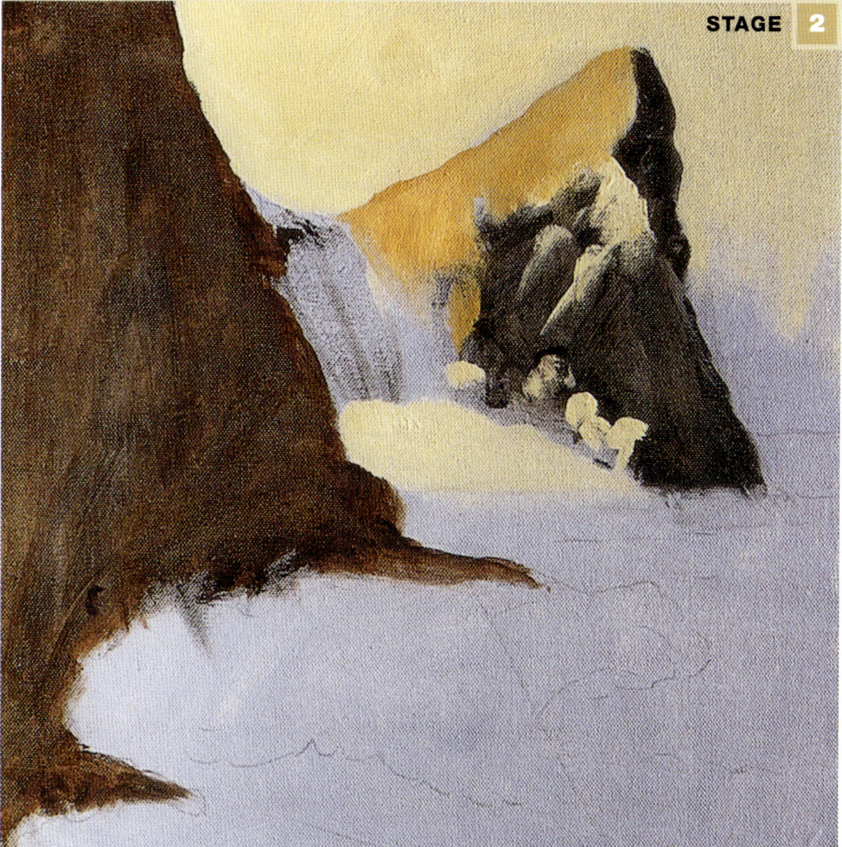

STAGE 2 Vary the direction of the brushwork.

3 STRENGTHENING THE DARKS

The dark cliffs are consolidated next by adding another layer of thicker, more opaque paint. The mix is made from cobalt blue with a little red iron oxide added.

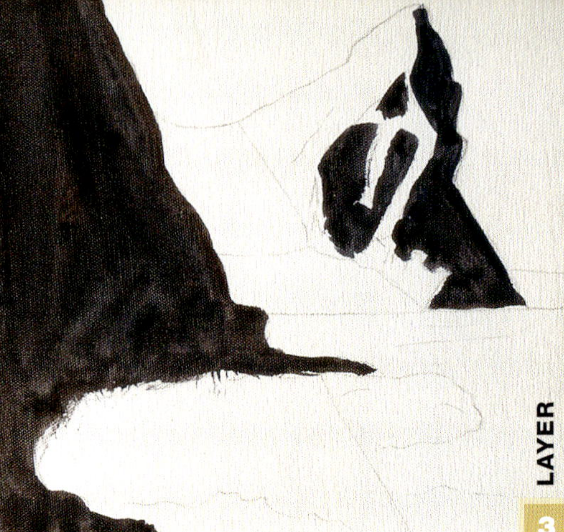

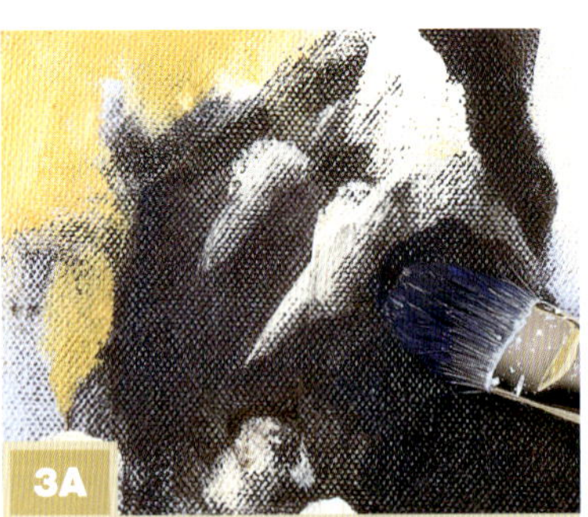

Work the paint around the light areas.

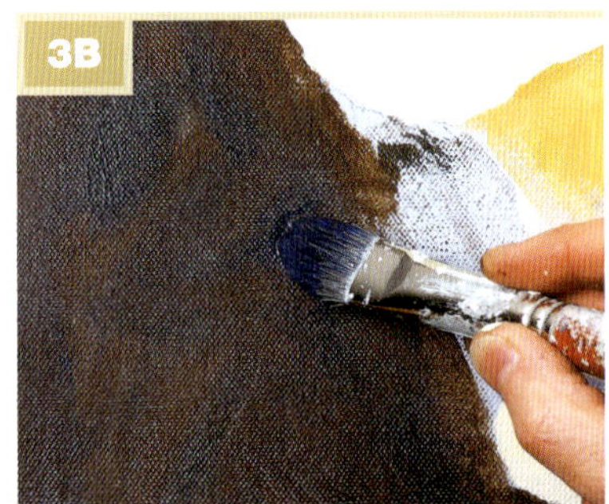

Use open brushwork.

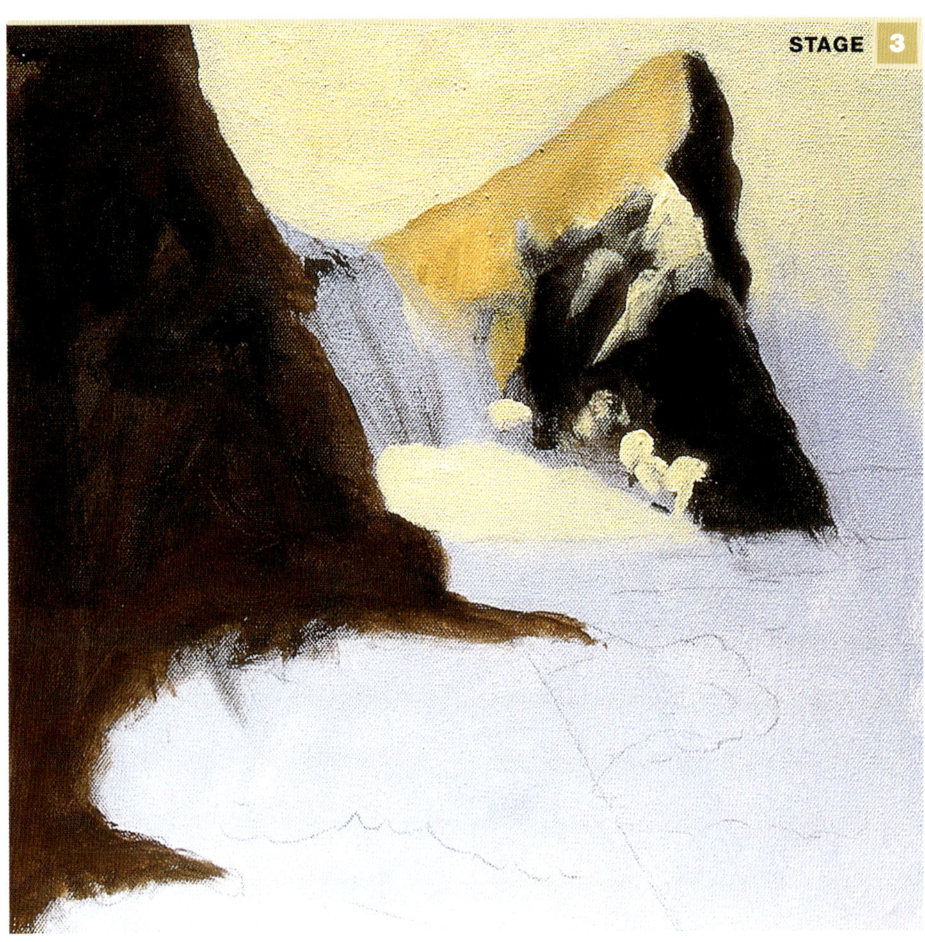

STAGE 3 The image looks more solid.

4 BEGINNING TO PAINT THE SEA

Attention now turns to the sea. The deep green is made using Hooker's green dark mixed with light blue-violet and white. For the sunlit sea, white is used to paint in the breaking waves. A cobalt blue and yellow ochre mix is then applied to the area that links the two outcrops of rock. A rich orange made using yellow ochre and red iron oxide is also worked into the strata of the central rock. Use the smaller #10 filbert brush.

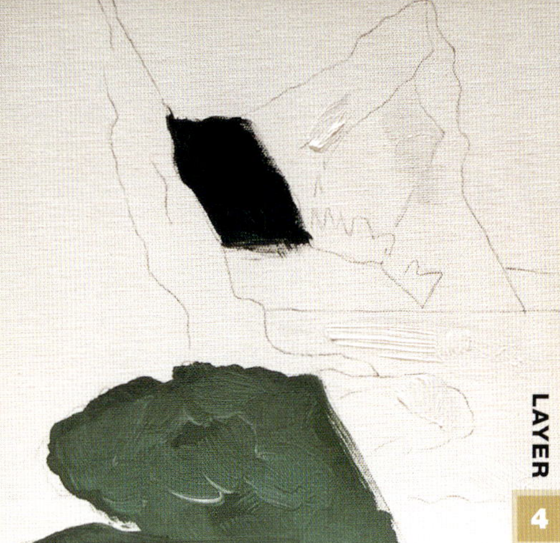

Apply the paint thickly and vary the direction of the brushstrokes.

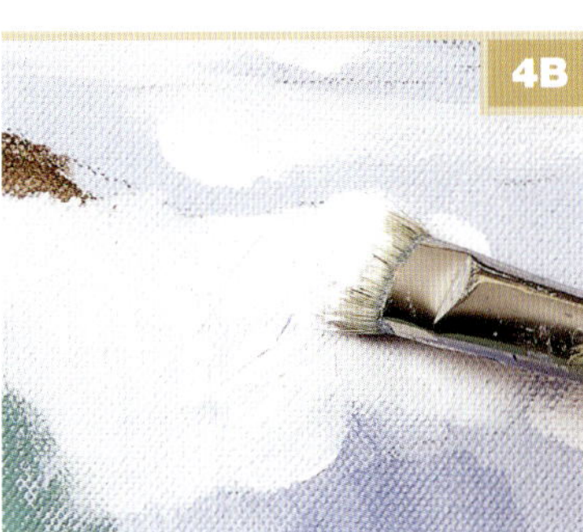

Use paint of the same consistency for the breaking waves.

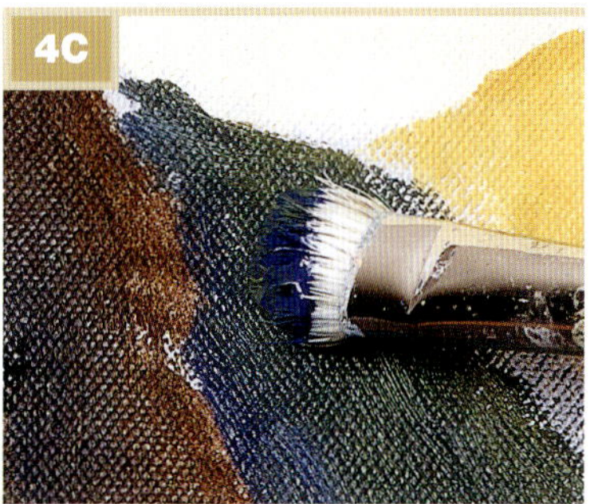

Use a thinner mix for the cliffside.

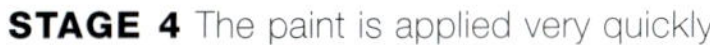

STAGE 4 The paint is applied very quickly.

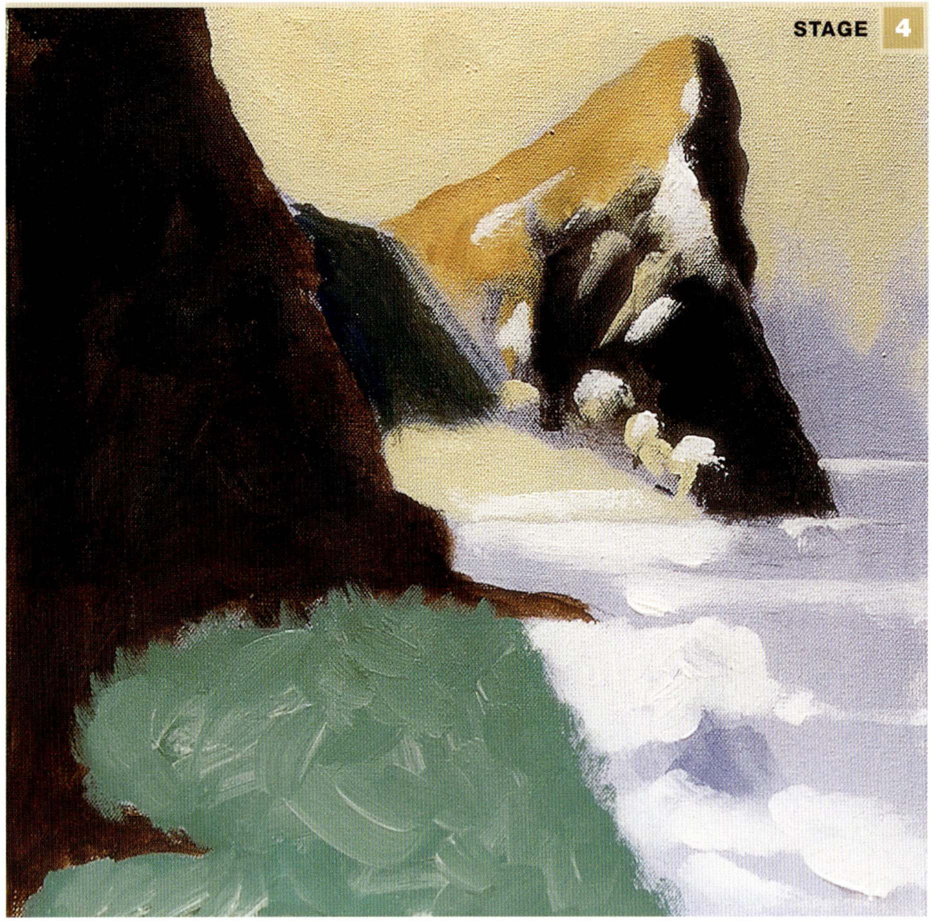

5 ADDING MOVEMENT

The sea is seen crashing against the rocks, falling back on itself, and throwing up foam. In order to show this, the artist works scumbled and loosely applied areas of paint into each other, while always allowing elements of previously applied layers to show through. The deep green is made using Hooker's green, cobalt blue, a little red iron oxide, and white.

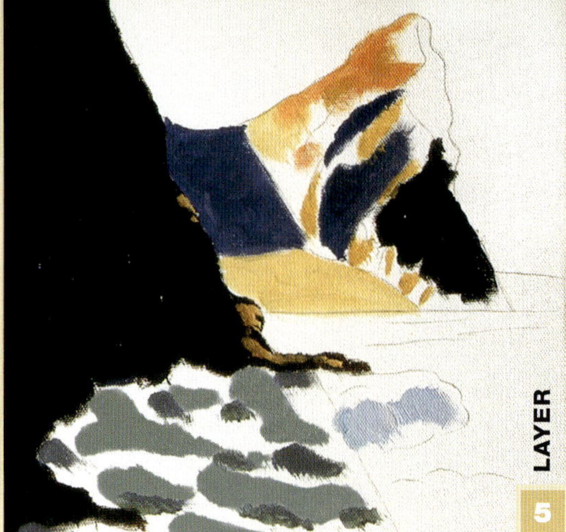

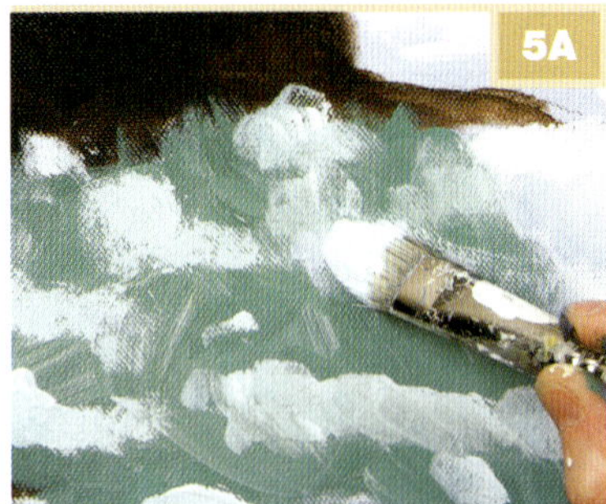

Apply white using open brushstrokes.

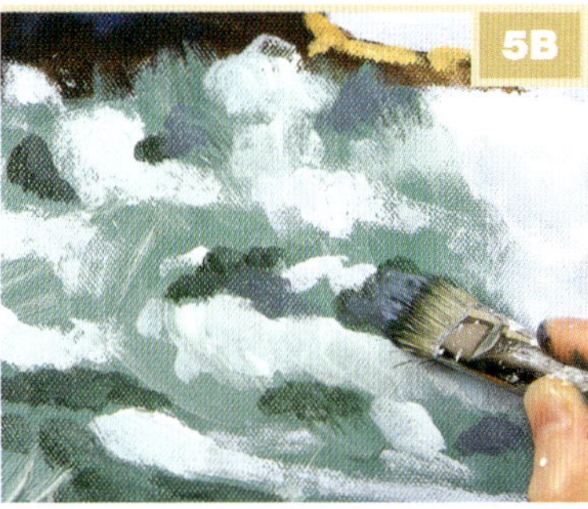

Intersperse areas of deep blue-green.

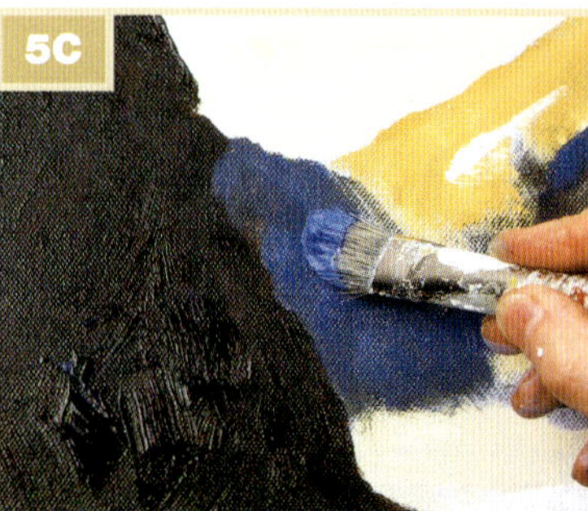

Cool the shadows on the rocks by adding cobalt blue mixed with white.

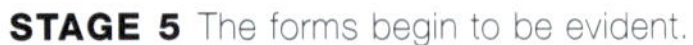

STAGE 5 The forms begin to be evident.

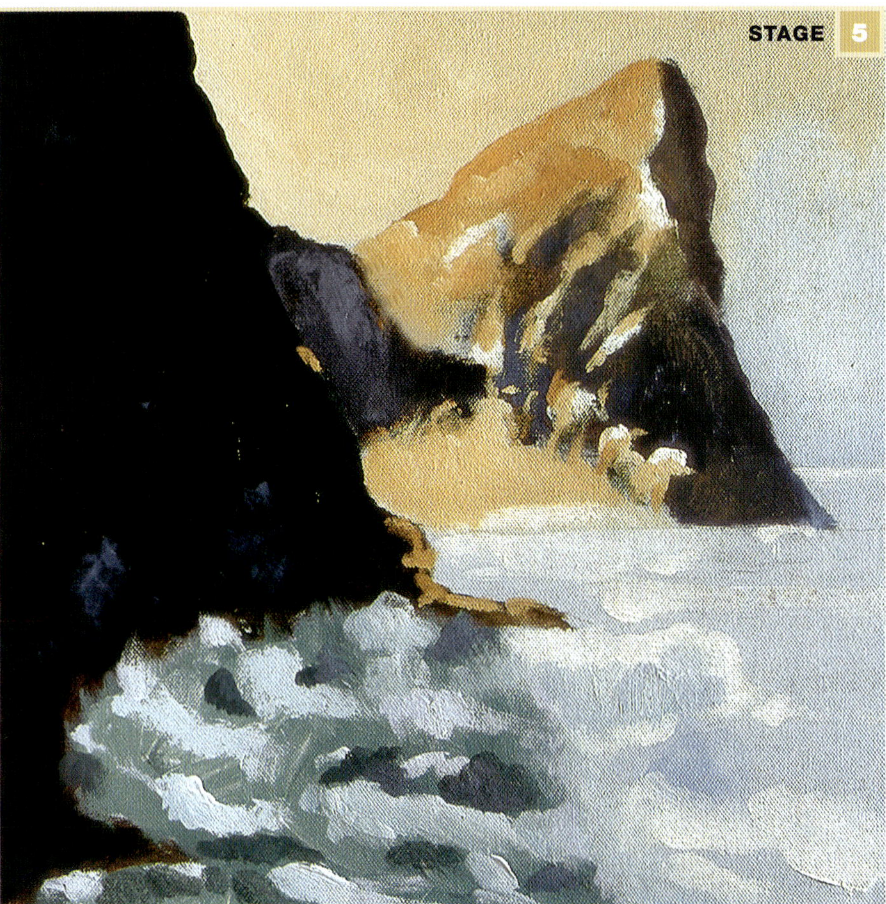

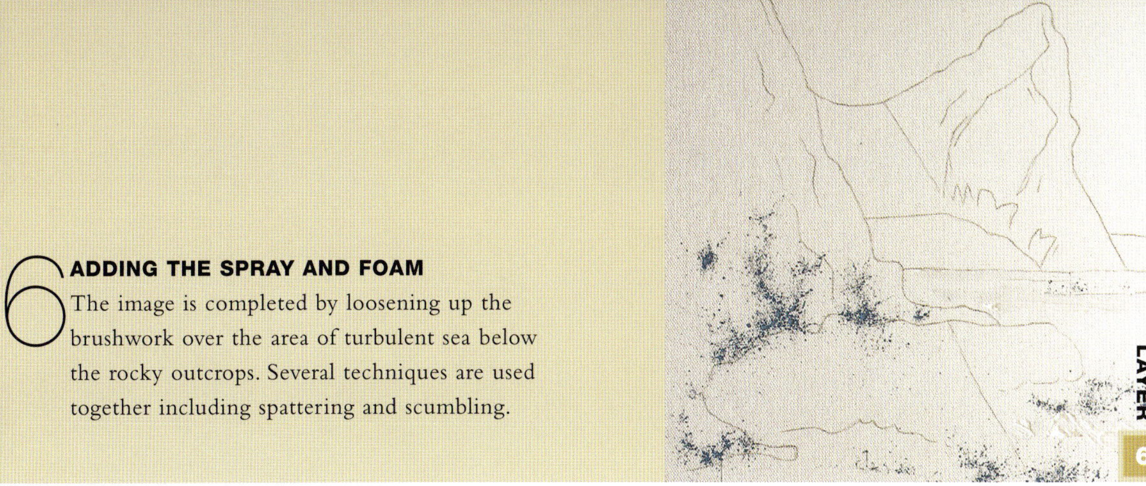

6 ADDING THE SPRAY AND FOAM

The image is completed by loosening up the brushwork over the area of turbulent sea below the rocky outcrops. Several techniques are used together including spattering and scumbling.

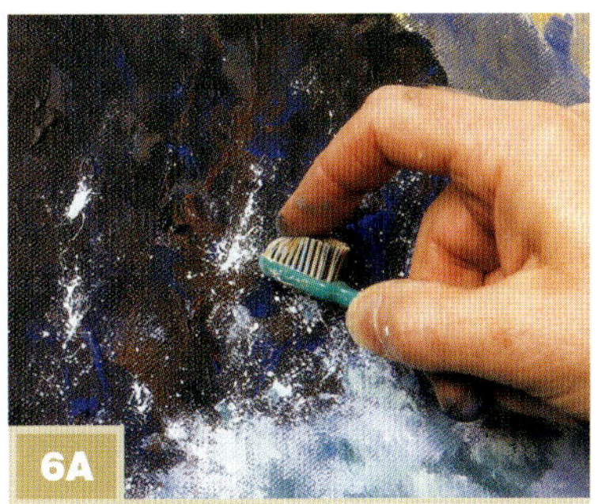

Use an old toothbrush to spatter paint.

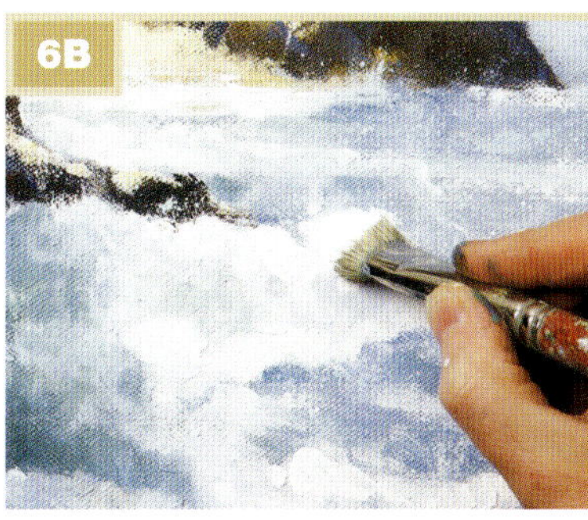

Use the front edge of the brush to achieve the shape of the waves.

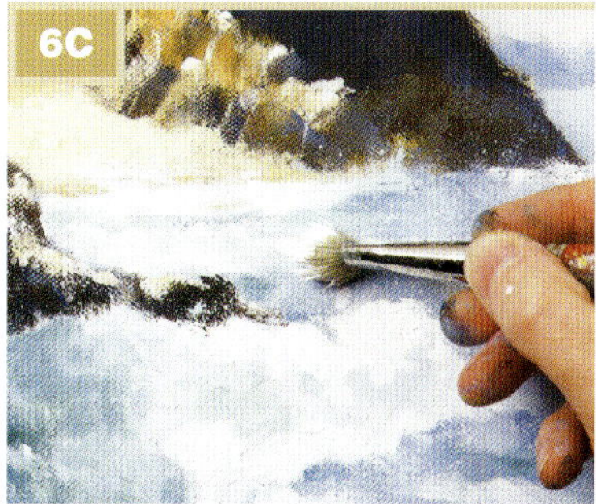

Drag stiff paint across the canvas surface.

STAGE 6 Added textures bring the image to life.

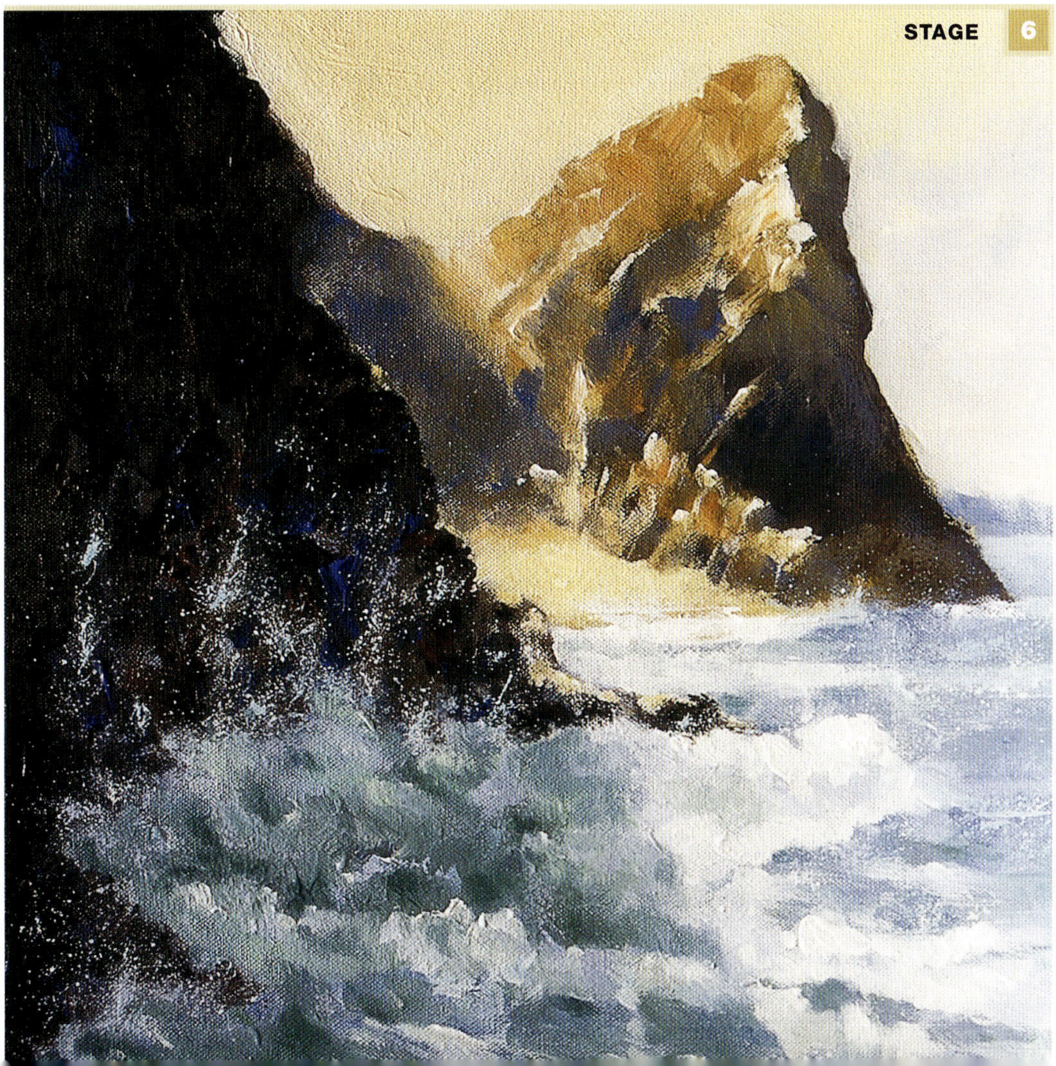

STAGE 6

MOOD

by STEPHEN RIPPINGTON

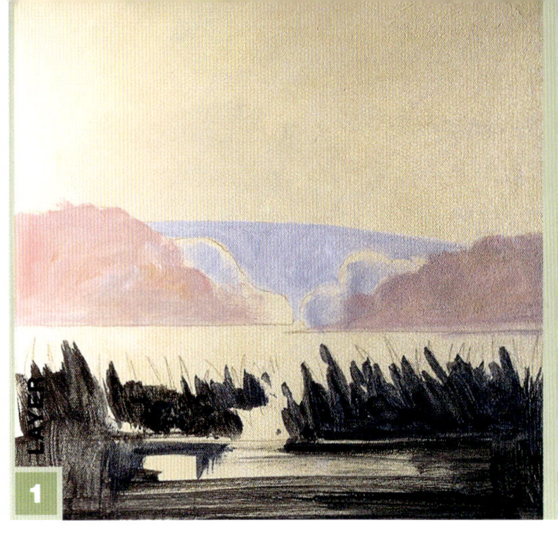

Mood is an important element in many paintings and can be an especially powerful tool in landscape paintings. Used successfully it can help suggest a real spirit of place, time of day or year, and can even induce the viewer into feeling hot or cold. Mood can be conveyed in several ways but the primary method is through the use of color. In this image, a misty ethereal quality is achieved by using pastel shades and indistinct distant shapes and edges.

1 THICK AND THIN COLOR

The artist has made a simple pencil drawing over a colored ground made by mixing Naples yellow, light blue-violet, and white. A cool pastel mix of light blue-violet and white establishes the distant hill, while a light blue violet, medium magenta, and white mix is applied to the treeline on the far banks of the river. An ultramarine blue and yellow ochre mix creates the base color for the reeds ranged across the foreground.

Apply the paint using a large bristle Filbert brush.

1A

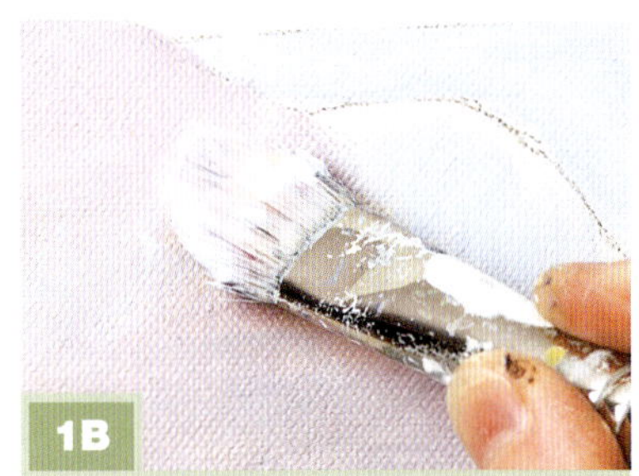

The color is relatively opaque.

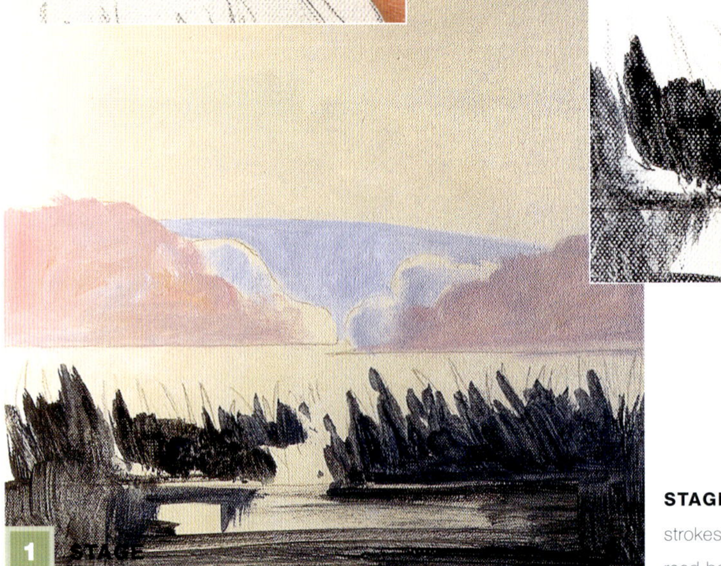

Apply semitransparent and fluid paint to the foreground.

STAGE 1 Directional strokes describe the reed bed.

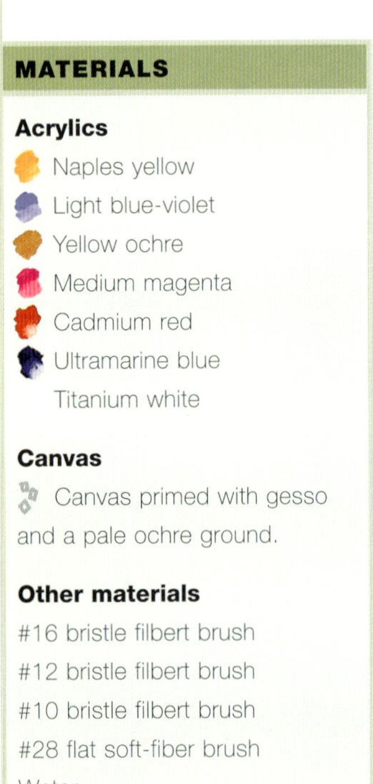

MATERIALS

Acrylics

- Naples yellow
- Light blue-violet
- Yellow ochre
- Medium magenta
- Cadmium red
- Ultramarine blue
- Titanium white

Canvas

Canvas primed with gesso and a pale ochre ground.

Other materials

- #16 bristle filbert brush
- #12 bristle filbert brush
- #10 bristle filbert brush
- #28 flat soft-fiber brush
- Water

2 ADDING DEPTH

A mix of Naples yellow, yellow ochre, and white is scumbled across the light magenta color used for the treeline, and a light blue-violet and white mix is scumbled over the sky. The reeds at the water's edge are strengthened by darkening the color.

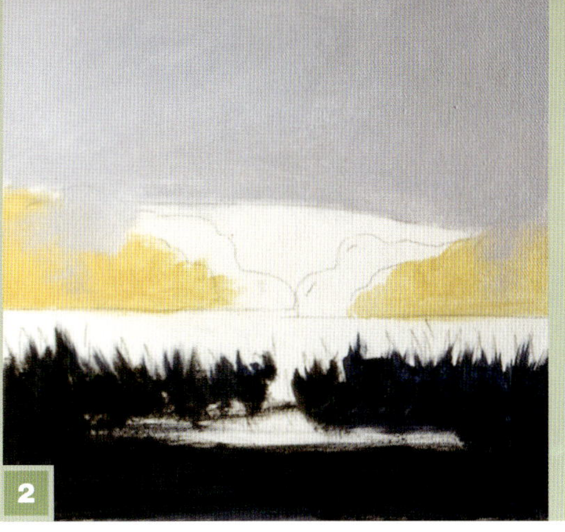

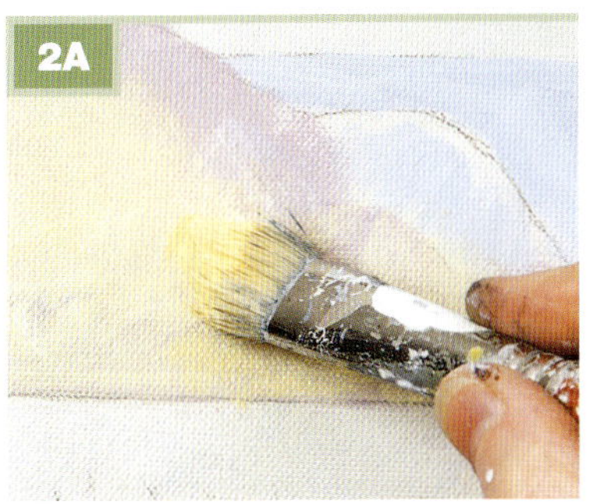

Allow the underlying color to seen.

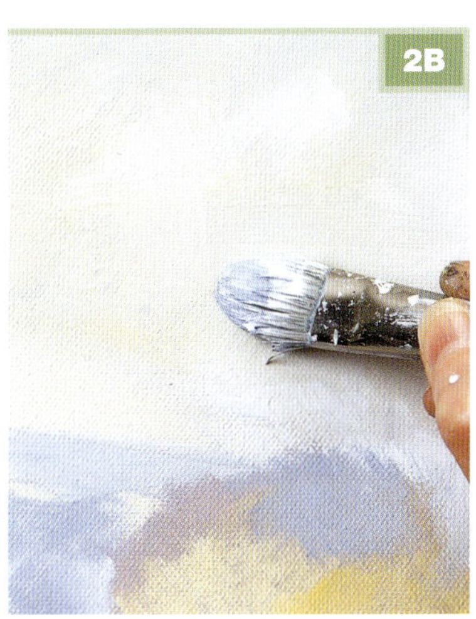

The sky is developed.

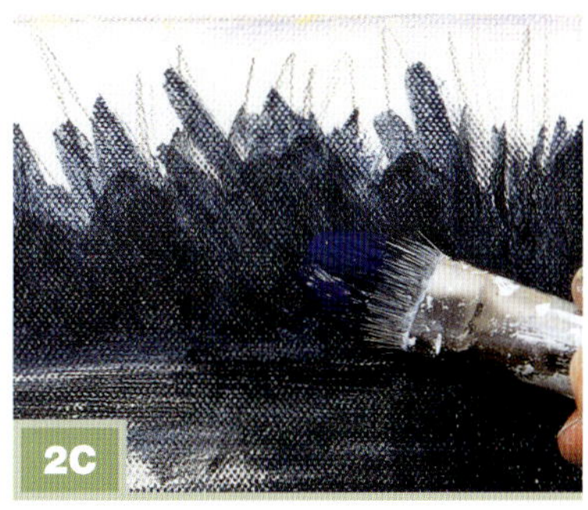

Apply paint to the reeds using loose, upward strokes.

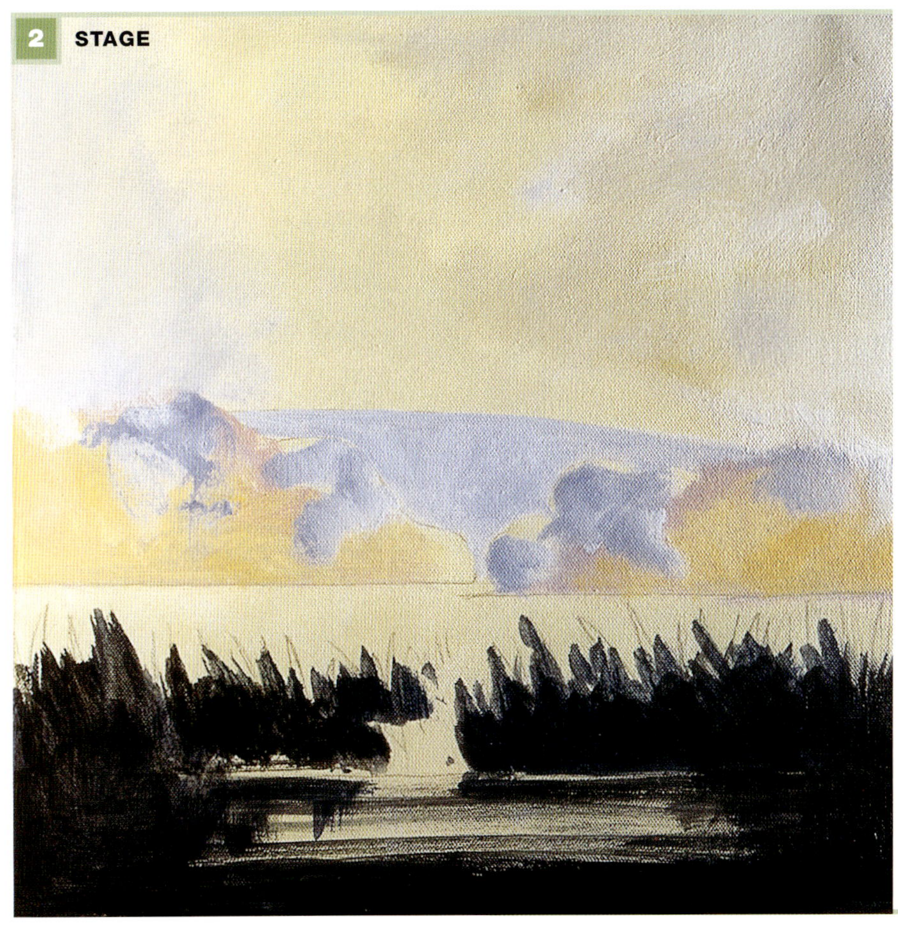

STAGE 2 Consolidating the color of the reeds makes them appear closer.

3 ASSESSING TONE

The addition of white to the river alters the tonal balance of the piece and makes the image appear lighter. This has the effect of making the far shore appear slightly darker and makes the bank of reeds in the foreground stand out.

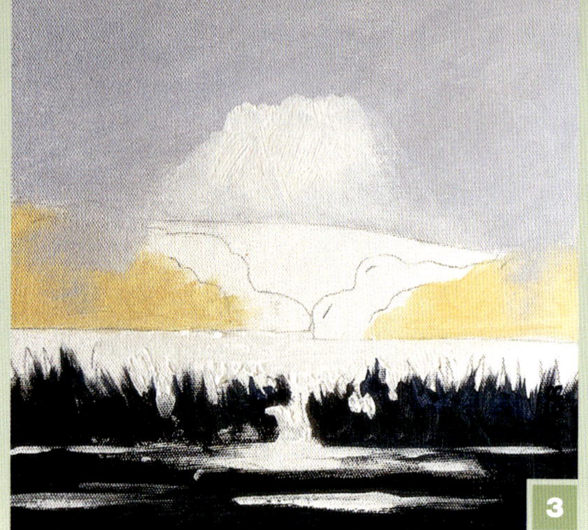

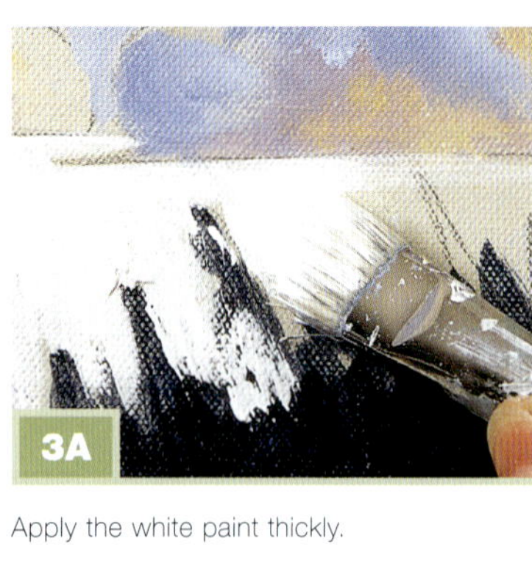

Apply the white paint thickly.

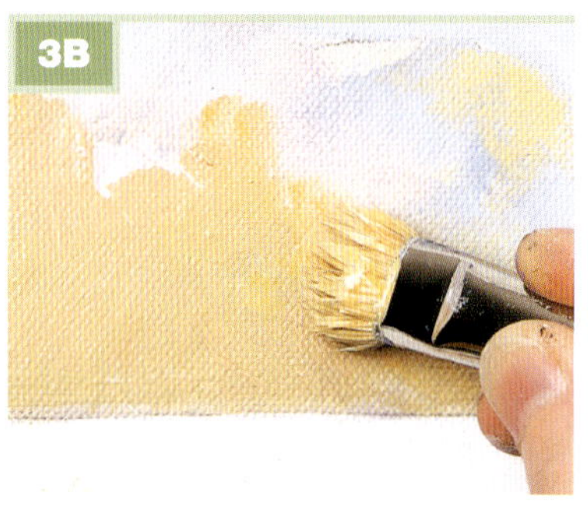

Mix yellow ochre and white, and apply it to the far bank of the river.

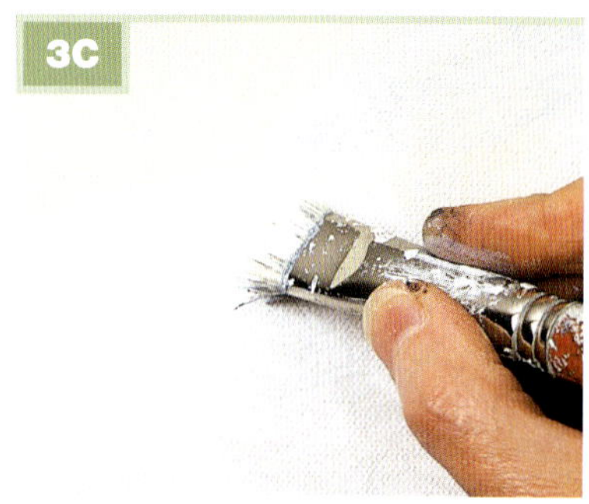

Use a looser, more fluid application of white to paint in the cloud.

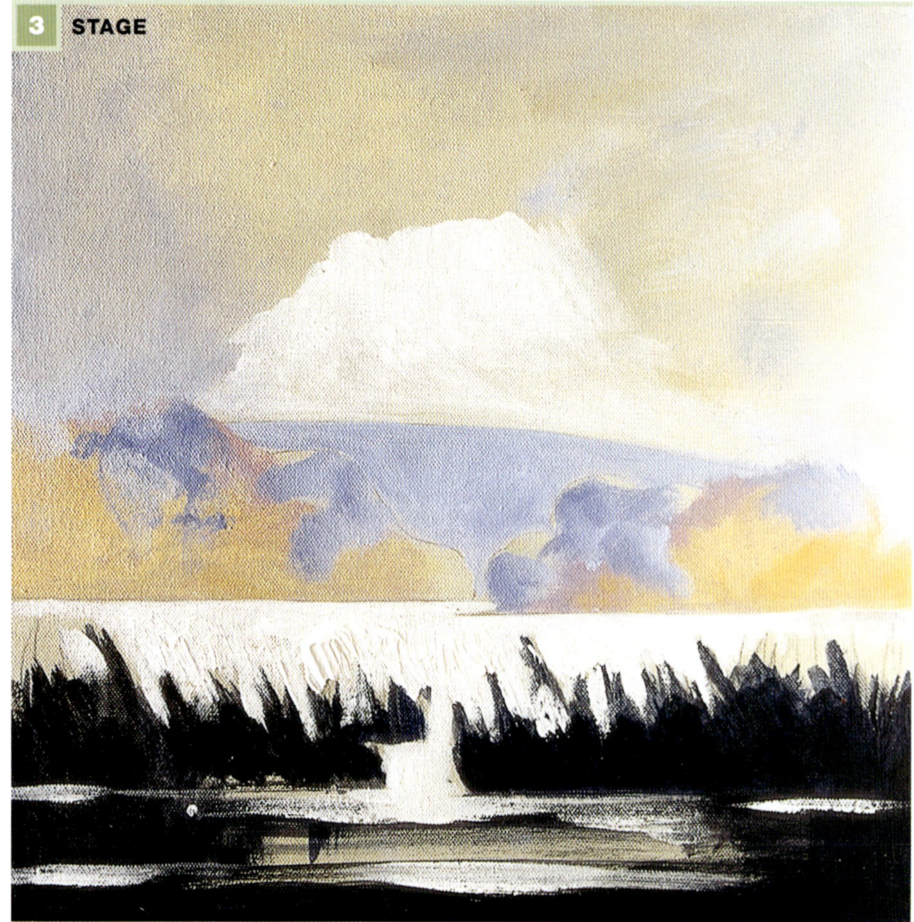

STAGE 3 The tonal balance has been altered.

4 ADDING COLOR

Warm ochre and pink mixes are introduced into the reed bank, which immediately pulls it forward and closer to the viewer, increasing the sense of space. The same ochre color is also dragged across the area of water between the reeds. The sky is then reworked using applications of Naples yellow, light blue-violet, and white mixes.

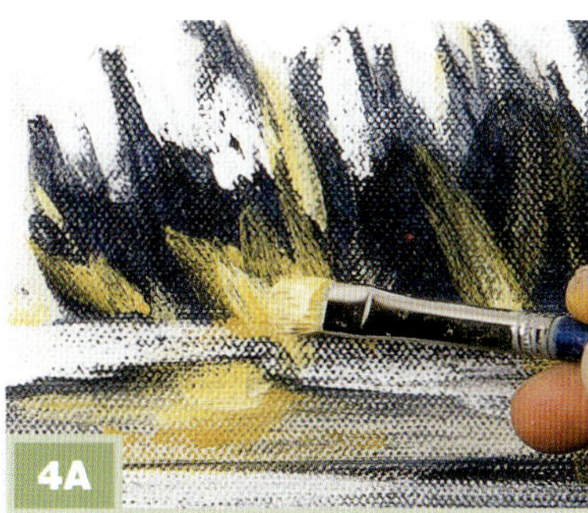

Use a small filbert to flick in color to the reeds.

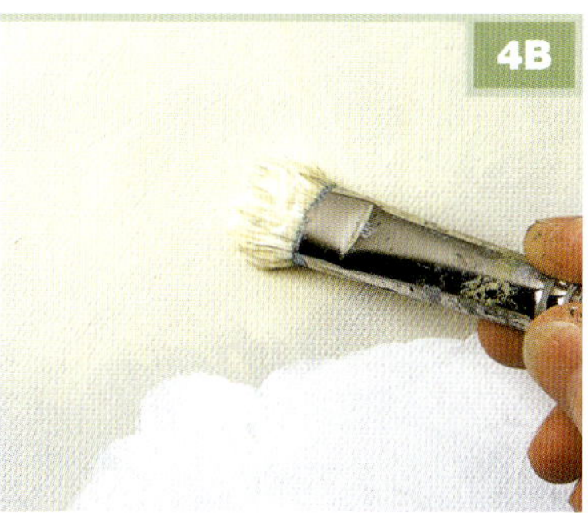

Work the sky colors into each other while they are still wet.

STAGE 4 Loose applications of color add interest to the reed bed.

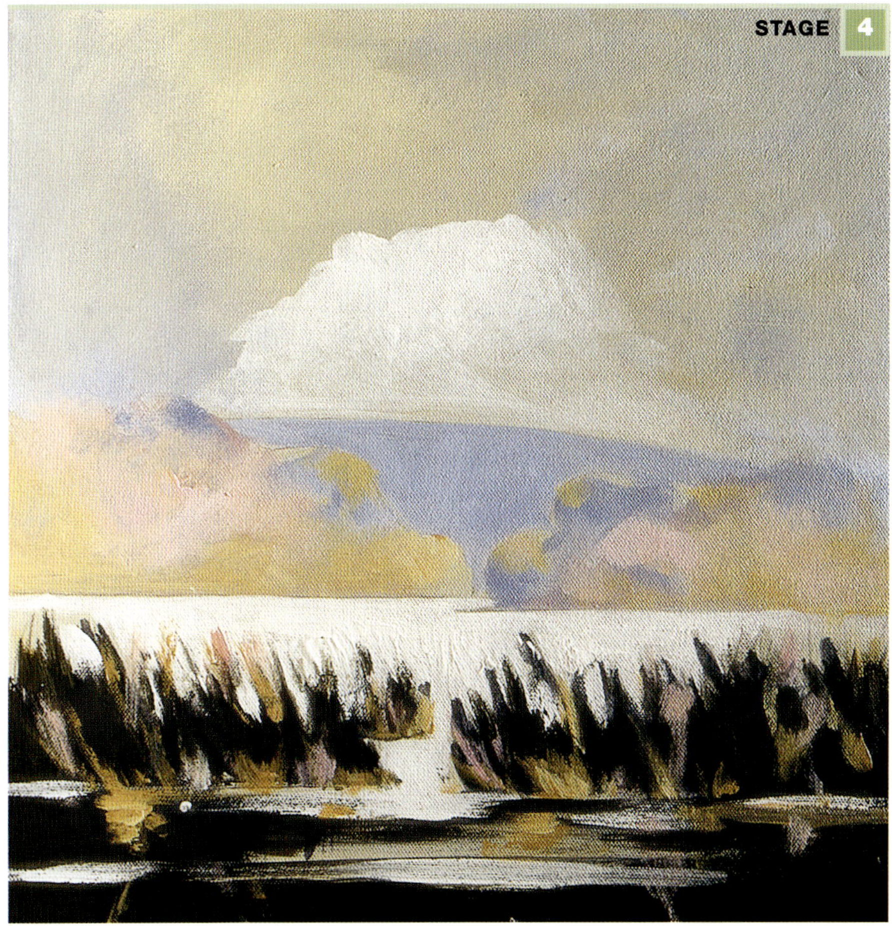

5

DEVELOPING THE FOREGROUND

The reeds are developed further with the application of more dark blue-green paint. Individual clumps of reeds are isolated using light ochre mixes and a pale pink made from medium magenta. Naples yellow and white mixes are worked over the trees on the far bank.

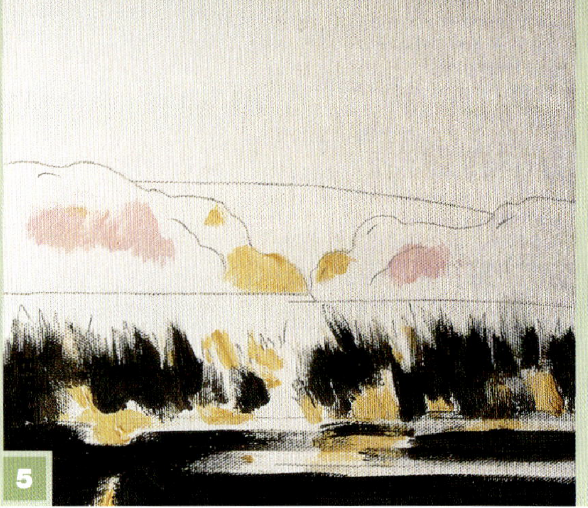

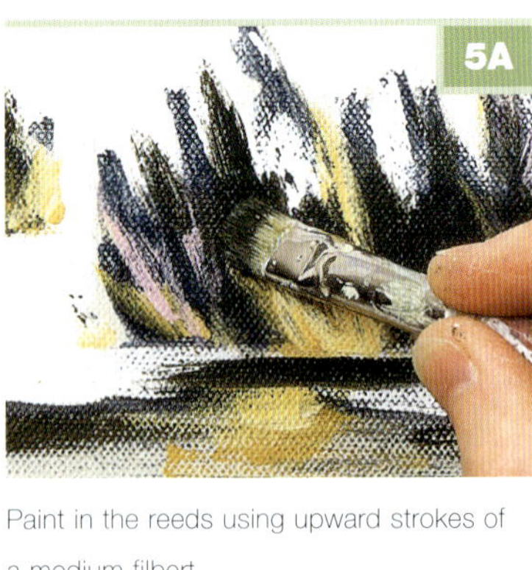

Paint in the reeds using upward strokes of a medium filbert.

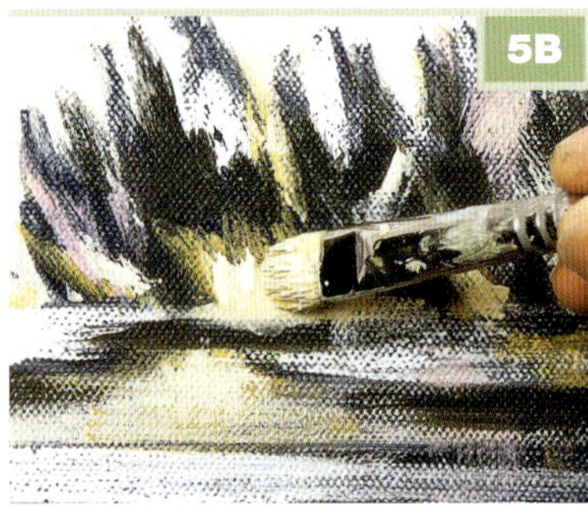

Light additions break up the dark mass.

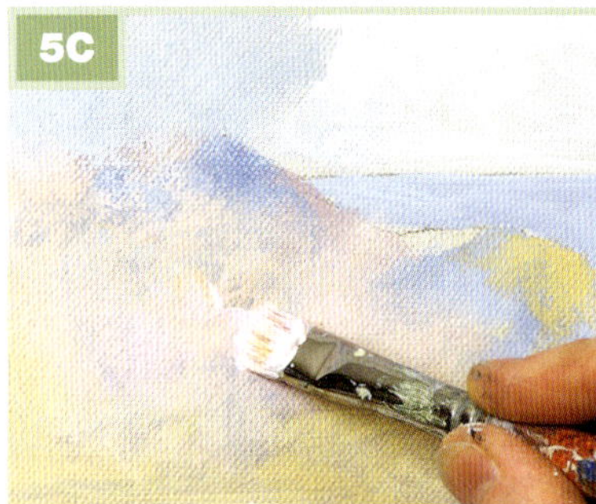

The colors in the distance are softened.

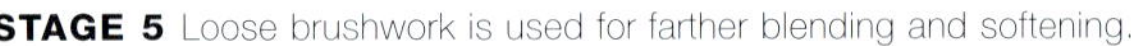

STAGE 5 Loose brushwork is used for farther blending and softening.

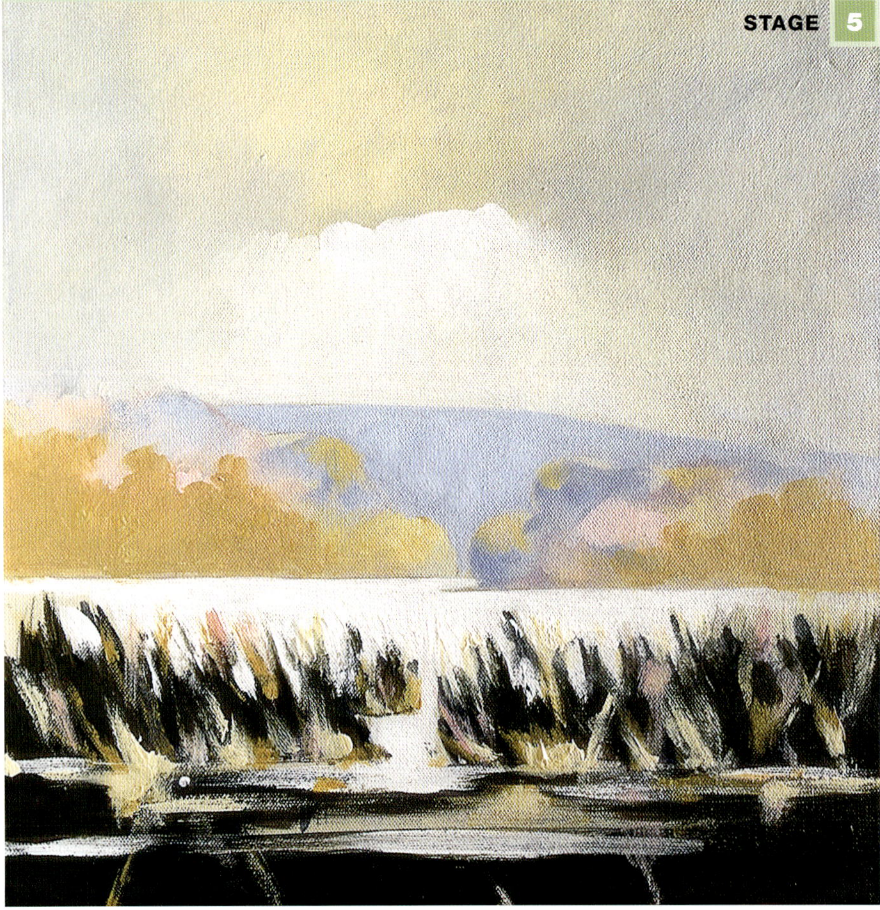

6 TWEAKING THE IMAGE

Finally, a halo of light is added to the trees in the distance to indicate where the soft, filtered light is catching the leaves. The reeds in the foreground are brought into sharp focus with a few precise brushmarks, and the introduction of a few dabs of warm pink and bright cadmium red pull this area firmly to the fore, and in so doing increases the feeling of space and distance.

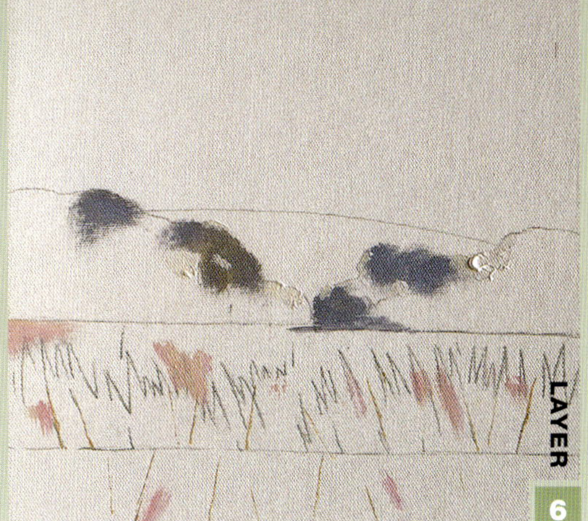

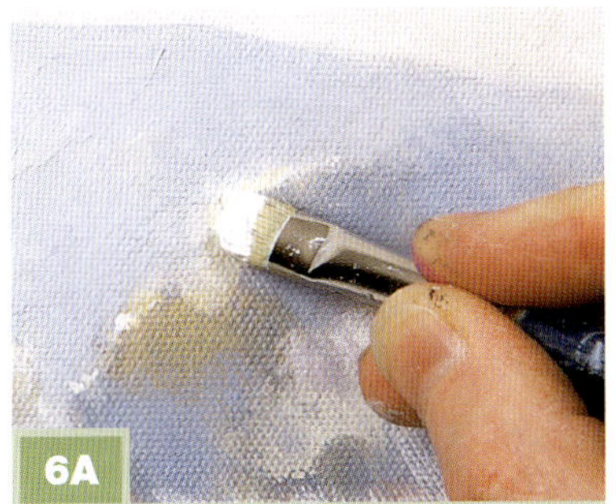

Stipple white paint onto the edge of the trees.

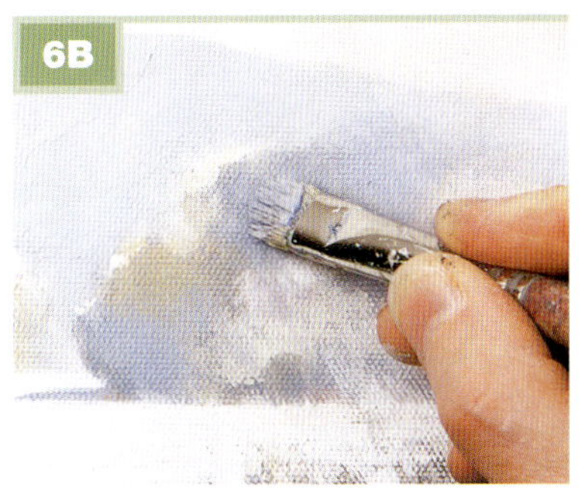

Introduce a little more blue into the tree canopy.

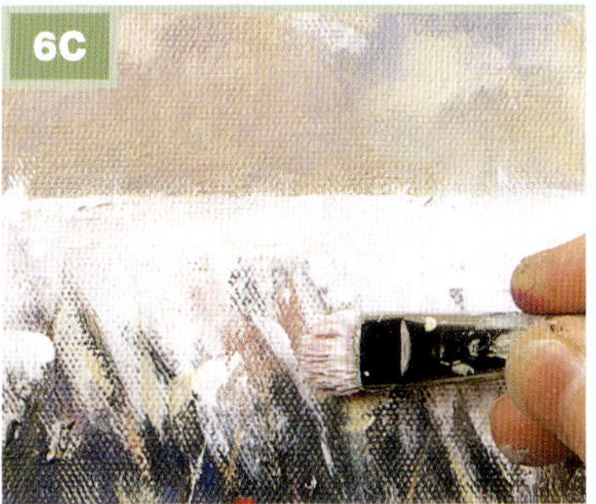

Add small dabs of pink and red.

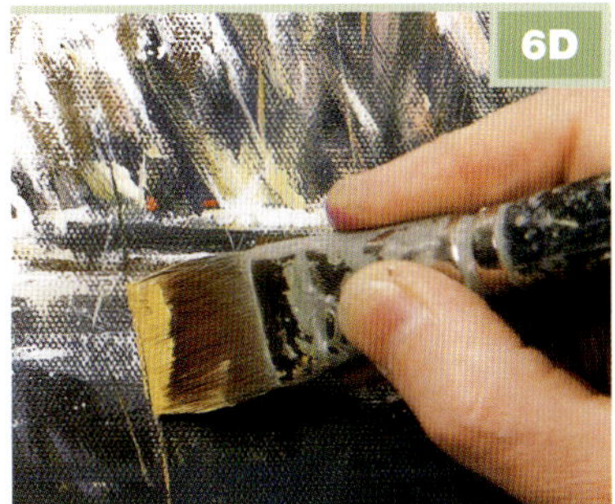

Use the very edge of a large, flat, soft-fiber brush to suggest individual reeds.

STAGE 6 A few carefully placed brushmarks bring the image to completion.

LIGHT TO DARK

by IAN SIDAWAY

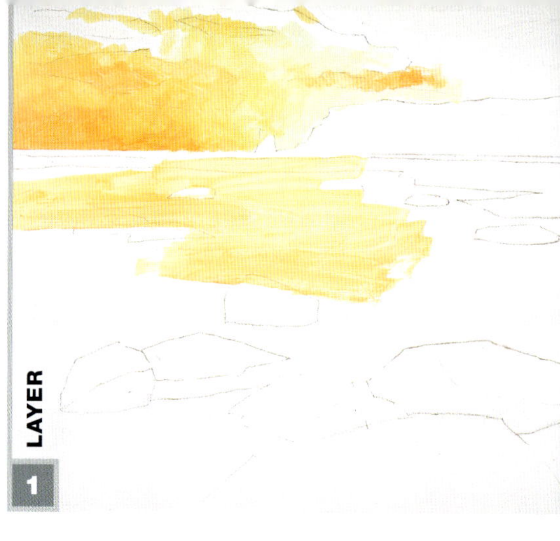

When mixed with water, acrylic paint becomes increasingly transparent and allows underlying images to show through. This transparency has its advantages because it allows the painter to retain intersecting lines and brushstrokes while building up color over them. As with watercolor, when using acrylic, work light to dark.

1 ESTABLISHING THE LIGHT SOURCE

The diffused sunlight originates from behind the dark solid coastline. Establish this light with a mix of lemon yellow and titanium white, applied with a ¼" (5 mm) flat soft-fiber acrylic brush. Gradually make the color more orange by adding acra crimson.

1A Paint the lightest areas first.

1B Paint outward from the light source, working the paint wet into wet.

1C Loosely apply a light orange mix to the sea.

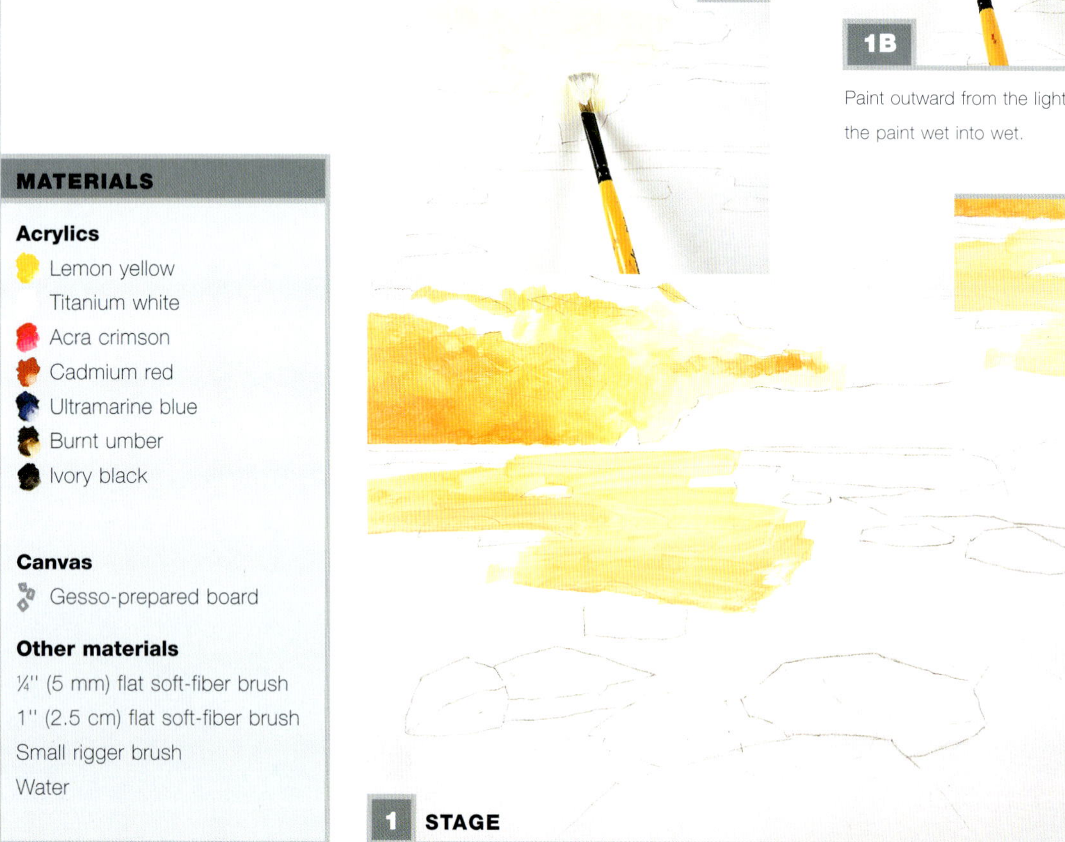

STAGE 1 These areas represent the lightest portion of the image.

MATERIALS

Acrylics

- Lemon yellow
- Titanium white
- Acra crimson
- Cadmium red
- Ultramarine blue
- Burnt umber
- Ivory black

Canvas

- Gesso-prepared board

Other materials

- ¼" (5 mm) flat soft-fiber brush
- 1" (2.5 cm) flat soft-fiber brush
- Small rigger brush
- Water

2 ADDING THE SKY AND THE SEA

Add cadmium red to the orange mix to darken it. Apply this mix to the edge of the clouds to make them appear illuminated from behind. Darken the mix with ultramarine blue, burnt umber, and acra red. Use this dull purple to establish the dark cloud mass. Paint the blue sky with a mix of ultramarine blue, titanium white, and a little lemon yellow.

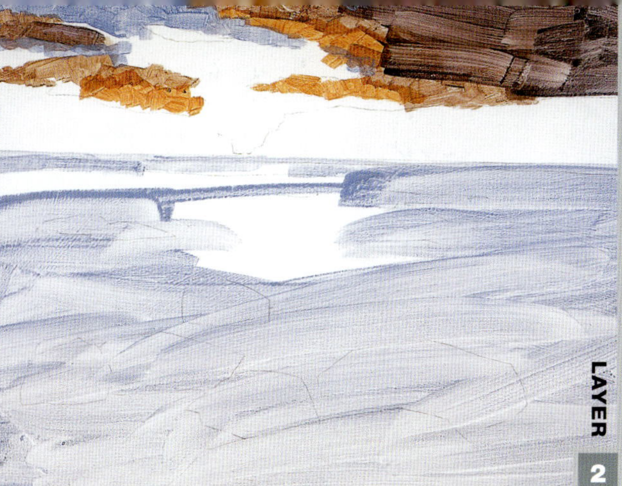

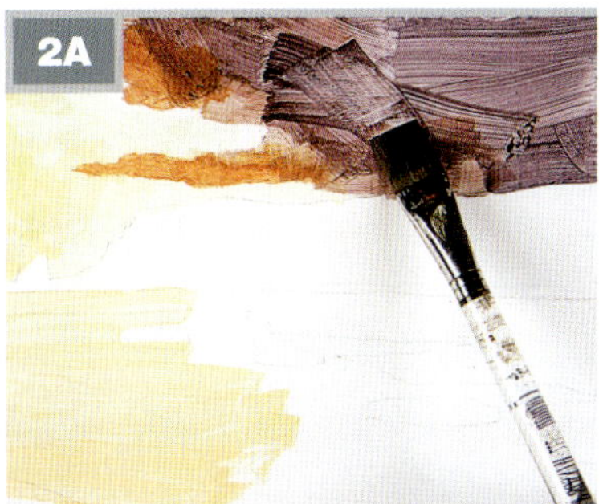

Paint in the cloud mass using the 1" (2.5 cm) flat brush.

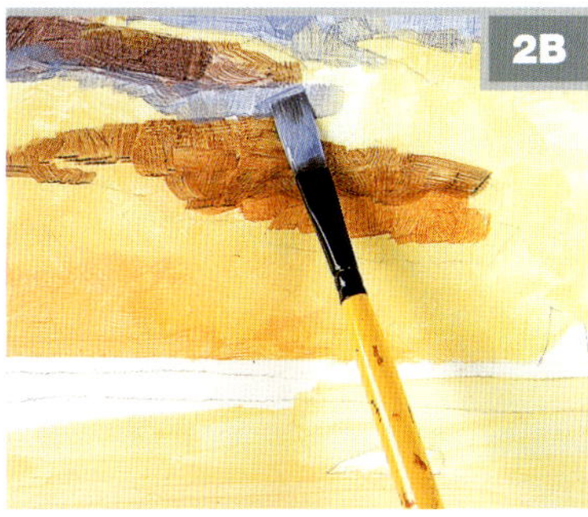

Work the blue paint carefully around the cloud shapes using the small flat brush.

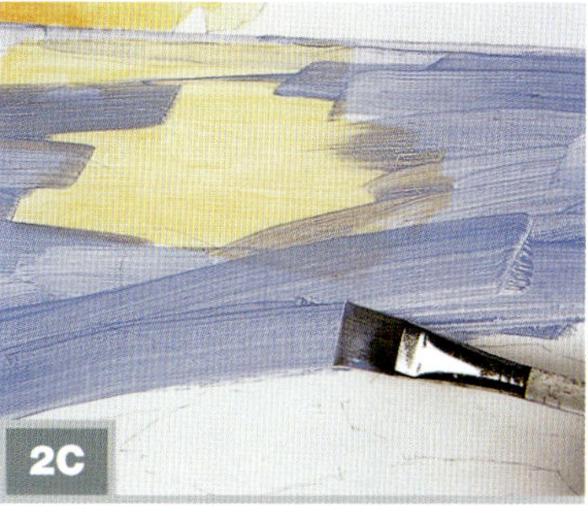

Loosely brush the color onto the sea area.

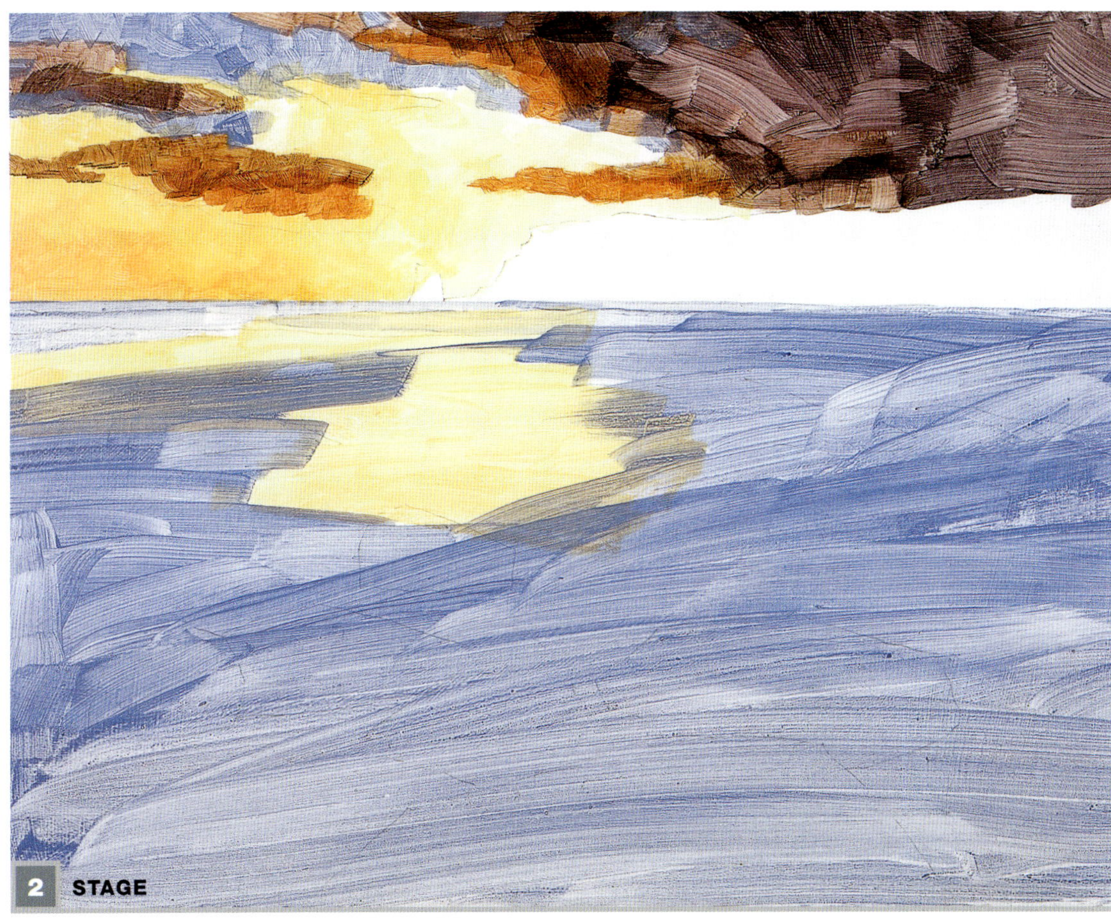

STAGE 2 The depth of the image increases.

3 DEVELOPING THE COLOR

Use the sky colors to create new mixes that unify and develop the existing colors in the clouds and the water.

LAYER 3

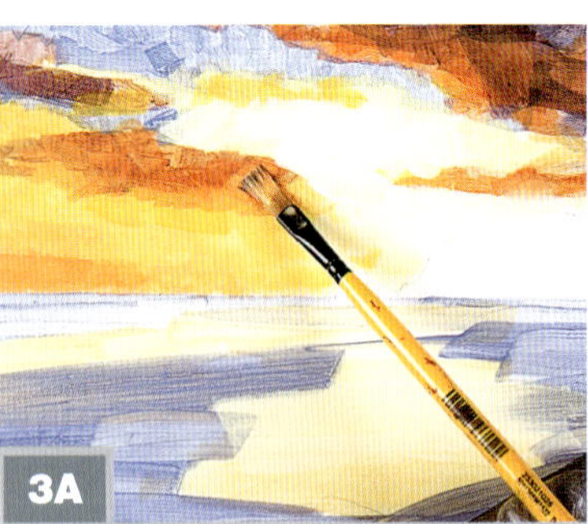

Consolidate the sky colors using multidirectional brushstrokes.

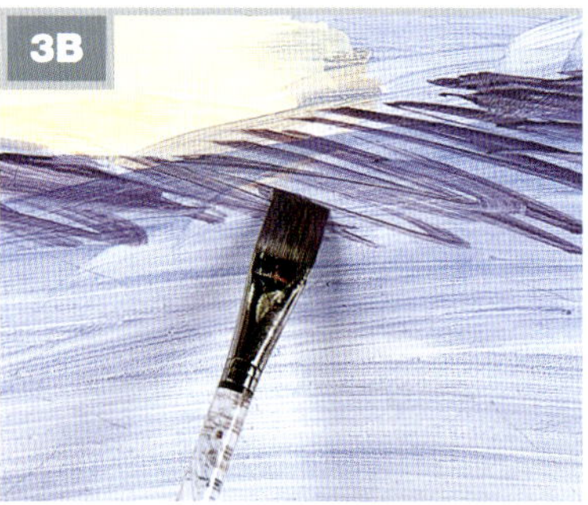

Use the edge of the larger brush to paint the small wave shapes.

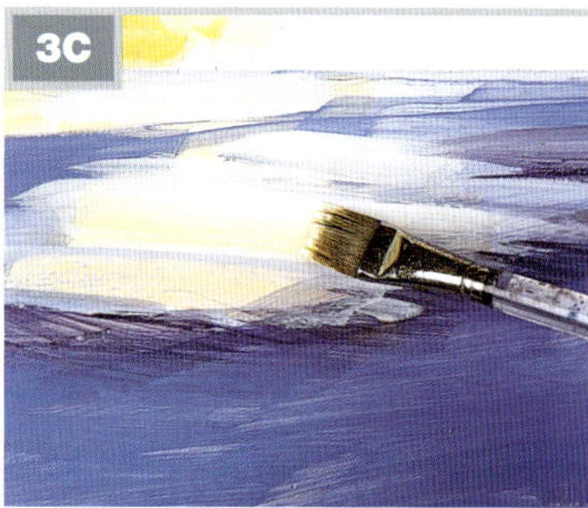

Rework the lighter colors using thin paint, worked wet into wet.

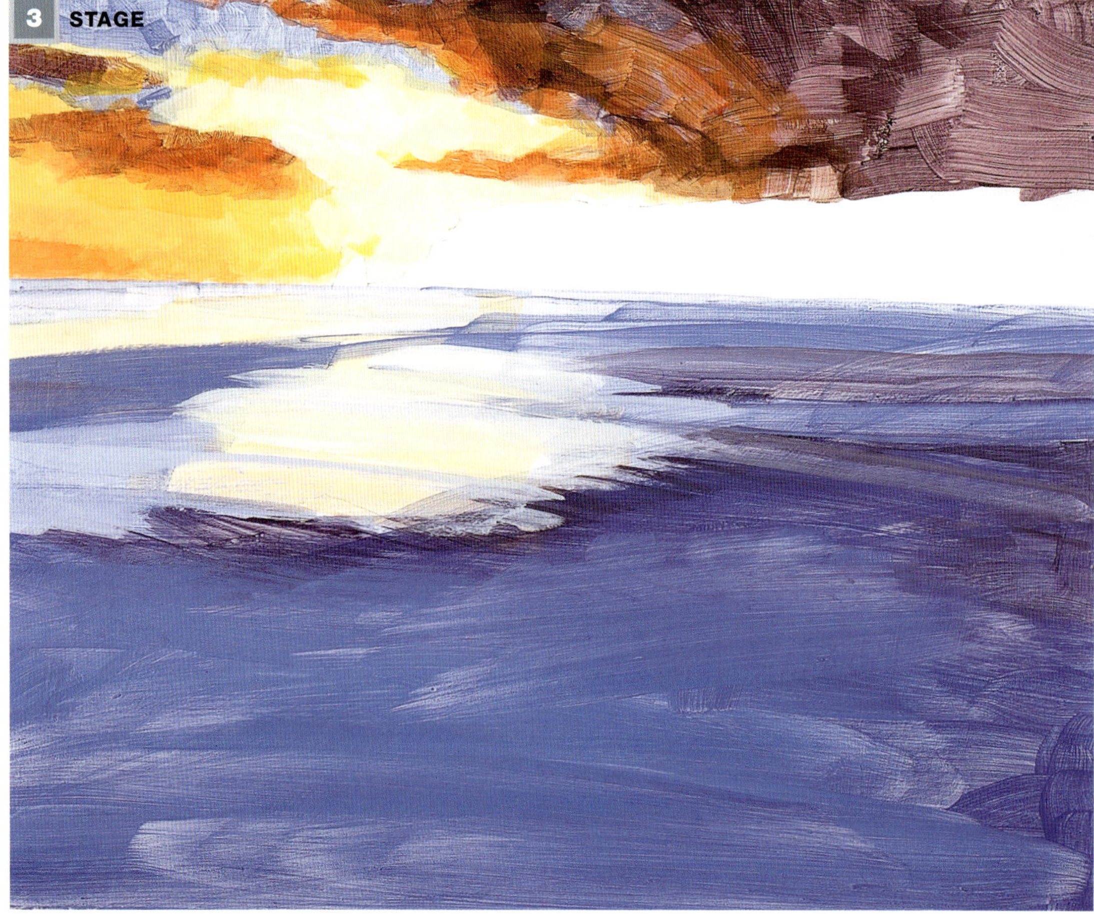

STAGE 3 The colors appear deeper and more intense.

4 POSITIONING THE ROCKS

Use a mix of ultramarine blue, acra crimson, and lemon yellow to develop the surface pattern on the sea. To emphasize the rocks, mix a blue-gray color from ivory black and ultramarine blue. Use the ¼" (5 mm) flat brush to paint in the dark bulk of each rock, and apply surface texture using the small rigger brush.

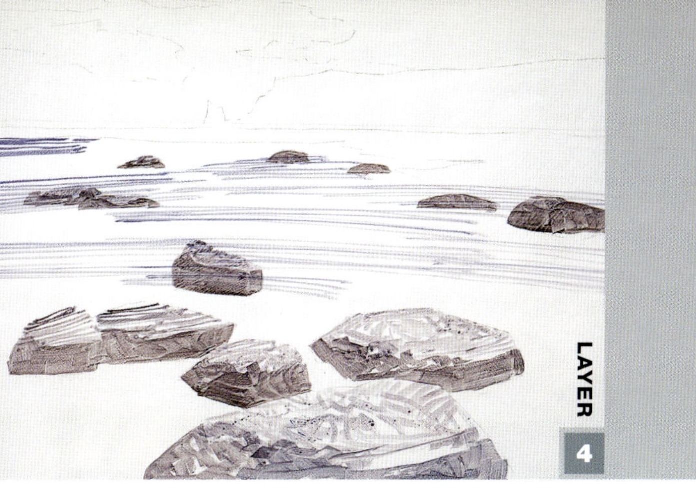

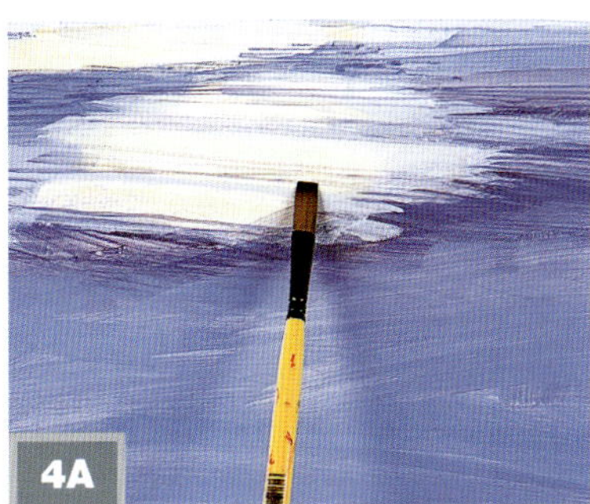

Use the end of the brush to make a series of thin lines.

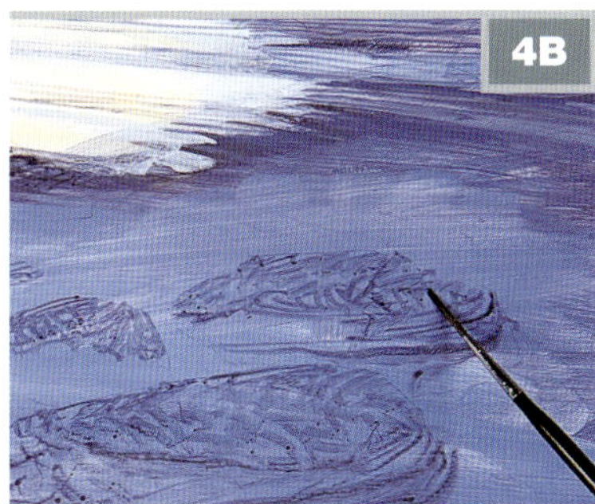

Use a thin mix to suggest surface texture.

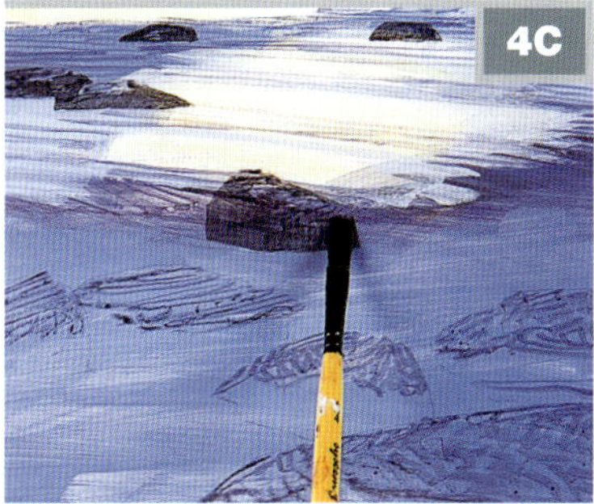

With the ¼" (5 mm) brush, apply short directional strokes to create shading.

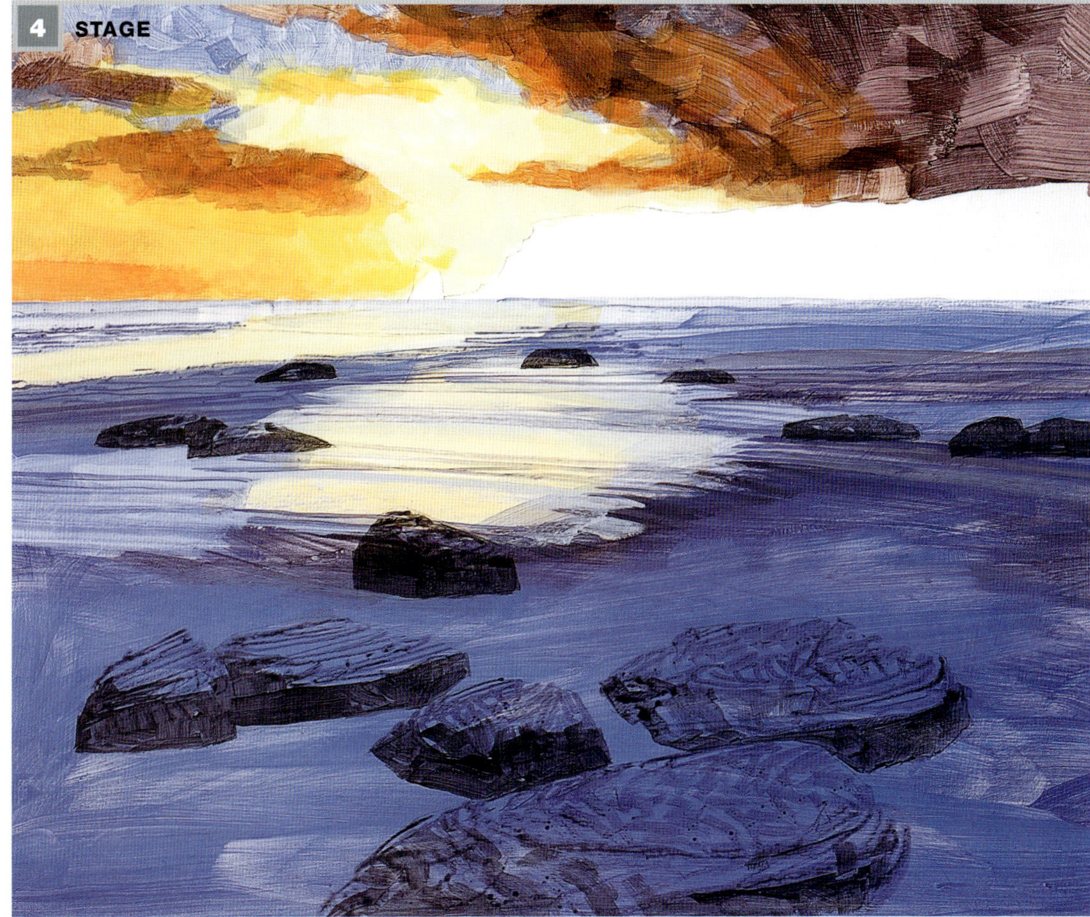

STAGE 4 The different-sized arrangement draws the eye to the horizon.

5 ADDING THE DARKS

Mix violet using ultramarine blue, acra crimson, and a little lemon yellow. Apply this mix to the coastline that runs across the top of the image. Darken the mix by adding more red, ultramarine blue, and a little ivory black. Use this new color to darken the exposed rocks in the middle distance. Add more ultramarine blue and ivory black to unify the color of the individual rocks scattered across the foreground.

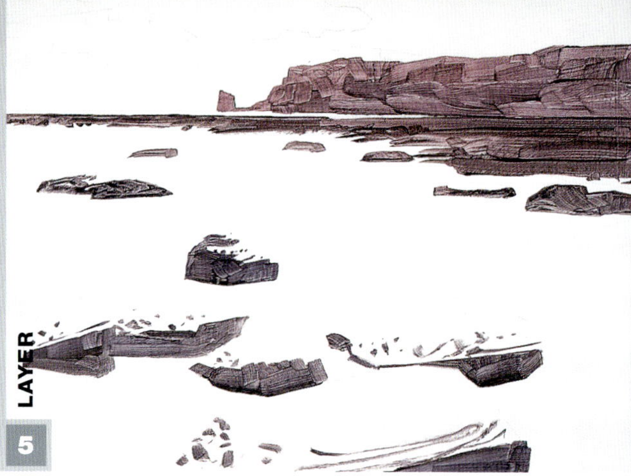

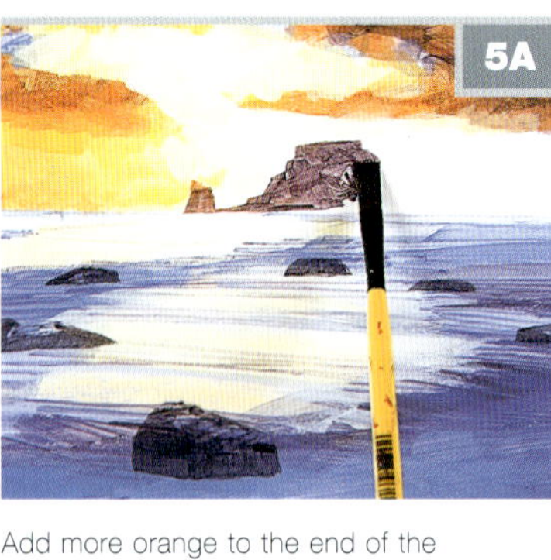

Add more orange to the end of the promontory.

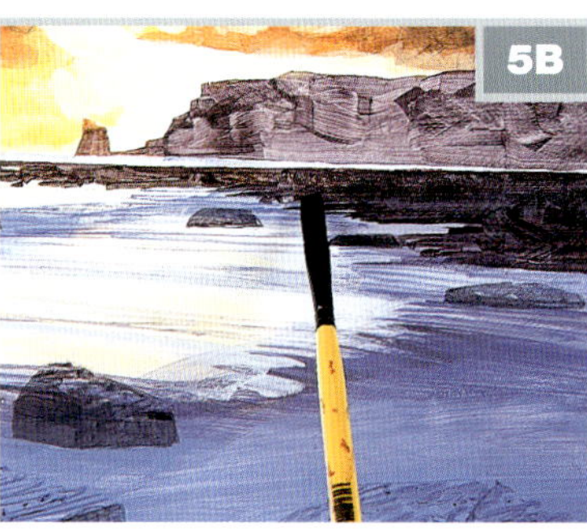

Use short brushstrokes and thinned paint to paint the band of dark rock.

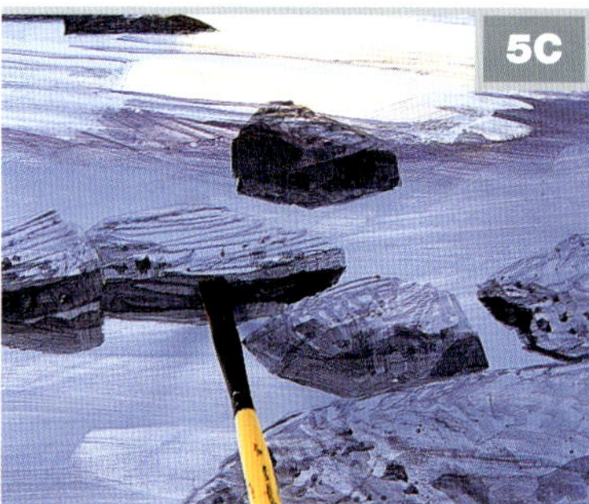

Add shadows beneath the rocks.

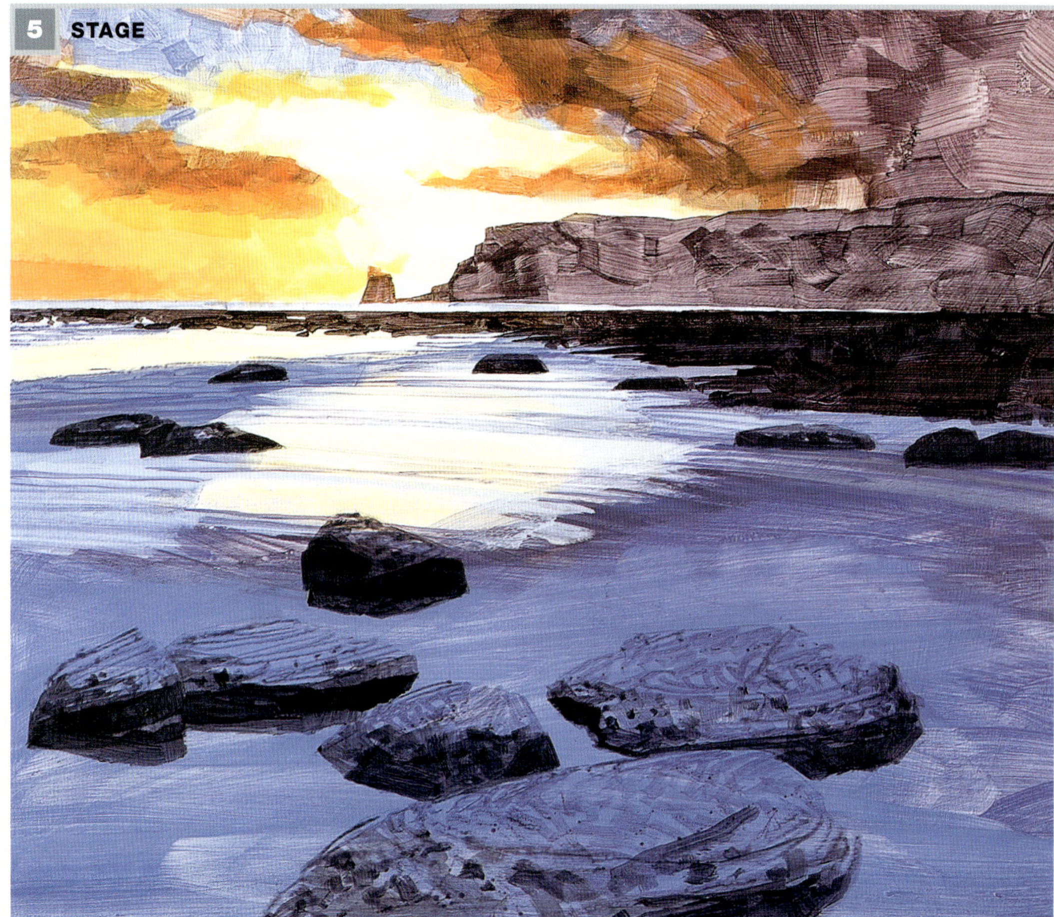

STAGE 5 The added dark sections emphasize the lighter areas.

6 THE FINAL ADJUSTMENTS

Unify the colors of the dark coastline with a combination of ultramarine blue and acra crimson. Use the same mixture for the rocky slab that breaks the surface of the water. Finally, lighten the sea around the rocks with a mix of ultramarine blue, a little lemon yellow, and titanium white.

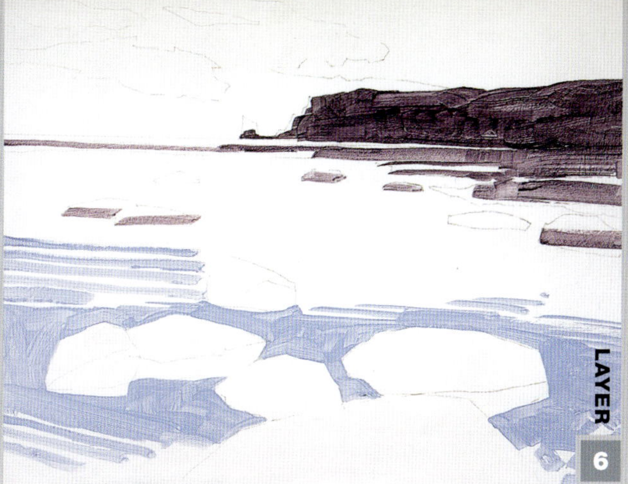

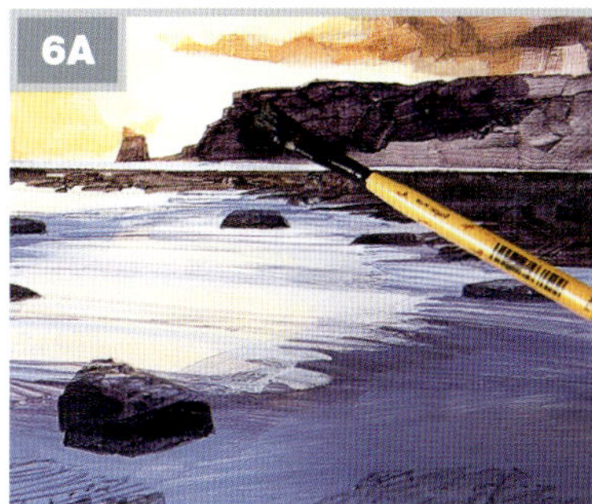

Leave the rock stack at the end of the promontory a deep orange.

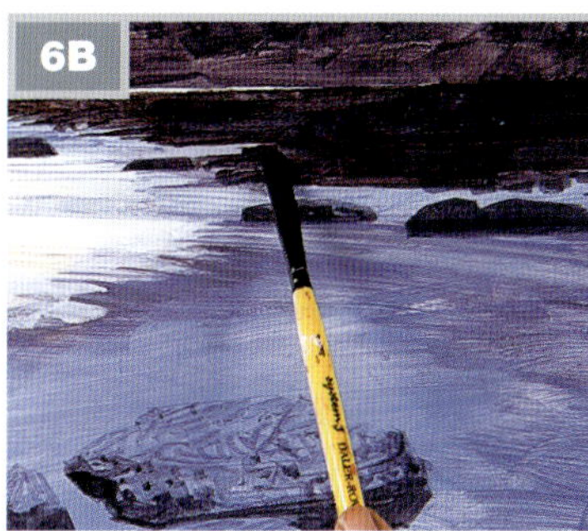

Break up the edge of the dark paint using short brushstrokes.

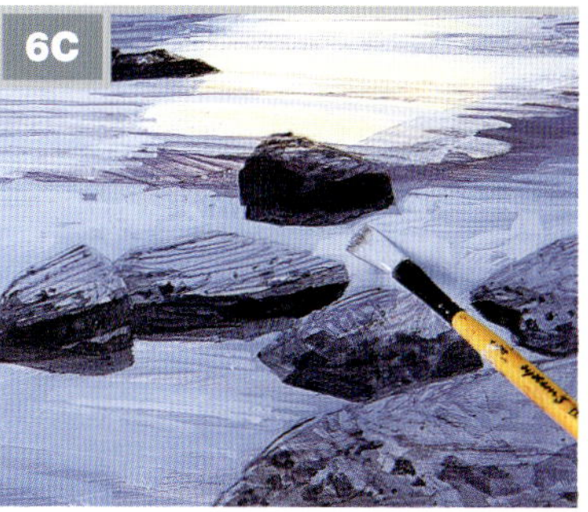

Use loose brushstrokes to suggest slight variations in sea color.

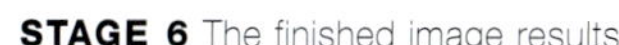
STAGE 6 The finished image results.

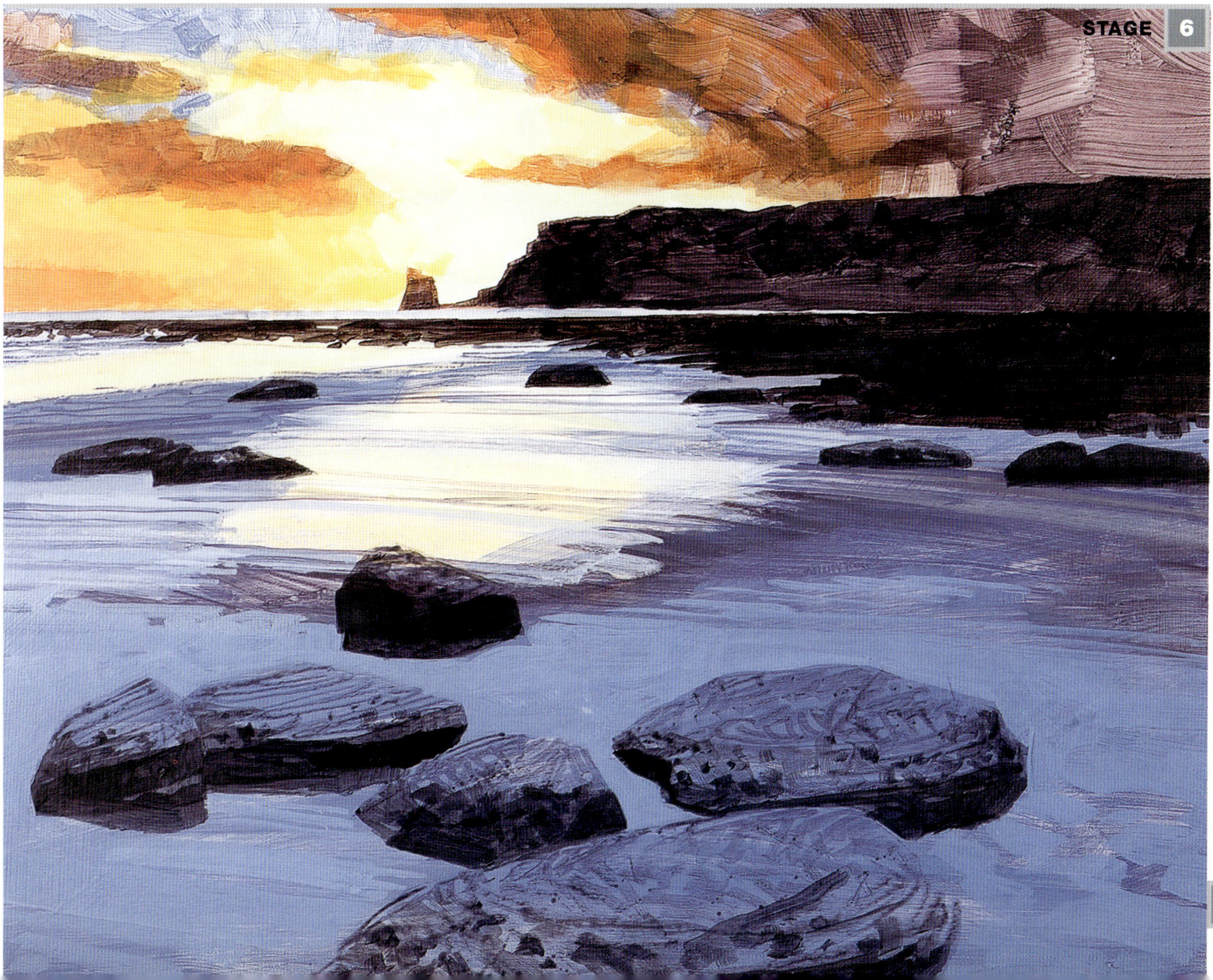

DESIGNING THE IMAGE USING TONE

by BOB BRANDT

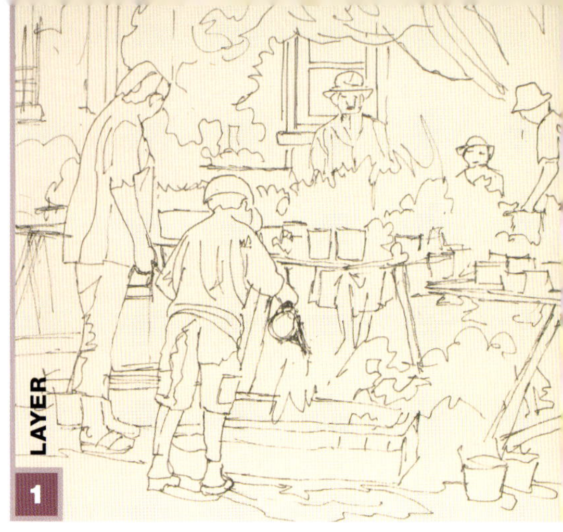

A grisaille is a tonal underpainting often used as a starting point for glazes. Here the artist has used a dark underpainting to help compose and design the space before committing himself to color. The underpainting not only indicates the design and the main areas of light and shade, but also adds depth to the subsequently applied colors.

1 ESTABLISHING THE DESIGN

A projector is used to reproduce the image onto the prepared painting support. Once the position and composition of the image is satisfactory, draw the main elements of the image using a fine-tip indellible marker.

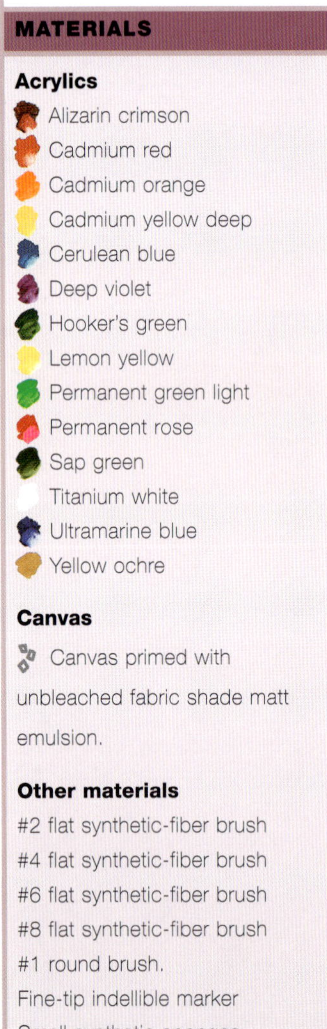

MATERIALS

Acrylics

- Alizarin crimson
- Cadmium red
- Cadmium orange
- Cadmium yellow deep
- Cerulean blue
- Deep violet
- Hooker's green
- Lemon yellow
- Permanent green light
- Permanent rose
- Sap green
- Titanium white
- Ultramarine blue
- Yellow ochre

Canvas

Canvas primed with unbleached fabric shade matt emulsion.

Other materials

#2 flat synthetic-fiber brush
#4 flat synthetic-fiber brush
#6 flat synthetic-fiber brush
#8 flat synthetic-fiber brush
#1 round brush.
Fine-tip indellible marker
Small synthetic sponges

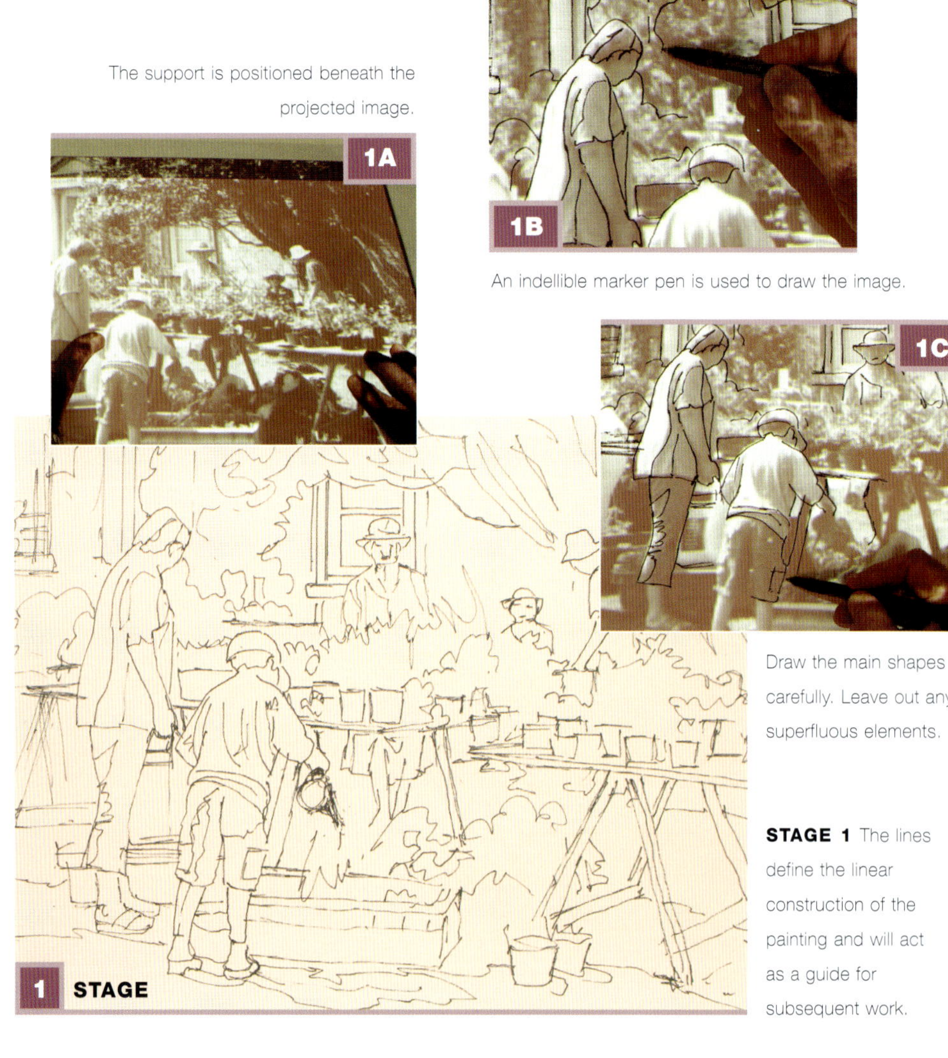

The support is positioned beneath the projected image.

An indellible marker pen is used to draw the image.

Draw the main shapes carefully. Leave out any superfluous elements.

STAGE 1 The lines define the linear construction of the painting and will act as a guide for subsequent work.

2 BUILDING THE BASIC TONAL STRUCTURE

Apply a deep violet color with a short #6 flat brush. Don't thin the paint with water, but keep the brush wet so that the paint spreads easily. Use the paint to establish the darker tonal passages seen in both the positive and negative shapes that make up the image.

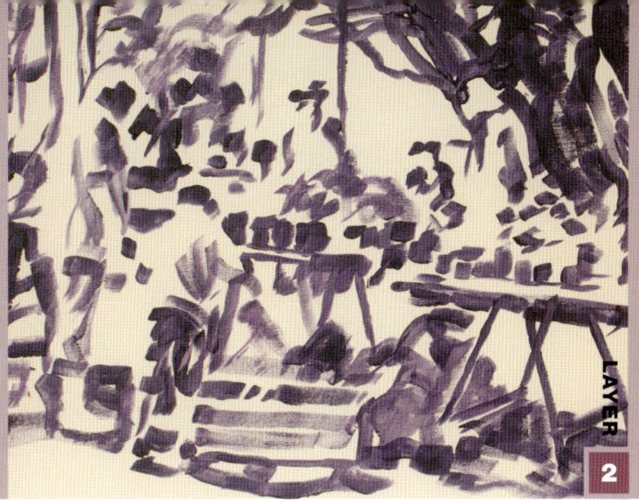

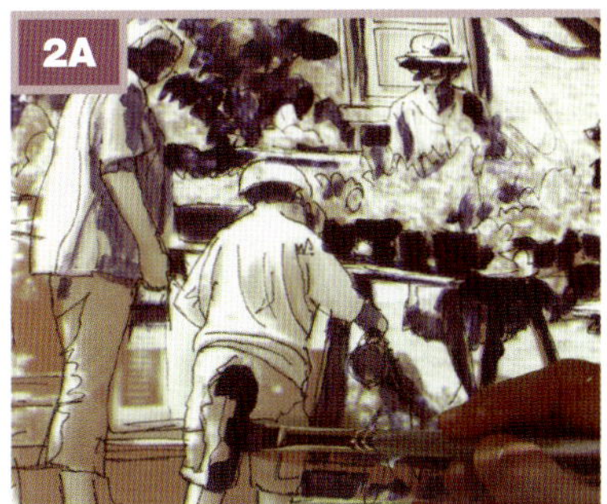

Use the projected image as a guide.

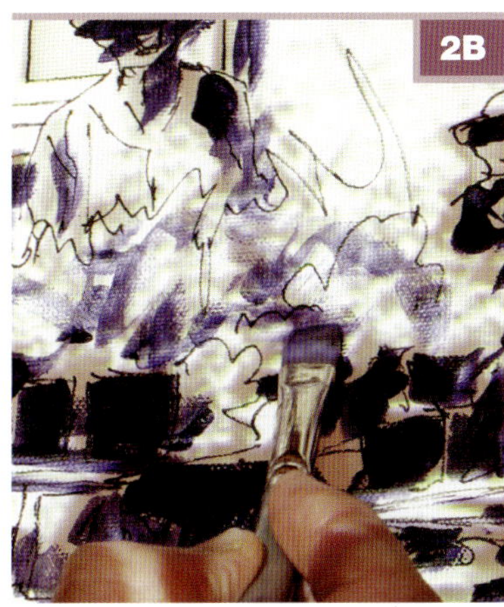

Less paint on the brush results in a lighter tone.

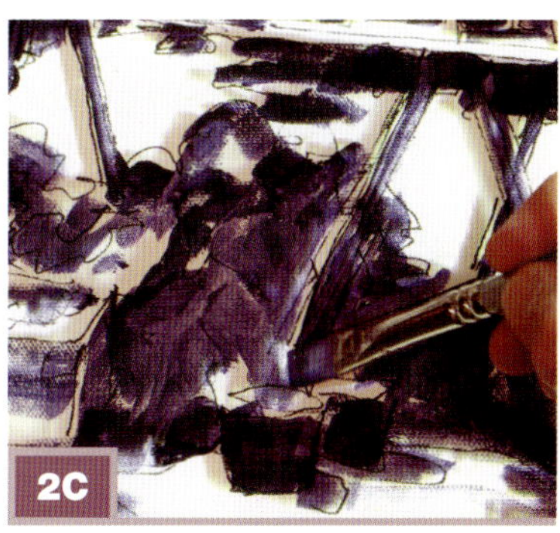

Keep the brushwork relatively loose.

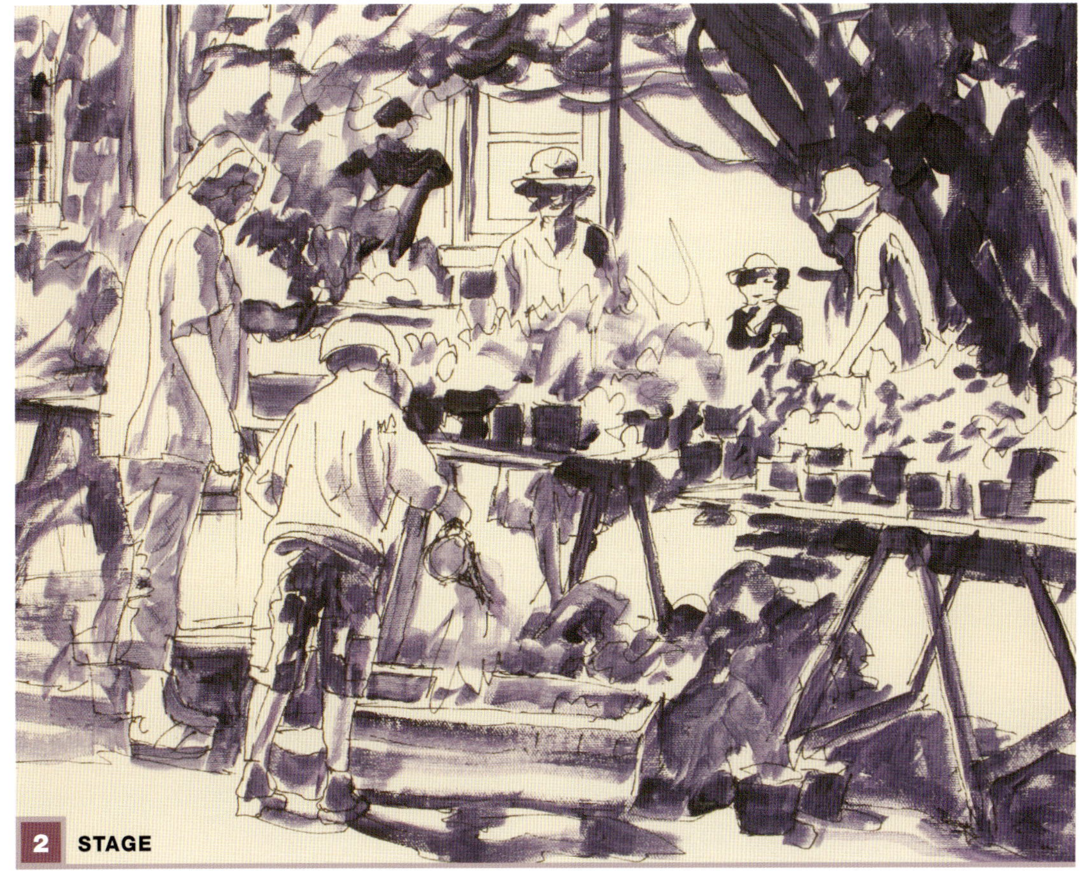

STAGE 2 The underlying tonal structure of the image becomes evident.

3 ESTABLISHING THE MAIN AREAS OF COLOR

Establish the main areas of color using small sponges. Also use the sponges to wipe away color if it is too bright. Apply a mix of permanent rose and cadmium orange to the top half of the image. Use lemon yellow and sap green for the lower half. Once the paint is dry, use the #6 flat brush to apply cerulean blue. Make a flesh color using cadmium red, cadmium yellow, and yellow ochre.

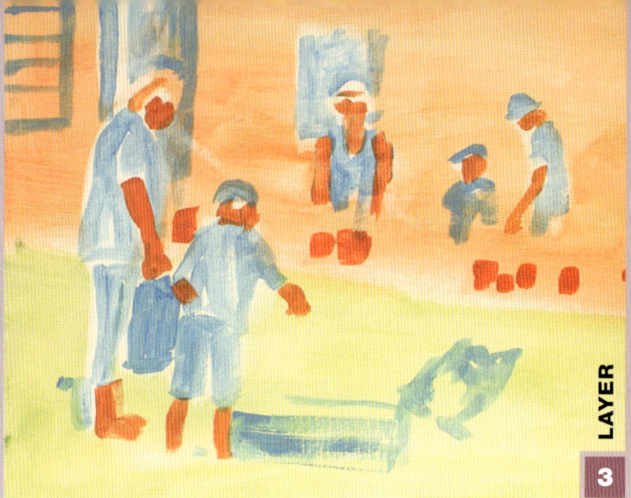

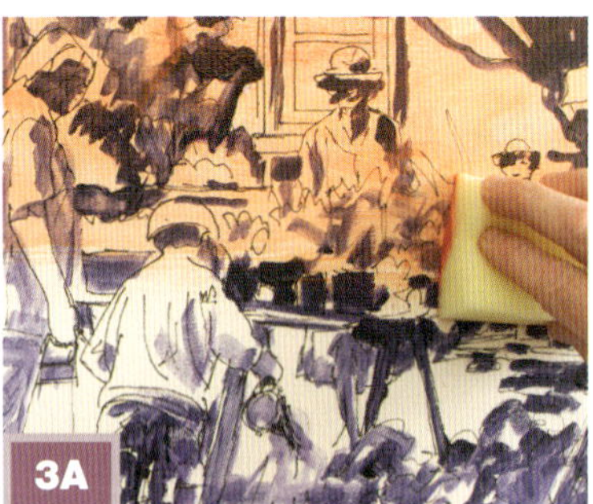

Apply the paint using a sponge.

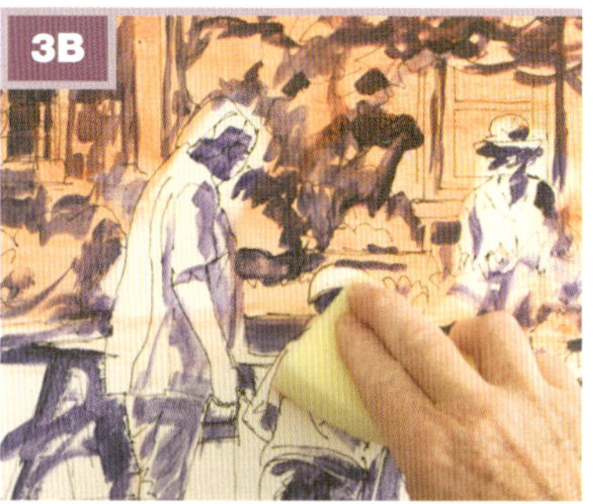

Use a sponge to remove color while the paint is still wet.

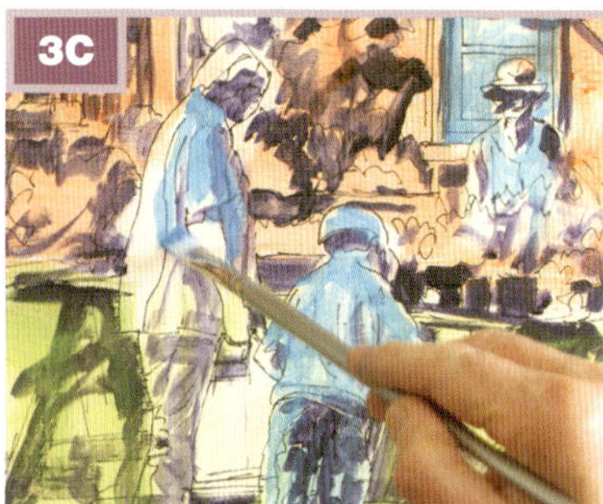

Use a brush to apply paint to precise areas.

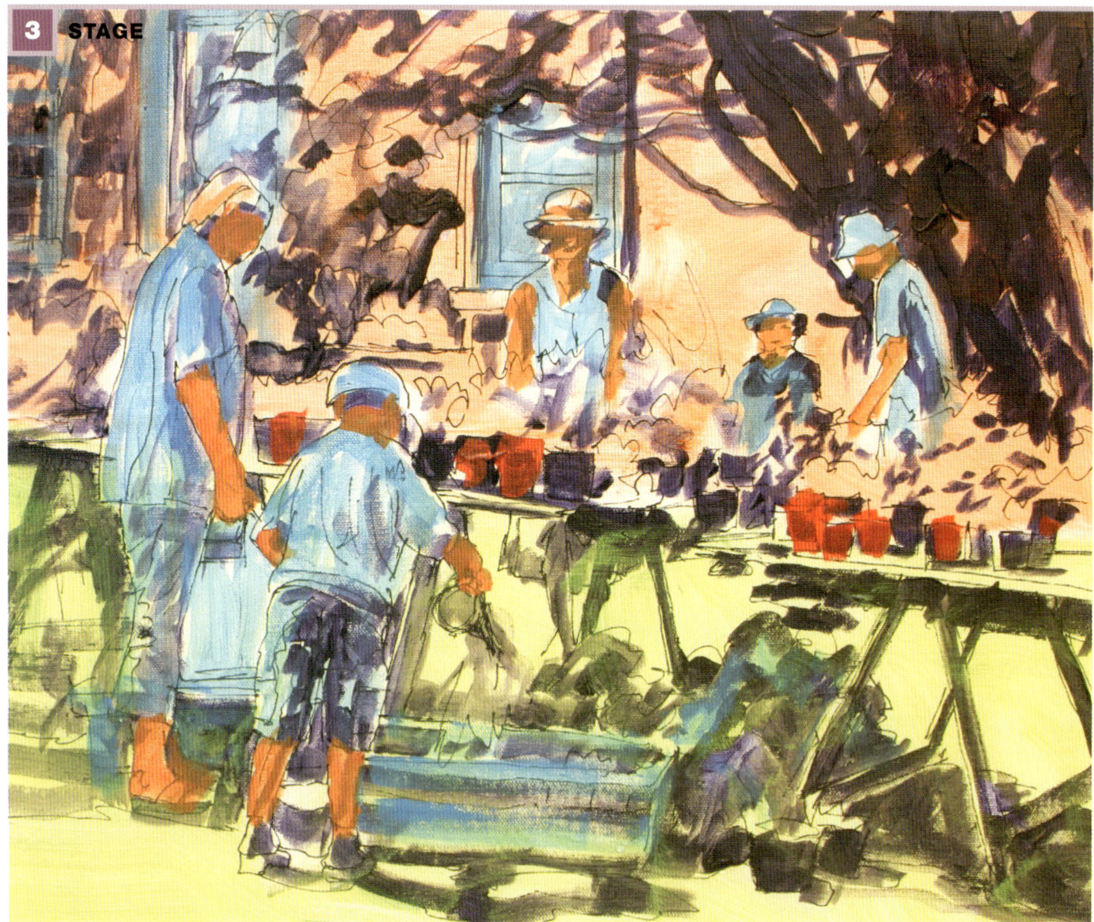

STAGE 3 The overall color and mood of the work is quickly established.

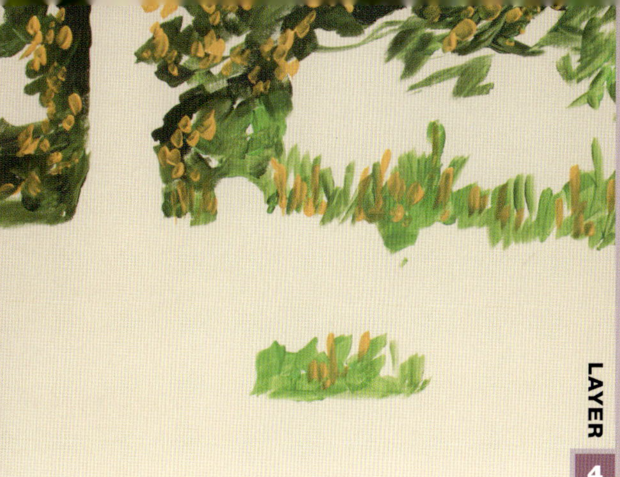

4 DEVELOPING THE COLOR STRUCTURE

Loosely apply mixtures of sap green, permanent green light, and Hooker's green with a #8 flat brush. Use the #6 flat brush to work cadmium yellow deep into the greens while they are still wet.

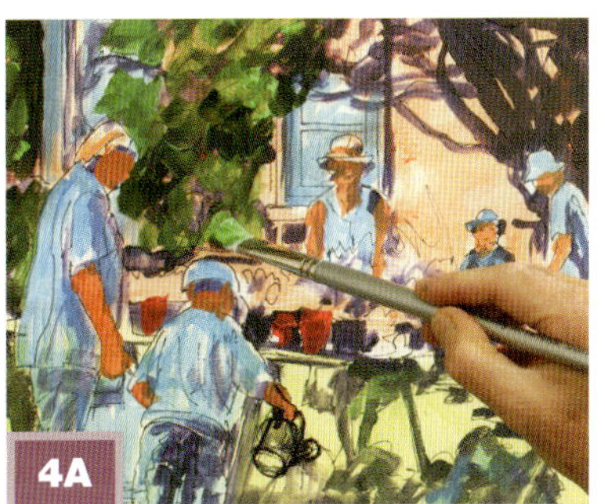

Apply the paint using direct brushwork.

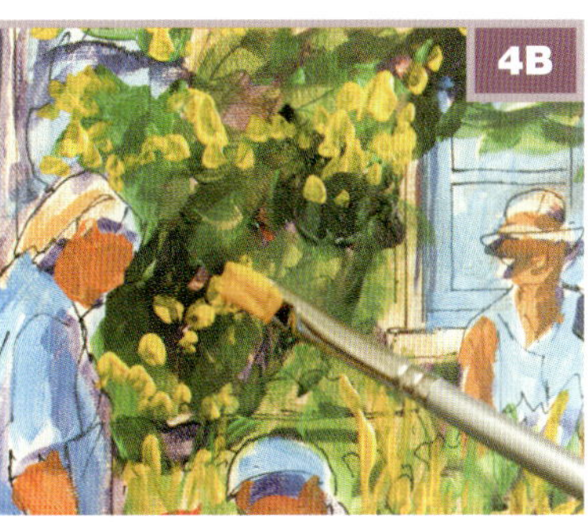

Apply small dabs of yellow into the greens.

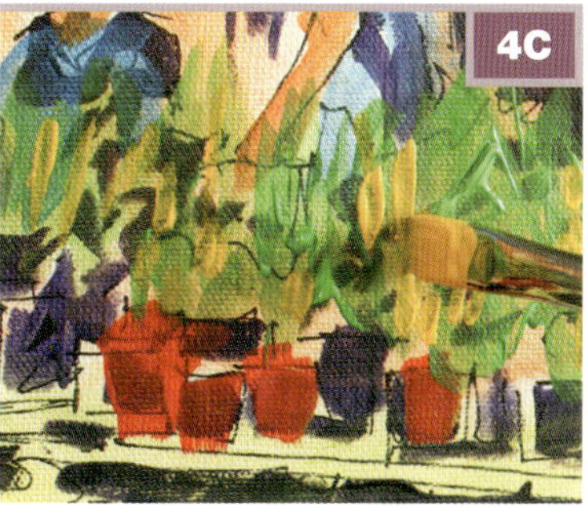

Modify the plants on the table.

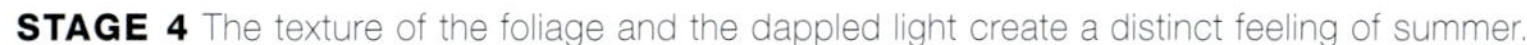

STAGE 4 The texture of the foliage and the dappled light create a distinct feeling of summer.

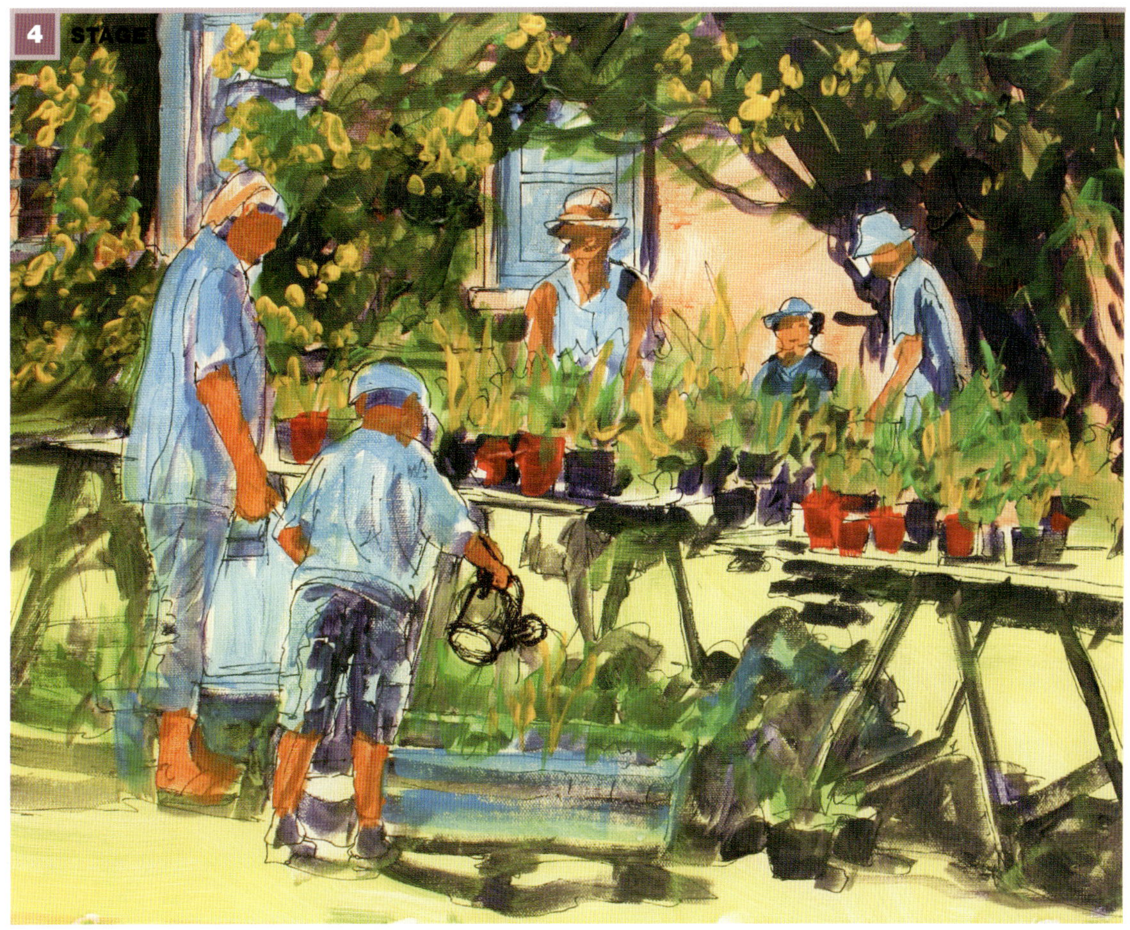

5 DEFINING THE DARK DETAILS

Adding the darker details results in an increase of tonal contrast. Make the dark using mixtures of ultramarine blue, alizarin crimson, and Hooker's green. Rather than mixing the colors on the palette, pick up the colors on the brush and work them directly onto the canvas. This results in a subtle "broken color" effect, with cooler mixes in the background foliage.

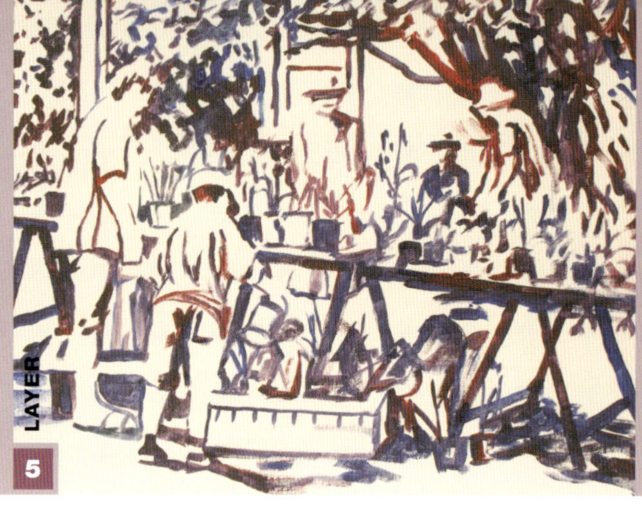

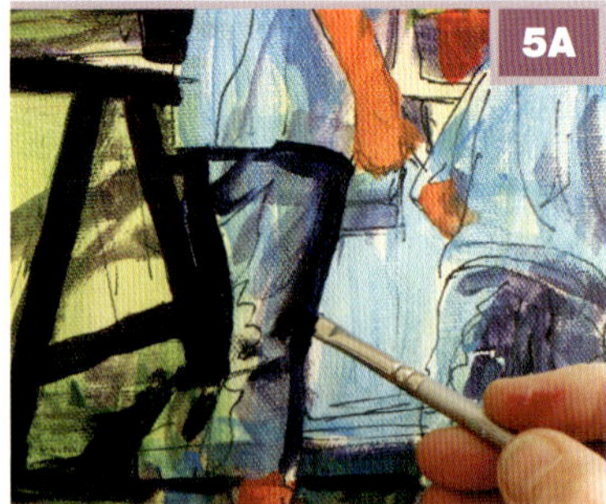

Use a #2 brush for making precise marks.

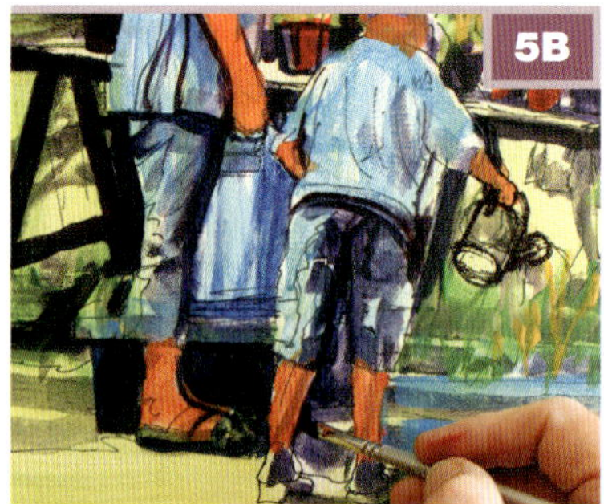

Define the lighter foreground shapes by painting the darker (negative) shapes around them.

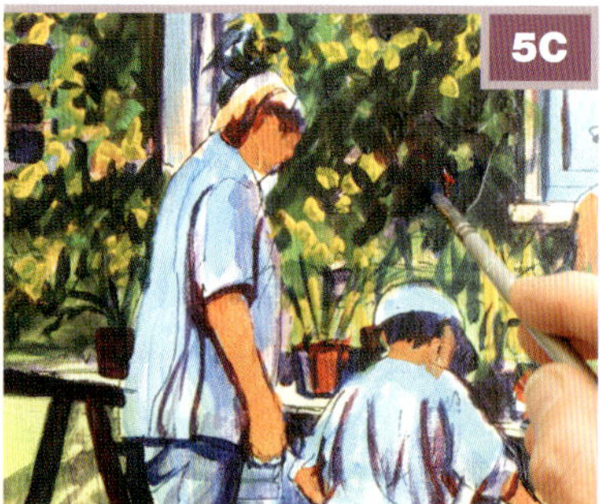

Use cooler mixes in the foliage.

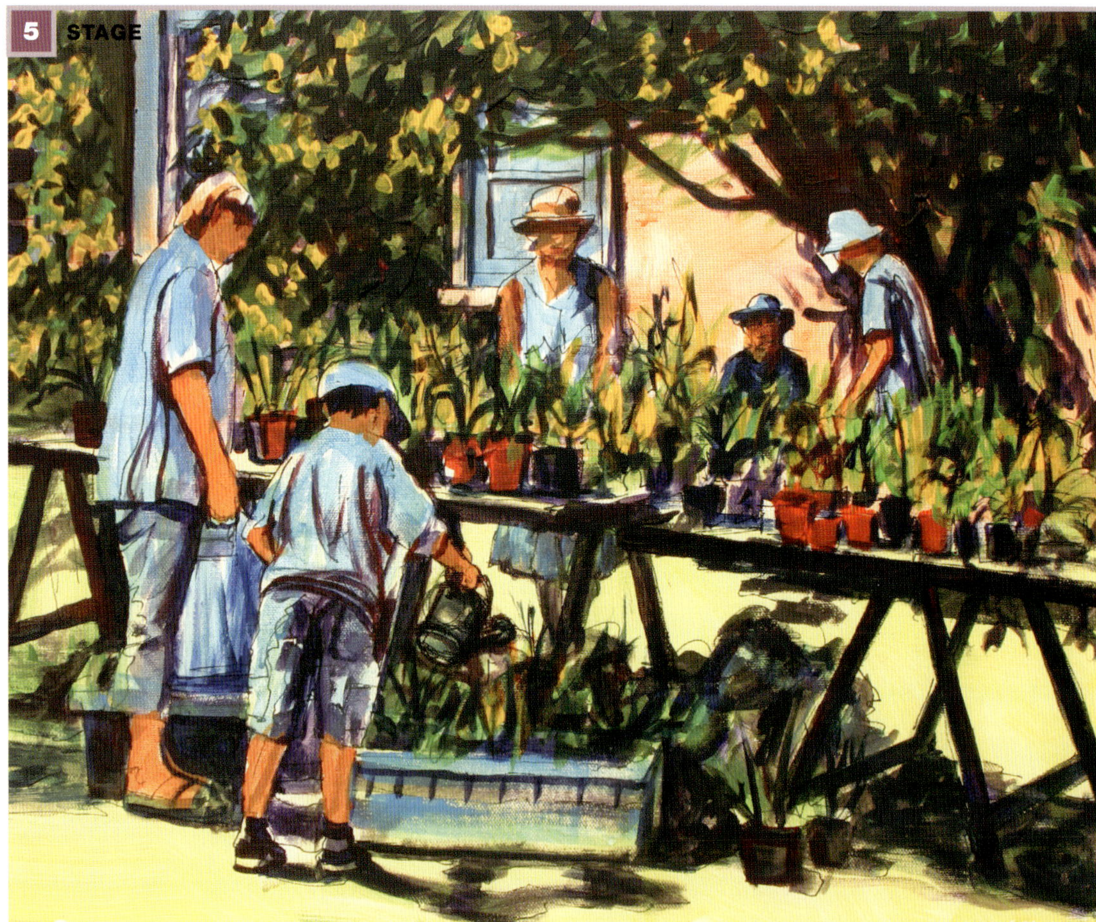

STAGE 5 The loose brushwork is maintained, increasing the effects of dappled light.

6 ADJUSTING THE COLOR AND ADDING HIGHLIGHTS

Base the highlights of the buildings and clothing on tints made using titanium white, permanent rose, and cobalt blue. Yellow ochre, cadmium orange, and cadmium red make up the stonework. Cerulean blue, yellow ochre, and permanent rose create the grays for the white clothing. The plant boxes are cobalt blue. Lemon yellow, yellow ochre, and sap green supply the grass color. A #4 flat brush is used throughout.

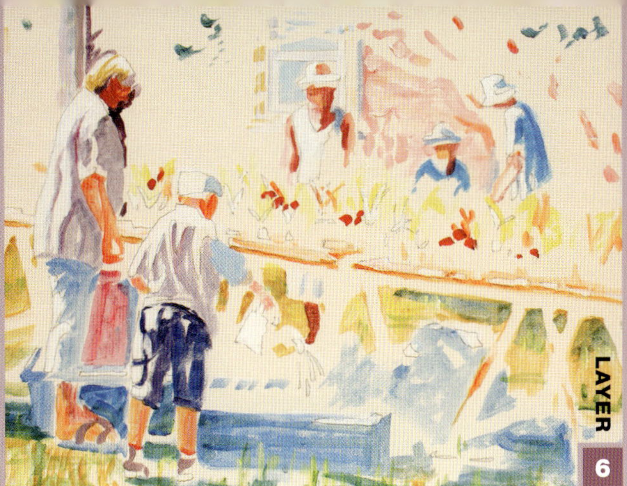

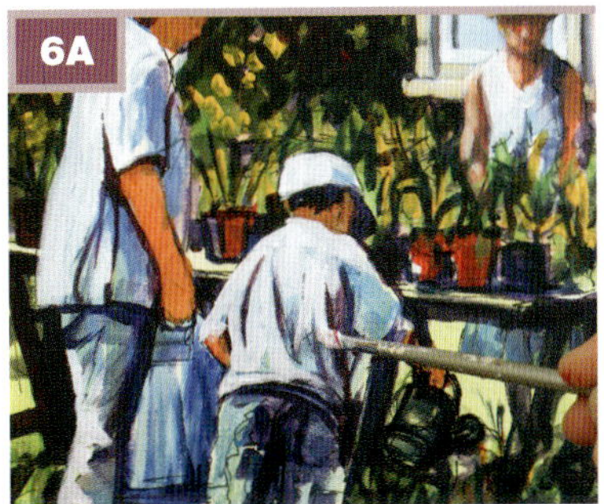

Paint the bright color of the clothing.

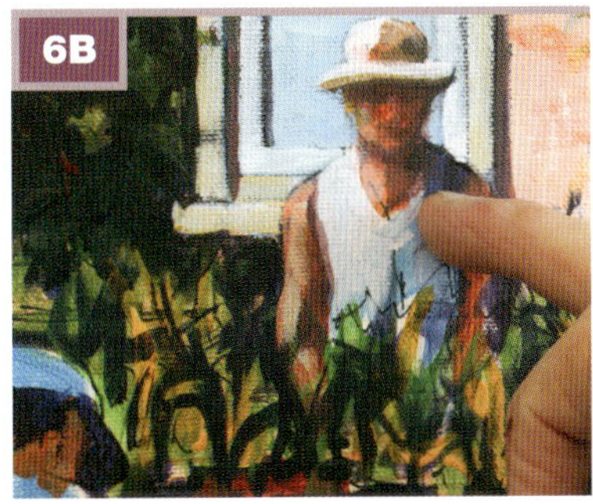

Blend colors and soften edges with a finger.

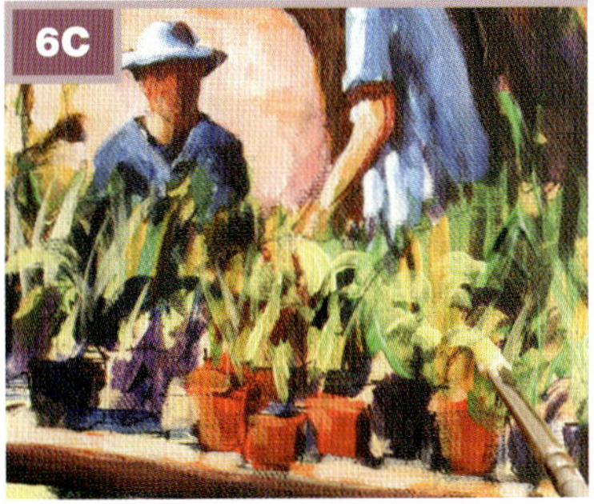

Brighten the plants on the table with dabs of color.

STAGE 6 Bright accents of color bring the image to life.

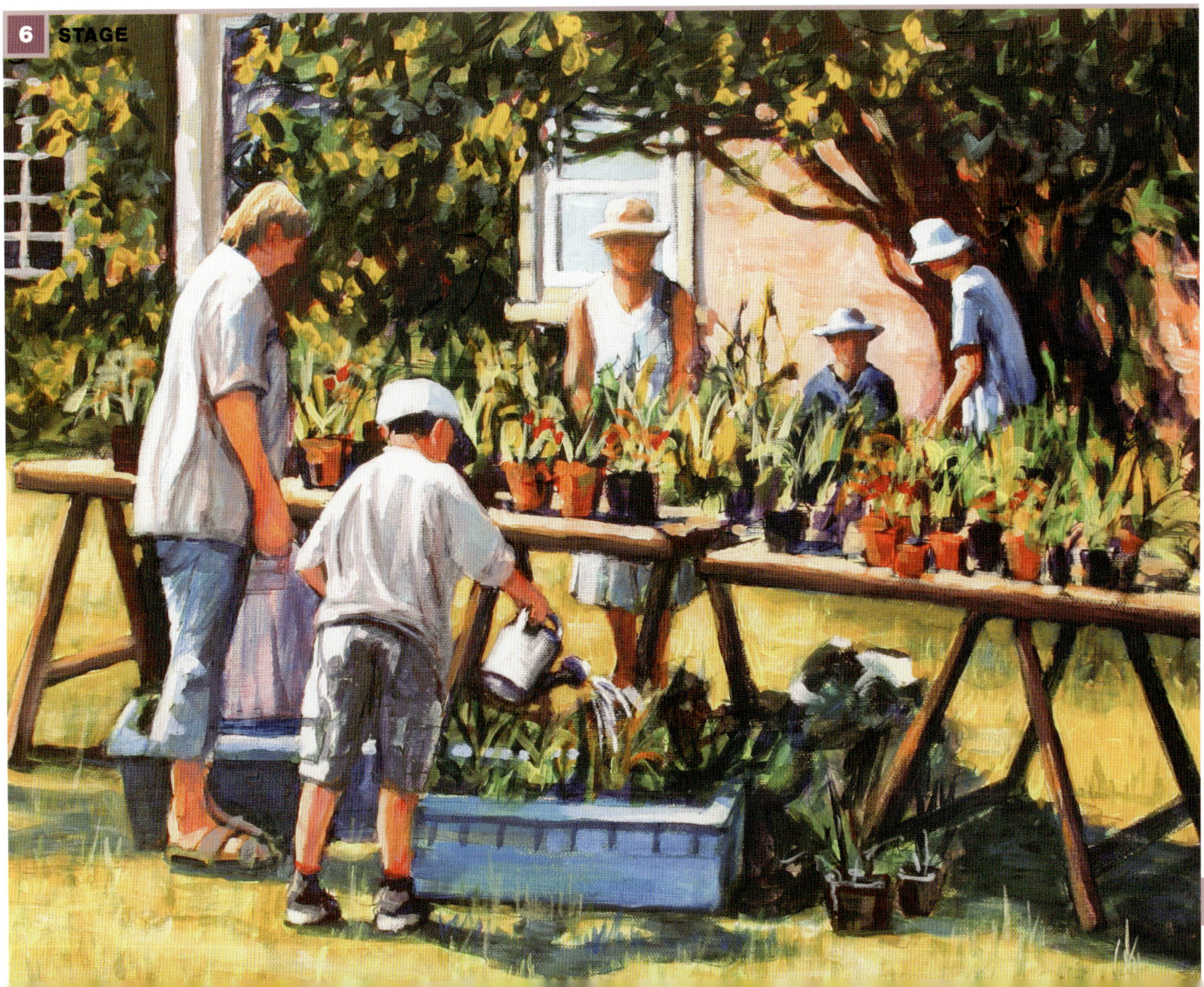

6 STAGE

WORKING ON A COLORED GROUND

by TONY PAUL

LAYER 1

A colored ground is known as an "imprimatura." This is usually applied as a thin wash over a previously prepared support. The ground color is usually chosen to complement the colors used in the actual work. Traditional imprimatura colors are green, gray, yellow, or brown. The top layers of paint are usually applied so that the underpainting shows through in places. This technique unifies the colors used in the finished work.

1 ESTABLISHING THE BACKGROUND

The figure is defined by first establishing its background and surrounding environment. A #10 flat synthetic-fiber brush is used to paint in the dull green behind the figure. This color is made using a phthalo green and burnt sienna mix. White is added to the mix and the tabletop established. A light gray made using cerulean blue and raw umber is mixed with white to paint the pages of the book.

MATERIALS

Acrylics
- Titanium white
- Phthalo green
- Burnt sienna
- Raw umber
- Red iron oxide
- Naples yellow
- Cerulean blue
- Ultramarine blue

Canvas
- Canvas board prepared using gesso and an imprimatura mixed using raw umber and white.

Other materials
- #10 flat synthetic-fiber brush
- #2 round synthetic-fiber brush
- Water

Use loose, multidirectional brushwork to build up the background.

1A

1B

Use slightly different tones of the same mix to add interest to flat surfaces.

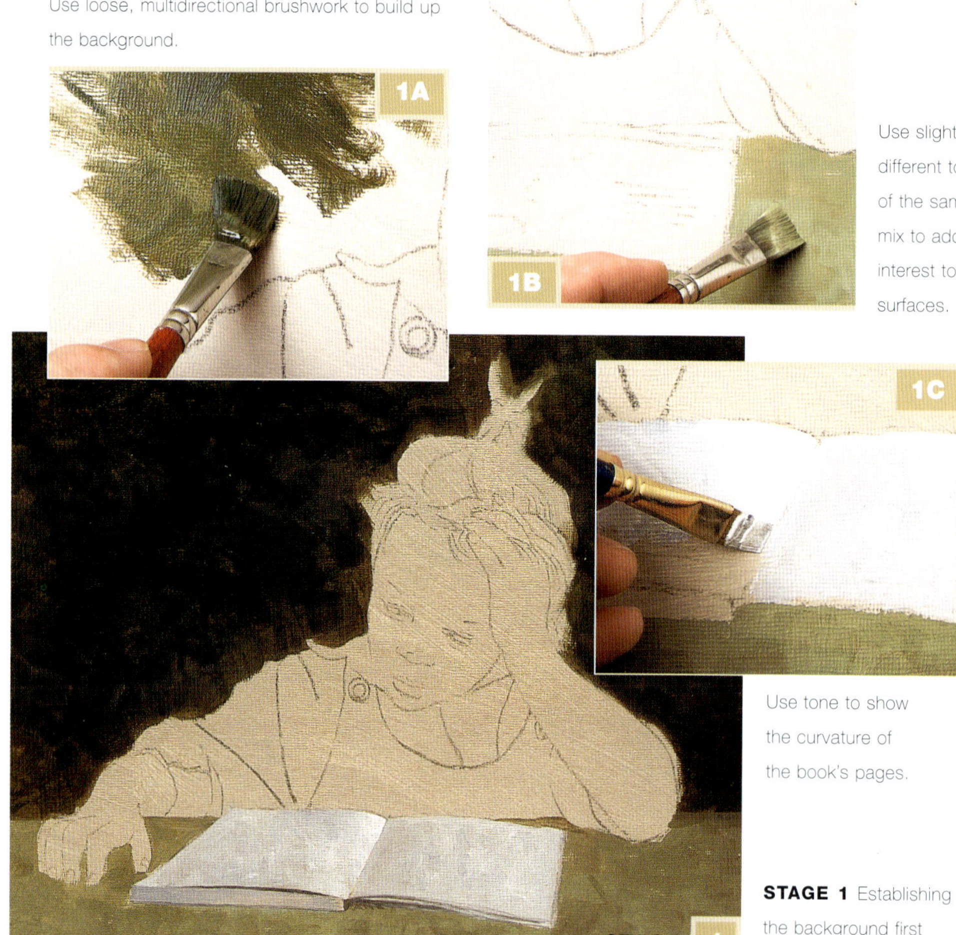

Use tone to show the curvature of the book's pages.

STAGE 1 Establishing the background first isolates the figure.

2 PAINTING IN THE LIGHTEST TONES

The light tones and highlights on the child's skin and hair are painted next. This appears to be white but is in fact a very light mix of white, red iron oxide, and Naples yellow. The #10 flat brush is used throughout.

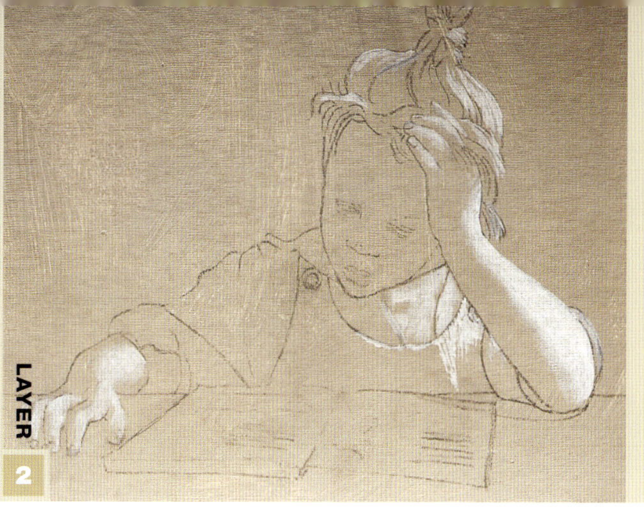

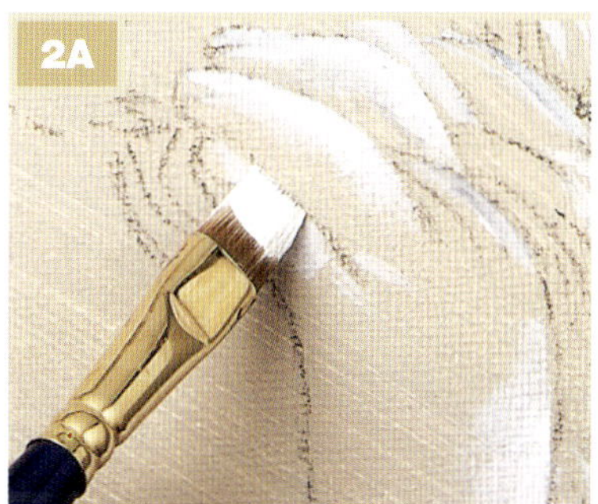

Use the edge of the brush to define the lightest bangs of hair and the highlights visible on the hand.

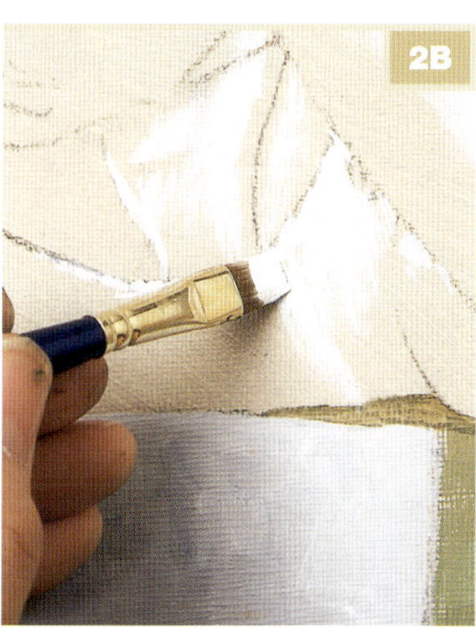

Use the same mix on the neck and arm.

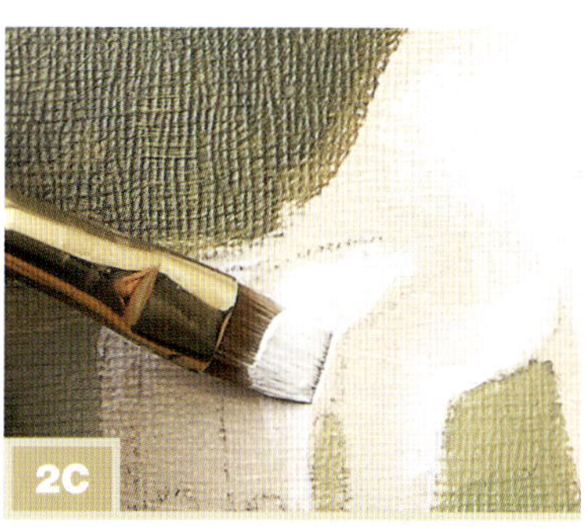

Carefully paint the right hand in the same way.

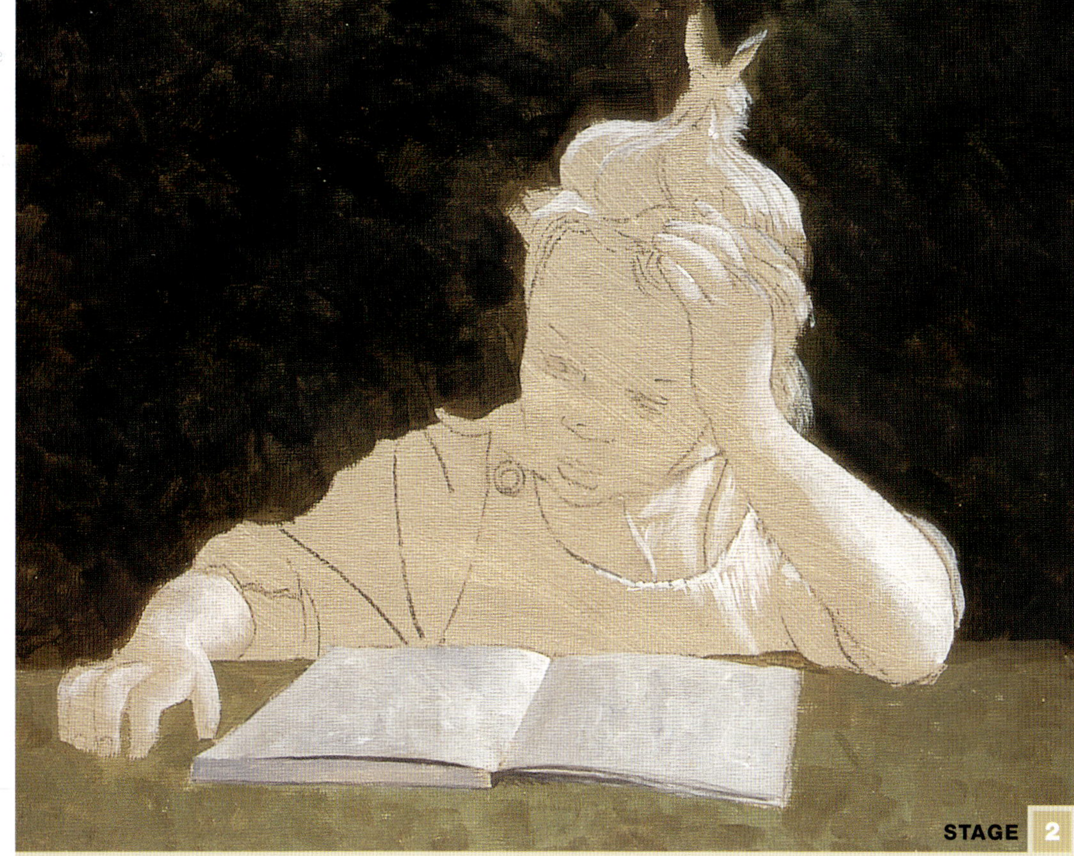

STAGE 2 The lights are established first.

3 PAINTING THE DARKS

A red iron oxide and ultramarine blue mix provides the dull red color that is used to paint in the darks on the child's face, hands, and clothing. The #10 flat brush is used throughout except when painting the features, where a small #2 round is used.

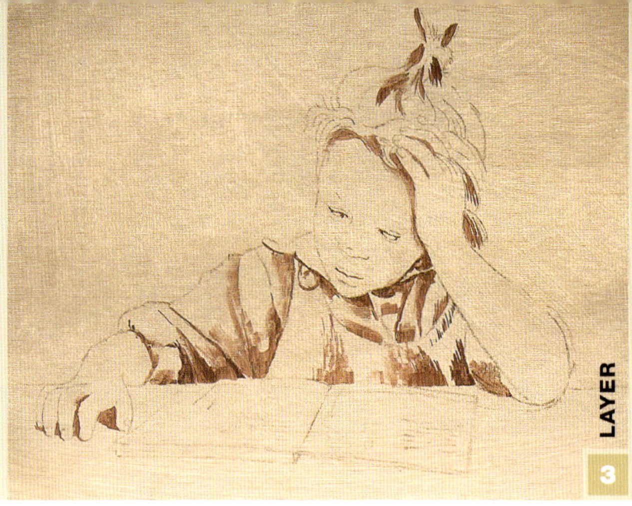

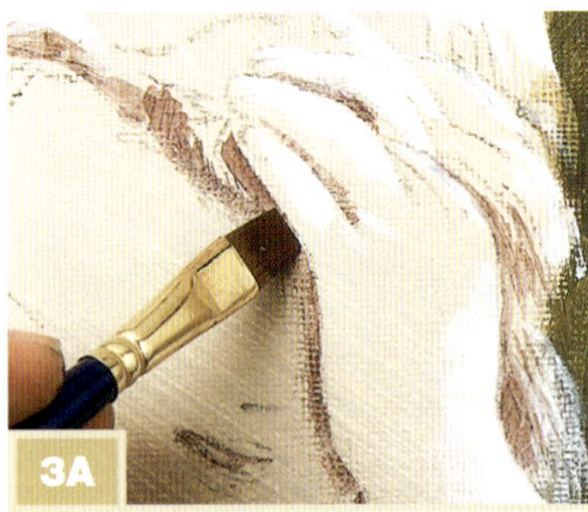

Angle the flat brush and use it on its edge to place the paint precisely.

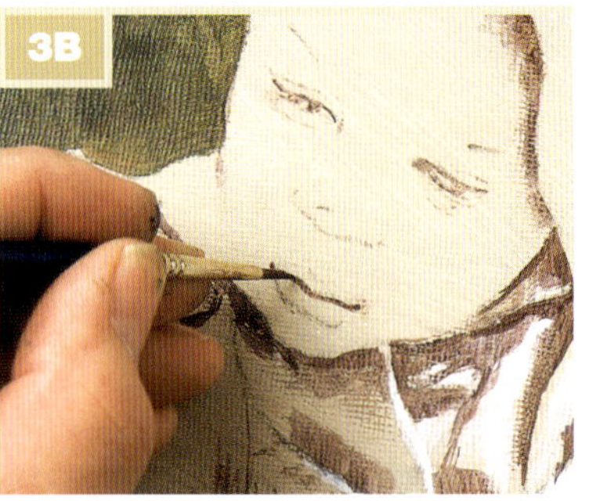

Use extra care when painting in the features.

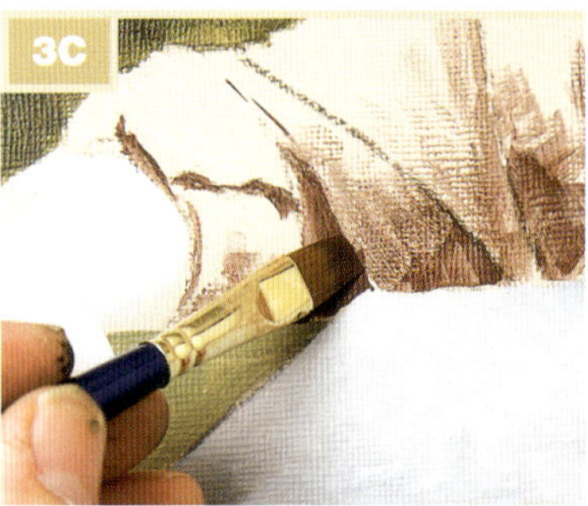

Scumble the paint slightly to give the fabric texture.

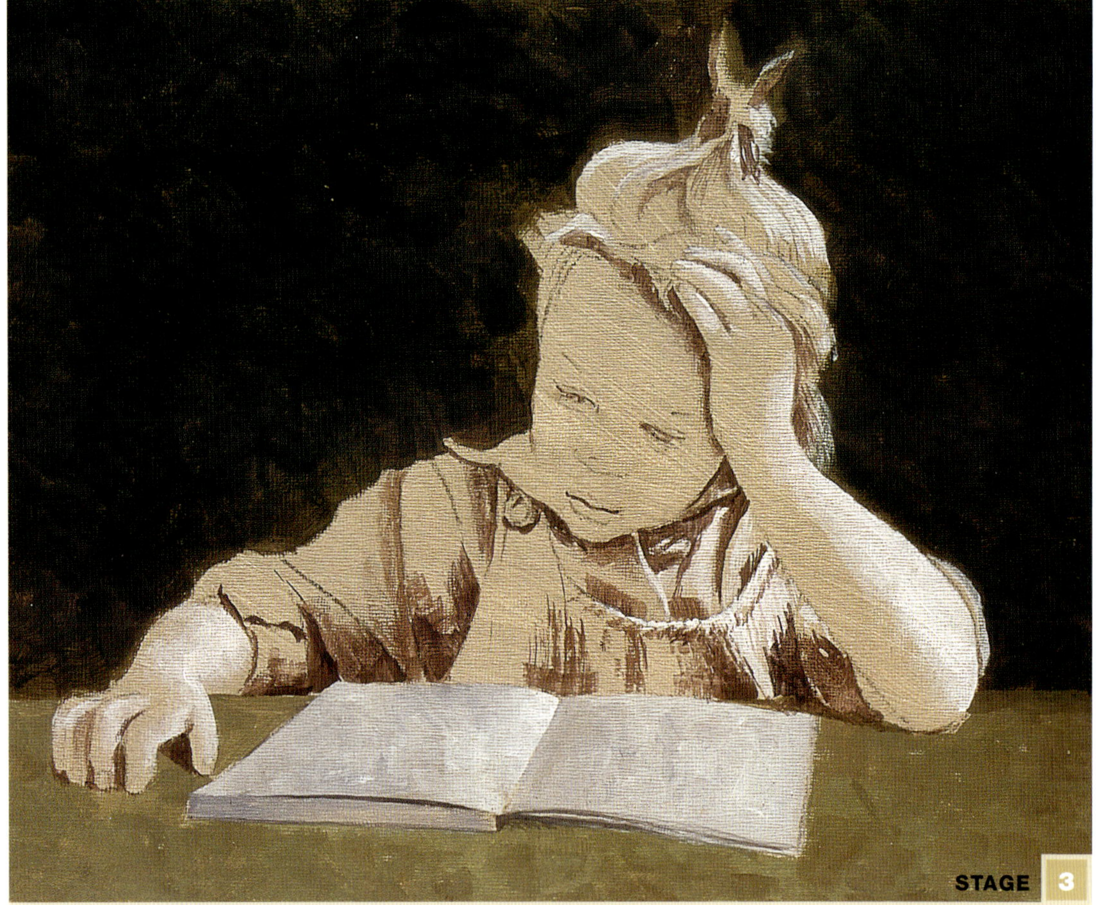

STAGE 3 The darks emphasize the two forms.

4 PATTERN AND TEXTURE

The intricate pattern and the texture of the fabrics are described using concise and precise brushwork. Even in these precisely painted areas the underpainting is never completely obscured but is instead allowed to show through. Ultramarine blue mixes are used on the corduroy dress.

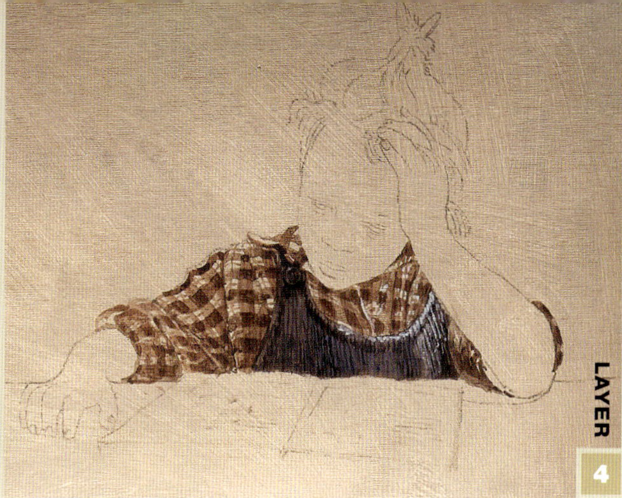
LAYER 4

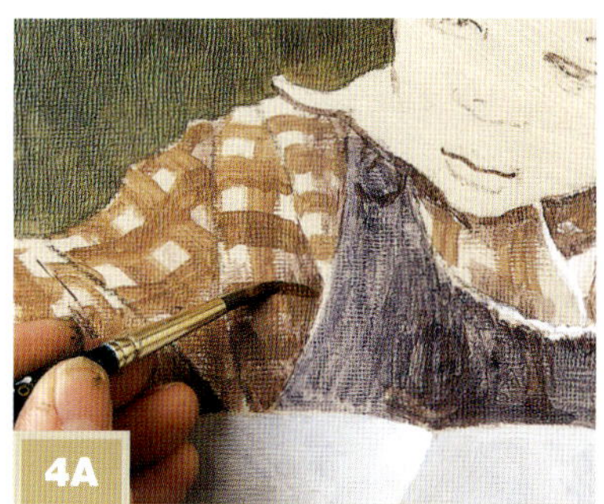
4A

Paint the broadest bands of pattern first, curving around the underlying form.

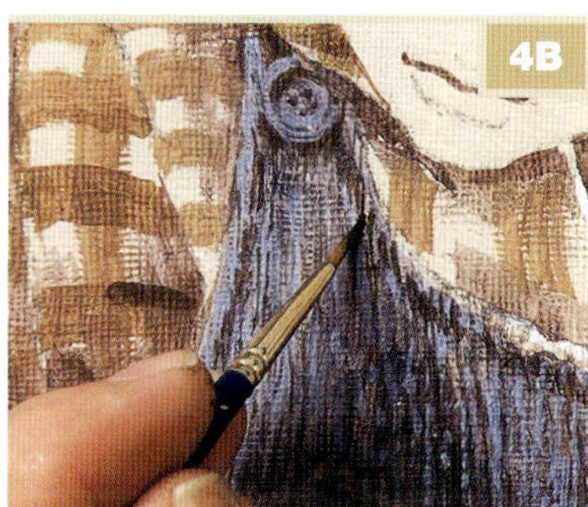
4B

Paint the pattern of the corduroy carefully using the #2 brush.

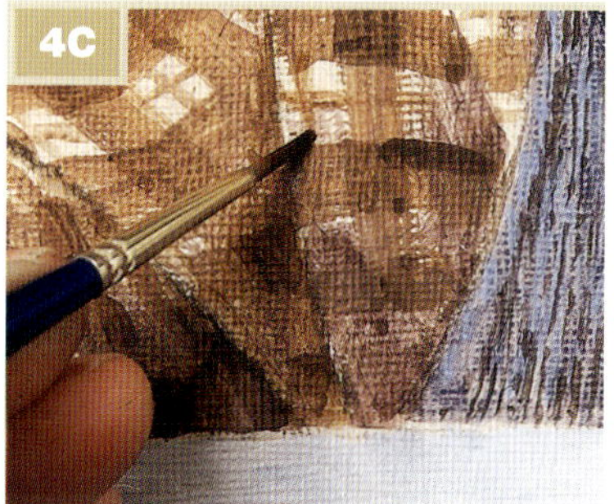
4C

Paint individual weave fibers in last.

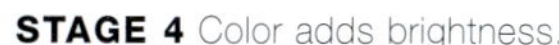

STAGE 4 Color adds brightness.

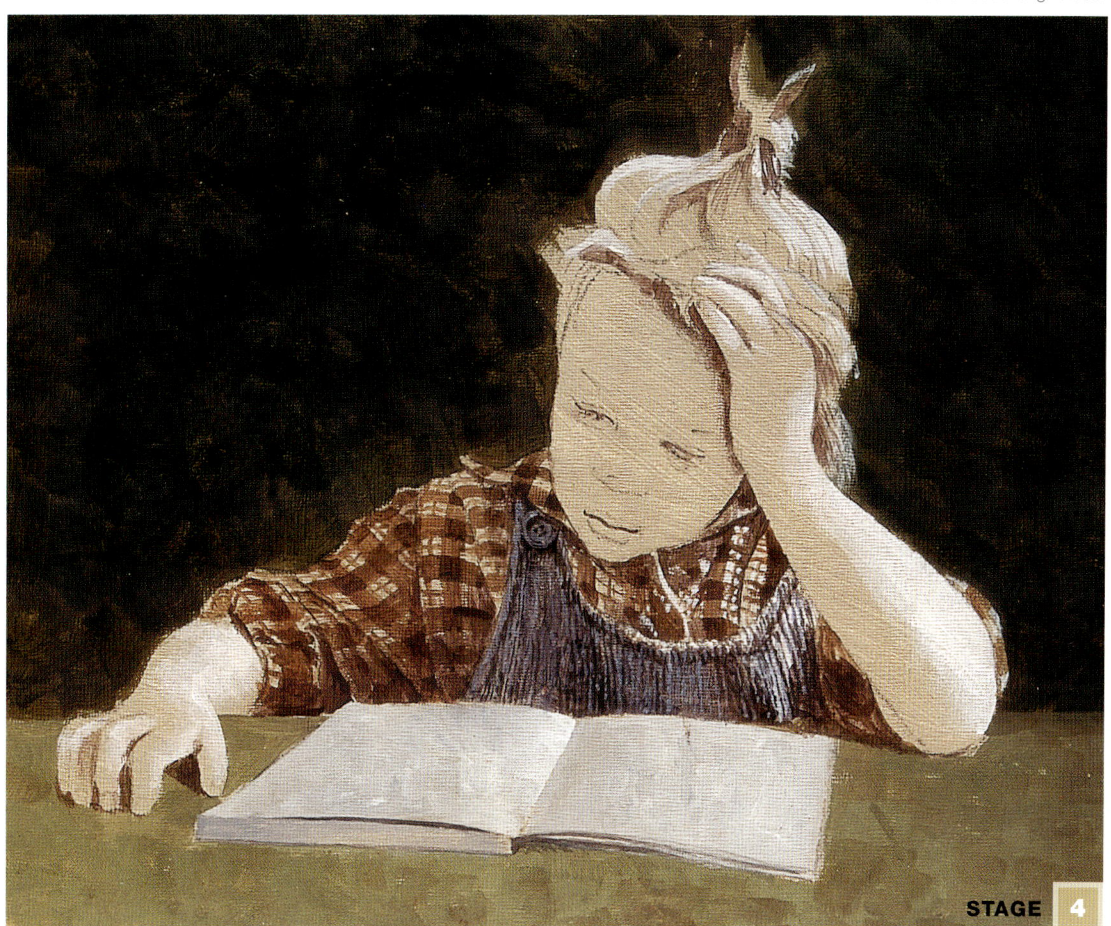
STAGE 4

5 DEVELOPING THE MIDTONES

The midtones link light and dark tones and create the form between. Mixes of red iron oxide, Naples yellow, and cerulean blue are lightened and modified using amounts of titanium white. Rather than using large brushstrokes, a small #2 round is used to knit a series of small marks together.

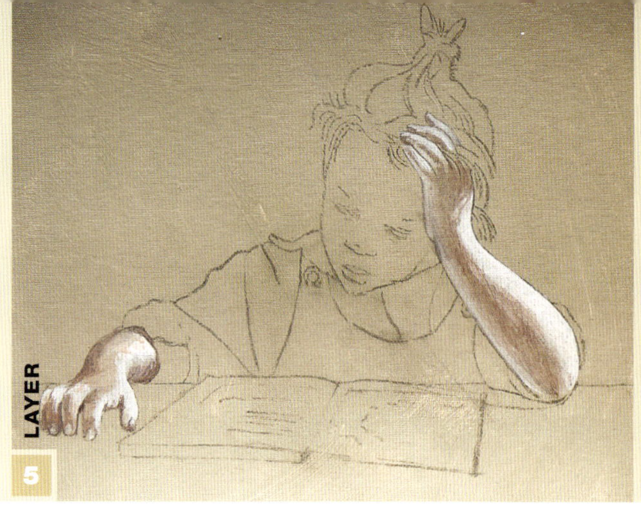

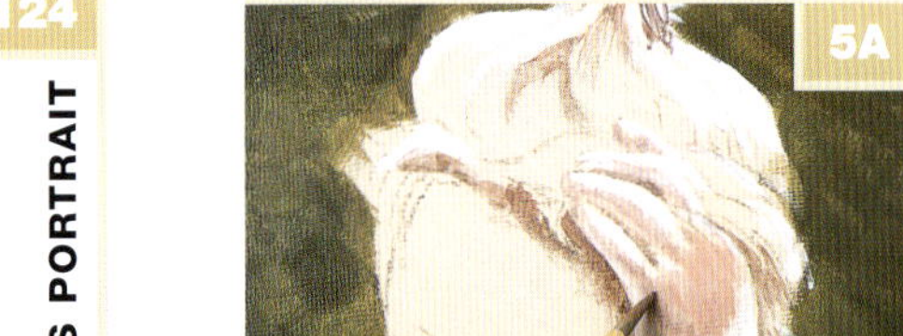

Carefully apply the paint to give shape to the hand.

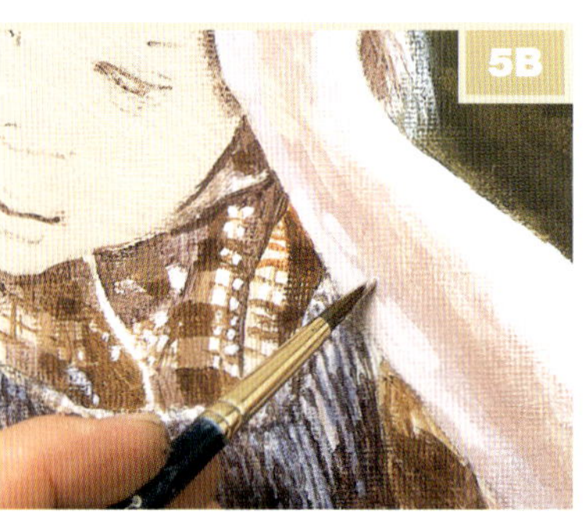

Lighten the mix by adding white, and use it to describe the area of light reflected beneath the arm.

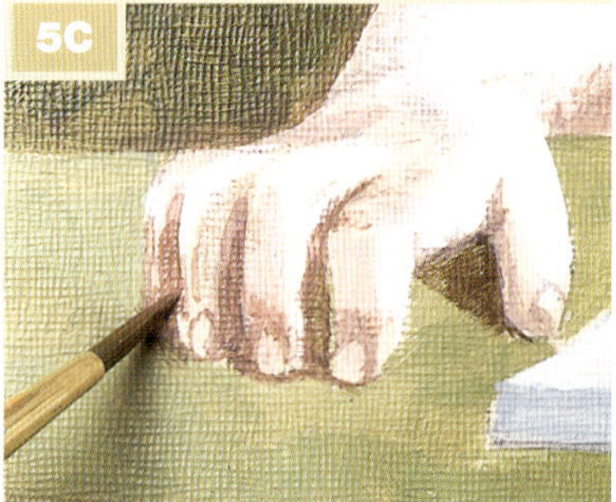

Paint the right hand in the same manner.

STAGE 5 The forms become more evident.

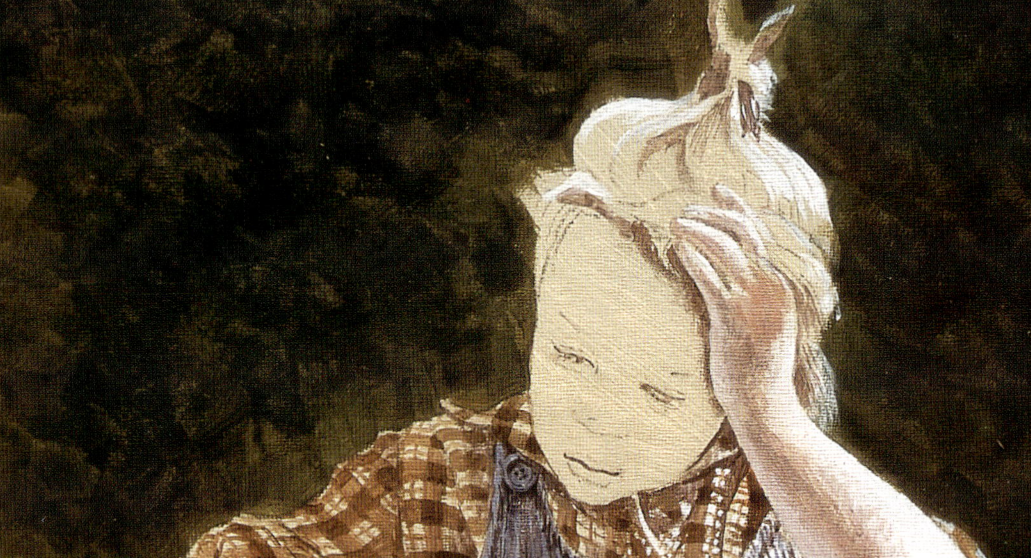

6 COMPLETING THE DETAILS

Details on the face and hair are painted last. Small brushmarks of red iron oxide, ultramarine blue, and white mixes provide the deep midtones on the face. Ultramarine blue is used on the bow in the hair and color is added to the face using red iron oxide, Naples yellow, and white mixes.

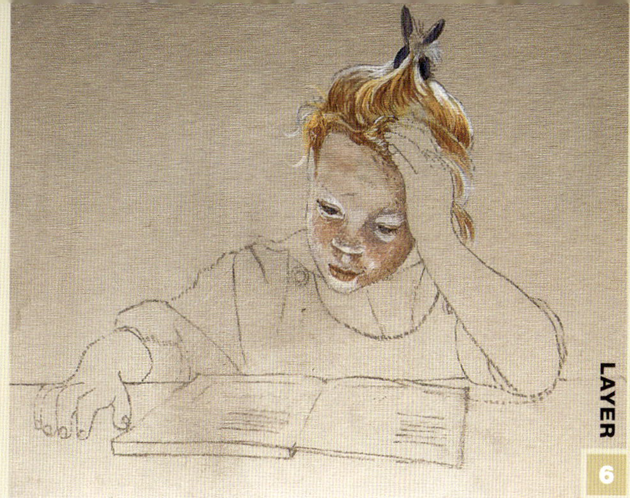

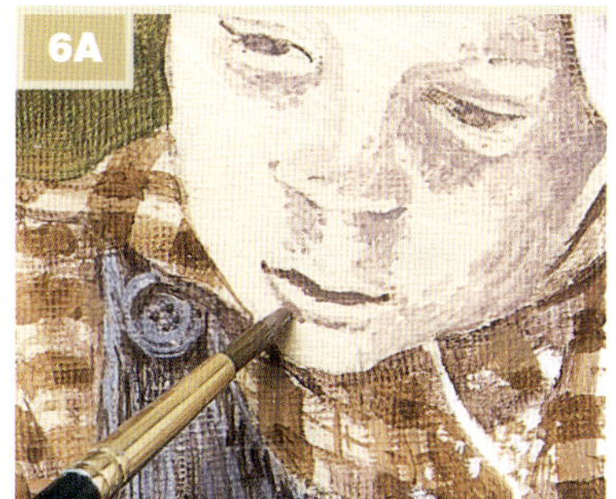

Build up the form using small dabs of color.

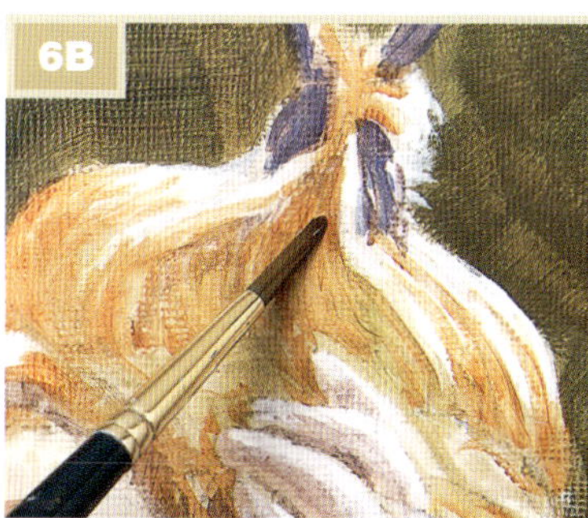

Raw umber and burnt sienna give color to the hair.

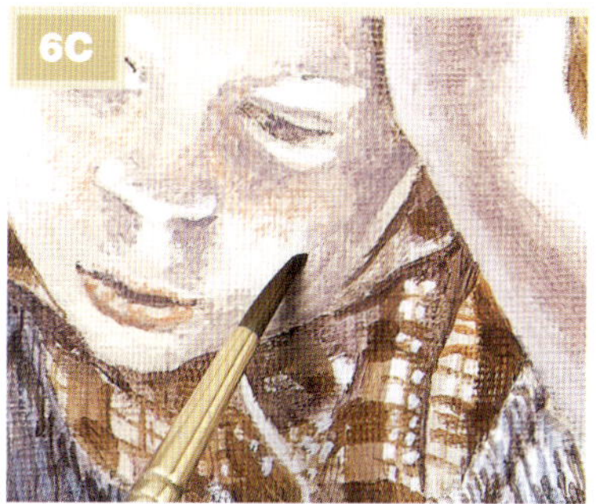

Add white to give the impression of reflected light bouncing off the pages of the book.

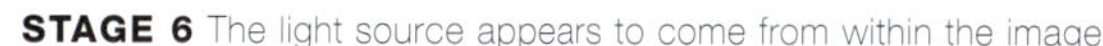

STAGE 6 The light source appears to come from within the image.

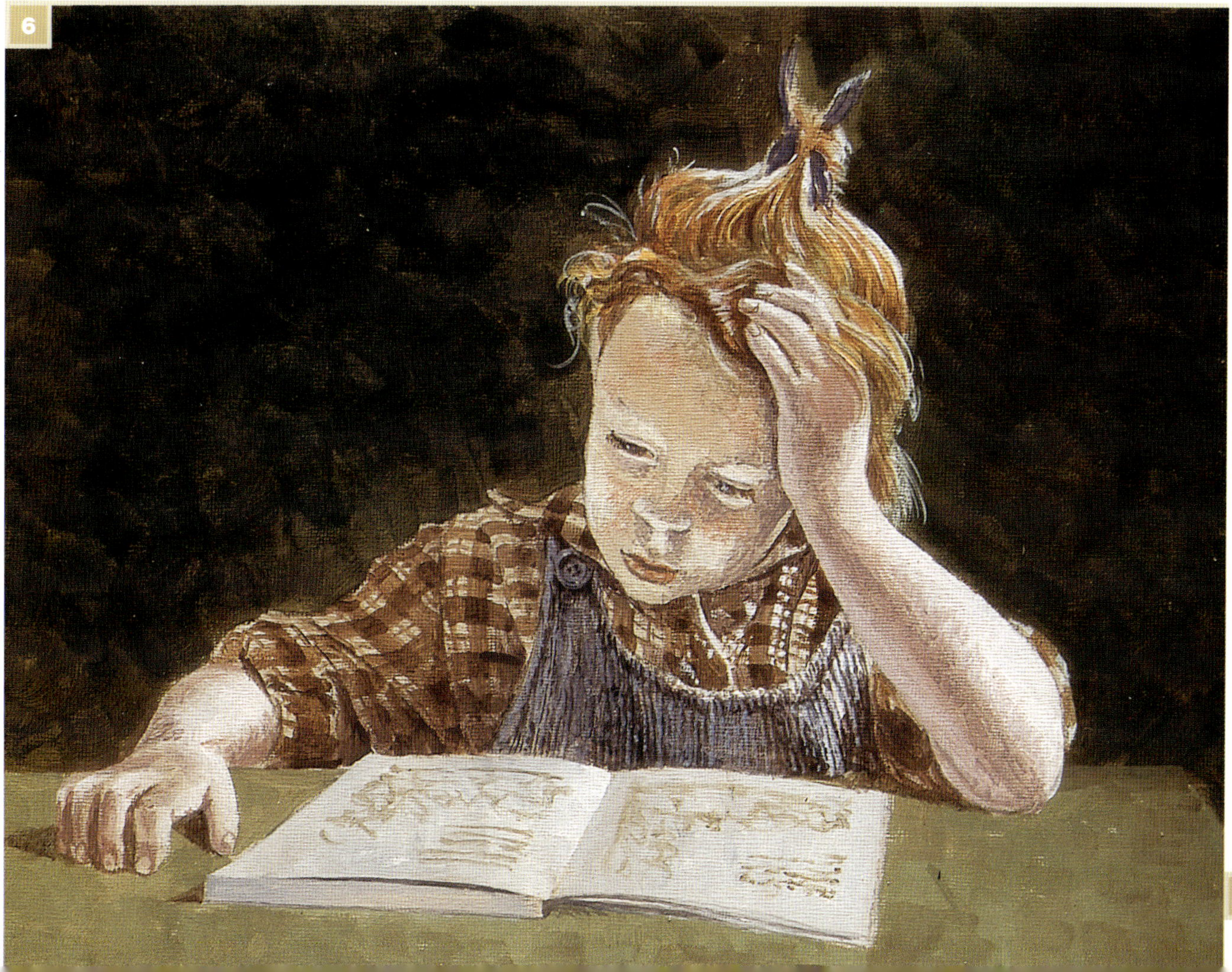

6

INDEX

CREDITS

The Artists

IAN SIDAWAY
Pages 52–57, 90–95, and 108–113

FREDA ANDERSON
Pages 58–63 and 64–71

STEPHEN RIPPINGTON
Pages 72–77, 96–101, and 102–107

TONY PAUL
Pages 78–83, 84–89, and 120–125

BOB BRANDT
Pages 114–119

Author acknowledgments

The author would like to thank Paula McMahon and Anna Knight for their help and understanding in bringing this book to publication.